MAPPING WORLD ANGLOPHONE STUDIES

This book explores core issues in the emerging field of World Anglophone Studies. It shows that traditional frameworks based on the colonial and imperial legacies of English need to be revised and extended to understand the complex adaptations, iterations, and incarnations of English in the contemporary world.

The chapters in this volume make three significant interventions in the field:

- First, they showcase the emergence of Anglophone literatures and cultures in parts of the world not traditionally considered Anglophone – Cuba, the Arab world, the Balkan region, Vietnam, Algeria, and Belize, among others.
- Second, they feature new zones of contact and creolization between Anglophone literatures, cultures, and languages such as Swahili, Santhali, Ojibway, and Hindi, as well as Anglophone representations of colonial encounters and contemporary experiences in non-Anglophone settings such as Cuba, Angola, and Algeria.
- And finally, the volume turns to Anglophone literary and cultural productions on new platforms such as social media and Netflix and highlights the role of English in emergent sites of resistance involving women, Indigenous populations, and queer and other non-heteronormative sexualities, as well as post-conflict societies.

Mapping linguistic transgressions and the transmigration of cultural tropes between Englishes, vernaculars, and a wide variety of other languages with a rich set of case studies, this volume will be essential reading for courses such as world literatures in English, postcolonial studies, anglophone studies, literature and culture, Indian Ocean worlds, Global Englishes, and Global South studies.

Pavan Kumar Malreddy (Goethe University Frankfurt) specializes in 20th- and 21st-century comparative Anglophone literatures and cultures with a regional focus on East Asia, Africa, and South Asia and with a thematic focus on conflicts, communal bonds, insurgencies, populism, public life, and migrancy. He co-edits *Kairos: A Journal of Critical Symposium*; his recent books include several co-edited volumes and the monograph *Insurgent Cultures: World Literatures and Violence from the Global South* (2024).

Frank Schulze-Engler was Professor of New Anglophone Literatures and Cultures at the Institute of English and American Studies at Goethe University Frankfurt and retired in 2023. His research and publications focus on African, Asian, Caribbean, Pacific, and Indigenous literatures and cultures; comparative perspectives on anglophone literatures in English; Indian Ocean Studies; "postcolonial" Europe; postcolonial theory; and transculturality in a world of globalized modernity.

Transdisciplinary Souths

Russell West-Pavlov
Universität Tübingen, Germany
Molly Brown
University of Pretoria, South Africa
Guadalupe Valencia García
Universidad Nacional Autónoma de México, Mexico City, Mexico
Philip Mead
University of Melbourne, Australia
Dilip Menon
University of the Witwatersrand, Johannesburg, South Africa
Sudesh Mishra
University of the South Pacific, Suva, Fiji
Sunita Reddy
Jawaharlal Nehru University, New Delhi, India
Fernando Resende
Universidade Federal Fluminense, Niterói/Rio de Janeiro, Brazil
Jing Zhao
Xi'an Jiaotong-Liverpool University, Suzhou, China

How might we theorize, think, articulate and critically/creatively inhabit the multiple and overlapping Souths of today's world? How do we enable these Souths to speak to each other, question each other, in ways that complement and expand the work upon which they are already embarked with each other? It is becoming increasingly clear that in order to better understand and contribute to the multiple processes and ways of becoming-Souths, a radically transdisciplinary approach to the study and analysis of, critical interventions in, and dialogues within and between Souths needs to be implemented. Intersectional thinking at the crossroads of race and ethnicity, class and labour, gender and corporeality, not to mention climate change and ecological destruction, demands a combination of perspectives and methodologies to deal adequately with complex planetary dilemmas. This series offers a hospitable forum for innovative intellectual inquiry that seeks to break out of extant disciplinary frameworks so as to address new questions emerging from contemporary Souths. Facilitating cross-border exchanges and polyglot negotiations between the most disparate fields of intellectual and scientific inquiry, thereby resisting the disciplining effect of enclave-thinking, the series aims to contribute to the transformation of knowledge production and associated practices across multiple Souths.

As a gesture of international solidarity, the editors of the series TRANSDISCIPLINARY SOUTHS donate the editors' royalties to the charitable organization PRO ASYL e.V. in Frankfurt am Main. PRO ASYL supports the cause of asylum seekers by providing public advocacy and legal advice.

Hospitalities
Transitions and Transgressions, North and South
Edited by Merle A. Williams

East and South
Mapping Other Europes
Lucy Gasser

Claiming the City in South African Literature
Meg Samuelson

Changing Theory
Concepts from the Global South
Edited by Dilip M Menon

Staging Revolutions and the Many Faces of Modernism
Performing Politics in Irish and Egyptian Theatre
Amina ElHalawani

The Order of Destruction
Monoculture in Colonial Caribbean Literature, c. 1640–1800
Heinrich Wilke

Mapping World Anglophone Studies
English in a World of Strangers
Edited by Pavan Kumar Malreddy and Frank Schulze-Engler

For more information about this series, please visit: www.routledge.com/Transdisciplinary-Souths/book-series/TRDS

"*Mapping World Anglophone Studies: English in a World of Strangers* is a rich and formidable contribution to scholarly research and debates in World Anglophone Studies. Emerging at the crossroads of contemporary postcolonial and world literary studies, 'World Anglophone' is a salutary correction to the term 'Global Anglophone,' with its limiting connotation of globalisation and its correlate commodities. The critical approach Malreddy and Schulze-Engler have adopted is immersive in relation to the lived realities and language worlds in erstwhile colonies and protectorates, within which Anglophone literature operates as a dominant minority. The scope of this collaborative volume is breathtakingly ambitious, with active forays into the local and 'vernacular' languages and literatures which have historically informed the emergence of Anglophone literature and continue to inflect it. The volume's outreach is matched with careful examinations of the specificities of and marked variations in Anglophone literature in each region under consideration. It adds new dimensions to World Anglophone Studies by not just recording the spread and sway of the World Anglophone but reenergising terms of exegesis such as the transnational and translingual, indigenous, and creole."

—**Ankhi Mukherjee,** *University of Oxford*

"This timely, diverse, and imaginative volume of essays sets the agenda for the rapidly emerging field of World Anglophone Studies. In engaging critically with English as it moves and morphs amidst proliferating circuits of cultures, peoples, and places – shaping a new cosmopolitics of 'strangers' – the contributors spotlight the myriad ways in which today's Anglosphere is characterised and complexified by conflict, combat, and contestation. Suspicious of both Anglophilia and Anglophobia, *Mapping World Anglophone Studies* reaches past well-worn notions of 'writing back' while refusing to reject English when committing to decolonising the mind. Instead, in tracking the polycentric networks where English is repeatedly transformed by the vernacularising agency of millions worldwide, time and again these essays unlock an expanding archive of impactful Anglophone endeavours that stubbornly contend with reterritorializing authorities and their oft-favoured nativist or nationalist imaginaries. Here English's global flow is newly prized not only in more familiar locations – Australia, Kenya, India, Trinidad – but also across the Anglosphere's novel domains: Algeria, Cuba, the Balkans. Ultimately, in gauging the global reach of the Anglosphere, its critique of as well as complicity in the world system, *Mapping World Anglophone Studies* entirely recalibrates how we might revalue English as newly minted critical world language."

—**John McLeod,** *University of Leeds, UK*

"For one who has been struck by the promiscuous, liminal, multi-platforming, transboundary, magnetising, mercurial, and adaptable character of certain languages (as well as their intent and capacity to survive, thrive and spread themselves like a useful weed), this book is a gift. A work that sets out to 'map the linguistic transgressions and the transmigration of cultural tropes between Englishes, vernaculars, and beyond' and which intends to capture the complex adaptations, iterations, and incarnations of English in the contemporary world is long overdue. English has transformed itself into a language rooted in many places of the earth, a lingua franca for our allusive multipolarity. It is a companion for the many rather than the one, propelled to this probably because it became the language of the seas, the air, of trade and exchange, a character trait that had once made Kiswahili a lingua franca of particular sea worlds before English installed itself with sound and fury. The book is also a testament to how a language domesticated itself to survive and thrive. You will find traces of this phenomenon in this book of rich texts, a brief yet thrilling cartography of English(es) in the world."

—**Yvonne Adhiambo Owuor**, *Kenya*

MAPPING WORLD ANGLOPHONE STUDIES

English in a World of Strangers

*Edited by Pavan Kumar Malreddy
and Frank Schulze-Engler*

Designed cover image: © Getty Images

First published 2025
by Routledge
4 Park Square, Milton Park, Abingdon, Oxon OX14 4RN

and by Routledge
605 Third Avenue, New York, NY 10158

Routledge is an imprint of the Taylor & Francis Group, an informa business

© 2025 selection and editorial matter, Pavan Kumar Malreddy and Frank Schulze-Engler; individual chapters, the contributors

The right of Pavan Kumar Malreddy and Frank Schulze-Engler to be identified as the authors of the editorial material, and of the authors for their individual chapters, has been asserted in accordance with sections 77 and 78 of the Copyright, Designs and Patents Act 1988.

The Open Access version of this book, available at www.taylorfrancis. com, has been made available under a Creative Commons Attribution-Non Commercial-No Derivatives (CC-BY-NC-ND) 4.0 International license.

Any third party material in this book is not included in the OA Creative Commons license, unless indicated otherwise in a credit line to the material. Please direct any permissions enquiries to the original rightsholder.

Disclaimer: The views and opinions expressed in this book are solely those of the authors and do not necessarily reflect those of the publisher. The analyses, data and figures based on research material are intended here to serve general educational and informational purposes and not obligatory upon any party. The authors have made every effort to ensure that the information presented in the book was correct at the time of press, but the authors and the publisher do not assume and hereby disclaim any liability with respect to the accuracy, completeness, reliability, suitability, selection and inclusion of the contents of this book and any implied warranties or guarantees. The authors and publisher make no representations or warranties of any kind to any person, product or entity for any loss, including, but not limited to special, incidental or consequential damage, or disruption alleged to have been caused, directly or indirectly, by omissions or any other related cause.

Trademark notice: Product or corporate names may be trademarks or registered trademarks, and are used only for identification and explanation without intent to infringe.

British Library Cataloguing-in-Publication Data
A catalogue record for this book is available from the British Library

ISBN: 978-1-032-38455-9 (hbk)
ISBN: 978-1-032-88663-3 (pbk)
ISBN: 978-1-003-46403-7 (ebk)

DOI: 10.4324/9781003464037

Typeset in Sabon LT Pro
by Apex CoVantage, LLC

To the memory of
Michael Wessels (1958–2018)

scholar, teacher, friend

CONTENTS

List of Contributors	*xiv*
Acknowledgements	*xix*

Introduction: Shouting Loudest Into the Anglophone
Pavan Kumar Malreddy and Frank Schulze-Engler   1

I
Rethinking World Anglophone Studies   21

1 Editing the Global Anglophone: Publishing History as a Framework for an Emergent Field
Ben Fried   23

2 "Now a Netflix Original Series": Indian TV Shows in World Anglophone Studies
Annika McPherson and Ashumi Shah   38

3 South African Fiction in English: From Post-Apartheid to World Anglophone
Deniz Gündoğan İbrişim   52

xii Contents

4 Questioning the Emergence of National Englishes: Non-Teleological Paths of Language Development in Contexts of Postcolonial Diversity 67
Britta Schneider

II
Deterritorializing the Anglophone 85

5 The Anglophone Imaginary and Agency in Contemporary Egyptian Literature in English 87
Pavan Kumar Malreddy and Stefanie Kemmerer

6 "Bilingual Silence"? New Anglophone Literature From the Balkans and Its Migrational Metamultilingual Mode 104
Miriam Wallraven

7 Invisibilising Feminism in Translation: Representation of Women in *Dreaming in Cuban* and *Soñar en cubano* 120
María Escobar-Aguiar

8 Decolonisation, Authenticity, and the Other: Talking in and About Englishes in Algeria 134
Camille Jacob and Leonald Kazibwe

III
Contact, Crossover, and Creolization 149

9 Performing Masculinities Using Sheng in Kenyan Popular Culture: The Billingsgate Genres 151
Alex Nelungo Wanjala

10 Situating Chick Lit of the Global South in Print and Online 166
Nicklas Hållén and Delphine Munos

11 "Too Much Joy, I Swear, Is Lost": Ambiguity in Ocean Vuong's *On Earth We're Briefly Gorgeous* 183
Elena Furlanetto

Contents **xiii**

12 Towards Shonglish?: An Analysis of Chenjerai Hove's
    Ancestors   197
    Tanaka Chidora

13 The Migrant Child: Doing the Puzzle of Home in
    Suneeta Peres da Costa's Novella *Saudade*   212
    Jean Page

IV
Embattled Englishes: Revolt, Emancipation, Transformation   **227**

14 "The Indian Queer": For Lack of a Better Term   229
    Umesh Patra

15 Tricksters, Hustlers, and Moral Saints: Students and
    Other Strangers in Post-Apartheid South African Literature   243
    Ibrahim Abraham

16 Spokeswomen: African Authors' Historical-Fictional
    Witnessing in the Literary Anglosphere   260
    Annie Gagiano

17 Toward a "Most Subtle and Fluent Self": Indigenous
    Englishes and the Pursuit of Self-Sovereignty in
    The Translation of Dr. Apelles   280
    Vanessa Evans

    Index   296

CONTRIBUTORS

Ibrahim Abraham is Lecturer in Sociology at Federation University Australia and Honorary Senior Lecturer in the Humanities Research Centre of the Australian National University. His books include *Race, Class and Christianity in South Africa: Middle-Class Moralities* (2021).

Tanaka Chidora lectures in the Department of Literary Studies at the University of Malawi and is also a research fellow at the University of the Free State (South Africa). He has a PhD in English from the University of the Free State and has further research interests in popular culture, world literature, transculturality, speculative fiction from Anglophone Africa, and Afro-diasporic writing. He is Co-Editor of *Matatu: Journal African Culture and Society* and Associate Editor for *Kairos: Journal of Critical Symposium* and *Feminist Encounters*.

María Escobar-Aguiar is a translator and lecturer at Universidad Nacional de La Plata (UNLP, Argentina). She has studied inter-American studies at Universität Bielefeld (Germany) and romance studies at Bergische Universität Wuppertal (Germany). Her current research focuses on the translation of archives, especially concerning militancy, gender, and memory of a dictatorial recent past. Since 2019, she has worked as a volunteer translator and researcher for Abuelas de Plaza de Mayo and Centro de Estudios Legales y Sociales (CELS), two renowned Argentinian human rights organizations.

Vanessa Evans (she/her) is a settler scholar and Assistant Professor of Indigenous Literatures at Appalachian State University. Her current research investigates how contemporary Indigenous novels from North America, Oceania, and South Asia represent and enact Indigenous resurgence. She is Co-Editor of *Cultures of Citizenship in the Twenty-First Century: Literary and Cultural Perspectives on a Legal Concept* (2023) and a co-managing editor for the *Journal of Transnational American Studies*.

Ben Fried is a British Academy Newton International Fellow at the Institute of English Studies, University of London. He has published widely on 20th-century Anglophone literatures; his first book manuscript, *The Empire of English Literature: Editing the Global Anglophone, 1947–1993*, explores the working relationships between editors in London and New York and authors from around the English-writing world, while his current research examines the impact of postwar migration on London's literary institutions.

Elena Furlanetto is a researcher in American studies at the University of Duisburg-Essen and Principal Investigator in the DFG Research Unit "Ambiguity and Difference: Historical and Cultural Dynamics." She is the author of *Towards Turkish American Literature: Narratives of Multiculturalism in Post-Imperial Turkey* (2017). Her research moves in transnational and postcolonial spaces and engages the intersections between the US and other cultures. Her most recent work focuses on early American literature, the 19th century, and ambiguity studies.

Annie Gagiano is a professor emerita in the English Department of the University of Stellenbosch in South Africa. She is the author of two books – *Achebe, Head, Marechera: On Power and Change in Africa* (2000) and *Dealing with Evils: Essays on Writing from Africa* (second ed. 2014) – and of numerous articles/book chapters mainly on Anglophone (or translated) fiction from various African regions. Her work reflects on the commemorative and evaluative functions of postcolonial (mainly African) literatures.

Nicklas Hållén is a lecturer and assistant professor at the Department of Languages, Literature and Intercultural studies at Karlstad University and a member of the African Literature Metadata research project based at Uppsala University, Sweden. His research is on ephemeral African literature.

Deniz Gündoğan İbrişim is a literary scholar who specializes in cultural trauma and memory studies, postcolonial theory, 20th- and 21st-century Anglophone literature, ecofeminism, and environmental humanities. Currently she is a visiting assistant professor of literature at Kadir Has University. She is currently working on her first book monograph, *Toward a Slow Wit(h)nessing in Anglophone World Literature*.

xvi Contributors

Camille Jacob's work focuses on how language as discourse and practices impacts other social and political issues, including narratives of identities, decolonization, and "development" in countries labelled "French-speaking." She is the Co-Editor, with Linda Gardelle, of *Schools and National Identities in French-speaking Africa: Political Choices, Means of Transmission and Appropriation* (Routledge). Her research has been funded by the UK's Arts & Humanities Research Council, the UK's Economic & Social Research Council, and the Leverhulme Trust.

Leonald Kazibwe holds a master's degree from the university of Padova, Italy, in historical sciences (mobility studies). His research focuses on South–South and South–North mobilities of students.

Stefanie Kemmerer studied cultural and literary studies in Mannheim and Alcalá de Henares (Spain). She earned her MA at Goethe University. Her thesis "Yogascapes – The Visual Politics of Transcultural Yoga" was awarded the GAPS Graduate Award 2022. She currently expands her research in this area in preparation for a PhD. Other research interests include Anglophone Arab literatures and South Asian literatures.

Pavan Kumar Malreddy specializes in 20th- and 21st-century comparative Anglophone literatures and cultures with a regional focus on East Asia, Africa, and South Asia and with a thematic focus on conflicts, communal bonds, insurgencies, populism, public life, and migrancy. He co-edits *Kairos: A Journal of Critical Symposium*; his recent books include several co-edited volumes and the monograph *Insurgent Cultures: World Literatures and Violence from the Global South* (Cambridge University Press, 2024).

Annika McPherson is Professor for New English Literatures and Cultural Studies at the University of Augsburg, Germany. From 2017 to 2019, she served as President of GAPS, the Association for Anglophone Postcolonial Studies. Her research and teaching areas include Anglophone World Literatures; Caribbean, West African, South African, Indian, and Canadian literatures in English; speculative fiction; postcolonial and diaspora studies; critical diversity studies; as well as global popular cultures and streaming media in comparative perspective.

Delphine Munos is Senior Lecturer in Anglophone Postcolonial Literatures at the University of Liège, Belgium. She is the author of *After Melancholia: A Reappraisal of Second-Generation Diasporic Subjectivity in the Work of Jhumpa Lahiri* (Brill/Rodopi, 2013) and co-editor, with Bénédicte Ledent, of the book series *Cross Cultures: Readings in Post/Colonial Literatures and Cultures in English* (Brill) and specializes in Anglophone postcolonial literatures and US ethnic literatures, with a special focus on "minor-to-minor" interactions.

Jean Page is a researcher at the University of Lisbon Centre for English Studies and works on its Representations of Home project in English-language literatures and cultures as well as with its Creative Journal ROAM. Her work focuses on Australian poetry (including her PhD on 20th-century Australian poet James McAuley) and short fiction. She has published in international and Australian journals and publications, drawing on postcolonial, ecocritical, language, and stylistics theory.

Umesh Patra is an assistant professor in the Department of English at Mahatma Gandhi Central University, Motihari, Bihar. He worked on a comparative analysis of an Odia folk theatre named Pala and Bertolt Brecht's epic theatre for his PhD dissertation. His research areas include theatre and performance studies, modern British literature, and queer theory. Some of his writings have been published in *Sanglap: A Journal of Literary and Cultural Inquiry*, *Research & Criticism*, *Muse India*, and *The Hindu*.

Britta Schneider is Professor of Language Use and Migration at European University Viadrina, Germany. Her main research interest is the study of language ideologies, with a focus on the discursive and material construction of languages in transnational, multilingual settings and in digital culture. Her book *Liquid Languages – Constructing Language in Late Modern Cultures of Diffusion* will be published by Cambridge University Press in 2024/2025, discussing polycentric language ideologies in postcolonial Belize.

Frank Schulze-Engler was Professor of New Anglophone Literatures and Cultures at the Institute of English and American Studies at Goethe University Frankfurt and retired in 2023. His research and publications focus on African, Asian, Caribbean, Pacific, and Indigenous literatures and cultures; comparative perspectives on anglophone literatures in English; Indian Ocean Studies; "postcolonial" Europe; postcolonial theory; and transculturality in a world of globalized modernity.

Ashumi Shah is a PhD graduate from the University of Augsburg, Germany. Having focused on fandoms of speculative television shows and web series, she now uses her powers for good in the areas of content marketing and video production.

Miriam Wallraven is Associate Professor at Julius-Maximilians-Universität Würzburg where she teaches English literature and cultural studies. Her current research focuses on literatures of migration and displacement in

xviii Contributors

a globalized world about which she is working on a book-length study. In this field, she has co-edited the volume *Configurations of Migration: Knowledges – Imaginaries – Media* (2023). She is a frequent contributor to peer-reviewed journals and international book projects.

Alex Nelungo Wanjala is a senior lecturer in the Department of Literature and French of the University of Nairobi, Kenya, and earned his PhD in French and comparative literature from Université de la Sorbonne Nouvelle-Paris 3. Wanjala's areas of specialization include postcolonial studies, gender studies, and cultural studies, with a focus on African literature in French and English expression. One of his most recent papers is titled "(East) African Postcolonial Ecocriticism: Revisiting Okot p'Bitek's Song of Prisoner" and was published in *Tydskrif vir Letterkunde*.

ACKNOWLEDGEMENTS

We would like to thank the Open Access Publication Fund, ConTrust Cluster Initiative of Goethe University Frankfurt am Main, and the German Research Foundation (DFG) for their financial support toward the research as well as the open access publication of this book.

INTRODUCTION

Shouting Loudest Into the Anglophone

Pavan Kumar Malreddy and Frank Schulze-Engler

English From Above, English From Below

In Timothy Mo's *Redundancy of Courage* (1991), the young Chinese protagonist Adolph Ng returns from Canada to his island as an Anglophone. At the time he arrives, the island is full of opportunities, and as a Chinese diasporic subject born on the island, Ng has always felt culturally neutral in relation to the Portuguese settlers, the natives of the island, and the mestizos – the Portuguese-native descendants. But soon after the Portuguese leave the colony, none other than its mighty neighbour (Indonesia) invades the island (East Timor), whose brutal occupation leaves no choice for Ng but to side with the native insurgents. Far from being a committed revolutionary, Ng is deeply suspicious of, if not disenchanted by, the insurgent cause: "The bastards had an unofficial Chinese exclusion policy."[1] Yet he becomes a full-time revolutionary for lack of a better choice and earns a reputation as a genius bomb manufacturer.

But soon the insurgents realize that they are fighting against a mighty and ugly enemy they cannot defeat, and the only war they can possibly win is the war of opinion in the international media. Though the island is swarming with Australian journalists, there is hardly anyone on the rebels' side who knows English and could propagate their version of the story. In this remote East Asian colony whose fortunes dwindle between four colonizers – the Portuguese, the Dutch, the Japanese, and the Southeast Asian Chinese diaspora – and their linguistic laundry, English becomes the ultimate contact zone, an indispensable transcultural glue that binds our protagonist to the island. The insurgents for their part recruit Ng not just for his skills in

DOI: 10.4324/9781003464037-1
This chapter has been made available under a CC-BY-NC-ND 4.0 license.

2 Pavan Kumar Malreddy and Frank Schulze-Engler

manufacturing explosives but see the man himself as an IED – not an improvised explosive device, but an improvised *English* device.

When East Timor eventually gained independence in 2002, it was a well-known fact that this was made possible by information wars and the diplomatic pressure exerted at the United Nations. But the fact that *Redundancy of Courage* was written ten years before actual independence makes Ng's vision all the more compelling. Ng, for his part, is anything but proleptic: he admonishes his fellow militants not to bark into every microphone they can get hold of to grab attention, but to "shout loudest into the anglophone."[2] In a world of Lusophone, Dutchophone, and Sinophone empires, shouting loudest into the Anglophone, as it were, has a greater purpose and value than a caravan of war tanks or a fleet of jet fighters.[3]

If not for such weaponized English, how then are wars waged, allegiances made, empires erected, or governments toppled with 140-character tweets, news-generating bots, or the botched syntax of social media campaigns? Ours is indeed a world in which English is everywhere and nowhere, just as in the Visual C++ code used to generate these words. It is everywhere, because it is the language of algorithms, artificial intelligence, and other prosaic rhythms we consume in media adverts between our visual meals. It is nowhere, because it seems to have lost a sense of metaphysical home or organic homeland. It also seems to lurk beneath the anticolonial critiques of yesteryear's national heroes and the reigning regimes of populists. In Egypt, for instance, English is at the apex of an Orwellian dystopia. The ruling elite labels anyone who speaks English with some confidence a Western or anti-national agent, yet has no qualms in sending their children to Ivy League schools in the States. Many members of the middle classes want to know just enough English to access tourist money and report anyone who indulges in this criminal tongue to the secret agents. The humourist Bassem Yousuf spells out this hypocritical treatment of English in the most trenchant manner:

And how does Big Brother drive masses? Simple.
Step 1: Create an enemy.
Step 2: Make sure it speaks English.
Step 3: Rinse and repeat.[4]

The Hindu nationalist regime in India seems to have internalized this principle: anyone who speaks grammatically sound English is an anti-national element or an urban Naxalite who aligns with liberal and radical left ideas from the 'West.' The Indian prime minister himself actively cultivates this image by proclaiming Hindi the one and only national language in order to foster an anti-establishment view of his identity: his humble origins as a *chaiwallah* (a tea seller) are dramatically cast against the 'crown prince' dynasty of

Introduction **3**

the Gandhis and their Oxbridge pedigree.[5] This is not to suggest that Hindu nativists such as Modi or the conservative Islamists of Egypt would reject English altogether. In Sri Lanka, the very proponents of the Sinhala Only Act, including the country's first prime minister, Sirimavo Bandaranaike, were English educated and even sent their children to universities in England. Ironically, the (rather cold) cultural wars over English resulted in two epic socialist uprisings in the South (in 1971 and 1987) by the Sinhala-speaking ethnic majority who saw the English-speaking Sinhalese in Colombo as their class enemies.[6] Even the Anglophobic nationalists of India, or the Salafists of Syria, seem to recognize the indispensability of English and, in some fashion, secretly admire it, if only to manipulate it to serve the interests of the state – be it in the name of International Yoga Day or human rights for Muslims worldwide.

This paradoxical if somewhat schizophrenic relationship between Anglophilia and Anglophobia has resulted in what Akshya Saxena identifies as two Englishes, one actively adopted by the state, with all its hegemonic undertones, and one vernacularized by its subjects, who perform English in myriad ways to resist such dominance.[7] If the state's use of English forms the basis for the *langue* of the law, or the vehicular language of *Ordnung*,[8] then vernacular English becomes the *parole* of the people. Just as nationalism becomes a competing narrative between the pedagogics of the state and the performance of the people,[9] Englishes, too, become a contested terrain of colonial powers and postcolonial aspirations, populist invocations and practices of the people, neoliberal arrogation and vernacular appropriation.

This collection is an attempt both to showcase these tensions in the emerging field of World Anglophone Studies and to move beyond the traditional frameworks based on the colonial and imperial legacies of English in order to understand the complex adaptations, iterations, and incarnations of English in the contemporary world. It does so by drawing attention to contexts in the Global South (and beyond) where Anglophone cultural capital lends deeper insights into the crimes not only of the colonial past but also of the postcolonial present – the everyday forms of domestic and vernacular hegemonies and the resistance against them. Such 'Anglophone imaginaries,' often internalized and vernacularized at the level of idioms, lexis, and metaphors, have significant heuristic implications for the formation of cultural networks and forms of filiation, affiliation, and agency in an age of interlaced digital pathways. As the chapters assembled in this volume show, World Anglophone Studies involves a philological transmigration into the vernacular worlds of Anglophone metaphors, symbols, and structures of expression to keep an arm-length distance from the familiar and the fraternal. Such distance distils a vision of clarity, if not a sense of suspicion, when it comes to the polarized discourses of Anglophobia and Anglophilia in the debates on world and vernacular letters today.

English in a World of Vernaculars

Consider, for instance, the celebration of October 25, the birthday of Lord Macaulay, as the awakening day of the English Goddess – a miniature bronze idol modelled after the Liberty Statue, with a book in hand in lieu of the flame torch – erected by the Dalits of Banka as a symbol of resistance against vernacular injustice and Brahminic domination. To read the very policies that became the founding objects of postcolonial critique – Lord Macaulay's *Minute on Education* or the Horton-Asquith models that predicated colonial educational policy in British-ruled Africa – as documents of liberation for marginalized postcolonial populations may seem counterintuitive, if not facetious. Yet using English against English, in the service of anti-colonial or anti-establishment movements, is nothing new. What is new, however, is the fear among the agents of the state that marginalized groups might use English more resourcefully, and that it might even poison the ordinary folk with liberal ideas and notions of law, justice, rights, and entitlements. There is indeed a modicum of truth to such fears, as Dipesh Chakrabarty observes: "the writings of the most trenchant critic [implicitly B.R. Ambedkar] of the institution of 'untouchability' in British India refer us back to some originally European ideas about liberty and human equality."[10] Apropos Chakrabarty's remark, English is both weaponized and vernacularized by Dalits and other 'backward castes' in India, not least because the author of the Indian constitution, a Dalit himself, wrote his treatise on the *Annihilation of Caste* in English,[11] and those who followed his footsteps went a step further by rejecting the oppressive tenors of the so-called organicity or vernacular authenticity of *mother* tongues in whose name *other* mothers and *other* tongues are created.[12] It is amidst this ceaseless collision and contradiction between the world and the vernacular that the World Anglophone Studies featured in this collection come to the fore.

This perennial contradiction, as epitomized by Ngũgĩ wa Thiong'o some four decades ago, still finds it resonances today. Consider Ngũgĩ's own relations to the English Canon and Shakespeare:

> My Shakespeare is always around me. Dickens is amazing in terms of the range of characters that he was able to conjure ... my criticism has nothing to do with the quality and worth of English Literature. What I take issue with is the hierarchical power relationships among languages and literatures, with English and other European languages seen as occupying the top of the hierarchy.[13]

Ngũgĩ's critique of the hierarchy of global language structures is well in tune with his life-long advocacy for the local and the vernacular, yet his focus on "Decolonizing the Mind" through a return to African languages[14] risks missing complex linguistic realities in Africa and elsewhere that often enough are characterized not by binary conflicts between the 'global' and the 'local' but by hybridized and mixed language practices, by a constitutive multi-lingualism that has created millions of English-language native speakers in Africa (and other parts of the world where English is still often thought to be a 'second language') that habitually navigate between several languages, and by the fact that global English today encompasses a host of vernacular Englishes that can no longer be primarily understood through the colonial genealogies that originally spread English throughout the world, but also fail to confirm to established patterns of 'national languages.'[15]

In these tangled constellations where cultural nationalist attempts to neatly separate 'mother' and 'other' tongues come up against myriad ways of 'doing English,' normative approaches to 'language justice' have to be attuned to the vagaries of linguistically constituted power relations. Just as much as vernacular languages are capable of instituting and even naturalizing hierar-chies, English, too, is capable of both reproducing and deconstructing such hierarchies. As Arundhati Roy enchantingly remarks:

> my mother was actually an alien, with fewer arms than Kali perhaps but many more tongues. English is certainly one of them. *My* English has been widened and deepened by the rhythms and cadences of my alien mother's other tongues. (I say *alien* because there's not much that is organic about her. Her nation-shaped body was first violently assimilated and then vio-lently dismembered by an imperial British quill. I also say *alien* because the violence unleashed in her name on those who do not wish to belong to her (Kashmiris, for example), as well as on those who do (Indian Muslims and Dalits, for example), makes her an extremely un-motherly mother.)[16]

While exposing the un-motherliness of the mother tongue in his provoca-tively titled autobiography *Why I'm Not a Hindu* (1998), Kancha Ilaiah likens English to a diagnostic device against the pathologies of vernacular hierarchies in his own mother tongue, Telugu:

> As I entered the B.A. course the medium of instruction shifted from Telugu to English. [...] The brahminical framework was replaced by a European one. European systems, whether of religion or society or politics, presented a world which was totally different from the brahminical one. While the brahminical lessons had been conspiratorially silent about our castes and our cultures, the English texts appeared to be doing the opposite. They spoke of classes in Europe, and the textbooks described the cultures of both the rich classes and poor classes. [...] As I look back, it is clear from the English textbooks that in class societies – which also have conflicting cultures – there is much less of a conspiracy of silence in comparison to

caste societies. In the Telugu textbooks the conspiracy of silence is as loud as a thunderclap.[17]

Ilaiah's description of mother tongues as harbingers of hierarchy or bearers of conspiratorial silence "as loud as a thunderclap" borrows – fittingly, yet ironically – from a 14th-century Middle English figure of speech to describe contemporary vernacular injustices. Yet the elevation of English to the language of liberation in all these appeals – the Dalits' penchant for the English Goddess; Roy's edict of English as a morally appropriate language to seek justice because of the injustices constituted in, and instituted through, that very language; or Dipesh Chakravarti's caveat that a sense of dignity and equality among the dispossessed subalterns is derived from European ideas of liberty and equality – is only one, if particularly important, facet of the social life of contemporary English. It would be naïve to assume that any language – whether imperial English or vernacular Anglophone – is devoid of hegemonies or could potentially operate at a zero level of oppression. The chapters presented in the present volume caution against any such romanticization of English – as well as any other language in a globally interconnected world – and present striking examples of writers, film-makers, cultural producers, and general language users that bend and transform English in every conceivable direction, doing (as Chinua Achebe prognosticated in the 1960s) "unheard of things with English"[18] in the process and utilizing it to communicate a seemingly endless variety of experiences, queries, and aspirations.

English in a World of Strangers

From Zimbabwe to South America, the Balkans to Canada, and Australia to the Middle East, the chapters featured in this volume locate English "in a world of strangers" (to use Anthony Appiah's compelling ethical formula that we have borrowed for the purposes of this collection),[19] a world in which English not only sinks its roots but spreads out as a global vernacular agent to express linguistic and cultural modernities emerging from both Anglophone and non-Anglophone worlds alike. These modernities are inextricably linked to cultures and lifeworlds in which matters of identity, questions of belonging, habitats of solidarity, and a resolute sense of being in the world are negotiated in perennially unfinished processes of transformation. Language, and the English language in particular, becomes a prime site and source of these processes and provides tropes of planetary modernities that can be found all over the globe, including the non-Anglophone parts of the world, in their internally differentiated, fractured formations. Anglophone studies thus need to be mapped not merely in a world of friends and fraternities but indeed also in a world of strangers.

This is vitally important, because English has also become a major language of migration and border-crossing. If English once migrated from Europe to various parts of the world in the wake of an unprecedented export of European populations to staff and settle European empires, it has long since come back to Britain in a process that Jamaican author Louise Bennett once jokingly called a "colonisation in reverse."[20] Migrant Englishes setting up cultural and linguistic interfaces with a wide variety of (former) home countries and mother tongues today can be found all over the globe from Europe to North America, Asia, and the Pacific and contribute to a further transformation of global English. As migrants over several generations settle down to become new citizens in (former) host countries, clear-cut distinctions between 'mother' and 'other' tongues become blurred, and what were once distinct migrant Englishes turn into new forms of British, American, Canadian, or Australian English.

Mapping World Anglophone Studies through the optics of multipolar power structures and transcultural flows thus turns a whole universe of discourse predicated on the question of who owns English on its head. As early as 2001, in his introduction to the essay collection *A New World Order*, Caryl Phillips predicted a reconfiguration of planetary communication "in which there will soon be one global conversation with limited participation open to all, and full participation available to none," and concluded that "in this new world order nobody will feel fully at home."[21] If English today finds itself in 'a world of strangers,' this is so because it has become a globally desirable medium of aesthetic expression and matters of political expediency, even for writers from traditionally non-Anglophone parts of the world such as Latin America, East Asia, the Arab World, or Eastern Europe. On the other hand, the grand notion of an 'anglophone world' is internally eroded by multilingual cultural configurations across the globe as well as by a revival of vernacular literatures in Africa or on the Indian subcontinent. This new dispensation arguably confronts Anglophone studies worldwide with the challenge to address the specific role of English as both a global and local medium of expression and social interaction. It also necessitates a self-reflexive reappraisal of established disciplinary protocols in cultural and literary studies as well as linguistics: how helpful are these routines – often enough mainly based on the colonial genealogies of English – for coming to terms with what Arundhati Roy, in her essay "What Is the Morally Appropriate Language in Which to Think and Write?", cited previously, has called the "mind-bending mosaic" of language politics – and practices – in the contemporary world?

Anglophone writing, even from the most marginalized communities, paradoxically occupies a privileged position within the global literary market. Indeed, at least since the turn of the millennium, Anglophone texts from the former colonies have become increasingly successful on the global market as cultural difference became an ever more attractive object of aesthetic consumption. The dominance of English as the universal language for coding and as the lingua franca of science, finance, and information technologies as well as the rise of digital literary cultures are further instances of the unique role of English in the contemporary world. What has often received far less attention, however, is the fact that English has also become the language of transitional justice and truth and reconciliation commissions, as well as – given its wider reach of national and transnational readerships – a preferred language of resistance and dissent for many subaltern and indigenous voices from Burma to Palestine and from Indonesia to Nigeria. This holds especially true for emerging genres of digital storytelling, social media narratives, television dramas, and streaming media which provide a global platform for hitherto untold narratives.

This volume takes up the challenge of exploring the current state and future development of World Anglophone Studies. In the past two decades, a host of new conceptual currents with seemingly mutual concerns, though with little or no mutual dialogue, have sought to move beyond the conventional postcolonial paradigm of "writing back" to the Empire by means of "appropriating" or "abrogating" English.[22] For instance, proponents of 'global literature' interrogate the homogenizing and universalistic tendencies of literary cultures enabled by the free market and transnational capital[23] and the resulting marginalization of vernacular letters.[24] The concept of "the world literary system" projects these homogenizing tendencies through the prism of global class *inequalities*, as opposed to cultural or vernacular tropes of *difference*.[25] Aamir Mufti's provocative study *Forget English! Orientalisms and World Literatures* draws attention to the contributions made by vernacular linguistic and cultural traditions that often remain overshadowed by Orientalist legacies of Anglophilia.[26] Within this global literary turn, the new variant of Global South studies (Mukoma wa Ngugi; Russell West-Pavlov) advocates the need for a South–South dialogue that does not triangulate the literary discourses of Asia, Africa and South America through Europe,[27] while Ottmar Ette muses about "literatures without a fixed abode" in *Writing-Between-Worlds*.[28]

Buoyed by Gayatri Spivak's call for a non-totalistic conception of "planetary literature,"[29] Mayo Miyoshi envisages a global literary field that is based on the ethos of inclusion, not of economic or cultural exclusion in the wake of collective global and planetary crises.[30] Ian Baucom's concept of "globallit" further elucidates these shared histories of inclusion and exclusion, arguing that the global in literature becomes a conceptual grid that brings together both the homogenizing ("centripetal") and differentiating ("centrifugal") effects of globalization in the metropolis and its margins.[31] Echoing this view, the debate on "global anglophone literature" initiated by scholars such as Ragini Srinivasan, Gaurav Desai, and Rebecca Walkowitz in a special forum of the journal *Interventions*[32] proposes to read literatures from former Anglophone colonies as both vernacularly grounded and globally anchored. Pheng Cheah's illuminating work *What Is a World? On Postcolonial Literature as World Literature* is an equally pathbreaking study that proposes a temporal conception of the "world" setting malleable, multiple, and non-normative perspectives against centrist spatial conceptions and coordinates.[33]

At the heart of all these enquiries lies a growing awareness that the focus on the colonial and imperial pasts of English is no longer sufficient to understand the complex role of multitudinous Englishes in the contemporary world. Yet neither the emergence of Anglophone literatures and cultures in parts of the world not traditionally considered Anglophone nor the multilingual and creolised ensembles in which English is reinventing itself as an extendable, if not elongated, tongue or the role of English on new media platforms and emergent sites of resistance involving women, indigenous populations, queer and other non-heteronormative sexualities has attracted much systematic attention so far.

Mapping World Anglophone Studies: Exemplary Case Studies

The four subsections of this volume – Rethinking World Anglophone Studies; Deterritorializing the Anglophone; Contact, Crossover and Creolization; and Embattled Englishes: Revolt, Emancipation, and Transformation – initiate such a systematic, if necessarily exemplary, mapping of World Anglophone Studies. Collectively, they bring forth the argument that World Anglophone Studies need to chart the influence of English beyond the British colonial/ Commonwealth axis, engage with the formation of hybrid contact zones between English and vernacular tongues as well as the vernacularization of English, and acknowledge the latter's ability to influence global circuits of the publication industry, streaming entertainment, and post-national cultural imaginaries. Furthermore, such a mapping of World Anglophone Studies can no longer be accompanied by a political charting of the field along the conventional coordinates of "writing back" to Empire. Instead, the agency of world anglophone texts and cultural practices lies as much in their appropriation of global market forces as in their capacity to "write back to self" (Mwangi),[34] with the English language time and again becoming a source of resistance and emancipation against oppressive tenors of local hierarchies as well as vernacular hegemonies.

The first section of this volume, Rethinking World Anglophone Studies, brings together incisive interventions in the theory and practice of World Anglophone Studies ranging from Trinidad to India, South Africa, and Belize and engaging with the role of transnational editing in the emergence of the global Anglophone as a field of literary practice and critique, transnational media practices and the politics of language, the role of English in the transition from post-Apartheid to world Anglophone literature and the complex interactions between English and Creoles in a globalized world.

Ben Fried's contribution to this volume inquires into the material practices and conceptual frameworks generated by the transnational production and reception of Anglophone literatures and argues that coming to terms with the reality of English literatures "spread and splintered across the globe" constitutes a challenge that cultural and literary studies cannot avoid, despite the manifold irritations raised by the shift of emphasis implied by the transition from 'postcolonial' to 'global Anglophone.' Focusing on the role of editing in the complex field formed by writers, readers and institutions, Fried argues that "a capacious, critical, and material framework for the global Anglophone" emerging from transnational commercial and aesthetic networks already exists. His case study of the intricate transmedial correlations between the editorial work of V.S. Naipaul in the BBC's *Caribbean Voices* programme and the beginning of his writing career in the late 1950s highlights the incessant transformation of a global language challenged and enriched by vernacular Englishes – and shows how habitual notions of "Imperial" English and its Others need to be overcome in order to make sense of Naipaul's creativity as well as the emergence of the global Anglophone.

Annika McPherson and Ashumi Shah delve deeply into a baffling media scenario in India involving global players such as Netflix producing popular web series in Hindi, Narendra Modi's "Digital India" flagship programme, and Shiv Sena ultra-nationalists castigating Netflix for its alleged defamation of Hinduism. Scrutinizing the Netflix adaptation of Prayaag Akbar's acclaimed debut novel *Leila* (2018) that transposes an English-language novel to a TV series with a Hindi and an English audio track as well as German, French, and Russian subtitles and of Dhruv Sehgal's *Little Things* (2016), which started as an English-language web series and was rebranded as a 'Netflix original' in 2018 that shifted from an English to a Hindi 'original' audio track with an English 'dubbed' version, the authors highlight the cultural, political, and linguistic complexity of Netflix productions in India. While there are excellent reasons to remain highly critical of the global marketing surge of web-based media giants such as Netflix and Amazon, the authors argue this complexity involves a high degree of translanguaging and critical content layers "that complicate easy assessments such as 'yet another Netflix show' based on the assumption of one-sided 'Westernization' or 'Americanization.'"

Deniz Gündoğan İbrışim takes the South African transition from post-Apartheid to world Anglophone literature as her test case for exploring the epistemic capacity of a world Anglophone perspective for the analysis of contemporary literatures and cultures. Her reading of Ahmat Dangor's *Kafka's Curse* seeks to nudge perceptions of contemporary South African literature out of "the strictures of the apartheid/post-apartheid binary" and situates Dangor's text within an Anglophone world literature which relies on multilingual encounters while "unfold[ing] into networks of diversified local epistemes and situated practices across the world." Anchoring its plot in an Arabic tale, Dangor's Anglophone novel thus creates "plural and non-Eurocentric worlds in which hierarchies between the intimate, local, regional, national, and the transnational blur."

BRITTA SCHNEIDER's take on the world Anglophone perspective unfolds through a critique of the widespread notion of 'national Englishes' on the one hand and an in-depth sociolinguistic study of the intricate relationship between English and Kriol in Belize on the other. Starting from the striking fact that all her interviewees rejected the existence of 'Belizean English,' the author unfolds a linguistic scenario where English is not necessarily projected as suppressive 'coloniser language,' and Kriol has acquired prestige as carrier of oral culture, linguistic creativity, and internal diversity and functions as an index of national belonging. As a result, English as a transnational medium of communication and Kriol as the lingua franca exist side by side, and speakers show little inclination towards wishing to 'decolonise' the Belizian linguascape. In coming to terms with the plurality of contemporary 'Englishing,' Schneider cautions, we should be wary of routinely nationalising Englishes and pay attention to the complexity of linguistic hierarchies within which English occupies a unique place.

The second section of this collection explores different trajectories of Deterritorializing the Anglophone and the emergence of anglophone literatures and cultures beyond the 'postcolonial' heritage of the British Empire. The case studies in this section address Egypt, the Balkans, Cuba, and Algeria and address issues such as the relationship between English and vernacular languages, Anglophone writing and migration, multilingualism and translation, as well as English as a contested means of decolonization.

PAVAN KUMAR MALREDDY and STEFANIE KEMMERER scrutinize the "uneasy encounter" of Arabic and English in Egyptian literature and show that the popular rhetorical juxtaposition of English as the alienating language of a small 'Westernized' elite and Arabic as the authentic language of the exploited masses misses much of the social, political, and literary dynamics of contemporary Egyptian society. By introducing the concept of an "Anglophone imaginary," the authors highlight the role of English and its associated cultural capital as "heuristic literary devices that lend deeper insights into the crimes committed in the name of local, vernacular, and national identities" and further "a distanced perspective of the familiar and the fraternal." Read through the lens of this "Anglophone imaginary," Saleem Haddad's *Guapa* (2016), and Bassem Youssef's *Revolution for Dummies* (2017) emerge as paradigmatic examples of a new phase of Anglo-Arabic writing inspired by the Arab Spring utilizing English as "a pivot from which the local and vernacular hierarchies can be critiqued, while simultaneously exposing its hegemonic tendencies." This polycentric writing neither engages in self-Orientalization nor in extolling the virtues of pan-Arabic nationalism, but has taken an "inward turn," deflating the "competing narratives of vernacular purism," and reflecting the spirit of "besieged, paralysed, and terrorised societies seeking radical uprooting and overhaul of the reigning systems."

Miriam Wallraven's chapter takes another look at a region of the world not traditionally associated with World Anglophone Studies and investigates the emergence of a new Balkan literature in English against the background of the contact zone caused by migration. Employing the concept of a "migrational metamultilingual mode" characterized by an accumulation of misunderstandings, loss of language, a self-reflexive "speaking about languages," and the thematization of authorship, the author investigates the complex negotiations of language and migration in Aleksandar Hemon's short story "Blind Jozef Pronek and Dead Souls" (2000), where Bosnia meets the US, and A.S. Patrić's novel *Black Rock White City* (2015), where former Yugoslavia encounters Australia. Both texts, the chapter argues, are characterized by an exploration of misunderstandings giving rise to communication problems and thematize the loss of voice resulting in a "bilingual silence" but also engage in "language-changing" strategies that allow them to develop multilingual voices utilizing English to explore "non-postcolonial" contexts and "expand the Anglophone literary canon."

María Aguiar-Escobar's chapter examines translation as yet another translingual contact zone, in this case between Anglophone and Hispanophone writing. Engaging with Cristina García, a Cuban–U.S. American woman writer, who as a "1.5 generation" author belongs neither to the "first" generation of people who migrated as adults nor to the "second" generation of children born in the new country, and her first novel *Dreaming in Cuban* (1992) as well as the Spanish translation *Soñar en cubano* (1993), the chapter builds on "feminist translation" as a key concept geared towards recovering women writers and translators invisibilized in dominant discourses, examining linguistic gender representation in translation and analysing feminist and sexist translations. While *Dreaming in Cuban* extends the hybridity of the Caribbean as "a linguistically and culturally fluid space" to the U.S., the chapter argues that it can also be considered a feminist novel, since "it brings to the spotlight women as subjects who have traditionally been silenced and excluded from history." By contrast, *Soñar en cubano* mutes the outspoken critique to be found in the Anglophone version, "dampens the feminist alliances forged in the English text," and deprives the Hispanophone world of a challenging transnational feminist perspective.

In the last chapter of this section, Camille Jacob and Leonald Kazibwe turn to yet another stranger shore of English – the sociolinguistic context of Algeria. Amidst prevalent calls for 'more English' in a society that often sees the continuing presence of French as a vestige of colonialism, this chapter uncovers a complex multilingual scenario in which " 'English' and Englishes are used to index decolonisation, authenticity, and Otherness in specific settings." While many commentators have perceived the linguistic dynamics in Algeria and other Francophone countries in terms of "a zero-sum game, with English 'replacing' French rather than adding to it," and "narratives of the world being threatened by 'l'anglo-américain'," the authors advocate an approach that takes language users' (often seemingly contradictory) positions seriously and focuses on the expansion of people's linguistic repertoire and the role of English as a medium of instruction and symbol of cultural capital. Yet language users in Algeria not only speak in English but often enough about it, projecting it as an "Other" spoken by "young people," "people in the South," or (non-Algerian) "native speakers." Talking about English, the authors conclude, is thus not only an index of language change but also a means of debating "history, belonging, and political priorities."

The third section of this volume investigates examples of Contact, Crossover, and Creolization in contemporary modes of "doing English." The chapters in this section focus on Sheng and popular culture in Kenya, chick lit in Nigeria and India, Vietnamese diasporic literature in the U.S., crossovers between English and Shona in Zimbabwean literature, and Goan-Angolan migration trajectories in contemporary Australian writing.

ALEX NELUNGO WANJALA's chapter on the role of Sheng in Kenyan popular culture opens this section with an impressive reminder of the complicated contestations of power that 'mixed' languages entail. Having emerged among lower-class Africans in Nairobi's Eastlands district in the 1930s, the Swahili/English crossover referred to as Sheng became a widely used marker of identity for urban youths in the following decades and today constitutes a vibrant mixed code used by its speakers as a means of "expressing conviviality among themselves as subjects" and counteracting the ethnolinguistic categorizations touted by the Kenyan nation-state which insists on its citizens identifying themselves as members of particular ethnic groups and communicating "either in one of the local languages, Kiswahili, or English." Drawing on Mikhail Bakhtin's concept of "Billingsgate genres," WANJALA analyses the widespread use of Sheng on social media platforms such as WhatsApp, Twitter, TikTok, and Instagram as contributing to the emergence of ribald, cheeky, and insolent forms of popular culture challenging 'polite' codes prevalent in Kenyan society and performing 'unruly' masculinities that confront conservative, 'traditional,' or commercialized gender norms.

Popular culture, although of a more transnational variety, also takes centre stage in DELPHINE MUNOS and NICKLAS HÅLLÉN's examination of chick lit of the Global South focusing on the strategic uses of different forms of English and their relationship to "the protagonists' as well as the authors' aspirational projects." Noting the emergence of chick lit imprints geared towards local and/or trans-regional audiences that are situated outside the Anglo-American literary market – still assumed to be the 'natural habitat' of chick lit by many critics – and the dynamic advance of social media and digital technologies that is rapidly transforming reading publics all over the world, the authors are particularly interested in the tensions between the roots of the chick lit genre "in the urban metropolis and in the English language" and narratives based in "globalising cities of the Global South" where English has often become "a language of aspiration." Their readings of Chetan Bhagat's *Half Girlfriend*, Olayemi Oyinkansola's *Finding Mr. Right*, and Joy Eju'ojo's *The Reunion* show that chick lit from the global South not only manages to combine rootedness in the local with identity constructions associated with transnational spaces, but also provides "fascinating insights into the palimpsestic language hierarchies and disparate thought-worlds at play in India and Nigeria."

In her chapter on Ocean Vuong's *On Earth We're Briefly Gorgeous*, ELENA FURLANETTO highlights the role of 'ambiguity aesthetics' in a migrant and queer text written in the contact zone between English and Vietnamese that is striving "to materialize the hesitations, stutters, silences, and slippages that happen in the blank spaces between languages, in the distance between the mother('s) tongue and the language of the everyday." Drawing on the key concepts of "language scarcity," which refers to contexts where language fails to express the experiences that fall in between two languages and their cultures, and "language excess," which signifies the new possibilities and expressions created by the "unexpected semantics" of multiple languages, the chapter investigates the complex manner in which Vuong's novel navigates between "the existential condition of being *neither-nor*" and "being *both-and*." If literary ambiguity unfolds through speechlessness, namelessness, and communication failures, the chapter concludes, it also generates spaces where languages compenetrate to build semantic bridges between each other and a new polysemous text can emerge through "the insistent knocking of Vietnamese below the surface of English."

TANAKA CHIDORA's contribution to this volume analyses Chenjerai Hove's experimentation with a Shonalized version of Zimbabwean English called Shonglish in his 1996 novel *Ancestors*. Hove's literary strategy of Shonalizing English, the chapter argues, aims at overcoming a "tourist gaze" that sees African characters as emblematic of "world minorities with a language not as worldly as English," but also eschews cultural nationalist renditions of continental or ethnic essentialism. In creative and communicative terms, Hove's "Shonglish" is "at par with standardised English," and becomes "a 'new' English" utilized by the author to cast a critical, self-reflexive eye on the role of women in Shona society. Employing techniques such as direct translation from Shona to English, the use of Shona words without definitions or glossaries, direct translations of proverbs into English, and constant borrowing from Shona oral history, Hove deftly communicates the oppression of Shona women "by using the linguistic idiom of the culture that oppresses them." Rather than waging a 'patriotic' war against English, the chapter concludes, Hove captures the nuances of Shona culture and language in "one of the many Englishes available in the world."

In the concluding chapter of this section, JEAN PAGE scrutinizes "the puzzle of home" and the role of food, clothing, and language in the formation of a diasporic migrant child in Suneeta Peres da Costa's novella *Saudade*, published in Australia in 2018. Portraying a "migrant minority family ambivalent about their own culture" and their diasporic affiliations to Goa, Angola, and Portugal in the 1960s, *Saudade* utilizes the protagonist girl's awakening consciousness to illuminate the complex cultural and identity affiliations produced by her family's trajectory within a crumbling Portuguese empire. In this case study, the English-language novel becomes host to a pluriverse of languages (Portuguese; the local Kimbundu spoken in Angola; and Konkani, the family's Goan regional language) interacting within the Anglophone imaginary set up in the text by the Goan-Australian author; if *Saudade*, shortlisted for the Australian Prime Minister's Literary Awards in 2019, is an example of "Australian migrant literature," it is so because of its author's migrant sensibility but neither because it features migrant experiences in Australia nor because it thematizes accommodating English into this pluriverse. Relexifying non-English languages into the Anglophone text, the chapter concludes, thus becomes a powerful tool for literary renditions of non-essentialist difference and a multilingual "mestiza consciousness."

The fourth and last section of this volume looks at Embattled Englishes: Revolt, Emancipation, Transformation and addresses representations of 'queerness' in India, post-Apartheid "Fallist" consciousness in the wake of the "Rhodes Must Fall" campaign, the role of Anglophone novels in projecting student activism in Africa, anglophone women's novels in Africa and their deep connections to the cultures and people they represent, and English as an invaluable mode of indigenous expression in Canada.

UMESH PATRA's chapter on the intricacies of representing queer communities and lifeworlds in India delves into the role of English as the predominant language of "the Indian queer" who – for historical and political reasons – have found it necessary to employ a language that in many respects jars with Indian cultural and linguistic realities. Due to "the lack of equivalent vernacular terms," the chapter argues, "the challenge of overthrowing a compulsory norm-assigning web" and of consolidating "a pan-Indian queer community united not only by a common cause but also a common tongue" has fallen upon English as "a necessary heuristic tool"; unlike the term 'Dalit,' however, which has managed to emerge as a widely accepted signifier for a wide array of caste-related grievances and sensibilities, 'queer' has remained untranslated and is sometimes hard to reconcile with specific forms of non-heteronormative gendered life in India. Amidst a burgeoning critique of 'Western' cultural influences voiced by conservative detractors of non-normative sexualities, the chapter concludes, the undeniable realities of queerness in India, emerging through academic discourse, a multimedia cultural presence, and a vibrant urban street life, are thus still struggling for an adequate linguistic expression.

In his chapter on the subjectivities of black South African students and young graduates in post-Apartheid *bildungsromane*, IBRAHIM ABRAHAM engages with Niq Mhlongo's *Dog Eat Dog* and *After Tears* and Songeziwe Mahlangu's *Penumbra*. Zooming in on three subjectivity types characteristic of the "Fallist" student movement in South Africa that emerged in the wake of the "Rhodes Must Fall" campaign – tricksters, hustlers, and moral saints – the chapter highlights the contours of black writing in "a democratic culture that now offers a cacophony of black voices" and "no longer even pretends to revere black writers." Given the fact that the "Fallist" student movement mainly championed English as their medium of expression, it is no coincidence that the *black bildungsromane* wrestling with the fallout of this movement in contemporary South Africa are Anglophone novels set in a "world of strangers" in which shared histories of oppression are no longer prominent, and that the protagonists of these novels "have not found settled places for themselves in their unsettled society in which individuals appear to hold ever less in common."

ANNIE GAGIANO's chapter on Anglophone African novelists as spokeswomen of specifically African perspectives contends that works such as Sefi Atta's *Everything Good Will Come* (2004), Aminatta Forna's *Ancestor Stones* (2006), and Maaza Mengiste's *The Shadow King* (2019) use their access to the literary Anglosphere to "decentralise colonial-era and postcolonial outsiders' histories and depictions of African societies." GAGIANO engages with the arguments of a spate of recent 'materialist' critics of African literature and argues that far from tailoring their tales to suit the tastes of 'Western readers' or the demands of 'the global publishing industry,' contemporary anglophone writers also address and have an impact upon readers native to the societies depicted in their works. Instead of fashionable dismissals of anglophone African writing as externally directed, the chapter concludes, what is needed are respectful critical engagements with the creative agency of contemporary African writers and the internal perspectives on specific, locally distinct histories, societies, and cultures projected in their works.

In the last chapter of this volume, VANESSA EVANS presents a critical reading of David Treuer's *The Translation of Dr. Apelles* (2008) that engages with the widespread assumption that "in speaking English Indigenous Peoples are complicit in their own erasure because English cannot be an Indigenous language." This assumption, the chapter argues, has emerged from long histories of colonial denigrations of 'deficient' indigenous cultures and today becomes recycled in the well-meant but highly detrimental notion of 'authenticity' that "occludes the reality that the very language used in processes of oppression can be taken back and reimagined as a means of strengthening Indigenous cultures." In unravelling the complex modes in which different narrative strands in Treuer's novel engage with the seeming impossibility of translating indigenous texts into English, the chapter shows that Dr. Appelles, the translated translator of the text, ultimately transforms English into a means of expressing his self-sovereignty as well as into a force of resistance against the mistranslations and misappropriations of colonial English.

As if heeding the curt instructions of Adolph Ng, the texts in this volume "speak loudest into the Anglophone" and etch their voices and visions into the English of our times: Instead of shouting back into the microphones of Empire – as epitomized in the metaphor of "writing back" that has long haunted the corridors of Anglophone literary gatherings – they shake up conventional modes of apprehending the Anglophone and delineate its transformation in various media, markets, and the publishing industry; they trace the deterritorialization of global Englishes and examine the vernacularization of English in a pluriverse of linguistic assemblages; and they probe the contact zones between English and other vernaculars and illuminate the dialogicity of languages within Anglophone texts.

Notes

1 Timothy Mo, *The Redundancy of Courage* (London: Vintage, 1991): 76.
2 Mo, *The Redundancy*, 400. See also Reed Way Dasenbrock, "Differentiating the Imperial and the Colonial in Southeast Asian Literature in English: *The Redundancy of Courage* and *The Gift of Rain*," *SARE: Southeast Asian Review of English* 50.1 (2017): 13–18.
3 Mo, *The Redundancy*, 13.
4 Bassem Youssef, *Revolution for Dummies* (New York: Dey Street Books, 2017): 24.
5 See Akshya Saxena, "Narendra Modi, Rohith Vemula and 'Vernacular English'," *The Wire.in*, 2022, https://thewire.in/books/narendra-modi-rohith-vemula-vernacular-english.
6 See Harshana Rambukwella, *The Politics and Poetics of Authenticity: A Cultural Genealogy of Sinhala Nationalism* (London: UCL Press, 2018): 31–35.
7 Akshya Saxena, *Vernacular English: Reading the Anglophone in Postcolonial India* (Princeton: Princeton University Press, 2022).
8 Gilles Deleuze and Felix Guattari, "What Is a Minor Literature?" *Mississippi Review* 11.3 (1983): 13–33.
9 See Homi K. Bhabha, "DissemiNation: Time, Narrative, and the Margins of the Modern Nation," in *Nation and Narration*, edited by Homi K. Bhabha (London: Routledge, 1990): 292.
10 Dipesh Chakrabarty, *Provincializing Europe: Postcolonial Thought and Historical Difference* (Chicago: Chicago University Press, 2008): 5.
11 Bhimrao Ramji Ambedkar, *Babasaheb Ambedkar: Writings and Speeches*, Vol. 6, compiled by Vasant Moon (Mumbai: Department of Education, Government of Maharashtra, 1998).
12 Arundhati Roy, "What is the Morally Appropriate Language in Which to Think and Write?" *Literary Hub*, 25 June 2018, https://lithub.com/what-is-the-morally-appropriate-language-in-which-to-think-and-write/.

13 Raut Tanuj, "Interview with Professor Ngũgĩ wa Thiong'o," *Myopia*, 11 December 2017. See also Simon Gikandi, "Traveling Theory: Ngugi's Return to English," *Research in African Literatures* 31.2 (2000): 194–209.

14 See Ngũgĩ wa Thiong'o, *Decolonising the Mind: The Politics of Language in African Literature* (London: Heinemann Educational, 1986). For a critique of Ngũgĩ's brand of 'decolonial' thinking as an "oversold promise" see Olúfémi Táíwò, *Against Decolonisation: Taking African Agency Seriously* (London: Hurst, 2022): 67–127.

15 See Brach Kachru, *World Englishes: Critical Concepts in Linguistics*, Vol. 4 (London: Taylor & Francis, 2006). For a critique of Kachru's model of 'national' World Englishes see Alastair Pennycook, *Global Englishes and Transcultural Flows* (Milton Park, Abingdon: Routledge, 2007).

16 Roy, "What is the Morally Appropriate Language in Which to Think and Write."

17 Kancha Ilaiah, *Why I am Not a Hindu: A Shudra Critique of Hindutva Philosophy, Culture and Political Economy* (Calcutta: Samya, 1996): 55.

18 Chinua Achebe, *Morning Yet on Creation Day: Essays* (London: Heinemann, 1975): 66.

19 Kwame Anthony Appiah, *Cosmopolitanism: Ethics in a World of Strangers* (New York: WW Norton & Company, 2006).

20 Louise Bennett, "Colonisation in Reverse," in *Jamaica Labrish*, edited by Louise Bennett (Kingston: Sangster, 1975): 179.

21 Caryl Philips, *A New World Order: Selected Essays* (London: Vintage, 2001): 5.

22 Bill Ashcroft, Gareth Griffiths and Helen Tiffin, *The Empire Writes Back: Theory and Practice in Post-Colonial Literatures* (London: Routledge, 1989).

23 Rajagopalan Radhakrishnan, "Globality is not Worldliness," *Gramma: Journal of Theory and Criticism* 13 (2005): 183–198; Suman Gupta, *Globalization and Literature* (London: Polity, 2009).

24 Ankhi Mukherjee, *What is a Classic? Postcolonial Rewriting and Invention of the Canon* (Stanford: Stanford University Press, 2013).

25 Neil Lazarus, "Cosmopolitanism and the Specificity of the Local in World Literature," *The Journal of Commonwealth Literature* 46.1 (2011): 119–137; Warwick Research Collective, *Combined and Uneven Development: Towards a New Theory of World-Literature* (Liverpool: Liverpool University Press, 2015).

26 Aamir Mufti, *Forget English! Orientalisms and World Literatures* (Cambridge: Harvard University Press, 2016).

27 Mukoma wa Ngugi, "Rethinking the Global South," *Journal of Contemporary Thought* 35 (2012): 40–46; Russell West-Pavlov, ed. *The Global South and Literature* (Cambridge: Cambridge University Press, 2018).

28 Ottmar Ette, *Writing-between-Worlds* (Berlin: de Gruyter, 2016).

29 Gayatri Chakravorty Spivak, *Death of a Discipline* (New York: Columbia University Press, 2003).

30 Masao Miyoshi, "Turn to the Planet: Literature, Diversity, and Totality," *Comparative Literature* 53.4 (2001): 283–297.

31 Ian Baucom, "Globalit, Inc.; or, the Cultural Logic of Global Literary Studies," *PMLA* 116.1 (2001): 158–172.

32 Ragini Tharoor Srinivasan, "Introduction: South Asia from Postcolonial to World Anglophone," *Interventions* 20.3 (2018): 309–316; Gaurav Desai, "Response: Postcolonial, by Any Other Name?" *Interventions* 20.3 (2018): 354–360; Rebecca Walkowitz, "Response: World Anglophone is a Theory," *Interventions* 20.3 (2018): 361–365.

33 Pheng Cheah, *What is a World? On Postcolonial Literature as World Literature* (Durham: Duke University Press, 2015).

34 Evan M. Mwangi, *Africa Writes Back to Self: Metafiction, Gender, Sexuality* (New York: State University of New York Press, 2009).

Introduction **19**

Bibliography

Achebe, Chinua. *Morning Yet on Creation Day: Essays*. London: Heinemann, 1975.

Ambedkar, Bhimrao Ramji. *Babasaheb Ambedkar: Writings and Speeches*, Vol. 6, compiled by Vasant Moon. Mumbai: Department of Education, Government of Maharashtra, 1998.

Appiah, Kwame Anthony. *Cosmopolitanism: Ethics in a World of Strangers*. New York: WW Norton & Company, 2006.

Ashcroft, Bill, Gareth Griffiths and Helen Tiffin. *The Empire Writes Back: Theory and Practice in Post-Colonial Literatures*. London: Routledge, 1989.

Baucom, Ian. "Globalit, Inc.; or, the Cultural Logic of Global Literary Studies." *PMLA* 116.1 (2001): 158–172.

Bennett, Louise. "Colonisation in Reverse." In *Jamaica Labrish*, edited by Bennett Louise. Kingston: Sangster, 1975: 179.

Bhabha, Homi K. "DissemiNation: Time, Narrative, and the Margins of the Modern Nation." In *Nation and Narration*, edited by Homi K. Bhabha. London: Routledge, 1990: 291–322.

Chakrabarty, Dipesh. *Provincializing Europe: Postcolonial Thought and Historical Difference*. Chicago: Chicago University Press, 2008.

Cheah, Pheng. *What is a World? On Postcolonial Literature as World Literature*. Durham: Duke University Press, 2015.

Dasenbrock, Reed Way. "Differentiating the Imperial and the Colonial in Southeast Asian Literature in English: *The Redundancy of Courage* and *The Gift of Rain*." *SARE: Southeast Asian Review of English* 50.1 (2017): 13–18.

Deleuze, Gilles and Felix Guattari. "What is a Minor Literature?" *Mississippi Review* 11.3 (1983): 13–33.

Desai, Gaurav. "Response: Postcolonial, by Any Other Name?" *Interventions* 20.3 (2018): 354–360.

Ette, Ottmar. *Writing-between-Worlds*. Berlin: de Gruyter, 2016.

Gikandi, Simon. "Traveling Theory: Ngugi's Return to English." *Research in African Literatures* 31.2 (2000): 194–209.

Gupta, Suman. *Globalization and Literature*. London: Polity, 2009.

Ilaiah, Kancha. *Why I am Not a Hindu: A Shudra Critique of Hindutva Philosophy, Culture and Political Economy*. Calcutta: Samya, 1996.

Kachru, Brach. *World Englishes: Critical Concepts in Linguistics*, Vol. 4. London: Taylor & Francis, 2006.

Lazarus, Neil. "Cosmopolitanism and the Specificity of the Local in World Literature." *The Journal of Commonwealth Literature* 46.1 (2011): 119–137.

Miyoshi, Masao. "Turn to the Planet: Literature, Diversity, and Totality." *Comparative Literature* 53.4 (2001): 283–297.

Mo, Timothy. *The Redundancy of Courage*. London: Vintage, 1991.

Mufti, Aamir. *Forget English! Orientalisms and World Literatures*. Cambridge: Harvard University Press, 2016.

Mukherjee, Ankhi. *What is a Classic? Postcolonial Rewriting and Invention of the Canon*. Stanford: Stanford University Press, 2013.

Mwangi, Evan M. *Africa Writes Back to Self: Metafiction, Gender, Sexuality*. New York: State University of New York Press, 2009.

Pennycook, Alastair. *Global Englishes and Transcultural Flows*. Milton Park, Abingdon: Routledge, 2007.

Philips, Caryl. *A New World Order: Selected Essays*. London: Vintage, 2001.

Radhakrishnan, Rajagopalan. "Globality is not Worldliness." *Gramma: Journal of Theory and Criticism* 13 (2005): 183–198.

Rambukwella, Harshana. *The Politics and Poetics of Authenticity: A Cultural Genealogy of Sinhala Nationalism*. London: UCL Press, 2018.

Roy, Arundhati. "What is the Morally Appropriate Language in Which to Think and Write?" 25 June 2018. https://lithub.com/what-is-the-morally-appropriate-language-in-which-to-think-and-write/ (last accessed 26 April 2024).

Saxena, Akshya. "Narendra Modi, Rohith Vemula and 'Vernacular English'." *The Wire.in*, 2022. https://thewire.in/books/narendra-modi-rohith-vemula-vernacular-english (last accessed 8 August 2023).

———. *Vernacular English: Reading the Anglophone in Postcolonial India*. Princeton: Princeton University Press, 2022.

Spivak, Gayatri Chakravorty. *Death of a Discipline*. New York: Columbia University Press, 2003.

Srinivasan, Ragini Tharoor. "Introduction: South Asia from Postcolonial to World Anglophone." *Interventions* 20.3 (2018): 309–316.

Táíwò, Olúfémi. *Against Decolonisation: Taking African Agency Seriously*. London: Hurst, 2022.

Tanuj, Raut. "Interview with Professor Ngũgĩ Wa Thiong'o." *Myopia*, 11 December 2017. https://projectmyopia.com/interview-with-professor-ngugi-wa-thiongo/ (last accessed 20 April 2024).

Walkowitz, Rebecca. "Response: World Anglophone is a Theory." *Interventions* 20.3 (2018): 361–365.

wa Ngugi, Mukoma. "Rethinking the Global South." *Journal of Contemporary Thought* 35 (2012): 40–46.

Warwick Research Collective. *Combined and Uneven Development: Towards a New Theory of World-Literature*. Liverpool: Liverpool University Press, 2015.

wa Thiong'o, Ngũgĩ. *Decolonising the Mind: The Politics of Language in African Literature*. London: Heinemann Educational, 1986.

West-Pavlov, Russell, ed. *The Global South and Literature*. Cambridge: Cambridge University Press, 2018.

Youssef, Bassem. *Revolution for Dummies*. New York: Dey Street Books, 2017.

I
Rethinking World Anglophone Studies

1

EDITING THE GLOBAL ANGLOPHONE

Publishing History as a Framework for an Emergent Field

Ben Fried

English is a literary language with two outsized capitals and many regions. Divided again and again by its common tongue, literature in English overflows national borders and the corresponding system of country classification by which, for the sake of convenience and some amount of cultural kinship, academic English studies traditionally understands the business of writing and reading. Yet it recedes before the furthest horizon of world literature, since a shared language and a wide, if widely various, experience of the British Empire have left a living legacy that deserves to be understood on its own terms. Those terms are, admittedly, complex. Successive scholarly models have partially mapped this uneven topography of mingled difference and affinity, but an encompassing framework for the English literatures that make up "English literature" has yet to emerge. Excluding the dominant Anglo-American axis, the now largely discarded umbrella of "Commonwealth literature" has been rejected precisely for reinscribing the imperial order and for imposing an outdated, condescending category with little remaining purchase on reality. Its passing coincides with the rise of postcolonial theory and of unsettled disputes over that term's proper ambit. "Some would deny it to white settler colonies," Stuart Hall observes, "reserving it exclusively for the non-western colonised societies."[1] For how can one extend the postcolonial sphere to both without advancing an equality of analysis that disguises profound inequality of experience? Anthologies and criticism which do so have a worrying tendency to "collaps[e] very different national-racial formations" and flatten historical discrepancies "with an easy stroke of the 'post.'"[2] The very attempt "to include all English literary productions by societies affected by colonialism" prunes postcolonialism of critical and political specificity. But, after all, Anglophone writing exists; ways must be found to discuss it

DOI: 10.4324/9781003464037-3
This chapter has been made available under a CC-BY-NC-ND 4.0 license.

fruitfully, despite and because of the great diversity it envelops. What conceptual architecture is equal to the fact of English literatures as they presently stand, spread and splintered across the globe? How can we understand the mingled motives of art and power that drive their expansion? Where do the literary centres lie, and who controls their means of production?

An opening for answers has arrived with the academy's latest disciplinary turn. Over the last decade, the "global Anglophone" has taken institutional, if not intellectual, hold in English Departments and MLA job listings. It offers the questionable benefits of breadth and imprecision, the opportunities and hazards that accompany a lack of definition. Blandly descriptive, the phrase specifies only a language; its adjective provides the opposite of qualification, inflating a linguistic field to its widest possible borders. Swallowing those territories once called Commonwealth and still studied under the postcolonial aegis, this new term provokes considerable resistance. In 2018 and 2019, special issues of *Interventions* and *Post45* canvassed young scholars on their shifting professional terrain and uncovered at best a grudging acceptance, at worst a sense that the postcolonial is being asset-stripped in the academic equivalent of a corporate takeover. Introducing the *Interventions* issue, Ragini Tharoor Srinivasan asks, "Who are we, if we are to be global Anglophonists and not postcolonialists?"[3] She answers, ambivalently, that this "renomination" at least leaves space for self-criticism, allowing the new Anglophonists to "work through and against English's hegemony in South Asia, its rapid global spread and omnipresence in the Academy."[4] Presenting the *Post45* series, Nasia Anam expresses a keener sense of what has been lost in rebranding, characterizing the buzzphrase as "more a marketing term than one reflecting an earnest shift in scholarly discourse," a heading that has no organic roots in "theoretical, generic, or disciplinary conversations."[5] In appropriating the territory of the postcolonial, the global Anglophone subjects it to a single measure: that of the English language, which is not quite the unifying principle the phrase seems to suggest. Starting from a fundamentally warped and warping premise, "the fact of an English-speaking world, not a world in which thousands of other languages, literatures and writers in those languages existed," the global Anglophone may be yet another addition to – if not the apotheosis of – what Mūkoma wa Ngũgĩ has named "the myth of the English metaphysical empire."[6] The ascendancy of this new field is indisputable, its utility much less so.

Yet the global Anglophone names a reality long distorted by piecemeal English studies: the spread of English writing and reading across the world, in conquest, resistance, and accommodation. Anam rightly spies the possibility for diminishment in this academic expansion. The act of "bring[ing] the U.S., Canada, Australia, and Ireland back into the fold without automatically necessitating an anticolonial perspective" may seem less like broad-minded analysis and more like a deliberate neutering of postcolonial dynamism.[7]

But leaving out those literatures generates a different set of limitations. It obscures the transnational networks of production and reception that do, in fact, give material and imaginative existence to a global Anglophone. As even its opponents acknowledge, this rising discipline will be moulded by its first generation of practitioners. Anam concludes by wondering whether we can "marshal the global Anglophone into becoming a politically and intellectually vanguard mode of critical inquiry" and replying that "in my view, we have no other option." Such a mode of inquiry could build on postcolonial foundations while incorporating Anglophone writing in all its varieties, attending to their imbalances while investigating the real relationships which bind them. This chapter is an attempt to outline that approach for future research, offering a theoretical justification for the global Anglophone and a case study against which to test it.

My argument is that a capacious, critical, and material framework for the global Anglophone is already available to us, although it has not yet been recognized and investigated as such: the field formed by the relations between its writers, readers, and institutions. To the extent that these commercial and aesthetic networks exist, a global Anglophone exists – the field of literary activity justifying the field of literary study. To map the topography of the global Anglophone is therefore to locate its editorial centres of gravity and track the changeable currents of literary goods circulating between them. Publishing history unites, and editorial activity reveals, the creative processes by which writing enters the world and reaches its readers. If we follow that history, we see where power and creativity intersect, along axes of domination and independence, via literary capitals whose organizational and artistic biases can be at once enabling and repressive. As acceptance and rejection belong equally to the study of editing and publishing, so an editorial analysis has the capacity to explain both what is illuminating and what is distorting about the global Anglophone. Conceived in this way, the emergent field need not reinforce a neo-colonial state of affairs; rather, it may house all those scholars seeking to understand the state of literatures in English today and the forces that have shaped them. Indeed, one might even suggest that the global Anglophone will only truly live up to its name when it encompasses American and English literatures too. We may thus answer the challenge thrown down by Salman Rushdie nearly four decades ago when refuting the existence of another academy-inspired category – and fulfil his vision of a more accurate and equitable critical dispensation.

A Framework for the Global Anglophone

Rushdie's 1983 essay "'Commonwealth Literature' Does Not Exist" unfolds the concept's emptiness and traces its pernicious edge. In practice, the term confines certain writers to a "ghetto," separated from the all-embracing genus

26 Ben Fried

"English literature."[8] Even on its own terms the distinction immediately lapses into incoherence. Rushdie asks why "South Africa and Pakistan, for instance, are not members of the Commonwealth, but their authors apparently belong to its literature" and notes that England itself, though actually part of the Commonwealth, is curiously not included.[9] Yet in rejecting this classification, he also makes the case for its renovation. Between national and world literature, the one inflating local specificity and the other diminishing it, there exists a common sphere of language and loose literary affinity developing both centripetally and centrifugally – orbiting old capitals of cultural power while establishing new ones. As Rushdie observes, "those peoples who were once colonized by the language are now rapidly remaking it, domesticating it."[10] He offers a glimpse of a more critical and pluralist framework, one large and open enough for the facts. "I think that if *all* English literatures could be studied together, a shape would emerge which would truly reflect the new shape of the language in the world."[11] But what is that shape?

Publishing history in the postwar era offers one path to a synoptic, cross-cultural view. The business of books – deciding what will be printed and read – is the chief means by which literary power is both maintained and challenged. As publishing charts the changing relationship between literary capitals and literary regions, therefore, it tells a twofold story. So complicated an evolution cannot be reduced to a simple contest between declining imperial influence and swelling literary self-determination. For one thing, cultural clout long outlasts direct rule. Books ensure the enduring dominance of London and New York, literary capitals by dint of their concentration of literary capital: the infrastructure of publishers and periodicals, agencies, and awards which, staffed by professional readers, support and distort the creative act. Centres of cultural gravity, they continue to set standards and bestow prestige, offering more reliable access to readers and remuneration, acting on the materials of writers and manuscripts drawn from around the world. Yet it would be equally mistaken to characterize the modes of cultural production as merely extending the hegemony of powerful metropoles over far-flung dependencies. The rise of Anglophone literatures is also a local affair, postwar booms in publishing and political independence combining to establish new channels for artistic creation much closer to home. These domestic publishers and magazines and broadcasters do not occupy a separate world to their larger counterparts but a cultural and commercial continuum. Individual works flow between these poles of production, mediated by them and mediating between them, testifying to the conditions of their publication even as they transcend them.

The power to publish manifests in the editorial prerogative of selection and its textual consequences: acceptance and rejection, revision, and distortion. The figure of the editor is therefore the prism through which this dynamic of converging power and creativity comes into view. Present at the gates of every domain of literary production, editors read, and by reading mediate between writer and public, text, and institution. It is the collaboration – and conflict – between authors and editors in the making of texts that allows us to map the fraught territory of Anglophone writing, its crossing and recrossing of frontiers, at once building newly confident national canons and deepening a transnational system of creation and circulation. In consequence, the reality of the global Anglophone requires a deeper account than literary scholarship has yet attempted of the nature and operation of editorial power. " 'Wouldn't it be interesting to write the history of the editor, as a figure not in the history of literature but in the history of knowledge?'" mused Jill Lepore in 2017.[12] The smaller task has only been seriously attempted – and quite recently at that – by Susan L. Greenberg.[13] Her account falls short, however, in its restricted conception of editing as simply "a stage in the making of texts."[14] Rather, it is an activity that blends reading and writing, linking and illuminating both ends of the literary exchange. From the wings, editors, and other agents of the editorial function, stage-manage the literary culture at large. Greenberg traces the growth of "a poetics that considers editing as a dynamic process with a built-in understanding of failure and a sense of the possible," but how do poetics translate into power, the shaping of texts into the shaping of taste?[15] At the crossroads of creation, editorial leverage exerts twin forces, the pull that gathers a circle of writers around an editor, the propulsion that directs writing outwards into society. Insofar as the editor's work can be reconstructed from archival material, that labour deepens our historical and theoretical understanding of writing and reading. It also reveals the shape of production and circulation that constitutes the global Anglophone's concrete purchase on literature.

To this end, an editorial framework for the global Anglophone builds on existing theoretical foundations, combining ideas of creative reading with analyses of the literary economy. Editorial activity clarifies, on the micro level, how reading kindles writing and, on the macro level, how literary institutions foster fields of production and reception. Thus, the editor demonstrates how the concepts of field and mediation – as defined by Pierre Bourdieu and John Guillory[16] – can be usefully integrated. Bourdieu leaves out two elements which happen to be related: the work of editing and a coherent account of creativity. His field is a scene of ceaseless competition for cultural prestige – a *"field of struggles"* occupied by a "whole set of agents whose combined efforts produce consumers capable of knowing and recognizing the work of art as such."[17] Yet one position is curiously neglected in Bourdieu's economy of art; the editor, that ink-stained reader wielding the most immediate influence over the text, is nowhere examined. The figure of the publisher *is* important to Bourdieu but precisely because it serves to undermine "the charismatic ideology of 'creation,'" a charisma which the sociologist replaces with the aura of *"consecration."*[18] Consecration aside,

28 Ben Fried

however, Bourdieu seems to have quite a limited understanding of a publisher's functions, declaring that "the publisher or the dealer can only organize and rationalize the distribution of the work." He passes over the making of the work to attend to its appraisal – revisions not of the text but of its value – and ignores the part played by middlemen in preparing literature for publication: their mediation between composition and reception. Attention paid to such editorial mediations can restore a vital theory of creativity to Bourdieu's social anatomy.

For a mediation is a transmission that is also a recreation. By drawing a text into a fresh context that partially absorbs and partially distinguishes itself against the old, mediation sets that text in motion – both within the individual imagination and through the social environment encompassing that imagination. John Guillory describes mediation as a process which imposes "*distance* (spatial, temporal, or even notional) between the terminal poles of the communication process," but whose "distanciation" is at the same time a form of "*transmission*," tying those poles together.[19] Though it "remains undertheorized in the study of culture," this concept can illuminate the long life of a piece of literature, the complexities of its creation, and the still unfolding intricacies of its reception.[20] Each work is produced and then sustained by a series of intermediary connections, between inspiration and creation, writer and reader, medium and remediation. And since "no cultural work comes to us except through such multiple categorical mediations," literature stands revealed as the sum of its relations. However, mediation does not merely occur between the work and the outside world; it is the constitutive operation of the work itself – beginning, in literature's case, with the act of translating speech into writing, experience into art. Mediation fuels creation, which in turn feeds further mediation.

We can therefore unite Guillory's understanding of how mediation generates literary genealogies with Bourdieu's understanding of how the interactions of a set of agents generate the field of production: mediation is precisely what those agents are up to. Furthermore, we can illustrate how these two theories of communication and power relations combine in practice by foregrounding the figure who escapes both Guillory and Bourdieu. The editor is a key representative of creative mediation, negotiating between commercial and aesthetic concerns at the portal to publication, and thus shaping the ensuing landscape of reception where further mediations proliferate. It remains to delineate how this conception of the field, animated by these editorial agents of mediation, applies to the particular domain of the global Anglophone. And here I take both my cue and my divergence from Pascale Casanova, who expands Bourdieu's blueprint to the largest possible scale in *The World Republic of Letters* (1999).[21]

An editorial framework for the global Anglophone must build on Casanova's exploration of "international literary space" – while challenging her treatment of the unequal power dynamics which form and deform this textual geography.[22] It is from Casanova's pioneering examination of the global literary economy that I derive my understanding of literary capitals, exerting their artistic-cum-commercial jurisdiction over "linguistic-cultural areas."[23] It is against her too-rigid conception of these capitals' dominion that I develop my own analysis of the global Anglophone's more supple and dialectical dynamic. For Casanova, the transnational field of literary production "is based on the opposition between a capital" and its "peripheral dependencies"; it therefore reflects "relations of force and a violence peculiar to them – in short, a *literary domination.*"[24] Indeed, Casanova's model of literary power is less a republic than an empire, one governed by traditional European centres and exerting a remarkably centralized degree of cultural control. She defines the " 'literature-world'" of capital-ruled "linguistic-cultural areas" as "a homogenous and autonomous sphere in which the legitimacy of its centralized power of consecration is unchallenged."[25] Yet the dynamism of a literature, let alone the numerous literatures in English, stems from its heterogeneity – from the many challenges that writers, institutions, and critics present to centralized power. I maintain that the real-world dynamic is more flexible than Casanova acknowledges. The imperial system of world literature certainly develops through relationships of centre and circumference – mediated by editors – but supposedly dominated writers can reshape a dominating literature in their own image. Homegrown operations and their editorial agents sometimes collaborate with capital counterparts, and sometimes defy them.

The inadequacy of certain critical judgments reveals the inadequacy of Casanova's analysis for the English-writing world. One of the most prominent literary targets in *The World Republic of Letters* is the Trinidadian-born, British-domiciled Nobel laureate V. S. Naipaul. Casanova gathers her criticism under the heading of "Naipaul: The Need to Conform."[26] Her particular argument – flowing from the overarching narrative of capital-based literary hegemony – posits Naipaul as "an outstanding example of a writer who wholly embraced the dominant literary values of his linguistic region." Without providing evidence from his early writing life, she nevertheless declares that from his arrival in England, Naipaul sought "to embody the most perfect Englishness."[27] That supposed conformity manifests in aesthetic conservatism, since "to write like an Englishman means having to conform to the canons of England." One would not know from this simplistic account that Naipaul's first literary outlet was the BBC radio programme *Caribbean Voices*; that those sonic surroundings encouraged him to use Trinidadian dialect and material; that Naipaul himself became, for a time, the programme's editor and a key figure in the London-and-BBC-based community of West Indian expatriate writers; or that in 1964, fourteen years after leaving Trinidad for England, he reflected on the influence of English canons over his

30 Ben Fried

literary development and came to the opposite conclusion to Casanova: "the English language was mine; the tradition was not."[28] The available literary "vision was alien, it diminished my own and did not give me courage to do a simple thing like mentioning the name of a Port of Spain street."

I will demonstrate that Naipaul's artistic motives, institutional surroundings, and literary results are far more mixed than Casanova's conceptual framework allows – and do so by briefly tracing the dynamic mediation between radio and print, writer and editor, Trinidad and London that ultimately did give Naipaul the courage to name and recreate a Port of Spain street in his first publishable book, *Miguel Street* (1959).[29] This case study offers evidence for Anglophone writing following a more complex material dialectic and arriving at more complex literary syntheses. Structured by relationships that extend outward from the text, each primary partnership between writer and editor containing and evoking the larger creative tension of capital and region, the global Anglophone is a necessary field of study, one which can do justice to the plurality of literatures in English and allow us to advance three interlocking levels of criticism: the textual, the institutional, and the global.

A Case Study: *Miguel Street*

During the second half of his life, in autobiographical essays and autobiographical novels, V. S. Naipaul would return to the story again and again, revising a tale that itself takes the form of creative return.[30] A young man from Trinidad, adrift and poor in the London of the early 1950s, sits in his place of part-time work – a BBC freelancers' room in the Langham Hotel – and suddenly writes the opening sentences of the book that confirms him in his vocation. The catalyst for this outpouring is the memory of a childhood sound; the book that emerges is *Miguel Street*, a sequence of linked short stories chronicling the noisy lives of a neighbourhood in Port of Spain. Meanwhile, the radio programme for which Naipaul was working at the time is *Caribbean Voices*, a weekly audio magazine that nurtured the postwar flourishing of West Indian literature from London, offering a wireless outlet, and network, for Anglophone Caribbean writers at a time when their venues and audiences for print were vanishingly small. The path of discovery is, in essence, a process of recovery, of finding within himself the resources of a writer. For in the beginning is a homecoming: "To become a writer, that noble thing, I had thought it necessary to leave. Actually to write, it was necessary to go back."[31]

Yet while these details are well-known, their coincidence – that Naipaul should find his voice while writing against the oral background of *Caribbean Voices* – has been disregarded by both the writer and his critics. Naipaul

Editing the Global Anglophone **31**

neglects to elaborate on either the apprenticeship on air which precedes this breakthrough or the editorship which accompanies it; critics remark on the divided language of *Miguel Street*, but none follow this discord back to the setting from which it emerges: radio.[32] I will read into the bifurcated form of Naipaul's book the divided setting which kindles his creativity, caught between the ambient orality of his radio room and the purposeful literacy of his typewriter, a mediation itself mediated by his relations with Henry Swanzy, the producer of *Caribbean Voices*. Combining the cacophony of its inhabitants, their dialogue and dialect, with the singular, retrospective, and standard English voice of its narration, Naipaul's short-story sequence demonstrates that mediation is a creative principle, one that structures the relationship between literary capital and literary region. At the origin of Naipaul's literary self-discovery lies the connection between radio and print – itself a proxy for the productive tension between Trinidad and London – overlapping and clashing and producing the passing unity of the work of art.

A magazine programme combining poetry, prose, reviews, and discussion – a "half-hour creative workshop around the craft of writing" – *Caribbean Voices* was broadcast over the BBC's Overseas Service every Sunday evening from 1943 to 1958.[33] Kamau Brathwaite speaks for an unwavering critical consensus when he calls *Caribbean Voices* "the single most important literary catalyst for Caribbean creative and critical writing in English" and names its "most influential producer (drive, enthusiasm, sympathy, critical acumen and length of service)" as the Anglo-Irish interloper and enabler "Henry Swanzy."[34] Naipaul's father, the would-be writer Seepersad, was one of the programme's many contributors. Introducing his father's posthumously published collection *The Adventures of Gurudeva* (1976), Naipaul expands on what programme and producer meant to the isolated writers of the West Indies. Into a territory deprived of paid avenues for literary expression, *Caribbean Voices* arrived and with it "there at last appeared a market."[35] Swanzy brought money, "standards and enthusiasm," taking "local writing seriously and lift[ing] it above the local." His praise spurred on Seepersad, "who had never been praised like that before."[36] What Naipaul sketches for his father is another variation on the tale of a writer's beginnings, though with the difference that he includes here what he disregards in his own case: the vital part played by *Caribbean Voices* – vital because it offered an outlet and an editor.[37] With "the stimulus of that weekly radio programme from London, my father, I believe, found his voice as a writer."[38] The same should be said for his son.

Naipaul began by writing stories for the programme as an undergraduate at Oxford, having them accepted, rejected, and revised by Swanzy. Through the early 1950s, Naipaul's letters to his father document how this editorial process directed the young writer towards a stripped-back style and a mining

32 Ben Fried

of his home material – towards stories for and of *Caribbean Voices*. "My story which is being broadcast in September has had its prosy parts knocked off. The conversation is being used"; Swanzy "ask[ed] me to rewrite the last page, which he thought was 'too literary'"; "I feel sure a three month stay in Trinidad would keep me writing for three years."[39] That Naipaul stays in England – while Trinidad remains at the centre of his early writing – is due, finally, to Swanzy's patronage. At the end of 1954, planning for his secondment to the Gold Coast Broadcasting System, Swanzy chooses Naipaul as his successor: twenty-five years later, Naipaul would say that the job " 'saved my life, really. I was living more or less at the limit of despair.' "[40] The details of Naipaul's editorship (1954–58) – and the contrast between his editorial style and Swanzy's – are a rich topic which must be left for another critical occasion. Here I will only suggest that while Naipaul's greater ambivalence about the programme and its medium may have made him a less generous editor,[41] that same ambivalence is at the root of a powerful divide shaping both the structure and the sound of his first finished book. In letters home, Naipaul deprecates his editing, for "what I am really working on is my writing, my own writing" – but that writing shares the sonic environment of *Caribbean Voices* and eventually becomes *Miguel Street*.[42] If his editing sinks below Swanzy's standard, Naipaul's art performs the work of mediation.

The friction between orality and composition which ignites Naipaul's creativity not only issues in the form of *Miguel Street*, it generates its thematic thrust – the failure which undoes the lives each story portrays in turn, a failure of learning and literacy which the narrator alone escapes, as he alone leaves Trinidad. Retrospectively, Naipaul presents the moment of his breakthrough as a call-and-response between the first sentence and the second.

> Every morning when he got up Hat would sit on the banister of his back veranda and shout across, "What happening there, Bogart?"
>
> Bogart would turn in his bed and mumble softly, so that no one heard, "What happening there, Hat?"[43]

"The first sentence was true. The second was invention."[44] If the movement between the two expresses the essence of Naipaul's creative departure, they also contain in miniature the sonic structure of the whole collection. The narrative voice is plain but grammatically conventional; within its frame, however, the characters speak a uniquely Caribbean tongue. The proportion of dialogue to narration on display in this opening exchange, along with the elision of auxiliary verbs, is true to all seventeen stories. Moreover, characters do not merely talk; they listen – and listen to, among other things, the calypsos that punctuate several stories with short bursts of song, a piece of sonic variety common to radio broadcasts. Twelve calypsos are heard over the course of the collection, refrains remembered by people for whom the songs

Editing the Global Anglophone **33**

are a chorus that makes sense of their lives, like "a calypso about Popo that was the rage that year. [...] *A certain carpenter feller went to Arima / Looking for a mopsy called Emelda.*"[45] But even more common than the calypsos are the white lines which punctuate each story, cuts and pockets of silence in which time passes and moods change. We hear an echo of Naipaul's spell as an editor, stitching together a programme from motley material. "His Chosen Calling" is about a boy named Elias and his many unsuccessful efforts to pass the Cambridge Senior School Certificate Examination. The descent of his ambition to be a doctor is measured out in blank space, subjected to a rapid series of transitions that progressively reduce him to a scavenger-cart driver, a furious exam failure who tells another man to "Shut your arse up, before it have trouble between we in this street."[46] The atmosphere of this book, like the atmosphere of its making, is highly tuned to the acoustic.

Yet "His Chosen Calling" indicates that orality is only half of the story. The vivid voice of Elias is shadowed by literacy, by the world of reading and writing which intersects with Naipaul's street life and stands ever-present in the narrator's retrospective style. Early in his career as an exam-taker, Elias confesses his weakness:

"Is the English and litritcher that does beat me."
   In Elias's mouth litritcher was the most beautiful word I heard. It sounded like something to eat, something rich like chocolate.
   Hat said, "You mean you have to read a lot of poultry and thing?"
   Elias nodded.[47]

This comedy of misunderstanding anticipates and explains Elias's failure. Several characters are similarly defeated by print. "Man-man" is "hypnotized by the word, particularly the written word, and he would spend a whole day writing a single word."[48] The madness that will later see him institutionalized emerges in his attempts to write, taking all day to chalk the word "school" on the pavement and never finishing. The poet B. Wordsworth claims to compose one line each month. Yet these lines are not written down, and his story ends with the confession that "All this talk about poetry and the greatest poem in the world, that wasn't true, either. Isn't that the funniest thing you have heard?"[49] Only the narrator has a comfortable relationship with writing – beginning with his part-time job as a sign-painter and leading to his success on the exam that Elias fails. *Miguel Street* ends with the one character who fully straddles the oral and the literate receiving a government scholarship to study in England: "I left them all and walked briskly towards the aeroplane, not looking back."[50]

Thus the narrator follows in his creator's footsteps – except that the creator does look back, for *Caribbean Voices*, and, in looking back, forges the stories of *Miguel Street*. The form Naipaul's first inspiration takes inscribes

34 Ben Fried

the dynamics of media, editing, and institution at play in its discovery. The oral-written dialectic within *Miguel Street* offers a synecdoche for the home-capital dialectic without – the editorial environment which shapes Naipaul and which he shapes in turn. By exploring the history of such overlapping environments, and by tracking the literary works they both foster and frustrate, scholars can recast the global Anglophone as a spacious, critical field for literatures in English.

Notes

1 Stuart Hall, "When was 'The Post-Colonial'? Thinking at the Limit," in *The Postcolonial Question: Common Skies, Divided Horizons*, edited by Iain Chambers and Lidia Curti (New York: Routledge, 1996): 246.
2 Ella Shohat, "Notes on the 'Post-Colonial,'" *Social Text* 31/32 (1992): 102.
3 Ragini Tharoor Srinivasan, "Introduction: South Asia from Postcolonial to World Anglophone," *Interventions* 20.3 (2018): 310.
4 Srinivasan, "Introduction," 312.
5 Nasia Anam, "Introduction: Forms of the Global Anglophone," in *Forms of the Global Anglophone*, *Post45*, 22 February 2019, https://post45.org/2019/02/introduction-forms-of-the-global-anglophone/.
6 Mūkoma wa Ngũgĩ, *The Rise of the African Novel: Politics of Language, Identity, and Ownership* (Ann Arbor: University of Michigan Press, 2018): 148.
7 Anam, "Introduction."
8 Salman Rushdie, "'Commonwealth Literature' Does Not Exist," in *Imaginary Homelands: Essays and Criticism, 1981–1991* (London: Granta Books, 1991): 63.
9 Rushdie, "Commonwealth," 62.
10 Rushdie, "Commonwealth," 64.
11 Rushdie, "Commonwealth," 70.
12 B. R. Cohen, "Public Thinker: Jill Lepore on the Challenge of Explaining Things," *Public Books*, 24 April 2017, www.publicbooks.org/public-thinker-jill-lepore-on-the-challenge-of-explaining-things/.
13 Once largely hidden in literary history, the editor is now the subject of a growing body of scholarship. See, for instance, Abram Foley's *The Editor Function: Literary Publishing in Postwar America* (Minneapolis: University of Minnesota Press, 2021). See also my article "'The Most Sympathetic Reader You Can Imagine': William Maxwell's New Yorker and the Mid-Century Short Story," *Post45* (July 2024), https://post45.org/2024/07/william-maxwells-new-yorker/– for a further elaboration of this chapter's theory of editorial power.
14 Susan L. Greenberg, *A Poetics of Editing* (New York: Palgrave Macmillan, 2018): ix.
15 Greenberg, *A Poetics of Editing*, 225.
16 Pierre Bourdieu, "The Field of Cultural Production, or: The Economic World Reversed," in *The Field of Cultural Production: Essays on Art and Literature*, edited by Randal Johnson (New York: Columbia University Press, 1993): 29–73; John Guillory, "Genesis of the Media Concept," *Critical Inquiry* 36.2 (Winter 2010): 321–362.
17 Bourdieu, "Field," 29, 37.
18 Pierre Bourdieu, *The Rules of Art: Genesis and Structure of the Literary Field*, translated by Susan Emanuel (Stanford: Stanford University Press, 1996): 167.
19 Guillory, "Genesis," 357.
20 Guillory, "Genesis," 354.

21 Pascale Casanova, *The World Republic of Letters*, translated by M. B. DeBevoise (Cambridge: Harvard University Press, 2004).
22 Casanova, *The World Republic*, xii.
23 Casanova, *The World Republic*, 117.
24 Casanova, *The World Republic*, 11, xii.
25 Casanova, *The World Republic*, 117.
26 Casanova, *The World Republic*, 205, 209.
27 Casanova, *The World Republic*, 210.
28 V. S. Naipaul, "Words on Their Own," *Times Literary Supplement* 3249 (4 June 1964): 472.
29 V.S. Naipaul, *Miguel Street* (New York: Vintage, 2002). *Miguel Street* was the first book Naipaul submitted to, and the third one issued by, his publisher. See Diana Athill, *Stet: An Editor's Life* (New York: Grove Press, 2000): 204–205.
30 See "Prologue to an Autobiography," in *Literary Occasions: Essays*, edited by Pankaj Mishra (New York: Knopf, 2003): 112–127; *The Enigma of Arrival* (New York: Knopf, 1987); *A Way in the World* (New York: Knopf, 1994); "Reading and Writing, a Personal Account," in *Literary Occasions: Essays*, edited by Pankaj Mishra (New York: Knopf, 2003): 3–34; "Two Worlds (The Nobel Lecture)," in *Literary Occasions: Essays*, edited by Pankaj Mishra (New York: Knopf, 2003): 181–195; *Half a Life* (New York: Knopf, 2001); and finally "Introduction," in *Collected Short Fiction* (New York: Knopf, 2011), vii–xiv.
31 Naipaul, "Prologue," 79.
32 See, for instance, Bruce King, *V.S. Naipaul* (London: Palgrave Macmillan, 2003): 25–29; and Fawzia Mustafa, *V.S. Naipaul* (Cambridge: Cambridge University Press, 1995): 14–34.
33 Philip Nanton, "London Calling," *Caribbean Beat* 63 (September/October 2003), www.caribbean-beat.com/issue-63/london-calling.
34 Edward Kamau Brathwaite, *History of the Voice: The Development of Nation Language in Anglophone Caribbean Poetry* (London: New Beacon Books, 1984): 87.
35 Naipaul, "Foreword to *The Adventures of Gurudeva*," in *Literary Occasions: Essays*, edited by Pankaj Mishra (New York: Knopf, 2003): 114.
36 Naipaul, "Foreword to *The Adventures of Gurudeva*," 115.
37 On Swanzy's editorial practice, see Glyne A. Griffith, *The BBC and the Development of Anglophone Caribbean Literature, 1943–1958* (London: Palgrave Macmillan, 2016); and Michael Niblett, "Style as Habitus: World Literature, Decolonization and *Caribbean Voices*," in *Bourdieu and Postcolonial Studies*, edited by Raphael Dalleo (Liverpool: Liverpool University Press, 2016): 119–136.
38 Naipaul, "Foreword to *The Adventures of Gurudeva*," 115.
39 Naipaul, *Letters between a Father and Son*, edited by Gillon Aitken (London: Little, Brown and Co., 2001): 154, 127, 361.
40 Patrick French, *The World is What it is: The Authorized Biography of V.S. Naipaul* (London: Picador, 2008): 139.
41 Griffith argues that under Naipaul's watch "the editorial focus of *Caribbean Voices* became less and less invested in casting a wide net for possible talent in the region." *The BBC*, 161.
42 Naipaul, *Letters*, 423.
43 Naipaul, *Miguel Street*, 9.
44 Naipaul, "Prologue," 58.
45 Naipaul, *Miguel Street*, 22.
46 Naipaul, *Miguel Street*, 44.
47 Naipaul, *Miguel Street*, 41.

36 Ben Fried

48 Naipaul, *Miguel Street*, 47.
49 Naipaul, *Miguel Street*, 65.
50 Naipaul, *Miguel Street*, 222.

Bibliography

Anam, Nasia. "Introduction: Forms of the Global Anglophone." *Forms of the Global Anglophone. Post45*, 22 February 2019. https://post45.org/2019/02/introduction-forms-of-the-global-anglophone/.

Athill, Diana. *Stet: An Editor's Life*. New York: Grove Press, 2000.

Bourdieu, Pierre. "The Field of Cultural Production, or: The Economic World Reversed." In *The Field of Cultural Production: Essays on Art and Literature*, edited by Randal Johnson. New York: Columbia University Press, 1993: 29–73.

———. *The Rules of Art: Genesis and Structure of the Literary Field*, translated by Susan Emanuel. Stanford: Stanford University Press, 1996.

Brathwaite, Edward Kamau. *History of the Voice: The Development of Nation Language in Anglophone Caribbean Poetry*. London: New Beacon Books, 1984.

Casanova, Pascale. *The World Republic of Letters*, translated by M. B. DeBevoise. Cambridge: Harvard University Press, 2004.

Cohen, B. R. "Public Thinker: Jill Lepore on the Challenge of Explaining Things." *Public Books*, 24 April 2017. www.publicbooks.org/public-thinker-jill-lepore-on-the-challenge-of-explaining-things/ (last accessed 30 March 2024).

Foley, Abram. *The Editor Function: Literary Publishing in Postwar America*. Minneapolis: University of Minnesota Press, 2021.

French, Patrick. *The World is What it is: The Authorized Biography of V.S. Naipaul*. London: Picador, 2008.

Fried, Ben. "'The Most Sympathetic Reader You Can Imagine': William Maxwell's New Yorker and the Mid-Century Short Story." *Post45* (July 2024), https://post45.org/2024/07/william-maxwells-new-yorker/.

Greenberg, Susan L. *A Poetics of Editing*. London: Palgrave Macmillan, 2018.

Griffith, Glyne A. *The BBC and the Development of Anglophone Caribbean Literature, 1943–1958*. London: Palgrave Macmillan, 2016.

Guillory, John. "Genesis of the Media Concept." *Critical Inquiry* 36.2 (Winter 2010): 321–362.

Hall, Stuart. "When was 'The Post-Colonial'? Thinking at the Limit." In *The Postcolonial Question: Common Skies, Divided Horizons*, edited by Iain Chambers and Lidia Curti. New York: Routledge, 1996: 242–260.

King, Bruce. *V.S. Naipaul*. London: Palgrave Macmillan, 2003.

Mustafa, Fawzia. *V.S. Naipaul*. Cambridge: Cambridge University Press, 1995.

Naipaul, V. S. *The Enigma of Arrival: A Novel*. New York: Knopf, 1987.

———. "Foreword to *The Adventures of Gurudeva*." In *Literary Occasions: Essays*, edited by Pankaj Mishra. New York: Knopf, 2003: 112–127.

———. *Half a Life*. New York: Knopf, 2001.

———. "Introduction." In *Collected Short Fiction*. New York: Knopf, 2010: vii–xiv.

———. *Letters between a Father and Son*, edited by Gillon Aitken. London: Little, Brown and Co., 2001.

———. *Miguel Street*. New York: Vintage, 2002.

———. "Prologue to an Autobiography." In *Literary Occasions: Essays*, edited by Pankaj Mishra. New York: Knopf, 2003: 53–111.

———. "Reading and Writing, a Personal Account." In *Literary Occasions: Essays*, edited by Pankaj Mishra. New York: Knopf, 2003: 3–34.

———. "Two Worlds (The Nobel Lecture)." In *Literary Occasions: Essays*, edited by Pankaj Mishra. New York: Knopf, 2003: 181–195.

———. *A Way in the World*. New York: Knopf, 1994.

———. "Words on Their Own." *Times Literary Supplement* 3249 (4 June 1964): 472.

Nanton, Philip. "London Calling." *Caribbean Beat*, 63, September/October 2003. www.caribbean-beat.com/issue-63/london-calling.

Ngũgĩ, Mũkoma wa. *The Rise of the African Novel: Politics of Language, Identity, and Ownership*. Ann Arbor: University of Michigan Press, 2018.

Niblett, Michael. "Style as Habitus: World Literature, Decolonization and Caribbean Voices." In *Bourdieu and Postcolonial Studies*, edited by Raphael Dalleo. Liverpool: Liverpool University Press, 2016: 119–136.

Rushdie, Salman. " 'Commonwealth Literature' Does Not Exist." In *Imaginary Homelands: Essays and Criticism, 1981–1991*. London: Granta Books, 1991: 61–70.

Shohat, Ella. "Notes on the 'Post-Colonial.'" *Social Text* 31/32 (1992): 99–113.

Srinivasan, Ragini Tharoor. "Introduction: South Asia from Postcolonial to World Anglophone." *Interventions* 20.3 (2018): 309–316.

2

"NOW A NETFLIX ORIGINAL SERIES"

Indian TV Shows in World Anglophone Studies

Annika McPherson and Ashumi Shah

Current media in globalized distribution contribute significantly to shifts in the practices and politics of representation of the Global South.[1] The subscription streaming service Netflix, one of the beneficiaries and drivers of neoliberal policies in the entertainment sector, makes available a broad and steadily increasing array of content via its voraciously globalizing platform. Its expansion over the last decade, especially across target regions of the Global South, has led to massive distribution packages as well as a steep increase in productions labelled "Netflix Originals." These are mostly shot in a local language, occasionally produced in several language versions, and frequently feature numerous language options for subtitles as well as multiple dubbed audio versions. In its dual role as distributor and (co-)producer, Netflix wields significant influence on the visibility of productions and, by extension, on the representation of cultural contexts that have long been marginalized in hegemonic patterns of global media distribution.

Based on user data, after viewing a film, series or performance production, the streaming service's algorithm will suggest other content tagged with similar genre markers and descriptions. This embedded affordance is characteristic of the intricate relationship between the different layers of new media, in which

> the computer layer will affect the cultural layer. The ways in which the computer models the world, represents data and allows us to operate on it; the key operations behind all computer programs (such as search, match, sort, filter); [...] – in short, what can be called the computer's ontology, epistemology, and pragmatics – influence the cultural layer of new media, its organization, its emerging genres, its contents.[2]

DOI: 10.4324/9781003464037-4
This chapter has been made available under a CC-BY-NC-ND 4.0 license.

"Now a Netflix Original Series" **39**

This "composite" culture which blends "human and computer meanings"[3] has a significant impact not only on distribution but also on the media product itself as well as on its audiences. The cultural layer, however, can be fraught with significant tension surrounding questions of cultural representation.

When the Netflix adaptation of Prayaag Akbar's acclaimed 2018 debut novel *Leila* was released in June 2019, a social media debate erupted based on precisely such questions of cultural representation. Following Shiv Sena member Ramesh Solanki's complaint against Netflix, in which he charged *Leila* and other series with the defamation of Hindus, the debate culminated in the Twitter campaign #BanNetflixInIndia.[4] The dystopian tale – in the televisual version tellingly set in 2047, one hundred years after Indian independence and partition – follows a mother's quest to find her daughter Leila who, in line with a governmental purity campaign in the fictional successor state Aryavarta, has been taken away on account of being the "mixed-blood" ("mishrit") child of a Hindu-Muslim marriage. Through its association with ancient texts that are commonly linked to orthodox schools of Hinduist thought, the adaptation's setting of Aryavarta allegorizes political aspirations of the Hindutva movement.[5] The protagonist Shalini, born Pathak and née Chaudhury,[6] is forced to revert back to her maiden name and identity in the government-sanctioned "Purity Centre" run by "Guru Ma" Dr. Iyer who aims to extinguish her transgressive marital identity by way of relentless indoctrination, Sisyphean tasks, and demeaning acts of submission that the women at the centre are continuously subjected to.

Alongside *Leila*, the acclaimed adaptation of Vikram Chandra's 2006 novel *Sacred Games* – Netflix's first directly produced and globally marketed Indian "original" series (2018–2019) – and other shows were also accused of misrepresentations. Taking its cue from this debate, the following discussion traces some of the adaptational shifts from Akbar's English-language novel to the Netflix series in its English and Hindi versions, with notable variations in terminology as well as allusive potentials. The political reverberations of *Leila* are contrasted to the romantic comedy series *Little Things* (2016), which depicts the everyday lives and globalized patterns of consumption of middle- and upper-middle-class "millennials" living in Mumbai. *Little Things* started as an English-language web series on Dice Media's YouTube channel and was picked up by Netflix in 2018. Rebranded as a "Netflix original," the second season shifted from an English to a Hindi original audio track with an English dubbed version. Significantly, in this process the translanguaging practices that are so common in the Indian context and many other multilingual areas largely disappear.[7] The two series' adaptational and language shifts in comparison to their previous literary and media versions complicate not only their labelling and "tagging" but also necessitate a reconsideration of the metonymic gap as commonly applied in postcolonial studies.[8] Taking into account questions of genre, author- and directorship, as well as current

40 Annika McPherson and Ashumi Shah

patterns of production, distribution, and reception, the analyzed shifts in the cultural layers of popular cultural representation are thus placed in conversation with broader debates surrounding World Anglophone Studies – which, as we argue, would benefit from a more nuanced focus on the multilingual dynamics of globalized contexts of production and consumption.

From Akbar's *Leila* to the Netflix Original Series and Back

In an article for *BBC Culture* tellingly titled "*Leila*: The Indian *Handmaid's Tale*," Rahul Verma explores the influence of streaming services on Indian film and television in relation to the debate surrounding Deepa Mehta's adaptation of Prayaag Akbar's novel.[9] Comparing it to Margaret Atwood's *The Handmaid's Tale* (1985) and its popular Hulu adaptation (2017–present), Verma writes:

> While [*Leila*] draws parallels with *The Handmaid's Tale* thanks to its depiction of a draconian, patriarchal state suppressing women and restricting their reproductive rights, *Leila's* central themes also include climate change and a deeply hierarchical society organised according to religion, caste and wealth.[10]

The way in which *Leila* politicizes religious themes, communal segregation, and social stratification rather unsurprisingly caused contention among viewers, some of whom have accused the show of being "anti-Hindu."[11] The calls for boycotts and censorship that shows such as *Leila* and *Sacred Games* have faced in India claim that they present a problematic picture of Hindus and India to the world. Especially *Leila*, whose portrayal Solanki describes as "a Muslim-hating, casteist, and bigoted nation," according to his complaint "went against the Indian supreme court's view that Hinduism is a way of life" (in Kapur, "Netflix"). What is at stake in these debates surrounding popular TV series in globalized circulation thus are different attitudes towards India's constitutional secularism, the precarity of which has become even more visible following the passing of the Citizenship Amendment Bill in December 2019 and the protests in its wake.[12] This renewed threat to India's precarious secularism received broad global media coverage, not least through Arundhati Roy's widely circulated article "The Pandemic Is a Portal," which links the uprising against the bill; the attacks on Muslims in Delhi by "Hindu vigilantes, backed by the police" in February 2020; and government responses to the Covid-19 pandemic as symptomatic of the physical and structural violence of Modi's populism.[13] In terms of state regulation, the government's order in November 2020 to place digital media and streaming platforms under the purview of the Ministry of Information and Broadcasting indicates a further push towards censorship procedures similar to the

"Now a Netflix Original Series" **41**

ones that have long affected Indian print media, audiovisual, and theatre productions.[14]

While *Leila* has been both a source and a symptom of political debates surrounding popular culture representations in and of Indian society, likening the series to *The Handmaid's Tale* positions it in a global comparative framework. The fact that Akbar's novel had raised significantly less controversy than the series can be attributed not only to the lesser reach of the book medium but also to significant changes made in its adaptation. Although its setting is projected into 2047, a few years into the regime change that brought about Aryavarta, the series' critics do not consider it a futuristic cautionary tale but – not least due the dystopian genre's thinly veiled allegory – indeed a mirror of current politics and social conditions in the vein of a film à clef, which is furthered by the show's cinematography.

Portrayed largely through protagonist Shalini's flashbacks along three timelines – her life before the despotic Dr. Joshi's coming into power, the events leading to her husband Rizwan's murder and their child's abduction, and her experiences in the Purity and Labour Camps – the regime change is symbolized most tellingly in the destruction of the Taj Mahal that is visualized in a futuristic holographic TV screen in the Chaudhury family's living room (E2, 29:00). The scene invokes the centuries-long controversy surrounding the site of the Babri Masjid Mosque in Ayodhya, at which both Hindus and Muslims claim previous historical religious structures. The mosque was demolished by Hindu nationalists in 1992, and the subsequent communalist violence left deep and lasting scars that in many ways were reopened by the 2019 and 2020 events and political developments linked in Roy's critique of the Modi government and its followers. During the flashback to the Taj Mahal's demolition in *Leila*, the diegetic newscast comments that "the symbol of love fell to hatred" (E2, 31:10), indicating the subjugation of Muslim culture in Aryavarta. On the level of the family, this is signified by Raziya Chaudhury, Riz's mother, whose aesthetic changes from the demolition flashback, in which she is dressed in bright yellow and wears make-up, to her later demure greyish pious attire and subdued body language (E2, 35:25).

The new regime's main goal is the segregation of society into distinct communities along religious and caste lines, ostensibly to guarantee peace. In the series, this is illustrated through the various sectors enclosed by unscalable walls, which leaves the destitute outside slum or "basti" ("colony") population in abject conditions, especially the so-called "Doosh" (E1, 04:30).[15] Roop, the "Doosh" girl who helps Shalini find her way back into Aryavarta after she escapes from a Labour Camp transport, invokes the trope of untouchability and contamination explicitly when she indicates that Shalini cannot drink from the same water container after her (E2, 28:10). Shalini's own outcast status as "Aryavarta's slave" (E2, 06:40) and Dr. Iyer's "property" is further entrenched when "Guru Ma" attests her to be "beyond purification" (E5, 05:15) and, following her unwillingness to have two other women "exterminated" in her first "Purity Test" aimed at atoning her own transgressions, also "beyond redemption" (E1, 39:35).[16] These transgressions are variously labelled as sins and crimes (e.g. E5, 03:35 and 05:40) and include marrying outside her own community, giving birth to a "mixed-blood" child and entering the "Doosh" sector. As "mishrit" children are considered a "burden" to be removed to "cleanse" and maintain the purity of Aryavarta (E1, 21:50), Dr. Iyer calls her a stigma (Engl. audio) or blemish (Engl. subtitles) (E 5, 04:30) on Aryavarta and its women. Rather than killing her, however, the intervention of the Labour Camp guard – who, as part of the resistance, has his own motivations for doing so – suggests that "rotting away as a slave" in the service of Rao Sahib is to be her punishment and penance (E5, 5:55). Through these and many other instances in which religious connotations are invoked, communalism along religious lines is foregrounded in alignment with Aryavarta's "motto" and description in the series' opening intertitle: "Peace by Segregation. Cities are divided into sectors with sky-high walls. Each sector has one community, free to practice their beliefs" (E1, 00:20–00:30). The language of contamination and purification thus is strongly associated with communal practices and beliefs that are frequently tied to food consumption and physical touch.

In the re-education camp, the chants "My lineage is my destiny" or "My duty defines my destiny" (E1, 04:45) serve to illustrate indoctrination. Nationalism under Mr. Joshi's regime is positioned as the binary opposite of Westernisation, as indicated in the poster "The Qualities of an Ideal Woman" which praises modest and compliant behaviour and, with a large red slash across the image of a woman dressed in "Western" clothing and holding a glass of wine (E1, 13:32), condemns such influence. Protest signs and slogans as well as the graffiti in the "Doosh" sector, however, point to the omnipresence of resistance and provide more ambivalent comments on nationalism.[17] Some of the slogans recall the Swadeshi ("indigenous"/"home-made") and Swaraj (self-rule) movements during India's struggle for independence from colonial power, thus recontextualising this remediated notion of nationalism in a politically charged manner that demonstrates the contradictory character of nationalism.[18]

The cultural layer of language in relation to the politics of representation features not only in the terminological choices highlighting religious contexts or nationalist sentiments but is also addressed directly on the diegetic level. In the Hindi version, for example, "Guru Ma" corrects himself when accidentally slipping into English (E1, 16:13), implying that to do so is a misstep and against the culture that the new leader "Joshiji" envisions for Aryavarta. In the English version, this distinction cannot be made, which is significant in so far as the Hindi version thus emphasizes the notion that all that is Western is bad. In the English version, this subtext is less prominent

"Now a Netflix Original Series" **43**

but still noticeable in Rao's correction of Shalini when she addresses him as "Sir" instead of "Sahib" (E5, 21:25) as well as in his – frequently ambiguous – statements on how the initial idea(l) of Aryavarta has been corrupted under Joshi's leadership, whose authority he constantly challenges and whom he wants to replace. Rao's love of singer Noor Jehan and poet Faiz Ahmed Faiz, whose poetry Shalini quotes (E5, 28:40), thus winning Rao's sympathies, indicates Rao's subversive potential and provides a further example of the series's cultural layering and invocation of subcontinental history.[19] Rao's love of Faiz's and Jehan's censored art signify his nostalgia for what was lost in the regime change that, to him, constitutes a failed revolution. Yet, he also points out "the achievements of Aryavarta" through the re-education of "women [who] had strayed from the right path" and "whose minds and values were corrupted" – in the English subtitle version "by Western values" (S6, 32:00) – in his final ploy to expose Joshi as a hypocrite and instead position himself as the true defender of purity and culture.

The series is furthermore focused on the trope of "trading places" between Shalini and Mrs. Dixit as well as with the Chaudhury's former maid Sapna. Numerous flashbacks illustrate that informal separation was already quite common and that the servant class faced discrimination and associations with contamination long before Aryavarta's formal institutionalization of communalist segregation, thus harking back to casteist attitudes and practices that have not disappeared from Indian society either. For example, in the opening sequence Sapna is shown to subversively sip from Shalini's wine glass just before serving it (E1, 01:50), and one of the Labour Camp women eats from the food they are preparing for Rao in his yard (E1, 17:05). After her own social downfall, Shalini recalls how she, too, had insisted that Sapna disinfect her hands before touching Leila and prohibited her kissing the little girl on her skin (E3, 12:55), just as she is told to sanitize her hands and is reprimanded for kissing Prasad (E3, 19:30). She is also suspected of having eaten "non-veg" food in the past and has to swallow Mrs. Dixit's condescending commands when she is sent to work as her maid.

While the switched social status between Shalini and Sapna is also elaborated towards the end of Akbar's English-language novel, the literary version dwells even more strongly on the symbolism of the walls separating communities. The first of these, "Purity One," has become a monument and shrine, its first brick a "holy centre to be worshipped" (Akbar 2). Shalini's social downfall is portrayed as a much longer process of political changes. Sixteen years after Leila has been taken away, Shalini's layered consciousness is portrayed in a first-person narration that frequently switches between the present and the past across passages of simultaneous narration as well as recollections triggered by her experiences. Narrative play with temporality signifies Shalini's state of mind, and she acts as a witness to the social and political divisions through the contrast to her recollections of her life

44   Annika McPherson and Ashumi Shah

"before" in a manner that highlights the gradual reinforcement of communalist segregation, not least through nostalgic portrayals of her erstwhile more tolerant and diverse social circle. Her ghostly husband's questioning commentary ("'Is this it – the culture they wanted?' Riz suddenly asked," Akbar 13) is juxtaposed to her own slow journey to (failed) rebellion in the quest to find her daughter. She now perceives what was invisible to – or, rather, conveniently ignored by – her in her privileged former life. While the TV series and the novel both feature variations of the Purity Camp, Shalini in the novel works at the Revenue Ministry and lives in the outcast sector of the fallen high-born "Tower women" and the "slummers" beyond the walls.

She recalls her family's reactions to the time of the building of the first walls ("Papa was right. These walls diminish us. Make us something less than human," Akbar 38), superimposed with the longer family memory of how her great-grandfather had been one of the "builders for the British, raising the new city" (Akbar 38) on Lakshmi Hill. In another remote invocation of colonial power dynamics, the novel links social segregation to old "laws written by colony builders" (Akbar 41) and their divide-and-rule philosophy that has been revived and brought to an extreme level by the new regime. Shalini's and Riz's "already complicated" (Akbar 75) courtship and marriage across religious lines prefigures the changes they cannot escape even after moving to the cosmopolitan and liberal "East End" that invokes the famed liberalism of cosmopolitan Mumbai. The changes they witness and experience in the East End signify the gradual encroachment of the new order and the "surgical vibrations of violence" (Akbar 114) that are epitomized in the series in the destruction of the Taj Mahal.

Many of Shalini's former friends support the new focus on community self-regulation in the sectors and negate its workings along the patterns set by casteism. In its reference to "Brahmin-only, Yadav-only, Parsi-only" real estate listings (Akbar 44) and the different sectors' "cast insignia" (Akbar 61), the novel alludes to existing practices and current appeals of communalist enclaves much more explicit than the TV series, foreshadowing a "purity" trajectory that culminates in the Skydome project's slogan "Must Your Children Share Their Air?" (Akbar 163). By bringing sectarian communalism to its logical conclusion of the threat of genocide of those cast out by the system, those who have "lived outside society for millennia" (Akbar 223), the Skydome's literal and metaphorical "hermetic setting" not only makes it "hard to think about outside" (Akbar 245) but demonstrates the willing sacrifice of disposable lives in a society in which the privileged go to extremes to serve their self-interest and secure scarce resources for themselves.

While both versions of the dystopian *Leila* ring rather eerily with the developments outlined in Roy's "The Pandemic Is a Portal," the TV series's language and adaptational shifts indicate a version whose potential to simultaneously appeal to global audiences and to alienate those who would prefer to invisibilize rather than topicalize deepening communalist tensions in popular culture has caused a significant backlash in the form of calls for censorship. By contrast, the very different genre of the romantic comedy series *Little Things* conveys another dimension of language politics in globalized popular culture.

"It's a Nath, Dhruv"— Millennial Cosmopolitanism in *Little Things*

Netflix marks the show *Little Things* as "Genres: Romantic TV Comedies, Hindi-Language TV Shows, Indian TV Shows" and describes it as follows: "A cohabiting couple in their 20s navigate the ups and downs of work, modern-day relationships and finding themselves in contemporary Mumbai." Although labelled as a "Netflix Original," *Little Things* (written by Dhruv Sehgal, who also plays the character Dhruv in the series) was originally developed by Dice Media, which produced the first season of the show and delivered it via YouTube as a web series in 2016. The shift in production to Netflix affects the series's content and language in significant ways.

Dice Media's bio on its official Twitter handle reads: "Sugar and Spice and all things Dice. A Premium storytelling platform from @PocketAcesHQ. We make high quality, relatable web series for Indian millennials."[20] Unlike Netflix's subscription service, Dice Media productions are available to view on YouTube, where episodes can be commented upon and up- or downvoted, marking the video's or the channel's popularity. The *Little Things* pilot episode titled "#FOMO" (an acronym for "Fear of Missing Out") has over 20 million views and 252,000 upvotes, while the production house Dice Media has over 4 million subscribers. This data points towards the affordances granted by social media platforms that demonstrate the propensity of audiences to interact with media texts and reconfigure viewings as a "social ritual" (Lee and Andrejevic 43).[21] The success of the web series led to Netflix picking it up for production and distribution from the second season onwards (2018–2019) with slightly longer episodes than the initial 15- to 17-minute first season ones. The first season, as is common among Indian millennials, is interspersed with dialogue in English that is suffused with Hindi terms and phrases, thus marked by frequent translanguaging. For example, the protagonists address each other and their friends as "dude," "man," and "bro" and use colloquial Hindi terms such as "Jugaad" (a resourceful "hack") as well as Hindi swear words and phrases, but their dialogue and social media communication also often features entire sentences in Hindi which at times remain untranslated in the subtitles.[22] While the show is distinguished by this seamless English-Hindi mix that colloquially is referred to as "Hinglish," the second and third seasons produced by Netflix instead provide a choice of Hindi dialogue (now marked as the "original" version) and English. Notably, however, the English audio version from the second season onwards is no longer characterized by translanguaging, but only features occasional Hindi terms that are usually picked up and explained in the dialogue, thus catering to a broader audience at the expense of linguistic idiosyncrasy.[23] Given that the series's protagonists Kavya and Dhruv negotiate not only their life as Indian millennials in the "big city," but also their respective regional, linguistic, cultural, and social backgrounds, the erasure of translanguaging clearly constitutes an intervention catering to global audiences who likely come to the show through algorithms based on genre as much as via regional context tagging.

The show features numerous references to global popular culture and patterns of consumption.[24] It follows the lives of Kavya, who hails from Nagpur and works at a company in a sales job that bores her and curtails her creative energy, which she most frequently expresses in drawings and social media memes, and Dhruv, a PhD candidate in maths from Delhi and dedicated Liverpool soccer fan, two years into their relationship after having met and moved in together in Mumbai. Referred to as Bombay throughout the first season in the common practice of maintaining its earlier name which designates its cosmopolitan legacy in the minds of many locals, the city is presented through their middle-class aspirational living and consumption. The show is suffused with references to "Little App," a local deals and cashback app catering to the millennial target audience, as well as to the Indian online custom jewellery company VelvetCase, both of which are listed in the show's credits, revealing the commercial interconnection between the creation of the show and these companies via product placement in a joint venture. The couple is constantly looking for "Little App" deals, which facilitate many of their experiences in the city – particularly of different types of food, with which Dhruv is rather obsessed. Kavya turns her days into Snapchat stories and envies her friends' travels and consumption, showing the embeddedness and preoccupation with everyday self-presentation on social media that again marks the show as representing the mindset of the Indian metropolitan millennial while pleading for less pressure in regard to the titular "Fear of Missing Out."

The couple's everyday life is marked by their patterns of consumption – from Disney movies and Netflix shows to Dhruv watching the Liverpool-Chelsea soccer game while Kavya is treating herself to a hair spa at Tony & Guy – and activities like going to the arcade on Sunday.[25] Their loving bantering and conflict resolution through social media memes negotiates their passage into adult life on their own in the city. When their sense of achievement is compromised, such as because they do not have the means to travel much or Dhruv's paper is not accepted at an international conference, they console and surprise each other with special food or catering to the other's preferences in terms of social activities and outings in the city (e.g., a "Taboo" games night at a friend's house when Dhruv would rather watch *Game of Thrones*, E4). As lovers and "best friends," they have created roles for each other, such as Kavya as the "Biryani Monster" of the story she draws for Dhruv. Her drawings illustrating their experiences are pinned to the wall in their apartment, a shot of which ends some of the episodes with the show's own global pop music-compatible acoustic guitar theme song.

The tender intimacy of the couple's largely unspectacular interaction and life together is interrupted more frequently in the subsequent seasons, for example, when the visit of a conservatively minded and homophobic school-friend from Delhi highlights the more liberal mindset of Bombay, when they travel back to their respective home towns, or have to make decisions about their relationship when their career paths diverge. In these seasons, just like through the erasure of translanguaging, the show arguably becomes more formulaic, following established patterns more closely, while continuously demonstrating the globalized nature and multi-directional interwovenness of current popular culture streaming media.

The Politics of Language and Cultural Representation in Popular Culture and World Anglophone Studies

The seismic shifts in global media over the last two decades are frequently seen – mainly from economic and political angles – as the victory of neoliberal capitalism and the market domination of a few villainous multinational corporations situated in the West, most notably Netflix and Amazon. While there is much truth to such critique, when zooming in on specific content and contexts, things arguably get a lot more complex and complicated. Whereas the company's insatiable global expansion is indeed cause for concern, in terms of content there are layers that complicate easy assessments such as "yet another Netflix show" based on the assumption of one-sided "Westernization" or "Americanization."

As a Netflix production with local units in Mumbai and Delhi, a renowned yet controversial diasporic director and creative executive producer working in tandem with local directors and teams, *Leila* is embedded not only in the Western media sphere that Netflix is often taken to embody, but also sits at the nexus of globalized production and distribution processes. As the complexity of its linguistic and cultural references transposed from an English-language novel to a TV series with a Hindi and an English audio track as well as German, French, and Russian subtitles has shown, the show's cultural layer sits in an equally ambivalent manner between national and global cultural politics and representational patterns.

The broad and continuously growing spectrum of India's portrayal and popular cultural contributions in globalized media can in many ways be seen as a by-product of Modi's 2015 flagship program "Digital India," whose objective to transform India into a digitally empowered society and knowledge economy not least through massive investments in digital infrastructure[26] has led to its increasing visibility in global popular culture beyond stereotypical associations with Bollywood. On the flip side, the agenda encompasses having government services accessible only via biometric mobile data and the so-called Aadhaar ID system that has been extended to banking and telecommunications with the goal to become the "world's first data democracy"[27] while raising much warranted concern regarding data security, privacy, and citizenship rights as well as the digital divide.

Somewhat ironically, the increased visibility and more globalized patterns of production and consumption facilitated by "Digital India" have also resulted in a loss of control over content. On the one hand, controversies such as those over *Leila* have resulted in the reactionary attempt to reign in the content of digital providers like Netflix via the governmental order to place digital media and streaming platforms under the purview of the Ministry of Information and Broadcasting. On the other hand, translanguaging in popular cultural media and the increase in the circulation of a broad variety of genres facilitates a reconsideration of approaches, concepts, and theories of World Anglophone Studies beyond reductive notions that mainly tie language use back to colonial influences. While the affordances of globalized media offer the potential to close the "metonymic gap" both literally and metaphorically for contemporary audiences, the shows alert us to the need to reconsider one-directional theories of globalization and advance more nuanced conceptualizations of cultural exchange and interwovenness.

Notes

1 For a critical discussion of the term 'Global South,' see, e.g., *The Global South Project*, Cornell University, www.globalsouthproject.cornell.edu.
2 Lev Manovich, *The Language of New Media* (Cambridge, MA: MIT Press, 2001): 46.
3 Manovich, *The Language of New Media*, 46.
4 Shiv Sena is a nationalist party associated with Hindutva fundamentalism. Solanki, according to his Tweet from September 4, 2019 (@Rajput_Ramesh), filed a police complaint against Netflix. See Manavi Kapur, "Netflix has Joined the List of Things that Indians Want Banned," *Quartz India*, 6 September 2019, https://qz.com/india/1703651/shiv-sena-man-wants-netflix-banned-for-sacred-games-leila-ghoul/.
5 While 'aryavat' can be translated as 'rising sun,' the name also invokes Āryāvarta, "the sacred land of the Āryans" as outlined in the *Monier-Williams Sanskrit-English Dictionary* 1899, www.sanskrit-lexicon.uni-koeln.de. Although the extension of the setting remains unclear in the adaptation and focuses largely on what seems to be more of a city state, Aryavarta is described as a 'nation' in the opening intertitle.
6 In the English subtitles, the family name is spelled Chaudhary, but in the credits as Chaudhury. Generally, discrepancies between audio tracks and subtitles are due to on-screen space and reading time, but in the case of *Leila* some of the word choices resonate quite differently.
7 Translanguaging has been defined as "the act performed by bilinguals of accessing different linguistic features or various modes of what are described as autonomous languages, in order to maximize communicative potential," Ofelia

García, *Bilingual Education in the 21st Century: A Global Perspective* (Oxford: Wiley-Blackwell, 2009): 140. The concept is mainly used in the context of bi- and multilingual education, in which it also designates a pedagogical approach while here, it is used to designate the multilingual oral interactions that in the present examples are colloquially frequently called 'Hinglish.' For a concise overview and outline of distinctions from concepts such as code switching and code mixing, see Jean Conteh, "Translanguaging," *ELT Journal* 72.2 (October 2018): 445–447, https://doi.org/10.1093/elt/ccy034.

8 According to the widely referenced description by Bill Ashcroft, Gareth Griffiths, and Helen Tiffin, the "metonymic gap is that cultural gap formed when appropriations of a colonial language insert unglossed words, phrases or passages from a first language, or concepts, allusions or references that may be unknown to the reader. Such words become synechdochic of the writer's culture – the part that stands for the whole – rather than representations of the world, as the colonial language might. Thus the inserted language 'stands for' the colonized culture in a metonymic way, and its very resistance to interpretation constructs a 'gap' between the writer's culture and the colonial culture. The local writer is thus able to represent his or her world to the colonizer (and others) in the metropolitan language, and at the same time to signal and emphasize a difference from it," *Post-Colonial Studies: The Key Concepts*, 2nd ed. (London and New York: Routledge, 2007): 122–123.

9 Deepa Mehta is widely known for her acclaimed 'Elements' movie trilogy *Fire* (1996), *Earth* (1998), and *Water* (2005) as well as the film adaptation of Salman Rushdie's *Midnight's Children* (2012). Especially *Fire* and *Water* had already stirred controversy and protests by Hindu fundamentalists, who also disrupted the filming of *Midnight's Children*. See e.g. David F. Burton, "Fire, Water and the Goddess: The Films of Deepa Mehta and Satyajit Ray as Critiques of Hindu Patriarchy," *Journal of Religion & Film* 17.2, article 3 (October 2013), https://digitalcommons.unomaha.edu/jrf/vol17/iss2/3. Mehta only directed the first two episodes of *Leila* but was creative executive producer and writer for the entire series. The other four episodes were directed by Shankar Raman and Pawan Kumar, who maintained the aesthetics set by Mehta.

10 Rahul Verma, "Leila: The Indian Handmaid's Tale," *BBC Culture*, 21 August 2019, www.bbc.com/culture/article/20190821-leila-the-indian-handmaids-tale.

11 See e.g. user reviews on the show's IMDb site www.imdb.com/title/tt9337588/reviews?ref_=tt_urv, where user 'ajay1609' writes: "Bhakts leaving 1star. You guys are not too far from forming an Aryavart of your own," www.imdb.com/review/rw4944364/?ref_=tt_urv. The term 'bhakts' refers to devout practitioners but has become synonymous with Hindu extremists. For a discussion of the term 'Modi Bhakts' in relation to the Prime Minister's followers, see Vipin Jos' reader's blog "Analysing the Mindset of an Average Bhakt," *The Times of India*, 8 May 2019, https://timesofindia.indiatimes.com/readersblog/vjc-blogs/analysing-the-mindset-of-an-average-bhakt-3411/.

12 The bill – which is linked to a proposed National Register of Citizens – grants citizenship to 'illegal' migrants from Afghanistan, Bangladesh and Pakistan who entered India before the end of 2014, provided they are Hindu, Sikh, Jain, Parsi, Buddhist, or Christian. As it does not mention Muslims or persecuted groups such as Sri Lankan Tamils, Rohingyas from Myanmar, or Tibetan refugees, it is widely considered to discriminate on the basis of religion and to thus undermine constitutional secularism.

13 Arundhati Roy, "The Pandemic Is a Portal," *Financial Times*, 3 April 2020, www.ft.com/content/10d8f5e8-74eb-11ea-95fe-fcd274e920ca. See also Roy's previous comments on the Delhi violence, which links these events to other examples of violence sanctioned by institutions of the state, "This is Our Version of the

Coronavirus. We are Sick," *Scroll.in*, 1 March 2020, https://scroll.in/article/954805/arundhati-roy-on-delhi-violence-this-is-our-version-of-the-coronavirus-we-are-sick.

14 Hannah Ellis-Peterson, "Indian Move to Regulate Digital Media Raises Censorship Fears," *The Guardian*, 11 November 2020, www.theguardian.com/world/2020/nov/11/india-to-regulate-netflix-and-amazon-streaming-content.

15 The term 'Doosh' appears first in the opening credits of the show in Hindi in the statement that translates as "Water is forbidden for the Doosh" (E1, 04:30). 'Dooshit' has numerous meanings in Hindi, including 'perverted,' 'polluted,' and 'contaminated.'

16 The 'purity test' ('shuddi pariksha') invokes Sita's 'agni pariksha' chastity test through the fire ordeal in the *Ramayana* as a commentary on the patriarchal order of Aryavarta. Those failing the purity test are relegated to labour camps.

17 Graffiti on the outer walls of Aryavarta includes slogans such as "As you progress, we burn," "Build humanity, not walls" or "Whose progress? Whose country?" (E2, 28:49).

18 In this context, "On the one hand, nationalism sought participation in the universalist promise of national development. On the other hand, it simultaneously expressed unease with modernity in a territorially grounded nativist particularism." Manu Goswami, "From Swadeshi to Swaraj: Nation, Economy, and Territory in Colonial South Asia, 1870–1907," *Comparative Studies in Society and History* 40.4 (October 1998): 609–636, www.jstor.org/stable/179304.

19 Both Faiz and Jehan opted to move to Pakistan but invoke the subcontinent at large since their careers spanned the history of 'British India' as well as the post-independence phase and post-partition divisions in complex ways. Jehan was a major star in the Indian film industry of the 1940s and later in Pakistan, while Faiz, who "was often hailed as an activist for human rights, civil liberties and social justice" and whose poetry was at times "denied access to the media, radio and television in Pakistan" went into temporary exile. Sarvat Rahman, "Poet of Love and Rage: Translating Faiz Ahmed Faiz," *India International Centre Quarterly* 26.3 (Monsoon 1999): 105–118, quote 105.

20 [@DiceMediaIndia], *Twitter*, https://twitter.com/DiceMediaIndia.

21 Hye Jin Lee and Mark Andrejevic, "Second-Screen Theory: From the Democratic Surround to the Digital Enclosure," in *Connected Viewing: Selling, Streaming and Sharing Media in the Digital Era*, edited by Jennifer Holt and Kevin Sanson (London and New York: Routledge, 2014): 40–60.

22 E.g. in Dhruv's text message "Yah! Say shava shava mahiya say mutton cutlet soniya!!" (E4, 0:31).

23 Furthermore, Netflix offers subtitles for the series in numerous languages including French, German, Russian, and Turkish.

24 For example, the first episode of the first series titled "#FOMO" includes a reference to the film *Taxi Driver* with its most famous line "You talking to me?", with further movie references popping up in the dialogue between the protagonists.

25 For example, they watch *Inside Out* on a lazy Sunday morning (E1) and *Master of None* (E3) when they cannot sleep at night.

26 About Digital India, 10 December 2022, https://digitalindia.gov.in/introduction/. See also www.india.gov.in/spotlight/digital-india-digitally-empowered-society-and-knowledge-economy#tab=tab-1.

27 See e.g. Nandan Nilekani, "India Must Become the World's First Data Democracy," *The Week*, 10 September 2017, www.theweek.in/theweek/specials/indiamust-become-the-worlds-first-data-democr-acy.html.

Bibliography

[@DiceMediaIndia]. Twitter. https://twitter.com/DiceMediaIndia.

"About Digital India." 9 April 2019. www.digitalindia.gov.in/introduction (last accessed 23 March 2024).

"Āryāvarta." *Monier-Williams Sanskrit-English Dictionary*, 1899. www.sanskrit-lexicon.uni-koeln.de.

Ashcroft, Bill, Gareth Griffiths and Helen Tiffin. *Post-Colonial Studies: The Key Concepts*, 2nd ed. London and New York: Routledge, 2007.

Burton, David F. "Fire, Water and the Goddess: The Films of Deepa Mehta and Satyajit Ray as Critiques of Hindu Patriarchy." *Journal of Religion and Film* 17.2, article 3 (October 2013). https://digitalcommons.unomaha.edu/jrf/vol17/iss2/3.

Conteh, Jean. "Translanguaging." *ELT Journal* 72.2 (October 2018): 445–447. https://doi.org/10.1093/elt/ccy034.

Ellis-Peterson, Hannah. "Indian Move to Regulate Digital Media Raises Censorship Fears." *The Guardian*, 11 November 2020. www.theguardian.com/world/2020/nov/11/india-to-regulate-netflix-and-amazon-streaming-content.

Garcia, Ofelia. *Bilingual Education in the 21st Century: A Global Perspective.* Oxford: Wiley-Blackwell, 2009.

The Global South Project. Cornell University. www.globalsouthproject.cornell.edu (last accessed 5 April 2024).

Goswami, Manu. "From Swadeshi to Swaraj: Nation, Economy, and Territory in Colonial South Asia, 1870–1907." *Comparative Studies in Society and History* 40.4 (October 1998): 609–636. www.jstor.org/stable/179304.

Johnson, Catherine. *Online TV.* Abingdon, Oxon and New York: Routledge, 2019.

Jos, Vipin. "Analysing the Mindset of an Average Bhakt." *The Times of India*, 8 May 2019. https://timesofindia.indiatimes.com/readersblog/vjc-blogs/analysing-the-mindset-of-an-average-bhakt-3411/.

Kapur, Manavi. "Netflix has Joined the List of Things that Indians Want Banned." *Quartz India*, 6 September 2019. https://qz.com/india/1703651/shiv-sena-man-wants-netflix-banned-for-sacred-games-leila-ghoul/ (last accessed 5 April 2024).

Lee, Hye Jin and Mark Andrejevic. "Second-Screen Theory: From the Democratic Surround to the Digital Enclosure." In *Connected Viewing: Selling, Streaming and Sharing Media in the Digital Era*, edited by Jennifer Holt and Kevin Sanson. London and New York: Routledge, 2014: 40–60.

Manovich, Lev. *The Language of New Media.* Cambridge, MA: MIT Press, 2001.

Nilekani, Nandan. "India Must Become the World's First Data Democracy." *The Week*, 10 September 2017. www.theweek.in/theweek/specials/indiamust-become-the-worlds-first-data-democracy.html.

Rahman, Sarvat. "Poets of Love and Rage: Translating Faiz Ahmed Faiz." *India International Centre Quarterly* 26.3 (Monsoon 1999): 105–118, quote 105.

Roy, Arundhati. "The Pandemic is a Portal." *Financial Times*, 3 April 2020. www.ft.com/content/10d8f5e8-74eb-11ea-95fe-fcd274e920ca.

———. "This is Our Version of the Coronavirus. We are Sick." *Scroll*, 1 March 2020. https://scroll.in/article/954805/arundhati-roy-on-delhi-violence-this-is-our-version-of-the-coronavirus-we-are-sick.

Verma, Rahul. "Leila: The Indian Handmaid's Tale." *BBC Culture*, 21 August 2019. www.bbc.com/culture/article/20190821-leila-the-indian-handmaids-tale.

3

SOUTH AFRICAN FICTION IN ENGLISH

From Post-Apartheid to World Anglophone

Deniz Gündoğan İbrişim[1]

Over many decades, the South African literary canon has primarily focused on the apartheid experience. However, in the aftermath of the establishment of the Truth and Reconciliation Commission (TRC) in 1995 in South Africa, which was the result of negotiations between Nelson Mandela's African National Congress (ANC) and F.W. de Klerk's National Party (NP), South African literature has focused on contradictory, alluring, and painful representations of the post-apartheid South African psyche. In their introduction to *SA Lit: Beyond 2000*, Michael Chapman and Margaret Lenta argue that the post-2000 period signals a difference, because "books tangential to heavy politics, or even to local interest, have begun to receive national recognition."[2] They cite texts that have received substantial attention, such as Anne Landsman's *The Rowing Lesson* (2008), J.M. Coetzee's suburban Australian novels, Imraan Coovadia's *High Low In-Between* (2009), Sally-Ann Murray's *Small Moving Parts* (2009), and Peter Harris's non-fictional narrative of human drama. In these narratives, the South African national formation and national identity have been fundamentally undermined. We encounter the possibilities of identity formations that become multiple, complex, shifting, and always contradictory.

The acclaimed critics of South African literature David Attwell and Barbara Harlow also examine contemporary South African literature and the state of what they call "post-apartheid narrative."[3] Attwell and Harlow argue that post-apartheid narratives are comparable to the postcolonial texts of other "liberated" nations in which people have their voices heard in election processes but at the same suffer from unequal economic conditions and oppressive class relations. They argue that post-apartheid writers such as Nadine Gordimer, J.M. Coetzee, Zakes Mda, and Sindiwe Magona posit challenges

DOI: 10.4324/9781003464037-5
This chapter has been made available under a CC-BY-NC-ND 4.0 license.

for literary and cultural critics who study the region according to the apartheid/post-apartheid binary and thus from a narrow perspective. To be able to understand South African post-apartheid fiction in all its complexities, Atwell and Harlow assert, novel and plural approaches and literary tropes beyond politicized and protest literature should be taken into consideration critically and creatively.[4] From this pluralistic perspective, I examine in this chapter how post-apartheid South African fiction unfolds into networks of diversified local epistemes and situated practices across the world. In particular, I argue contemporary South African literature epitomizes Anglophone world literature, which relies on translational, provincial, multilingual, and worldly affiliations and encounters.

Monica Popescu's work, loosely following the trajectory of South African history from apartheid to post-apartheid and highlighting the debates around anti-apartheid resistance, the years of transition to democracy, and the challenges of pluralism in the early 1990s, is pivotal in terms of its relational and pluralistic approach to South African fiction. In her book *South African Literature Beyond the Cold War* (2010), Popescu advances a novel framework for understanding the complex and nuanced relationship between South Africa and Eastern Europe as well as between postcolonialism and postcommunism in ways that immensely enrich and complicate our current understanding of South African literature. She argues: "South African and the Eastern European populations turned their back on some of the world's most repressive regimes and expressed their hopes for democracy almost at the same time."[5] For Popescu, contemporary South African literature reflects a fascination with Russian and Eastern European stories of revolution and transformation as well as resistance to state oppression. Through this relational analysis, I suggest, Popescu breaks the stranglehold of the dominant political reality and overwhelming oppression of the apartheid time that had an unrelenting impact on South African writers.

These pluralistic interventions regarding contemporary South African literature allow me to undertake an analysis which offers a nuanced alternative to dominant understandings of South Africa. In this chapter, I move away from the long-lasting logic of black and white, good and bad, past and present, modern and pre-modern, and consider multitextured and multidirectional perceptions of the country's language and culture. Specifically, I argue that writers like Achmat Dangor critically and strategically juxtapose varied Western and non-Western cultural registers (i.e., Afrikaans,[6] Dutch, Hindi, Arabic, Persian, and Turkish) alongside literary English and classical allusions. Taking Dangor's *Kafka's Curse* (1997) as a case study for my investigation,[7] I examine in this chapter how the novel crosses literary borders by punctuating the very negotiation between the singular and the plural, between the modern and traditional, and thereby encourages us to read the text as "Anglophone world literature." In what follows, I first provide a brief

54 Deniz Gündoğan İbrişim

overview of Anglophone world literary studies as a field in order to better understand the material circumstances of Dangor's text. Second, I focus on how Dangor offers a cosmopolitan, transnational, and hybrid vision of South African life that encourages the reader to consider the text as Anglophone world literature rather than as a narrative within the strictures of the apartheid/post-apartheid binary.

Anglophone World Literary Studies

Gauri Viswanathan in her seminal article dating back to 1987 ponders on the location of English literature and asks: "Where is English literature produced?"[8] To be sure, her answer is "not in England," attracting our attention to the genealogy of postcolonial theory and its development within the British Empire and other territories outside England. She underscores the dynamic relationship between "sites of cultural production and institutionalization," as well as the particular way that "English literature" in the broad sense constitutes both a mode of analysis and a vast collection of works in the world. Viswanathan argues that there is no English literature before institutionalization. Put another way, cultural products surface and consolidate themselves as fields through disciplinary norms.[9] Here, Viswanathan substantiates the Gramscian idea of the relation between culture and power, arguing that cultural hegemony best serves British political and commercial interests and the establishment of English Literature as a discipline in India. Thereby, her question "Where is English literature produced?" encourages the reader to contemplate the particular practices through which works are classified and given social as well as cultural purpose.

From a 21st-century perspective, we can broaden Viswanathan's claims and add more questions on the practices of English literature: how does English literature circulate? Where is English literature read and through which linguistic and cultural practices it is received? How has the global circulation of English shaped the forms of its appearance? I argue that these questions underscore circulation rather than the issue of mere production, thereby emphasizing the worldly understanding of English in literary studies. In a similar vein, Rebecca L. Walkowitz's *Immigrant Fictions*, which is a paradigm-changing collection bringing together studies of world literature, book history, narrative theory, and the contemporary novel, expands and challenges methods of critical reading based on national models of literary culture, suggesting that contemporary literature, and in particular English texts, cannot be imagined to exist in a single literary system but might exist, now and in the future, within several literary systems, through various and uneven practices of world-making. Walkowitz argues that Anglophone works of immigrant fiction are not always produced in an Anglophone country and that some immigrant fictions produced in an Anglophone country are not originally Anglophone. All these variations, Walkowitz argues, challenge the assumed national monolingualism, reminding us that there has always been a non-conformist relationship between the national and linguistic capacities of the tradition we call "English literature."[10] Walkowitz claims that this phenomenon is not new, because for many centuries, works of Anglophone literature have been produced outside of England, including Scotland, Ireland, Wales, India, Nigeria, Antigua, the U.S., Canada, and so forth. Thereby, contemporary literature has been read within and beyond several national traditions and national systems, allowing us to reflect on different literary histories that are put tandem with each-other.

To be sure, these questions concerning literature also relate to and reflect on the significance of the concept of world literature,[11] which has come to acknowledge the heterogeneity and discontinuity of national cultures, as well as the emergence of novel networks of tradition and the relational social processes through which those networks have been established. In particular, Haun Saussy's influential contribution to the American Comparative Literature Association's decennial report (2004) signals and elaborates on this heterogeneity. One should underline that although, for Saussy, the term "world" marks a hegemonizing, homogenizing, and systematizing perspective, perhaps a phantasm for novel spaces of difference and plurality,[12] it also surfaces as a comparative category, a mode of looking into relationality between subjects and objects, nations and globes, particularities and totalities as well as literary texts and the plural worlds they build or remake.

It is precisely the emphasis on the poietic world-making aspects of literature that transgresses the contours of what Aamir Mufti calls a one-world reality which must engage with the "critical-historical examination of a certain constellation of ideas and practices in its accretions and transformations over time."[13] In a similar way of understanding the network of interconnections that shape the multilingual landscapes of literatures at large and of Anglophone literatures in particular, Mufti challenges us to reconfigure canon-making itself. Mufti argues the project of philological Orientalism, from the microscopic level of the text to the macroscopic one of the library, produces an entire hermeneutics which "may be understood as a set of processes for the reorganization of language, literature, and culture on a planetary scale that effected the assimilation of heterogeneous and dispersed bodies of writing onto the plane of equivalence and evaluability that is (world) literature."[14] Seen in this light, Anglophone world literature then engages with the world-making potentialities of literature critically and thereby fosters processes of exchange that both thrive on and transcend locally diversified literary traditions.

Bearing in mind the world-making potentialities of literature here, I would like to turn to the recent discussion of Anglophone world literature, which I understand as both a global and local medium of expression

56 Deniz Gündoğan İbrişim

and world-building/making practice as well as an attentiveness to the recognition of the plurality of aesthetic expressivity beyond Eurocentric frames in specific locales. This attentiveness neither puts much emphasis on topographical singularities nor exclusively highlights global inequalities. Instead, it foregrounds the concept of world-building in both its temporal and spatial dimensions. In particular, world-building gets the most important share in *What Is a World?* (2016) by Pheng Cheah, a leading theorist of cosmopolitanism. Cheah tackles the tensions between universalist normative ethics and local modes of being-in-the-world through his readings of postcolonial literature, including works by Michelle Cliff, Amitav Ghosh, Nuruddin Farah, Ninotchka Rosca, and Timothy Mo. These texts, as Cheah argues, illuminate a globally conceived and administered humanist ethos that can conflict with local needs. To illustrate, Ghosh's novel provides an in-depth account of the international project of creating a wildlife preserve for tigers in the Sundarbans, the mangrove forests of West Bengal, which was carried out by the Indian government with exceptional violence against local villagers.

Cheah insists that there must be something about what literature is or, more importantly, what literature with its world does that cannot be accounted for in purely rational, sociological, or political terms. I would say that by world, Cheah means one of many worlds. For him, our normalized idea of the world is a capitalist and colonial construction, built and maintained by temporal structures (i.e. time zones). Cheah's world and worlding refer to "how a world is held together and given unity by the force of time. In giving rise to existence, temporalization worlds a world."[15] For Cheah, then, what is most troubling about our concept of time is that it is ultimately driven by capitalism and a fast-paced thinking that spread via European colonialism. For him, postcolonial literature is worlding new (postcolonial) worlds in a literal sense and challenging a capitalist world.

I find Cheah's argument neither romantic nor an idyllic return to literature's autonomy. Instead, one of the results of his intervention which I find most fruitful for my analysis here is drawing attention to a global and local medium of expression and world-building/making practices. It is my contention here that contemporary South African literature, and in particular Dangor's *Kafka's Curse*, illuminates new worlds through its demonstration of heterogeneous and planetary topographies as well as intertwined histories of non-Western cultures. As I will discuss in the following sections, *Kafka's Curse* focuses on imaginative manoeuvres, such as the creation of non-Eurocentric networks of reciprocal exchange and the entanglement of heterogeneous spatio-temporal realms. In this way, it reworks the concept of the "Anglophone" and the "world" within and from multidimensional contexts where centre-periphery, local-global, universal-particular, diaspora-native, individual-collective frameworks become reductive. This hybrid constellation reveals the idea that we need a stronger notion of the

South African Fiction in English **57**

world of world literature (hence I would say world literature itself) that would allow us to diversify its semantic and practical content to undermine the Eurocentric connotations and at the same time to facilitate other modes of agentic capabilities of literature. I suggest that this fosters a more inclusive move from a mere production to circulation with its varied forms including both the dissemination and translation of local and culturally specific stories and knowledge. In what follows, I will discuss *Kafka's Curse* and pay particular attention to the literary processes of world-making that emphasize the range of local contexts and imaginative creations of other worlds that are in Schulze-Engler's words "by no means restricted to transcultural interactions with Europe or the West"[16] but extend to capture multidirectional flows beyond the transnational and the East/West divide.

Worlds of *Kafka's Curse*: Beyond Singular Acts and Responses

Short-listed for the Booker Prize in 2004, *Kafka's Curse* presents South African culture, where complex identities and sedimented traumatic histories are envisioned and re-envisioned in a state of constant renegotiation. *Kafka's Curse* interrogates the apartheid-era doctrine of racial purity, separation, and segregation, posing questions about how apartheid practices are rewritten in the post-apartheid nation. The story revolves around the Khan family. Omar Khan is an Eastern Indian Muslim who claims to be a Jew in order to pass for white. He changes his name to Oscar Kahn, crossing the colour line, and marries Anna, an English-descended wife. The protagonist's name thus appears as Omar/Oscar throughout the novel. Omar/Oscar's devout Muslim brother Malik and his wife Fatgiyah do not approve Omar/Oscar's changed name and his new lifestyle. Eventually Omar/Oscar dies in the aftermath of his mysterious metamorphosis, becoming dust in the end. After Omar/Oscar's death, the rest of the book is told from the perspective of multiple characters, jumping back and forth in time by bringing in Omar/Oscar's fractured family portraits. As we navigate the complexly layered family stories, the knots of perverse sexuality embedded in each character as well as incestuous bonds come to light. Each character is revealed to be other than what she/he claims. We learn that Anna is sexually abused by her brother Martin, and Anna's white colonial father has a second, "secret" family that is Muslim and black. The Khan family, with its complex history of mixed blood in several generations, endures recurrent tragedies, as every character seems to be alienated from society. Omar/Oscar's English-descended wife Anna is sexually abused and does not know Omar/Oscar was born Muslim until after he dies; Omar/Oscar's brother Malik falls into an affair with Omar/Oscar's therapist, Amina Mandelstam, who is also a secret Muslim; Omar/Oscar's free-spirit son Fadiel falls in love with a Boer descendant, blonde Marianne. *Kafka's Curse* is rife with themes of love across racial barriers, suicide, and pervasive

58 Deniz Gündoğan İbrişim

sexual relationships. In this context, the novel's ambition is twofold. First, it seeks to reimagine the stories of interracial relationships within the capacious narrative of South African history, and second, it problematizes the value and use of such stories in the production of a new South Africa.

Dangor reworks the Arabian myth of a gardener, Majnun, whose forbidden love for a princess, Layla, causes him to be turned into a tree. The original theme of the myth passed and circulated from Arabic roots to Persia, Turkey, and India. The famous Persian poet Nizami Ganjavi (1141–1209) adopted the myth in his composition of the story of love between Khosrow (the Persian king of the Sasanian era) and Shirin (the Armenian princess) in 1192. At least forty Persian and thirteen Turkish versions based on Nizami's poetic narrative style are known, and there are over a hundred versions in those two languages alone. Among these, the melodic rendition of the story of Layla and Majnun by Fuzûlî, one of the greatest Azeri-Turkish poets, became immensely popular in the 16th-century Ottoman Empire. The allegorical romance of Fuzûlî depicts the attraction of Majnun (the spelling appears as "Mejnun" in his version, meaning the ultimate human spirit) to Layla (the spelling appears as "Leyla" in his version, meaning the divine beauty). However, Fuzûlî's story diverges from Nizami's version in that Nizami's male protagonist might refer to a real man who directs all his feelings to his earthly beloved, whereas Fuzûlî's version highlights a love for an ideal source, an abstraction. Fuzûlî's version also depicts Majnun's pilgrimage to Mecca and his contemplation of Al-Mubdi, the one who is the originator of all creation.

I argue here that Dangor responds to Fuzûlî and poses questions that have yet to be addressed within the South African context at large. Dangor specifically and provocatively adds a South African element (both the spelling and the metamorphosis into a willow tree) into Fuzûlî's version in order to indicate how history and literature work together through multiple entry points both culturally and linguistically. Thereby, Dangor encourages us to look at (Anglophone) world literature from the concept of literature as being multitemporal and multilingual, allowing for an understanding of literature as being always in the making. One can claim that Dangor's gesture re-politicizes world literature and connects South Africa with popular myths as well as the global with the local.

The power to create new, open and plural worlds in *Kafka's Curse* surfaces with Omar/Oscar's mysterious transformation into a "beautiful and sensitive" willow tree right in his own bedroom. The parts of his body that remain are nothing but unidentifiable patterns of roots, dust, and crust at the foot of his bed:

> Look at my skin. As coarse and grainy as the bark of some ancient tree. The itching has stopped though. The merciful death of the skin beneath this bark. Smell the dust in the air, moistened by my exhaled breath, until

everything is damp. All sort of organisms come to life, spores grow from the walls, and lichen covers the floorboards. In the kitchen and bathroom, green damp has invaded the concrete floors, licking at tiles and establishing homes in the warm vaginas of the taps. Perhaps that's why you didn't come back. You were frightened off by the virulent forests of my dementia.[...] Yesterday a group of clappers landed in the nettling of my hair.

(58–60)

Omar/Oscar is of Indian descent. He is of mixed Muslim Indian, African, and Dutch origin and undergoes a metamorphosis. At the beginning, Omar/Oscar is a successful architect who lives in the wealthy white suburb of Johannesburg with his wife Anna. However, as seen from the previous excerpt, his transformation occasions a traumatic collapse in which the old and familiar order suddenly disappears and the world is turned upside down. As Omar/Oscar takes to his bed, his skin hardens into bark; he begins inhaling carbon dioxide and exhaling oxygen. He moves from the human to the vegetative state, becoming a willow tree in tumultuous post-apartheid South Africa.

The moment of metamorphosis is important on two levels, as it illuminates a number of poetic practices and transcultural aesthetics that bring together different literary traditions (such as reworkings of the Arabian myth) that crisscross the world and that cultivate relationality and interdependency with the transformative force of locality. First, the metamorphosis in *Kafka's Curse* is based on an imaginative utilization of the Northern Arabic and Ottoman-Turkish myth "Layla and Majnun,"[17] which originally pivots around an unattainable love between an ordinary gardener and a wealthy princess. Dangor strategically utilizes this story as a form of counter-storytelling to portray a specific kind of suffering and struggle in post-apartheid South Africa and thus creates transnational and transcultural polycentric networks and relations among texts as well as their world-making capacities. In this context, if we understand literature in Wai Chee Dimock's terms as a "continuum which extends, across space and time, messing up territorial sovereignty and numerical chronology,"[18] *Kafka's Curse* illustrates this with the story of Layla and Majnun, the most well-known tales in Islamic literature, emerging from legends, tales, poems, songs, and epics hailing from the Caucasus to Africa and from the Atlantic to the Indian Ocean.

Second, the metamorphosis Omar/Oscar goes through makes the reader rethink a particular collective trauma: the trauma of the South African Muslim Indians who are caught between a Muslim Indian identity and a South African one. As will be further discussed, the willow tree in *Kafka's Curse* marks a contingent sense of belonging, bringing into light the complex dynamics involved both in the trauma of individual displacement and the trauma of environmental uprooting in post-apartheid South Africa. In addition, this metamorphosis illuminates a new paradigm for discontinuous

60 Deniz Gündoğan İbrişim

transformations of historically fixed subjectivities regarding South Africa. Like the gods and mortals in Ovid's *Metamorphoses*, the characters in Dangor's *Kafka's Curse* always transform – from Muslim to Jew, from black to white, from man to tree, in order to write themselves anew beyond established dichotomies.

Omar/Oscar's metamorphosis clearly draws our attention to socio-historical and cross-cultural traumatic contexts (such as the plight of diasporic Muslim Indian and South African people) in a novel way in the fictional world of post-apartheid South Africa. While Omar/Oscar describes his metamorphosis into the willow tree through the Majnun story, we are drawn into a creative imagination that unsettles the established anthropocentric subjecthood and generates fluid and resistant archives vis-à-vis rigid colonial histories, hierarchies, and temporal scales.

> I allowed the myth Leila and Majnoen to lie a little bit more than necessary. Imagine a man turning into a tree as he waits for a lover who will never arrive. A well-deserved fate, if you ask me, for a lowly gardener waiting for a princess. In any case, there are no great forests in all of Arabia. So, what are the real origins of the legend? Heroic propositions by slaves from India or Malaysia to sustain themselves? A coping mechanism – that's what you call it, no? It might have been African? [...] You see, the myth really warns against the madness of Majnoen, or is it against Majnoen the Madness? An insanity that strikes those who dare to stray from their life station, that little room which you are told at birth is yours. You may expand it a bit, add a loft or a garden, and build a bigger fence than the one you inherited. But you leave it at your peril. In fact, you are punished for leaving. [...] Making this tale African would have been too obvious. Everybody wants to make our little room theirs, make their destiny ours. [...] It was Muslim, that much I know.
>
> *(30–31)*

Omar/Oscar's monologue reveals here the discursive hierarchies in histories of colonialism and dehumanization, thereby identifying the violence and trauma of Indian slavery in the enterprise of colonialism. Dangor blurs the myth's origin and inserts his own version of the tale so that South African history, with its hidden turbulences such as the arrival of Indian slaves and Muslim Indian slavery, can be revealed to the reader. Moreover, Omar/Oscar provocatively emphasizes that there are no great forests in all of Arabia. This provocation, and more importantly his transformation into a willow tree, suggest that the myth travelled to South Africa through the Indian Ocean slave trade that encompassed Africa, Asia, and the Middle East, with people from these areas involved as both captors and captives.

Dangor's intervention here aligns with the importance of narrativity in resisting dominance by anchoring both the discursive and the material through oral stories. Stories undoubtedly become a bridge in the transmission of native and exilic legacies from a troubled past. Omar/Oscar, who becomes a trickster in his passing as a Jew, doubles his trickster abilities to let the Layla and Majnun tale "lie a little more than necessary," expanding the spatio-temporal realm pertinent to its Ottoman-Arabic origins. Through a particular engagement, Omar/Oscar rejects histories of dominance and skilfully plays with power structures. The novel thus constitutes a profound narrative attempt to reclaim the unsolved and largely overlooked phenomenon of Indian slavery in South Africa. Storytelling here encourages us to rethink dominant discourses in colonial and postcolonial structures in order to promote both the production and more significantly the circulation of overlooked histories and untold stories. In this way, it would be fair to claim that *Kafka's Curse* foregrounds a number of poetic practices and translocal as well as transcultural aesthetics that bring together different literary traditions that crisscross the world and that cultivate relationality, exchange and interdependency.

Such an exercise in reading can be fruitful in several respects. First, *Kafka's Curse* rejects the strictures of pre-set value systems such as identity, history, past, and politics. Instead, the novel remodels a world which rests on a variable range of materiality, connecting multiple violent histories, roots, and routes in post-apartheid South Africa. Second, by showcasing the multiple processes of loss and individuation, *Kafka's Curse* rewrites a priori, fixed subjects and demonstrates a creative and imaginative leap beyond the status-quo. By attuning himself to a porous vision, Omar/Oscar is defined by his material relations and his connections to land (landscapes, plants, air, water, and space) and other beings. Omar/Oscar, a heterogeneous assemblage of the human and the nonhuman, is far away from his apparent white and privileged subjectivity through which we come to know him at the beginning of the novel. As a willow tree, he possesses the curious ability to act and to produce dramatic and subtle effects for reworking Indian Muslim and South African memory writ large. One can claim that Omar/Oscar establishes a "glocal" memory here which captures the dynamic, contingent, and two-way dialectic between global and local concerns regarding humans, nonhuman others, matter, language, and space in a historical context. Seen in this light, *Kafka's Curse* exceeds national boundaries to include indigenous, tribal, and other vulnerable histories, creating a cross-cultural pollination beyond a national and compartmentalized context. The novel thus moves beyond a mere apartheid/post-apartheid division and dualist definition and situates itself in terms of Anglophone world literature or world Anglophone text, criticizing narrative teleology.

Reading With Hyperlinked Histories

One of the major examples of a cross-cultural pollination in *Kafka's Curse* can be seen in the character Malik and his relations. In contrast to the trickster figure Omar/Oscar, Malik is a successful local politician who remains devoted to his Muslim religion and heritage, despite the hardships that someone with his identity faces within the apartheid state. However, starting with his brother Omar/Oscar's death, Malik begins to experience a psychological trauma that breaches his own integrity and sheltered world. Malik undergoes a symbolic metamorphosis, if not a physical one, based on self-reflexivity and a critical reflection of his ancestral roots. This symbolic metamorphosis, I suggest, is best illustrated through the love affair between Malik and Amina (Omar/Oscar's former therapist). After making love, Malik and Amina talk about their families and past secrets. At that moment, Malik gives Amina a novel called *Memed, My Hawk*, by Yaşar Kemal, the Turkish author and human right activist of Kurdish origin.[19] Upon receiving the novel, Amina reacts:

> Memed, that's Mohammed? Why is it spelled so funnily? Turkish. Maybe it's the translator. What do they know about Islamic culture? His face, that willful clamp of mouth and furrowed forehead, impresses on her the importance of the book to him. She finds Memed's adventures too earnest, his heroism coy. [...] Yet the very fact that he read the book betrays a more sensual Malik, a lover of fiction, an imbiber of conjured images. She imagined Malik as a brigand.[20]

This passage is intriguing on two levels. First, there is a remarkable connection between Turkish and South African literary contexts. This moment constitutes a link between South African and Turkish literature in their overlapping fictional portrayal of atrocity and human rights abuses as well as their formal strategies to overcome them. For Malik, Mehmed[21] becomes a role model of survival against domination and victimhood in South Africa. Malik's fondness for Yaşar Kemal's *Memed, My Hawk* denotes active resistance and repudiation of dominance against obtrusive themes of tragedy and victimhood. Yaşar Kemal's young protagonist Memed manages to reclaim a transformative collective space for both himself and his community. Here, Malik also establishes an analogy between himself and Memed. This analogy is vital for Malik as he works through his loss (both the loss of his brother and the loss of the everyday familiar world in which he used to live) by keeping Memed's adventures by his side, navigating his way in the post-apartheid era.

Second, I contend that the dialogue between Amina and Malik brings to light an overlooked phenomenon of cross-cultural repressed histories. Malik's sarcastic answer: "Turkish. What do they know about Islamic culture?" is key to this repressed history. I propose that Dangor's intervention implicitly

South African Fiction in English **63**

refers to the Ottoman imperial legacy and the assimilation of Malay Muslims into Ottoman-Islamic hegemony in Cape Town during the 19th century.[22] The history of the Ottoman presence in South Africa has hardly been a topic of debate in the contemporary novel. In 1869, Ottoman-Kurdish Abu Bakr Effendi (who was born in the Ottoman province Şehrizur and was an Ottoman Magistrate) was sent to Cape Town by the Ottoman Sultan Abdülmecid I in order to teach Islam and assist religious matters in the heterogeneous Muslim community of Cape Malays, which comprised of Southern Indian and South East Asian Muslims. Abu Bakr Effendi had a massive impact on Islam at the Cape. His greatest contribution to Cape Muslim society was his "Bayannuddin" ("the explanation of the religion"), which was one of the earliest and most comprehensive books written uniquely in Arabic-Afrikaans, with prefaces in Turkish, Arabic and Afrikaans. He introduced fezzes to be worn by men and the face-covering attire to be worn by Cape Muslim women.

Despite his efforts of communal unity, Abu Bakr Effendi faced strong resistance from the Cape Malay Muslims, as his Ottoman Islamic reforms were oriented toward eradicating local and indigenous practices among the community.[23] Thus, although Abu Bakr was a distinguished figure, he was controversial because of his strict sanctions which created conflict in the Cape community. In this framework, I suggest that we circle back to Amina's question here "What do they know about the Islamic culture?" To be sure, this question emerges as rhetorical, and yet, it resonates with the Cape Malay Muslim community and Abu Bakr's 19th-century prescriptions in South Africa. Through a narrative that integrates the Turkish-Kurdish fictional character Memed into his fiction, Dangor forges a mnemonic link between the contested belonging and the forgotten indigenous history of Cape Malay Muslims. He thus places the minor Cape Muslim voice at the centre of his narrative of the complex and continuously traumatic history of South Africa.

This continuum allows for a space that is open to a wide diversity of positions from which to study or address hyperlinked histories that might foster worlds of their own if we follow Cheah's footsteps here, being attentive to alternative worlds that can shed critical light upon the existing world. While *Kafka's Curse* renders a world informed by Afrikaans and English, Ottoman-Arabic as well as Turkish cultural registers, it generates an array of imaginative gestures such as the creation of overlooked non-Eurocentric narratives based on the specificity and singularity of the individual literary text as well as its transnational trajectories.

Conclusion

This chapter has discussed how *Kafka's Curse* epitomizes a circulatory phenomenon which can be read across geographical, historical, cultural, and linguistic boundaries through a combination of Afrikaans and English,

Ottoman-Arabic, and Turkish. In particular, the novel foregrounds a translation of the Arabic tale *Layla and Majnun* and specifically introduces non-Western modes of storytelling for generating worlds constantly in a state of becoming. Additionally, the text invites the reader to an engagement for channelling the traumatic memory of apartheid/post-apartheid into other overlooked stories such as Cape Malay Muslim's repressed history.

Kafka's Curse, then, is cross-cultural, globalized, and transcultural. At the same time, it is highly shaped by multiple and entangled local expressive traditions and regionally grounded experiences. Thereby, I suggest that the novel is agentic in creating plural and non-Eurocentric worlds in which hierarchies between the intimate, local, regional, national, and the transnational blur. In this way, it gestures toward a literary world-making which includes a number of poetic practices, translocal and transcultural aesthetics that bring together different literary traditions that crisscross the world. It would be suggestive to remember Cheah's arguments that narrative fictions do not simply reflect on the conflictual state of a globalized world, but also carry a significant and normative power to create and shape alternate worlds. Literature then becomes an inexhaustible resource for world-making, as Cheah suggests. *Kafka's Curse* makes visible literary processes of both creativity and world-making within and more significantly outside Western frameworks.

Notes

1 This study has been supported by the Horizon EU 2020-MSCA-IF fellowship (grant number 101025604).
2 Michael Chapman and Margaret Lenta, eds., *SA Lit: Beyond 2000* (Pietermaritzburg: The *University of KwaZulu-Natal Press*, 2011): ix.
3 David Attwell and Barbara Harlow, "Introduction: South African Fiction after Apartheid," *Modern Fiction Studies* 46.1 (Spring 2000): 1–9.
4 See also, for example, Mark Sanders, *Complicities: The Intellectual and Apartheid* (Durham: Duke University Press, 2002) and Achille Mbembe, "Provisional Notes on the Postcolony," *Africa: Journal of the International African Institute* 62.1 (1992): 3–37.
5 Monica Popescu, *South African Literature Beyond the Cold War* (London: Palgrave Macmillan, 2010): 4.
6 Afrikaans is a creole language that evolved during the 19th century under colonialism in southern Africa. It had its roots mainly in Dutch, mixed with seafarer variants of Malay, Portuguese, Indonesian, and the indigenous Khoekhoe and San languages. It was generally spoken by peasants, the urban proletariat, and the middle class of civil servants, traders, and teachers.
7 Achmat Dangor, *Kafka's Curse* (New York: Pantheon Books, 1999).
8 Gauri Viswanathan, "The Beginnings of English Literary Study in British India," *Oxford Literary Review* 9.1/2 (1987): 22.
9 Viswanathan, "The Beginnings," 20.
10 Rebecca Walkowitz, *Immigrant Fictions: Contemporary Literature in an Age of Globalization* (Madison: University of Wisconsin Press, 2007): 529–530.

11 This chapter does not discuss the concept and genealogy of world literature at large due to limitations of scope and space. Since Goethe's coining of the term *Weltliteratur* in the early 19th century, the amorphous and expansive term of world literature has undergone a constant revision and redefinition. Erich Auerbach's anxiety and pessimism about standardization, David Damrosch's conceptualization of world literature as "a mode of circulation and of reading," Franco Moretti's formulation of world literature as "one and unequal" or Pascal Casanova's "Gallocentric" model in which so-called peripheral writers derive their aesthetic innovation, creativity and expressivity from the centre, have influenced recent debates on Anglophone world literatures. There has been a significant effort in opening up the Eurocentric canon and investing literary studies through more "worldly" urgency.

12 Haun Saussy, "Comparative Literature: The Next Ten Years," State of the Discipline Report, March 2014, https://stateofthediscipline.acla.org/entry/comparative-literature-next-ten-years.

13 Aamir R. Mufti, *Forget English: Orientalisms and World Literatures* (Cambridge, MA: Harvard University Press, 2018): 19–20.

14 Mufti, *Forget English*, 145.

15 Cheah, *What is a World?* 8–10.

16 Frank Schulze-Engler, "Theoretical Perspectives: From Postcolonialism to Transcultural World Literature," in *English Literatures across the Globe: A Companion*, edited by Lars Eckstein (Paderborn: Fink, 2007): 20–32.

17 Rather than the more familiar Arabic spelling "Layla and Majnun," Dangor uses "Majnoen and Leila" in his novel. "Layla and Majnun" begins in the Arabian desert in the latter half of the 7th century. It belongs to the Udhri love story of the Bedouin poet Qays İbn Al-Mulawwah and his beloved Layla.

18 Wai Chee Dimock, "Literature for the Planet," *PMLA* 116.1 (2001): 175.

19 Yaşar Kemal, *Memed, My Hawk*, translated by Edouard Roditi (New York: New York Review of Books Classics, 2005).

20 Dangor, *Kafka's Curse*, 143–144.

21 Published in original Turkish in 1955, and later translated into forty languages, including English, German, Spanish, and French, *Memed, My Hawk* has been praised as a masterpiece of Turkish oral storytelling. Set in the 1930s, during the early years of the tumultuous Turkish Republic in the aftermath of the fall of the Ottoman Empire, the novel centres on Memed, a young boy from an Anatolian village.

22 Islam first arrived in South Africa though slavery, which began in the mid-1600s to the mid-1800s when the Dutch sent slaves and political prisoners to the Cape Colony from Indonesia and other Asian countries. The second wave of Muslims arrived from India as indentured labourers to work in sugar cane farms for the British in the late 1800s. The South African legacy of colonial occupation, slavery, and indentured labour is intricately connected to every-day lives of the Muslims and to their long history of struggle of recognition and justice.

23 Abu Bakr strictly criticized the daily eating practices of the Cape Muslim community. In 1869, he declared certain seafood, including snoek and crayfish, forbidden ("haram") for Shafi'i Muslims in Cape Town, whose diet was mainly dependent on this particular seafood. This pronouncement created a rift between Abu Bakr and the local community. See Martin van Bruinessen, "A Nineteenth Century Kurdish Scholar in South Africa," in *Mullas, Sufis, and Heretics: The Role of Religion in Kurdish Society: Collected Articles*, edited by Martin van Bruinessen (Piscataway: Gorgias Press, 2011): 133–142.

66   Deniz Gündoğan İbrişim

Bibliography

Auerbach, Erich. *Introduction to Romance Languages and Literature: Latin, French, Spanish, Provençal, Italian*, translated by Guy Daniels. Jenkintown: Capricorn Books, 1961.

Attwell, David and Barbara Harlow. "Introduction: South African Fiction after Apartheid." *Modern Fiction Studies* 46.1 (Spring 2000): 1–9.

Casanova, Pascale. *The World Republic of Letters*, translated by M. B. DeBevoise. Cambridge, MA: Harvard University Press, 2004.

Chapman, Michael and Margaret Lenta, eds. *SA Lit: Beyond 2000*. Pietermaritzburg: The University of KwaZulu-Natal Press, 2011.

Cheah, Pheng. *What is a World? On Postcolonial Literature as World Literature*. Durham: Duke University Press, 2016.

Damrosch, David. *What is World Literature?* Princeton: Princeton University Press, 2018.

Dangor, Achmat. *Kafka's Curse*. New York: Pantheon Books, 1999.

Dimock, Wai Chee. "Literature for the Planet." *PMLA* 116.1 (2001): 173–188.

Kemal, Yaşar. *Memed, My Hawk*, translated by Edouard Roditi. New York: New York Review of Books Classics, 2005.

Mbembe, Achille. "Provisional Notes on the Postcolony." *Africa: Journal of the International African Institute* 62.1 (1992): 3–37.

Moretti, Franco. "Conjectures on World Literature." *New Left Review* 1 (January–February 2000): 54–68.

Mufti, Aamir R. *Forget English: Orientalisms and World Literatures*. Cambridge, MA: Harvard University Press, 2018.

Popescu, Monica. *South African Literature beyond the Cold War*. London: Palgrave Macmillan, 2010.

Sanders, Mark. *Complicities: The Intellectual and Apartheid*. Durham: Duke University Press, 2002.

Saussy, Haun. "Comparative Literature: The Next Ten Years." *State of the Discipline Report*, March 2014. https://stateofthediscipline.acla.org/entry/comparative-literature-next-ten-years.

Schulze-Engler, Frank. "Theoretical Perspectives: From Postcolonialism to Transcultural World Literature." In *English Literatures across the Globe: A Companion*, edited by Lars Eckstein. Paderborn: Fink, 2007: 20–32.

Van Bruinessen, Martin. "A Nineteenth Century Kurdish scholar in South Africa." In *Mullas, Sufis, and Heretics: The Role of Religion in Kurdish Society: Collected Articles*, edited by Martin Van Bruinessen. Piscataway: Gorgias Press, 2011: 133–142. https://doi.org/10.31826/9781463229887-009.

Viswanathan, Gauri. "The Beginnings of English Literary Study in British India." *Oxford Literary Review* 9.1/2 (1987): 2–26.

Walkowitz, Rebecca. *Immigrant Fictions: Contemporary Literature in an Age of Globalization*. Madison: University of Wisconsin Press, 2007.

4

QUESTIONING THE EMERGENCE OF NATIONAL ENGLISHES

Non-Teleological Paths of Language Development in Contexts of Postcolonial Diversity

Britta Schneider

Introduction: Non-Teleological Language Orientations

In the study of World Englishes, *the nation* has formed a central and mostly unquestioned descriptive entity – concepts of the social as 'naturally' materialising in territorial, national settings[1] have framed many of our analyses of English in language repertoires worldwide.[2] Yet non-national connections, such as transnational social ties or prestige associated with transnational realms, have existed for a long time. Particularly for postcolonial speakers, non-national entanglements are neither new nor exciting. Thus, for example, the language ideologies of the European nation-state,[3] among them notions of 'proper' language and ideals of homogenous standardised language in culturally homogenous spaces, continue to impact, often in paradoxical manners, on the sociolinguistic make-up of postcolonial societies today. At the same time, practices of *translanguaging*, that is, creative uses of language resources from what Western speakers understand as different *languages*,[4] have a long tradition in multilingual postcolonial contexts. In light of current translingual theorising, colonial settings, constituted in transnational interactions of language and discourse, appear as avant-garde samples of contemporary language entanglements of globalisation. In order to understand post-colonial 'Englishing,' we cannot limit ourselves to narratives of English as 'indigenising' in national contexts[5] and should not ignore the complex local, national, transnational, and non-territorial dynamics that may shape language practices. Postcolonial settings, where the myth of national monolingualism has never been naturalised, with their transnational and multilingual histories, are an ideal context to overcome modernist, nationalist, and colonial epistemologies, which have shaped linguistic concepts and methods.[6]

DOI: 10.4324/9781003464037-6

This chapter has been made available under a CC-BY-NC-ND 4.0 license.

The aim of this chapter is to discuss discourses on language in a multilingual and transnationally embedded postcolonial context. This shows that the emergence of national varieties of English is by no means a necessary or even 'natural' development, not even in contexts where English is established and officially recognised. Rather, speakers in complex and globalised multilingual contexts may orient towards linguistic prestige that does not derive from national institutions or may oppose the idea of a homogenous and nationally shared standard. Standard language culture's ideals of stable normativity may exist besides other prestige orientations where, particularly in traditions of oral culture, ideals of creativity and internal diversity may be valued. Thus, there is no teleological path towards the emergence and stabilisation of national varieties of English.

In the following, I present data from an ethnographic field study conducted in a village in Belize, Central America. The participants of the study reject the existence of a national variety of Belizean English. This relates to transnational discourses of prestige, specific national conditions, and local linguistic complexity. In particular, the role of the Anglophone creole language *Kriol*, functioning as an index of national belonging, means that the Belizeans interviewed in this study feel no need to develop a national variety of English. At least in the local setting observed, speakers orient towards international standards of English, which they do not understand as suppressive. This relates to the fact that Belize is surrounded by Spanish-speaking countries and hosts a large number of Spanish speakers so that Spanish, not English, is constructed as 'threat' to local culture.[7] At the same time, local language ideologies pertaining to the mostly orally used language Kriol, with its ties to African oral traditions,[8] do not venerate a nationally shared, homogenous standard. Interviewees argue that the non-standardised, constantly shifting, and expressive nature of Kriol is what defines its character.

Overall, the observations lead to a questioning of Western epistemologies that typically construct teleological paths towards the stabilisation and standardisation ('indigenisation') of languages on national levels. In this context, postcolonial speakers are often assumed to strive for national norms, which is not conjectured from speakers who are classified as 'foreign language learners' from the 'expanding circle.'[9] Besides the fact that prestige orientations may not necessarily be based on a desire to develop norms of nationhood, language practice is not always framed in ideals of standard monolingualism. The ethnographic study of language ideologies[10] indicates the relevance of multiple historical and contemporary prestige orientations in understanding English in postcolonial settings. At the same time, it illustrates that the concept of an orderly, specific, shared, and standardised language that indexes territorial belonging should not be treated as universal but as an outcome of culturally specific discourses that emerged in the age of European modernist literary print culture. In this sense, the study aims to contribute to 'provincialising Europe'[11] by uncovering the social and historical conditionality of many of the methodologically nationalist approaches of the discipline of linguistics.

In the following, I introduce discourses on English as colonial and as a global language and elaborate on the idea of *languages* as discursively constructed categories. In the section "Ethnographic Approaches to Non-National Language Ideologies in a Caribbean Village," the methodological approaches of the study and the research context are introduced. The subsequent section discusses data that illustrate discourses on language in the setting inspected. The chapter ends with a short discussion and conclusion.

National Englishes and 'Languages' as Western Constructs

In the linguistic study of World Englishes, the most famous model to conceptualise English in the world is Braj Kachru's *three-circle model*.[12] Here, a distinction is made along the lines of 'native English' as spoken in the UK and in former settler colonies ('inner circle,' 'norm-providing'), English as 'second language' ('outer circle,' 'norm-developing' – typically former colonies), and English as 'foreign language' ('expanding circle,' 'norm-dependent' – typically no history of colonisation). The original aim of Kachru was to support the status of non-metropolitan (that is, non-UK, non-US) norms as legitimate varieties of English at a time when a very limited range of variation was considered legitimate. An array of other models followed, most of which conceptualised English as appearing in national contexts.[13] Later on, the relevance of non-national planes became more visible.[14] Overall, the main interest of linguistic research on World Englishes lies in describing linguistic features that have developed in specific national contexts. The language of national elites (that is, mostly speakers who have attended university, in other words, institutions that follow Western ideals of education) is regarded as representative for the respective nations. Their practices, if distinct from metropolitan norms, are classified as emerging national norms that serve to index national identities.[15]

In the context of literary studies, there has been a vital debate on the usage of English in postcolonial literature, often understood as a form of colonial subjugation. Wa Thiong'o supports the idea that indigenous languages are important in anti-imperialist struggles.[16] Yet there are different interpretations of the symbolic functions of English in postcolonial contexts. In a study on language policies during British colonialism, Pennycook, for example, shows that colonised speakers do not always interpret the use of English as colonial subordination, particularly where colonisers aimed to limit access to this important resource of power.[17] Similarly, Adejunmobi argues that postcolonial speakers' use of metropolitan norms of English (or, for that matter, other European-derived languages) does not necessarily mean the colonial subjugation of speakers. In a study on language in West Africa, she criticises that "[s]cholarly conversations about language and identity in the postcolonial world often take as their premise the prior existence of an ideal monolingual order, centred around mother tongues and disrupted by the violent processes of colonization."[18] She instead draws an image of West African speakers as "people [who] had come to terms with life as polyglots in a multilingual world," where "colonialism, and later still, globalization entailed using different languages for different purposes."[19] Consequently, she cautions "readers against systematically interpreting a willingness to use non-native language as evidence of a desire for identification with cultures previously thought of as foreign."[20] In this light, 'returning' to monolingual indigenous orders or striving for national norms of English may both be interpreted as based on European fantasies of ordered, monolingual language spaces and thus reproducing Western national language ideologies.

Particularly in the context of linguistic anthropology, the notion of fixed and standardised languages, representing territorially based identities, has been discussed as European language ideology.[21] In the history of European language discourses, standard languages have been constructed as representing rationality, in line with hegemonic constructions of modernity.[22] At the same time, the emergence of national standard languages is in a dialectical relationship to the emergence of national public spaces. Dominant public voices turn into 'voices from nowhere,' as their hegemonic position renders their language practices unmarked and neutral.[23] The distribution of this 'neutral' standard language in national publics is inconceivable without the printing press and mass literacy, so that the technologies of the 'Gutenberg Galaxy'[24] have to be seen as foundational in the overall assemblage of national language ideologies.[25] Thus, to summarise a central insight of language ideology research, we can maintain that "[l]anguages are no more pregiven entities that preexist our linguistic performances than are gendered or ethnic identities. Rather they are the sedimented products of repeated acts of identity."[26]

A related strand of research that considers *languages* as discursive constructs is associated with applied linguistics and focuses on the term *translanguaging*. It is here a central tenet that "speakers engage, first and foremost, in 'languaging,' that is, combine sets of linguistic resources that may, or may not, agree with canonically recognized languages, codes or styles."[27] In the context of World Englishes, the notion of translingualism also gained traction in recent years,[28] as both, World Englishes research and translanguaging approaches have been "interested in language diversity that goes beyond dominant linguistic models based on territorialization and native speaker-hood."[29]

In the following, I aim to contribute to understanding non-European, non-national discourses associated with language(-ing) in a multilingual postcolonial setting.

Ethnographic Approaches to Non-National Language Ideologies in a Caribbean Village

This chapter aims to gain access to language ideologies in a postcolonial village while questioning that there are stable and clearly defined languages, that language practices that *are* classified as representing particular languages are necessarily associated with national levels, and that the prestige associated with particular languages is based on ideologies of standardisation. As a consequence, the research design of the study assumes that links between social and linguistic categorisation are neither clear nor pregiven. Qualitative, ethnographic approaches thus have been applied. These ensure openness towards the documentation of unexpected cultural meanings.[30]

The ethnographic documentation of language ideologies took place in a multilingual village in Belize. Belize belongs to the Commonwealth and was a British colony until 1981. English is the official language, used in formal settings and in education. Kriol is the national (oral) lingua franca with African ties, developed under slavery in colonial times.[31] Due to specific historical developments, people of interracial Afro-European descent – so-called *Creoles* – had a relatively high social status in the area surrounding Belize City already in the 19th century.[32] The language Kriol, even though it is today an index of belonging for Belizeans of all ethnicities,[33] is historically associated with the national Creole elite. Spanish is the numerically most widely spoken language, specifically in the peripheral regions of the country,[34] and a rather large number of languages function as minority languages.[35] The village I study has about 1,500 inhabitants and is located on a small island that was inhabited by Spanish and Yucatec speakers since the mid-19th century. As an effect of rising economic opportunities on the island in the fishing industry and in tourism since the 1970s, there has been an increase of Kriol, Garifuna, and other Spanish speakers from within and from outside of Belize; an increase of speakers of internationally recognised forms of standard English; and an increase of speakers of other European and Asian languages from different locations worldwide. Thus, the island was Yucatec and Spanish dominant until the 1970s and is now very diverse.

In the complex language context of Belize, language is not considered a straightforward index of ethnicity – as a matter of fact, ethnic belonging is not stable and rarely discussed as central social category. It is not uncommon, for example, that siblings from the same family declare they belong to different ethnic groups. Many consultants are not able (or willing) to say to which ethnic group they belong. Categorising Belizeans according to ethnicity is discussed by some of my consultants as a colonial strategy to divide the people. Others report that they only learned in school that there is such a thing as ethnicity. Most consultants say that they use at least three languages (English, Kriol, and Spanish being the most frequently mentioned

72 Britta Schneider

ones). Social categorisation does exist, however. It seems to be rather fluid and is linked to racial ascriptions. While individuals of Maya and Hispanic descent who show no obvious traits of African descent are usually classified as *Mestizo* or *Spanish* (the latter locally carries negative connotations), individuals whose phenotype suggests that they may be of African heritage are understood as *Creole*[36] or *Garifuna*.[37] These categorisations are not based on ethnic essentialist ideologies, as all of these categories are understood as based on cultural mixing and contain members who have ancestors from different groups. Furthermore, there is no clear link to language, as it is assumed that all Belizeans learn English at school and speak Kriol at home or in semi-public settings and that many have Spanish as one home language and, potentially, a number of other languages. National language ideology that assumes a link between ethnic membership and language is of little relevance. Instead, what Le Page and Tabouret-Keller already observed in their seminal study on Belize in the 1970s, that we have to do with a *diffuse* language culture,[38] is still applicable.

The ethnographic field study was undertaken in spring 2015 and in spring 2017 for three and a half months in total. It comprises field notes of participant observation in public space, in a school, and in a kindergarten and photographs and a collection of printed material that give access to the overall sociolinguistic context. To elicit overt language ideological discourse, I conducted 19 qualitative in-depth interviews of length from 30 minutes to 2.5 hours and recorded two group discussions with pupils on the role of language in Belize of 1-hour length each. I also recorded 20 hours of school interaction inside and outside of class. In this way, language ideologies as found in explicit talk but also as indicated in language choice and language practice were documented. Furthermore, I collected quantitative material on language attitudes by interviewing 10% of the permanent residents of the village about their language use across domains (family, friends, work). Since 2012, the on-site data collection has been supplemented by observation of online interaction and media (radio, newspaper, television) and by the study of the history of Belize and of Belizean literature. I analyse language choices and social discourses on language and what they tell us with regard to whether and how linguistic and social categories are interrelated. The observations show that local language ideologies are not framed in national discourses that would strive for an eventual congruence of territory, people, and language use. Rather, multilingual practices, social diversity, oral traditions, and transnational orientations bring about complex discourses about language, with different, simultaneously existing conceptualisations of linguistic prestige.

Non-National Language Concepts in a Multilingual Belizean Village

A first indication of the fact that the official language of Belize, English, is not conceptualised according to national language ideology can be found in interview quotes that display an opposition towards the idea that there is such a thing as Belizean English. For example, in the following quote, a male, middle-aged high school teacher of English explains in a straightforward fashion that the concept of a national variety of English is not acceptable in Belize:

Excerpt 1

Belizeans are completely against ... having Belizean English
Because they wanna speak Proper English

The consultant is engaged in language activism that supports the use of Kriol and also teaches African drumming at school. When I observed one of his lessons in school, I was surprised about the many Kriol features he used in class talk. It is generally common that the boundaries between English and Kriol are unclear. Fused, non-standard forms have their own prestige (which I discuss subsequently). Yet the consultant is very aware of the dominant language discourse on English in Belize, where practices of English that indicate localness are not considered prestigious. The concept of *Proper English* is a relevant and often used emic term that relates to the language standards as they are taught in school, which are based on the norms of the Caribbean Examination Council. These orient towards traditional written norms of US English. A general orientation towards US but also UK norms, also in pronunciation, is noticeable in Belize, which has to do with the fact that a large community of Belizeans resides in the US (more than 90% of the pupils in the high school I observed have relatives in the US), with tourism being the most central economic sector, and with the fact that the most prestigious private high schools in Belize City were founded by British and US American religious institutions.

The transnational entanglements of the Belizean elite in social, economic, religious, and educational terms contribute to an awareness of transnational hierarchies. Continuing colonial hierarchies are displayed in the following quote from an interview with a Ministry employee who works in the context of national language planning. He has not grown up in Belize and has more of an outsider perspective.[39] As a sociolinguistically educated person, he is very positive towards the idea of internal norms of English (and towards multilingualism) and asks himself why the idea is so unpopular within Belize:

Excerpt 2

So why is Belizean English such an (1) unpalatable idea?
And here's a totally off the wall theory
Belize became independent in 1981
So in some ways it's a fairly immature country (2)
Part of showing that you are a member of the international elite

74 Britta Schneider

And that Belize is not full of uneducated simpletons
Is this ability to speak in the international high-status language.

He assumes that the recency of independence explains why Belizeans want to symbolically show that they are 'members of the international elite' via their language performance. Later during the interview, he also considers that the small size of the country may contribute to the perception of Belizean attributes being of little symbolic value in an international context. To confirm his hypothesis, he reports on a conversation he had previously had with a member of the national educational elite who had a leading role in Belizean tertiary education.

Excerpt 3

I said to her why don't we go further down this line of Belizean English
And her reaction was hostile
It wasn't even mildly ...
It was like ... that was a totally unacceptable thing to even raise in polite conversation

The interviewee's interaction partner was someone who is very much in favour of supporting Kriol culture as an expression of Belizean belonging, so her negative attitudes towards local forms of English cannot be explained by general negative attitudes towards local Belizean culture. The rather strong affective reactions that are described in the previous quote may, however, not only be based on the marginality of the Belizean state due to its young age and small size. Belize is the only country in Central America that has English as an official language and Belizeans are generally proud of this. To be able to speak English not only differentiates my interviewees from their Hispanic neighbours, but, as in the following quote, it is perceived as 'elevating' them:

Excerpt 4

If I'm able to speak English ... or if (1)
Perhaps ...
You know, even ...
That if English is the official language of this country
It elevates us ... over our Central American counterparts.

As there is an unresolved centuries-old border conflict between Belize and Guatemala, which does not recognise the status of Belize as an independent nation,[40] Belizean discourses typically present Hispanic neighbouring countries as a threat. The British colonisers, in this discursive context, are considered as protecting Anglophone (English as well as Kriol) forms of living and, as a matter of fact, the British Army is still based in Belize,[41] which Belizeans perceive positively. This situation may contribute to positive attitudes towards exogenous standards of English.[42]

The positive attitudes towards exogenous norms of English have an effect on language practices. Those Belizeans who have access to elite education are trained in contexts where exogenous, mostly US English is spoken. In the following quote, a young woman who resides in the village but has been educated in the elite school St. Catherine's Academy (where many teachers are from the US), displays negative affect towards local pronunciation forms. She elaborates on her own use of English and of that of her friend; both are present during the interview. The friend's father is from Scotland, the speaker's parents are both from Belize, and both have never left Belize. Both speak, in terms of pronunciation and grammar, what I would define as US American English.

Excerpt 5

I don't know where I got it or where we got it
Well I know where she got it
I don't know where I got it from
But I have a hard time speaking English with an accent
I cannot do it
It makes me cringe

The interviewee wonders where their orientation towards non-local forms of English derives from. She is apparently not aware of the influence of her own elite schooling, as it is not the majority of Belizeans who are able to produce US American English in their daily speech practices. She not only says that it is difficult for her to use 'English with an accent' (by which she means local pronunciation practices with influence from Spanish, Kriol, or other languages), but her report on negative bodily reactions when she tries to – 'it makes me cringe' – indicates that anti-local attitudes are strong.

Overall, discourses on English in Belize do not suggest that the national 'indigenising' of English is likely. The reasons for this are found in the cultural history and political situation of Belize and in its specific transnational relations. National language ideologies – which have often informed linguistic research and which assume the development of national norms – are not adequate to understand this linguistic context.

A second relevant aspect that has an impact on the overall sociolinguistic context of Belize is the specific symbolic role of Kriol. In particular, Kriol's popular function as index of national belonging implies that English is not understood as expressing Belizeanness. Discourses on Kriol differ strongly

76 Britta Schneider

from those on English. All of my interviewees relate highly positively to Kriol, and there is generally a strong emotional attachment to the language. People usually start to smile when asked about Kriol, and the language is not tied to discourses of ethnic belonging. Thus, even interviewees who do not use the language in home settings, that is, who would be defined as *non-native speakers* in the discourses of national language ideology, are proud speakers of Kriol. The impression that ethnic heritage is not relevant for being a legitimate speaker of Kriol is also shared in this quote from a Kriol language activist of Creole heritage:

Excerpt 4

It doesn't matter if you're Chinese Haitian Arab Indian Mestizo
Kriol is the common language

The groups mentioned are with and without historical ties to the Belizean territory. The Chinese represent a sizable community in Belize who run more or less all supermarkets, Haitians are considered culturally close, as they also use a creole language (even though it is French-lexified), and migration from Haiti to Belize has been observed after Hurricane Matthew in 2016. Arab relates to a minority group within Belize whose ancestors came from Lebanon in the early 20th century, some of whose members hold elite social positions (e.g., former Prime Minister Said Musa). There are also Belizeans of Indian descent who came as indentured slaves, and several respondents mention that the creole language spoken in Trinidad (which displays influence from languages spoken in India) is related to Belizean Kriol. *Mestizo* is the name to refer to people who are or appear to be of Maya and/or Hispanic descent. The previous quote shows that Kriol is tied to a discourse in which concepts of native speakerhood are not hegemonic. Furthermore, the mentioning of Haitians and Indians may be interpreted as an understanding of 'creoleness' as something characteristic of the entire Caribbean region and not only of a national, Belizean context.

The ethnic inclusiveness and transnational relations associated with Kriol do not imply indexical meanings of social distance (e.g., Kriol as a functional language for cross-ethnic interaction), but the language is tied to the creation of a close-knit community, as demonstrated in the following quote from a female high school teacher (who, by the way, strongly rejects the idea of using Kriol in school):

Excerpt 6

When it comes to like Kriol
It's more of a like a community (2)
You think at it

> You think about it not as a country
> But mostly as a like a community
> Where, in which you can ahm you're more ahm
> Linked to each other or you're more close to each other ... talking Kriol

Kriol holds the function of creating a community and is described as if the language itself forms a community. The interviewee explicitly argues that the language is, in her imagination, not linked to 'a country,' that is, Kriol is not discursively linked to governmental institutions or official norms. Instead, she associates it with feeling socially 'close' to others. What has been described as *diglossia*[43] seems to be applicable here. Kriol is described with features typical for the 'L-code' – diglossia models argue that in bilingual communities, there may be a 'L(ow)-code' and a 'H(igh)-code,' where the L-code is associated with solidarity and social closeness. The H-code, in contrast, is reserved for formal communication and expresses social distance. While the diglossic relation of Kriol and English in Belize is, in this sense, not unusual, the overall construction is still different from traditional national language ideologies. English as H-code relates to a transnational sphere, with exogenous norms being prevalent. Kriol, on the other hand, is the language of group solidarity that indexes belonging, irrespective of the individual's social, ethnic or linguistic background; it is unlinked to the national institutions of the government and it is associated with creole cultures in the entire Caribbean region. The construction of the links between territorial space, language use, and social affiliation are here different from what has been naturalised in Western national language concepts.

Finally, and maybe because Kriol is not understood as the language of a mono-ethnic, territorially bounded group, it is conceptualised as a non-standardised language. The appraisal of creativity and change in language was observed in Belize already in the 1970s.[44] The following quote by a young female village resident illustrates the idea of a non-formal, constantly changing, and internally diverse concept of language vividly:

Excerpt 7

> There is no proper Kriol
> Nothing in Kriol is proper at all
> Nothing is set
> Everything is just
> It's a sound
> It's very phonetic
> That's it
> That's about it
> And it changes ...
> And that the culture of Kriol is to have no standard

78 Britta Schneider

Because it develops
And everyone can be individual
And be much more creative with the language
Than if you have the actual idea that you have one

Kriol is tacitly opposed to English through the term *proper* – 'Proper English,' as shown in Excerpt 1, is the idea of internationally recognised, standard, and formal English. The speaker has a positive evaluation of instability ('nothing is set'), change, non-standardisation ('the culture of Kriol is to have no standard'), idiosyncrasy ('And everyone can be individual'), and creativity in relation to the language Kriol.

The contrast of language ideological concepts tied to English and to Kriol enforces the non-development of a Belizean variety of English. While Kriol is understood as inclusive code that allows for individual appropriation, English is associated with international prestige, educational status and 'properness.' There remains a lot to say about the discursive development of these contrasts and their roots in colonial modernist European concepts of formality and African traditions of verbal poetry, and yet it is clear that norms, stability, and formality are not what Belizeans understand to define 'their' community culture.

Discussion

Overall, in the discourses inspected in this chapter, exogenous English is not understood as a colonial threat to local forms of culture and belonging. Rather, in this specific setting, non-Belizean English is constructed as prestigious tool. In other words, exogenous English is a social practice that links to European-derived understandings of formal prestige and "[i]n the same way in which hip hop is one way of realizing socio-political rebellion through a set of musical resources, [...] English is one way of realizing social activities [linked to formality] via a set of linguistic resources."[45] The language situation of Belize is not framed in the idea of a monolingual norm for the entire population and for all social domains. What we find here is a multilingual context where different codes have different symbolic values that are not based on national concepts of *one language – one culture – one territory*. Instead, different (constructs of) languages relate to different transnational spheres and are embedded in different language ideological discourses, where normed formality but also creative multiplicity are culturally valued. The idea that one and only one language is indexical of local identity does not fit into this multilingual setting, where speakers construct their linguistic realities on the basis of multiple linguistic resources that are symbolically tied to national as well as transnational spheres, to ideals of formality as well as creativity.

What can be generally taken from this is that in order to understand the symbolic meanings of languages in specific cultural contexts, it is problematic to take Western discourses as *a priori*. These typically assume that humans live in ethnically homogenous groups that strive for homogenous, group-internal language norms. While this may well be the case in some contexts – and while national varieties of English therefore may well be a symbol for emancipation in some settings – it is not a universal phenomenon. In this light, the assumption that communities in general value monolingualism, homogeneity, and linguistic regularity can be interpreted as European provincialism. In order to overcome this, we have to inspect discourses on language in non-European but also in newly emerging globalised cultures. Ethnographic, qualitative approaches are indispensable to get insights into language ideologies where a hegemonic Western discourse derived from European modernism cannot be taken for granted. Diverse discourses on language have to be studied empirically and with methods that allow for the documentation of unexpected ideas and values.

Understanding a positive evaluation of UK or US language norms as a general sign for colonial subjugation can be interpreted as a form of *methodological nationalism*.[46] It tacitly assumes monolingual speakers who construct identity on the basis of one language only, while the Caribbean speakers presented in this chapter use different languages for different purposes, with partly national and partly transnational orientations. And despite the fact that US and UK language norms do carry colonial baggage, in settings of multilingual complexity, the appraisal of exogenous forms of English and the refusal to develop national varieties of English does not necessarily indicate colonially oppressed minds. Instead we should recognise that an understanding of multiplex and culturally conditioned language orientations may help to overcome nationalist simplifications.

Conclusion

In this chapter, I have discussed discourses on language as documented in the multilingual context of postcolonial Belize. Against the background of current linguistic anthropological theorising that takes *languages* to be discursive categories, I have presented data that has been collected ethnographically in a Belizean village. In this specific context, the emergence of a national variety of English is mostly rejected. Rather, speakers display orientations towards the linguistic prestige of internationally recognised standard norms of English. This has to do with the particular political and linguistic situation, where the troublesome relationship towards Guatemala leads to a positive evaluation of Belize's continuing ties to the former coloniser. Additionally, the language Kriol is positively valued as language of community and inter-ethnic solidarity. Yet the idea of a homogenous and nationally shared standard of Kriol is not constructed as cultural value, as Kriol is associated with ideals of creativity and diversity. The discourses associated with Kriol imply that there is no need for a nationally standardised variety of English. The main argument of this chapter is therefore that there is no teleological path towards the emergence and stabilisation of homogenous national varieties of English, nor of any other language, for that matter. The deconstructive questioning of national epistemologies of language that have shaped much of linguistic theorising lately, and a sensitive consideration of potentially widely differing, culturally framed discourses on language, will be important for linguistics in the 21st century – for linguistics in a world of strangers – where further sociolinguistic complexities in transnational and digital interaction are to be expected.

Notes

1 Andreas Wimmer and Nina Glick Schiller, "Methodological Nationalism and Beyond: Nation-State Building, Migration and the Social Sciences," *Global Networks* 2.4 (2002): 301–334.
2 Britta Schneider, "Methodological Nationalism in Linguistics," *Language Sciences* 76 (2019).
3 See Benedict Anderson, *Imagined Communities* (London: Verso, 1985).
4 Ofelia García and Li Wei, *Translanguaging: Language, Bilingualism and Education* (Basingstoke: Palgrave Macmillan, 2014).
5 As in e.g. Edgar W. Schneider, *English around the World* (Cambridge: Cambridge University Press, 2011).
6 Richard Bauman and Charles L. Briggs, *Voices of Modernity: Language Ideologies and the Politics of Inequality* (Cambridge: Cambridge University Press, 2003); Monica Heller and Bonnie McElhinny, *Language, Capitalism, Colonialism* (Toronto: University of Toronto Press, 2017).
7 For similar phenomena in Gibraltar and Hong Kong, see Daniel Weston, "The Lesser of Two Evils: Atypical Trajectories in English Dialect Evolution," *Journal of Sociolinguistics* 19 (2015): 671–687.
8 R. French and K. T. Kernan, "Art and Artifice in Belizean Creole," *American Ethnologist* 8 (1981): 238–258.
9 On the 'circle model,' see Braj Kachru, "Standards, Codification and Sociolinguistic Realism: The English Language in the Outer Circle," in *English in the World: Teaching and Learning the Language and Literatures*, edited by Randolph Quirk and H. G. Widdowson (Cambridge: Cambridge University Press, 1985): 11–30.
10 Paul V. Kroskrity, "Language Ideologies," in *Handbook of Pragmatics Online*, edited by Jef Verschueren, Jan Blommaert and Chris Bulcaen (Amsterdam: Benjamins, 2009).
11 Dipesh Chakrabarti, *Provincializing Europe: Postcolonial Thought and Historical Difference* (Princeton: Princeton University Press, 2000).
12 Kachru, "Standards, Codification and Sociolinguistic Realism."
13 E.g. Edgar W. Schneider, *Postcolonial English: Varieties around the World* (Cambridge: Cambridge University Press, 2007); see Kingsley Bolton, "World Englishes: Approaches, Models and Methodology," in *Bloomsbury World Englishes: Paradigms*, edited by Britta Schneider and Theresa Heyd (London: Bloomsbury, 2021): 9–26 for an overview of models.

14 Christian Mair, "World Englishes: From Methodological Nationalism to a Global Perspective," in *Bloomsbury World Englishes: Paradigms*, edited by Britta Schneider and Theresa Heyd (London: Bloomsbury, 2021): 27–45.

15 See e.g. the Dynamic Model in Schneider, *English around the World*: 34; for a critique, see e.g. Mario Saraceni, *World Englishes: A Critical Analysis* (London: Bloomsbury, 2015); for a collection of studies that overcome national framings, see Britta Schneider and Theresa Heyd, eds., *Bloomsbury World Englishes: Paradigms* (London: Bloomsbury, 2021).

16 Ngũgĩ wa Thiong'o, *Decolonising the Mind: The Politics of Language in African Literature* (London: Heinemann, 1986).

17 Alastair Pennycook, *English and the Discourses of Colonialism* (London: Routledge, 1998).

18 Moradewun Adejunmobi, *Vernacular Palaver: Imaginations of the Local and Non-Native Languages in West Africa* (Clevedon: Multilingual Matters, 2004): viii.

19 Adejunmobi, *Vernacular Palaver*, viii.

20 Adejunmobi, *Vernacular Palaver*, viii–ix.

21 Dell Hymes, "Linguistic Problems in Defining the Concept of 'Tribe,'" in *Essays on the Problem of the Tribe: Proceedings of the 1967 Annual Spring Meeting of the American Ethnological Society*, edited by June Helm (Washington: University of Washington Press, 1968): 23–48; Judith T. Irvine and Susan Gal, "Language Ideology and Linguistic Differentiation," in *Regimes of Language: Ideologies, Polities and Identities*, edited by Paul V. Kroskrity (Santa Fe, New Mexico: School of American Research Press, 2000): 35–83.

22 Bauman and Briggs, *Voices of Modernity* on e.g. the writings of Bacon, Locke or Herder who contributed to the idea of the language of women, non-Europeans or the poor as 'pre-modern.'

23 Susan Gal and Kathryn A. Woolard, *Languages and Publics: The Making of Authority* (Manchester: St. Jerome, 2001).

24 Marshall McLuhan, *The Gutenberg Galaxy: The Making of Typographic Man* (London: University of Toronto Press, 1962).

25 Walter J. Ong, *Orality and Literacy: The Technologizing of the Word* (London: Routledge, 1982); Britta Schneider, "Posthumanism and the Role of Orality and Literacy in Language Ideologies in Belize," *World Englishes* 42.1 (2022): 150–168, https://doi.org/10.1111/weng.12612.

26 Alastair Pennycook, "Performativity and Language Studies," *Critical Inquiry in Language Studies* 1 (2004): 15.

27 Jürgen Jaspers, "The Transformative Limits of Translanguaging," *Working Papers in Urban Language & Literacies* 226 (2017): 4.

28 Suresh Canagarajah, *Translingual Practice: Global Englishes and Cosmopolitan Relations* (London: Routledge, 2013).

29 Jerry Won Lee and Suresh Canagarajah, "Translingualism and World Englishes," in *Bloomsbury World Englishes: Paradigms*, edited by Britta Schneider and Theresa Heyd (London: Bloomsbury, 2021): 99.

30 Miguel Pérez-Milans, "Language and Identity in Linguistic Ethnography," *Tilburg Paper in Culture Studies* 132 (2015): 1–15.

31 Geneviève Escure, "Belizean Creole Structure Dataset," in *Atlas of Pidgin and Creole Language Structures Online*, edited by Susanne Maria Michaelis, Philippe Maurer, Martin Haspelmath and Magnus Huber (Leipzig: Max Planck Institute for Evolutionary Anthropology, 2013), http://apics-online.info/contributions/9 (accessed 19 October 2016).

32 Richard Wilk, *Home Cooking in the Global Village* (Oxford: Berg, 2006).

82 Britta Schneider

33 R. B. Le Page and Andrée Tabouret-Keller, *Acts of Identity: Creole-Based Approaches to Language and Ethnicity* (Cambridge: Cambridge University Press, 1985).
34 Britta Schneider, "The Multiplex Symbolic Functions of Spanish in Multilingual Belize," in *When Creole and Spanish Collide: Language and Cultural Contact in the Caribbean*, edited by Glenda-Alicia Leung and Miki Loschky (Leiden and Bosten: Brill, 2021): 253–276.
35 E.g. Mopan, Yucatec, Q'uechí, Garifuna, German, Hindi, Mandarin, Cantonese; for a detailed account of the complex language situation see Britta Schneider, *Liquid Languages – Constructing Language in Late Modern Cultures of Diffusion* (Cambridge: Cambridge University Press, in preparation).
36 Note that the term relating to people of Afro-European descent is spelled *Creole*, whereas, according to the choices of the *National Kriol Council*, the associated language is spelled *Kriol*.
37 People of Afro-Carib descent, Geneviève Escure, "Garifuna in Belize and Honduras," in *Creoles, Contact, and Language Change*, edited by Geneviève Escure and Armin Schwegler (Amsterdam: Benjamins, 2004): 35–65.
38 Le Page and Tabouret-Keller, *Acts of Identity*.
39 Belize has only about 360,000 inhabitants; because of ethical concerns I give as little personal detail as possible, as it would otherwise be possible to identify individuals.
40 World Politics Review, "Why Belize is Likely to Prevail in its Territorial Dispute with Guatemala," 23 May 2019, www.worldpoliticsreview.com/insights/27884/territorial-dispute-between-belize-and-guatemala-who-is-likely-to-prevail (last accessed 3 April 2024).
41 J. Vitor Tossini, "British Forces in Belize – a Military Partnership in Central America," *UK Defence Journal* (2018).
42 See Weston, "The Lesser of Two Evils," for similar phenomena in Gibraltar and Hong Kong, where Spain and China are understood as aggressors and where therefore the British are understood as 'protector.'
43 Charles Ferguson, "Diglossia," *Word* 15 (1959): 325–340; Joshua Fishman, "Bilingualism with and without Diglossia; Diglossia with and without Bilingualism," *Journal of Social Issues* XXIII (1967): 29–37.
44 French and Kernan, "Art and Artifice in Belizean Creole."
45 Saraceni, *World Englishes: A Critical Analysis*.
46 Wimmer and Schiller, "Methodological Nationalism and Beyond."

Bibliography

Adejunmobi, Moradewun. *Vernacular Palaver: Imaginations of the Local and Non-Native Languages in West Africa*. Clevedon: Multilingual Matters, 2004.
Anderson, Benedict. *Imagined Communities*. London: Verso, 1985.
Bauman, Richard and Charles L. Briggs. *Voices of Modernity: Language Ideologies and the Politics of Inequality*. Cambridge: Cambridge University Press, 2003.
Bolton, Kingsley. "World Englishes: Approaches, Models and Methodology." In *Bloomsbury World Englishes: Paradigms*, edited by Britta Schneider and Theresa Heyd. London: Bloomsbury, 2021: 9–26.
Canagarajah, Suresh. *Translingual Practice: Global Englishes and Cosmopolitan Relations*. London: Routledge, 2013.
Chakrabarti, Dipesh. *Provincializing Europe: Postcolonial Thought and Historical Difference*. Princeton: Princeton University Press, 2000.
Escure, Geneviève. "Belizean Creole Structure Dataset." In *Atlas of Pidgin and Creole Language Structures Online*, edited by Susanne Maria Michaelis, Philippe Maurer,

Martin Haspelmath and Magnus Huber. Leipzig: Max Planck Institute for Evolutionary Anthropology, 2013. http://Apics-Online.Info/contributors/escuregenevieve (last accessed 22 April 2024).

———. "Garifuna in Belize and Honduras." In *Creoles, Contact, and Language Change*, edited by Geneviève Escure and Armin Schwegler. Amsterdam: Benjamins, 2004: 35–65.

Ferguson, Charles. "Diglossia." *Word* 15 (1959): 325–340.

Fishman, Joshua. "Bilingualism with and without Diglossia; Diglossia with and without Bilingualism." *Journal of Social Issues* XXIII (1967): 29–37.

French, R. and K. T. Kernan. "Art and Artifice in Belizean Creole." *American Ethnologist* 8 (1981): 238–258.

Gal, Susan and Kathryn A. Woolard. *Languages and Publics: The Making of Authority*. Manchester: St. Jerome, 2001.

García, Ofelia and Li Wei. *Translanguaging. Language, Bilingualism and Education*. Basingstoke: Palgrave Macmillan, 2014.

Heller, Monica and Bonnie McElhinny. *Language, Capitalism, Colonialism*. Toronto: University of Toronto Press, 2017.

Hymes, Dell. "Linguistic Problems in Defining the Concept of 'Tribe.'" In *Essays on the Problem of the Tribe: Proceedings of the 1967 Annual Spring Meeting of the American Ethnological Society*, edited by June Helm. Washington: University of Washington Press, 1968: 23–48.

Irvine, Judith T. and Susan Gal. "Language Ideology and Linguistic Differentiation." In *Regimes of Language: Ideologies, Polities and Identities*, edited by Paul V. Kroskrity. Santa Fe, New Mexico: School of American Research Press, 2000: 35–83.

Jaspers, Jürgen. "The Transformative Limits of Translanguaging." *Working Papers in Urban Language & Literacies* 226 (2017): 1–17.

Kachru, Braj. "Standards, Codification and Sociolinguistic Realism: The English Language in the Outer Circle." In *English in the World: Teaching and Learning the Language and Literatures*, edited by Randolph Quirk and H. G. Widdowson. Cambridge: Cambridge University Press, 1985: 11–30.

Kroskrity, Paul V. "Language Ideologies." In *Handbook of Pragmatics Online*, edited by Jef Verschueren, Jan-Ola Östman, Jan Blommaert and Chris Bulcaen. Amsterdam: Benjamins, 2009.

Le Page, R. B. and Andrée Tabouret-Keller. *Acts of Identity: Creole-Based Approaches to Language and Ethnicity*. Cambridge: Cambridge University Press, 1985.

Mair, Christian. "World Englishes: From Methodological Nationalism to a Global Perspective." In *Bloomsbury World Englishes: Paradigms*, edited by Britta Schneider and Theresa Heyd. London: Bloomsbury, 2021: 27–45.

McLuhan, Marshall. *The Gutenberg Galaxy: The Making of Typographic Man*. London: University of Toronto Press, 1962.

Ong, Walter J. *Orality and Literacy. The Technologizing of the Word*. London: Routledge, 1982.

Pennycook, Alastair. *English and the Discourses of Colonialism*. London: Routledge, 1998.

———. "Performativity and Language Studies." *Critical Inquiry in Language Studies* 1 (2004): 1–19.

Pérez-Milans, Miguel. "Language and Identity in Linguistic Ethnography." *Tilburg Paper in Culture Studies* 132 (2015): 1–15.

Saraceni, Mario. *World Englishes: A Critical Analysis*. London: Bloomsbury, 2015.

Schneider, Britta. *Liquid Languages – Constructing Language in Late Modern Cultures of Diffusion*. Cambridge: Cambridge University Press, in preparation.

———. "Methodological Nationalism in Linguistics." *Language Sciences* 76 (2019). https://doi.org/10.1016/j.langsci.2018.05.006.

———. "The Multiplex Symbolic Functions of Spanish in Multilingual Belize." In *When Creole and Spanish Collide: Language and Cultural Contact in the Caribbean*, edited by Glenda-Alicia Leung and Miki Loschky. Leiden and Bosten: Brill, 2021: 253–276.

———. "Posthumanism and the Role of Orality and Literacy in Language Ideologies in Belize." *World Englishes* 42.1 (2022): 150–168. https://doi.org/10.1111/weng.12612.

Schneider, Britta and Theresa Heyd, eds. *Bloomsbury World Englishes: Paradigms*. General Editor Mario Saraceni. London: Bloomsbury, 2021.

Schneider, Edgar W. *English around the World*. Cambridge: Cambridge University Press, 2011.

———. *Postcolonial English: Varieties around the World*. Cambridge: Cambridge University Press, 2007.

Tossini, J. Vitor. "British Forces in Belize – a Military Partnership in Central America." *UK Defence Journal* (2018). https://ukdefencejournal.org.uk/british-forces-in-belize-a-military-partnership-in-central-america/.

wa Thiong'o, Ngũgĩ. *Decolonising the Mind: The Politics of Language in African Literature*. London: Heinemann, 1986.

Weston, Daniel. "The Lesser of Two Evils: Atypical Trajectories in English Dialect Evolution." *Journal of Sociolinguistics* 19 (2015): 671–687.

Wilk, Richard. *Home Cooking in the Global Village*. Oxford: Berg, 2006.

Wimmer, Andreas and Nina Glick Schiller. "Methodological Nationalism and Beyond: Nation-State Building, Migration and the Social Sciences." *Global Networks* 2.4 (2002): 301–334.

Won Lee, Jerry and Suresh Canagarajah. "Translingualism and World Englishes." In *Bloomsbury World Englishes: Paradigms*, edited by Britta Schneider and Theresa Heyd. London: Bloomsbury, 2021: 99–112.

World Politics Review. "Why Belize is Likely to Prevail in its Territorial Dispute with Guatemala." 23 May 2019. https://www.worldpoliticsreview.com/insights/27884/territorial-dispute-between-belize-and-guatemala-who-is-likely-to-prevail (last accessed 3 April 2024).

II

Deterritorializing the Anglophone

5

THE ANGLOPHONE IMAGINARY AND AGENCY IN CONTEMPORARY EGYPTIAN LITERATURE IN ENGLISH

Pavan Kumar Malreddy and Stefanie Kemmerer[1]

Introduction

In an episode of self-aggrandizing satire titled "English as Criminal Language," the autodiegetic narrator of Bassem Youssef's *Revolution for Dummies* (2017) recounts the hypocrisy of Egypt's ruling elite who treat English as the language of spies and foreign agents but send their children to Ivy League universities in the United States. This almost schizophrenic relationship to English may seem benign, but for many Egyptians it is a matter of public crisis, if not the crisis of the public sphere itself: "speaking English in Egypt can improve your chances of getting arrested and visiting an Egyptian jail."[2] The same people who see tourists as a boon for the economy and might learn just enough English to do their business would probably report those who speak slightly more proficient English to the secret service. Things are much worse elsewhere; in India, one would be labelled a Maoist or terrorist sympathizer if one spoke perfectly grammatical English.[3]

Implicit to both these founded and unfounded fears about English, at least from the ruling elite's point of view, is that it intoxicates the ordinary populace with liberal ideas and notions of law, justice, rights, and entitlements. There is indeed a modicum of truth to such fears, as Dipesh Chakrabarty concedes: "the most trenchant critic of the institution of 'untouchability' in British India refer[s] us back to some originally European ideas about liberty and human equality."[4] Apropos Chakrabarty's remark, the English language is seen as the language of emancipation by many subaltern groups in India, especially the Dalits, against the oppressive tenors of the organic 'mother

DOI: 10.4324/9781003464037-8
This chapter has been made available under a CC-BY-NC-ND 4.0 license.

tongues' of the organic 'mother nations,' in whose name other tongues are created. Arundhati Roy, for instance, writes:

> my mother was actually an alien, with fewer arms than Kali perhaps but many more tongues. English is certainly one of them. *My* English has been widened and deepened by the rhythms and cadences of my alien mother's other tongues. (I say *alien* because there's not much that is organic about her. Her nation-shaped body was first violently assimilated and then violently dismembered by an imperial British quill. I also say *alien* because of the violence unleashed in her name on those who do not wish to belong to her (Kashmiris, for example), as well as on those who do (Indian Muslims and Dalits, for example), makes her an extremely un-motherly mother.)[5]

Although Egypt was exposed to English less intensely (but no less systematically) than India, its centrality to British colonialism cannot be undermined. Yet the very alien treatment of the English language in popular media, particularly in times of social upheavals and crises, as the enemy's agent or an anti-national instrument, takes Rasa, the protagonist of Saleem Haddad's *Guapa* (2016) by surprise[6] when accused by his own friends and political allies of speaking more English than Arabic and for copying Western mannerisms rather than the local swag and slang. The post-Arab Spring treatment of English and the associated "western espionage" is probably more conservative than the sort of nativism advocated by anticolonial intellectuals of the early 20th century – from Gandhi to Nasser – who were the beneficiaries of English education and had a calculated appreciation for the role of the English language and 'Western' ideas in shaping postcolonial modernities. Rasa, our American returnee, finds himself equally ill at ease when navigating the forked path paved by the Anglo-Arab cultural encounter in the wake of, in the shadow of, and in the name of the Egyptian revolution of 2011, also known as the Arab Spring.

This chapter attempts to grasp the ways in which recent Anglophone writers from Egypt use the English language to tease out, and at times pathologize or even unlock, its uneasy encounter with all things local, vernacular, and national in the context of the Arab Spring uprisings. By proposing the concept of an Anglophone imaginary, the chapter argues that the English language and its associated Anglophonic cultural capital in the two texts selected for analysis – Saleem Haddad's *Guapa*, and Bassem Youssef's *Revolution for Dummies* (2017) – manifest themselves as heuristic literary devices that lend deeper insights into the crimes committed in the name of local, vernacular, and national identities. By Anglophone imaginary, we refer not only to the signification of English at the lexical or metaphorical level but also to a certain cultural capital attached to such linguistic and symbolic heritage typically associated with, or pitted against, the local, the vernacular, and the national – Arabic. An Anglophone imaginary, in that sense, operates as an inside out perspective of the vernacular contexts in question, in which a certain detachment from the latter into a world of Anglophone metaphors, symbols, and structures of expression lends itself to a distanced perspective of the familiar and the fraternal. Such distance, as the Somali writer Nuruddin Farah puts it, "distils and makes ideas worth pursuing. I think I have learned a lot more about Somalia by questioning myself and my country from afar. One needs to extricate oneself from the daily needs and demands of living at home."[7]

For the lead characters of the two novels in question, Rasa and Bassem, this very distanced perspective of home is enabled by English and its attendant Anglophone imaginary. While Rasa is a returnee from America, Bassem embraces the American dream, as it were, in a desperate attempt to escape the Egyptian nightmare. The result is a surprising set of observations about and critiques of Egypt which help them to "extricate" themselves from the "burdens and demands of living at home."[8] In a sense, both the physical distancing produced by their diasporic experience, as well as an imagined distance produced by the self-imposed exile of the lead characters in the texts, enable them to confront the ambiguities, contradictions, and hidden ossifications within and among Egyptian social classes. Turning English into a third protagonist, the novels sift themselves through the filter of the Anglophone imaginary, thus dissecting the Arab Spring, its protagonists and antagonists, its benefactors and detractors, in ways the vernacular or local imagination that is subject to censorship under dictatorship regimes cannot. English, in other words, becomes a "morally appropriate"[9] language precisely because it gestures towards the sites of its moral bankruptcy – the lexical sources of law, ideologies, and doctrines that were used not only to justify colonialism but to *actualize* it – and provides an opportunity to issue a course correction to the latter. It does so, as we demonstrate through selected examples, in three ways: by importing notions of justice and rights from a larger milieu of Anglophone cultures and struggles, by disrupting the parochialist tendencies within the vernacular traditions by virtue of the latter imports, and by holding global power structures equally responsible for the political instability at home.

The encounter between English and vernacular languages throughout colonialism, however, has not been an easy one, and can neither simply be read nor rendered as a matter of 'cancelling cultures,' 'hybrid encounters,' or 'contact zones.' Not all English imports are ideologically or culturally innocent, nor are all vernacular traditions pure, unsullied, and romantically egalitarian or libertarian. As Arundhati Roy cautions, the treatment of Urdu in India as an outsider's language, or as an object of resistance to the imposition of Hindi as the national language, gestures towards the hierarchies inherent to all linguistic traditions contained inside of national or regional maps.

This holds true for the Arab Anglophone context as well: whereas a number of women novelists tend to orientalize their homelands (Ahdaf Soueif's *In the Eye of the Sun*, 1993),[10] English translations from Arabic (e.g. Rajaa Alsanea's novel *The Girls of Riyadh*, 2007)[11] do the reverse; they sacrifice certain vernacular formulations (of lexis, landscapes, or objects) and westernize their female characters so as to cater for a global readership.[12] At the same time, writers operating from their home countries are either subjected to censorship regimes or self-censor their work in a climate of fear and persecution. In his illuminating piece, "Living in Arabic,"[13] Edward Said points to the distinction between classical Arabic – a preferred language of writers across the Arab world which in fact binds the Arab-speaking world – and the more demotic, regionally spoken variants which have much less in common with one another. However, some of these variants might be more influential than others, for example, Egyptian Arabic, which takes the throne for being the "TV language" simply because most soap operas in Arabic before the millennium were produced in Egypt. Given the rich tradition of the Arabic language to construct new vocabulary based on its grammatical roots and the roots of those roots, and given the minuteness of its variations,[14] the Arab-speaking world's relationship with English or other colonial languages has not been a smooth one, which calls for further explanation.

Arabic and English: An Uneasy Encounter

Anglophone Arab writing emerged in the early 20th century against the backdrop of the collapse of the Ottoman empire, the consolidation of French and British colonialism in the region later followed by US-American imperialism, and the rise of Arab nationalism.[15] During this time, the influence of the novel in Arabic or Anglophone Arabic writing was at its nascent stage, as poetry remained the primary medium of expression during the colonial rule in parts of the Arab world.[16] This has changed as a result of decolonial struggles. Accompanying these processes were negotiations of nationality, displacement, and questions of belonging which found their expression in the *Mahjar* – a name given to the literary movement founded by the Arab diaspora in America at the turn of the 20th century. This group of writers initially wrote in Arabic and turned to English towards the end of their lives and careers. As a result, their works were shaped by a sense of cultural and linguistic nationalism that is pan-Arabic, laced with a sense of the religious sublime, and a spiritual quest for the lost home rather than the (Arab-American) diasporic predicament that may be more palatable to an Anglophone readership. It is thus not overstating the matter to say that the *Mahjar* writers did not "write back" to anyone but "wrote to themselves," to use Evan Mwangi's expression,[17] and to a readership that is as opaque as the themes of their work: primitive goodness and transcendental homelessness.[18]

The Anglophone Imaginary and Agency **91**

Written in the first half of the 20th century, Anglophone Arab writings were highly autobiographical and focused on the individual experience of emigration in which economic factors played a decisive role. While the works of the aforementioned authors published in Arabic were much more political and nationalist in character, their Anglophone works idealized American life and tried to accommodate their Arab identity through "strategies of containment and distancing."[19] The depiction of personal circumstances together with economic and political trepidations in the authors' countries of origin appealed to "a readership disenchanted by the growing materialism of the West and lamenting a purer, virginal, pre-industrial world,"[20] which required these authors to situate themselves within and towards a pre-existing, orientalized discourse in their adopted countries to find acceptance. Such self-orientalization led a number of these writers to deliver "to America a thoroughly domesticated Orient that hardly challenged [America's] modes of perception or its self-image."[21]

After the end of World War II, the motifs of home, nation, pan-Arab nationalism, exile, and displacement dominated the literary responses between 1950–90. Laila Al-Maleh points out that since the 1970s, Arab Anglophone writing has become increasingly "hybrid, hyphenated, transcultural, exilic/diasporic."[22] Works like Fadia Faqir's *Pillars of Salt* (1996) and Samia Serageldine's *The Cairo House* (2000),[23] for instance, negotiate aspects of time, place, and language, and intend to "liberate ideas of fixed identities."[24] Following the 9/11 attacks, however, readers in North America and Western Europe turned to Arab Anglophone literature as a source for understanding Islam.[25] The post-9/11 Euro-American market for Arab stories relied primarily on the Orientalist association of the terrorist with that of a pan-Arab identity at the expense of its plurality and diversity as well as internal fractures. Yet the literary production emerging out of the Arab-speaking world – especially Iraq, Syria, Kurdistan, and Palestine – in the post-9/11 era has not only marked a departure from pan-Arabism but represents an "inward" shift towards the national and local tyrannies that bred fundamentalist or potentially anti-Western attitudes, in an attempt to "deconstruct the government's rhetoric of anticolonial resistance as a binding force to hold society together."[26] This 'inward' turn from the pan-Arabic to the national and local may well be seen as a response to the Orientalist association of the figure of the terrorist with the Arab community, as represented in the immediate literary responses by Arab Anglophone novelists to the 9/11 attacks: Laila Halaby's *Once in a Promised Land* (2008), Rabih Alameddine's *The Hakawati* (2008), and Alia Yunis's *The Night Counter* (2009).[27]

These developments have also led to a new wave of novels dissecting local power asymmetries, including sectarianism and patriarchy, most notably in Fadia Faqir's *Willow Trees Don't Weep* (2014) and Rabih Alameddine's *An Unnecessary Woman* (2013).[28] Hisham Matar's two novels *In the*

Country of Men (2006) and *Anatomy of a Disappearance* (2011), as well as his memoir *The Return* (2016),[29] belong to this introspective turn towards the political pathos of national and local power in Libya. Within this move from pan-Arabism to the local and vernacular, a new generation of novelists such as Sinan Antoon, Saleem Haddad, and Hassan Blasim began to experiment with irrealism or magical realism as well as Gothic sub-genres in an overt attempt to "articulate the unspeakable, lost, repressed, or deliberately silenced narratives of victims of this structural violence."[30] In doing so, they variously portray insurgencies, resistance, and resilience reflecting the spirit of besieged, paralyzed, and terrorized societies seeking radical uprooting and overhaul of the reigning systems, as do the two Anglophone texts under discussion in this chapter.

The Anglophone Imaginary in *Guapa* and *Revolution for Dummies*

Against the backdrop of the Arab spring protests, Saleem Haddad's *Guapa* covers 24 hours in the life of Rasa, who returns from America having trained in translation. The plot is intricately woven into Rasa's childhood, including characters such as his grandmother with whom he shares an apartment in a middleclass neighborhood of Cairo, and his neighbor and lover Taymour. Upon his return, Rasa, the center of the action, reconnects with some of his friends from his young years and cultivates a community of radical anti-establishment youth at the old cinema which becomes a popular meeting point for the gay community. The tightening grip of the state, however, leads to the raiding and closing of the cinema, and the abduction of Rasa's best friend Maj by the authorities. While Rasa tries to make sense of his place and positioning in his country by roaming the streets of fictionalized Cairo, he finds himself constantly othered, if not estranged, due to his sexual orientation. When the protests Rasa joins with great hope and anticipation are being infiltrated and eventually taken over by an unnamed political force (the allegorical Muslim Brotherhood), Rasa turns his back, feeling there is nothing left worth fighting for. Rasa's subsequent journeys throughout the novel – anchored in the memories of his childhood; his years of studying abroad; and the many nights spent at his favorite bar, Guapa – enable him to draw a comparison between his personal alienation and that of the politically marginalized and, more importantly, to see his country through the eyes of a diasporic returnee:

> My American education had given me a way to analyze my people. I felt I was mixing with the true salt of the earth, the authentic Arab voice. But like an old lover, as the years pass and the complaints remain the same, that rose-tinted vision has cleared. The problems they complain about are now my own problems, and problems are much less glamorous when they

are yours. Anyway, today of all days I don't have the energy to bestow sympathy. I have my own troubles to deal with. I need my own space to think. But the driver talks and talks, invading my thoughts. I look out the window to avoid any pretence of conversation.[31]

Rasa's musings are not only replete with the Anglophone imaginary of American education, especially the latter's emphasis on carving out a sense of individual space and emancipation from traditional expectations – demonstrated through the repetitive use of first person address – but they are well in tune with Anglophone modernities' unresolved tension between the tyrannies of tradition and the agency of the individual. The diasporic gaze enabled by Rasa's Anglophone cultural capital, as evinced in the 'cab-side' view of his own country, instills in him a savior syndrome of sorts privy to many American novels and films on the region:[32] "I could probably help these people, share some of my savings, my English skills, direct them to the good NGOs, the right UN agencies. I could be of use to them somehow. They would take me in" (38). This savior syndrome is laid to rest as soon as Rasa finds himself as a semi-insider of the same system he intends to reform. The resulting inside-out perspective enabled by a diasporic Egyptian is neither disabling nor debilitating but lends unique insights into the naturalized, fossilized, at times even forged notions of home, tradition and national belonging.

As a translator working for a journalist of an American newspaper, Rasa situates himself both literally and figuratively between the untranslated zones of two cultures. In an interview conducted by the American journalist with a family of victims who lost their child in the protests, Rasa is challenged through a stream of perspectives by the family in question which praises the revolution (and criticizes the president), but blames the Western cultural influence as the greatest threat to Egypt and the holding up of the promises brought forth by the Arab Spring. Lost in translation, Rasa reflects intermittently in the awkward pauses in the conversation with the family:

Another thought occurs to me, the realization that we are from the same country, the same city even, yet we never truly knew each other. I want to tell Ahmed some things and to ask his opinion of many more. I want to agree with some of his views and challenge him on others. I want to tell Um Abdallah that my best friend is also being held by the regime for who he is, for who he wants to be, but I cannot find the words to do so. How will they react if I tell them Maj was arrested while at the old cinemas? How can I explain that I am like them, misunderstood, vilified by the regime and the media? I don't have the words to say any of this, and the brief moment of deep solidarity I feel dissipates before my eyes.

(86)

The tropes of his stream(s) of consciousness, and the soliloquy-like confessions which are marked characteristics of the literary modernities of the Anglophone tradition, manifest themselves in the narrative as a critique of unchecked euphoria surrounding the events of the Egyptian revolution of 2011, thereby serving as proleptic devices that guard against political complacency forged through polarized ideologies of 'Egypt vs. the West.' Instead, these soliloquies draw attention to the polarities within Egypt often buried under the utopia of revolution. Rasa's diasporic flânerie, for instance, charts the city's topography, which is depicted in the most Manichean, apartheid terms: the Western suburbs are home to an English-speaking, affluent elite endorsing the president's secular, "Western oriented" yet authoritarian politics. In contrast, the slum of al-Sharqiyeh to the East is poor, lacking critical infrastructure, and rejects presidential politics on the grounds of rising food prices and infrastructural neglect. Its citizens are granted only controlled access to the city sphere and are treated as second-class denizens, as reflected in the frequent denouncing of them as terrorists.

Amidst the jostling of multiple political stakeholders – between the fall of Hosni Mubarak in February 2011 and the hijacking of the revolution by the Muslim Brotherhood-backed President Mohamed Morsi – including the military, state police, and the Islamists, for Rasa and his comrades, taking to the streets becomes an existential gesture of belonging to the city: "We were not just taking back the streets, we were taking back our lives" (51). In this process, however, downtown, especially the *midan*, begins to lose the vibrant political image it once had, instead representing a "landscape of discontent"[33] with neither the model of the Western suburbs – seemingly more liberal but also home to corrupt politicians and entrepreneurs depleting the country – nor the religiously motivated city development plan offered by Sheikh Ahmad as prospective alternatives:

> Looking around, I began to think: If we did manage to bring down the president, and if we tore down every damn picture and statue from the city, what would we replace him with? The protests had felt like the most authentic thing I had done in my life. Now they felt like a martyrdom operation to help a new generation of dictators come to power.
>
> *(82)*

If the deferred sense of agency implied in Rasa's meditations on the failed attempt at symbolically reclaiming the revolution is inflected by his own marginalized position as a rejected sexual minority in Egyptian society, it is also enabled by the Anglophone imaginary which lends piercing insights into the tyrannies of the vernacular. As a translator to an American journalist, Rasa sums up his subject position in the most unambiguous fashion: "I am her bridge, her reliable Oriental guide. I speak both Arabic and English and understand how Americans see us" (73). Yet Rasa does not reject or refute his Arab(ic) legacy. Instead, his Anglophone imaginary enables him to recover the pleasure and politics of the vernacular, as he concedes that if speaking English made him a critical person, speaking Arabic made him "a kinder person somehow, more passionate and human" (166). In light of this epiphany, Rasa reflects on how it all went wrong with his Arabic heritage as a child:

> The feeling was very different from how I felt growing up. [...] In English class we read the Famous Five, Judy Blume, *Lord of the Flies*, *Robinson Crusoe*, all that stuff. I saw myself in the characters and could feel what they were feeling. Arabic, on the other hand, was like a dead world. We only had one large textbook, which had short vignettes of Quranic verses and old nationalist poems that were boring as hell, and the grammar was too damn difficult. It wasn't even the Arabic I spoke, which was free-flowing and malleable. The Arabic that was shoved down our throats was rigid and alien. So Maj and I would feign illness or else spend the hour hiding in the bathroom cubicle, which smelled of piss but at least we could joke and speak however we wanted.
>
> *(166–167)*

Edward Said would have testified to Rasa's discomfort with the sort of frozen, fossilized, Qur'anic Arabic and the eloquence the language had achieved after having been fused into its multiple regional iterations across the Arab speaking world. Like Said's own unique positioning between European and Arabic linguistic traditions, Rasa uses his own in-between position as the translator to his advantage:

> But when I see that the words I am asked to translate are blatant lies then it is my job to do something. Because if the lies come out of my mouth, if they pass through me even if they belong to someone else, am I not complicit in them? In those situations I misinterpret.
>
> *(76)*

Rasa's tactical use of English serves as an antidote to the Anglophobia of his interview partner Sheikh Ahmad, who is fluent in English but refuses to speak it on the grounds that "it would be treacherous" to speak the language of the estranged elite rather than Arabic. Echoing Ngũgĩ wa Thiong'o's rejection of English as a decolonizing strategy,[34] Ahmad's refusal to entertain English aligns with – albeit inadvertently – the reactionary attitudes of the local elites who speak Arabic at home to mobilize people under the auspices of Arab and Arabic unity but amass the means to send their children to Ivy League universities in America.

For Rasa, the politics of an Anglophone imaginary reflect another order of negotiating (sexual) identity: the televised coming out of an American pop singer provides Rasa with a word and language to name his self-perceived deviance: "Gay. That's the word, I thought" (92). Thus, English initially offers him a sense of empowerment which is quickly replaced by the search for more vernacular expressions (94), realizing that "both English and Arabic have so many words that explored every dimension of what I was feeling, and yet not one word that could encapsulate it all" (97).

After his return to the US where he hopes to finally explore his otherwise embargoed sexuality, Rasa finds himself confronted with a new identity made visible by the lingering presence of post-9/11 Islamophobia. For Rasa, the "temporary positions or pivots"[35] from which to evaluate new aspects of being and identity are shaped by the choice of language and eventually place, thus manifesting in the polycentricity – a signature theme of Arab Anglophone writings – that allows for writing back to self, the local, the vernacular vis-à-vis imperialist power hierarchies.

Similarly, the Anglophone becomes the stage for setting, if not plotting, the entire narrative in Bassem Youssef's satirical text *Revolution for Dummies* (2017), with the autodiegetic narrator singling out his readership and declaring his intention from the get-go:

> Picture this: an Arab man (played by Javier Bardem with an accent because, you know, Hollywood's diversity problem) grows up to save a *few lives* as a heart surgeon, but when a whole region experiences the biggest clusterfuck in its history, he saves the *whole nation* with his jokes. The writers may have to take some liberties in order to write a happy ending and appeal to an American audience, but enjoy your second Oscar, Javier.[36]

Youssef prefaces and concludes his book by consciously choosing his reader, the reader exposed to Anglophone journalism and academic knowledge about the Middle East in the West, and takes on the think tanks and popular media that dominated the representation of the region since the Six-Day War, and even more aggressively after 9/11. He writes:

> There are dozens of these books claiming they've got the "answer" for what the hell is happening there [...] yet the Middle East is still a big mess. So either no one is reading these books or even heavily funded policy institutions don't know jack shit about us.
>
> *(ix–x)*

Thus, Bassem disrupts the seemingly self-orientalized presentation to directly address his assumed Anglophone readers, repeatedly drawing parallels between Egypt and the West by rhetorically asking: "Sound familiar?" (72).

With a twist of irony, Youssef challenges the readers not to sacrifice their aesthetic palate for populist rhetoric or insipid fads and research findings about Egypt but to tag along with him with the same vigor for truth – and be entertained by him. The trick here is that *he* – Bassem the comedian – will replace Javier Bardem as the Arab hero in Hollywood and try to save the nation through humor. Forfeiting the Oscar here may be taken as disowning Hollywood Orientalism of the white-Arab heroes as well as their white-man salvaging narratives.

Youssef's treatment of Hollywood's management of the Arab image calls for the mediation of the Anglophone imaginary precisely because, as Arundhati Roy reminds us, English provides an opportunity to rectify the wrongs committed under the aegis of imperialism and Orientalism in that very language. In tune with the 'distanced' view of the diasporic subject of the Anglophone imaginary, Bassem sees the world through the eyes of a self-imposed, if not forced, exile as he begins his narrative with his exodus from Egypt: "How did it come to this? Why did I have to flee, while tyrants and thieves got to stay? I didn't steal, didn't abuse my powers, and certainly didn't hurt anyone. All I did was tell jokes" (4). Thus Bassem reconstructs his entire struggle throughout the Arab Spring and his career as a popular comedian through the eyes of a detached exile. He does so with the full awareness of cultivated literary rhetoric, which he uses against an Islamist in a TV debate: "I reminded him that in the 'Western media' there is no person above satire and sarcasm" (132). His reference to western media here is exclusively Anglophonic, especially when invoking the American political satire of Jon Stewart's *The Daily Show*. Youssef not only idolizes and models his own career in Egyptian television after Jon Stewart with his own show *Al-Bernameg*, but he utilizes the American political situation as a satirical reference to understand present-day Egypt:

> Through it [the book] you will see how ignorance, xenophobia, racism, and everything that Donald Trump stands for can transcend borders, cultures, and religions. You will find how easy it is to brainwash masses of people, however well informed they think they are, without the funding of Fox News, the pure hatred that is Ann Coulter, or the Bible. After the fame and the short-lived celebrity life I had in Egypt, my story is all I have left.
>
> *(xi)*

The sort of Anglophone imaginary that Youssef deploys to broach the subject – Trump, American conservative figures, religious metaphors and their implied propaganda doctrines that beckoned the colonial civilizing mission – is pressed into the service of demystifying Egypt not as an arcane, unique, or fossilized culture but one that is part and parcel of historical and global power dynamics. Bassem's cheeky references to popular fads such as the "Salafi sheikhs were under the control of the Egyptian equivalent of the NSA" (41) or one such Salafi sheikh's belief that "the reason the Titanic sank was because Kate Winslet posed nude for Leonardo DiCaprio" (65) more than serve this purpose. They also show that Egypt is implicated in the world Anglophone imaginary by virtue of its history and, more importantly, as an active, if not willing consumer of global culture. Such hybrid, globalectical comparisons, to use Ngũgĩ wa Thiong'o's term,[37] reach their peak in the characterization of a mullah who, as it were, can be best described as a character walking out of a handbook on Anglophone popular culture:

> Think of a zealous religious conservative like Mike Huckabee with his extreme fundamentalist quotes and his adorable smile. Then add some Michelle Bachman's non-fact "facts." Then mix that with the bigotry of Donald Trump and the self-serving beliefs of Ted Cruz. Then go ahead and wrap everything up in the crazy that is Sarah Palin. Add a dash of twisted religious interpretation and a scary Islamic beard and now you have Abu Ismail.
>
> *(143)*

The charm, verbosity, imprudence, and bigotry that characterize the figures mentioned above are all imports of the Anglophone imaginary that *necessitate* the characterization of a local figure, who is no more, and no less, than a hybrid monster made up of global populist icons. The hybrid figure in question here is fully aware of, and deeply imbricated in, the Anglophone imaginary that he is made of:

> He was known for his ability to uncover the Western conspiracies against Islam. One of his famous television lessons showed him explaining that the soda company Pepsi had led a conspiracy. Yes, Pepsi. The one related to child obesity, sugar addiction, and Beyoncé. He said that Pepsi was an acronym for *Pay Every Penny to Save Israel*.
>
> *(144, original emphasis)*

Here, the parading of the symbols of popular culture both to explain the victimological position of Egypt and to criticize American hegemony bespeaks of an ambiguity that is endemic to the Egyptian populace for whom America was "the reason for everything evil that happened during the revolution" and yet they would "kill" to get an American visa (29). Youssef, however, is careful not to treat his adopted Anglophone imaginary – enabled by his exilic vision and diasporic distance – which exposes the hypocrisies of the Egyptian ruling elite in relation to the larger world as a means of forging emancipatory insights or inroads into the Egyptian cultural psyche. Instead, like Rasa, he treats both Anglophobia and Anglophilia with a sense of suspicion when he finds them inadequate to capture the complexities of vernacular cultural

The Anglophone Imaginary and Agency **99**

formations. For instance, drawing parallels between the willing believers of state propaganda in Egypt and Trump supporters in the US, Bassem subverts the criticism to expose the hegemonic pedagogies of the Anglophone imaginary:

> We receive $1.3 billion in military aid each year from America, plus more money to 'support democracy.' Big mistake! In order for Egypt to get the $1.3 billion in deadly weapons, we needed to appear as if we were financially supporting free speech and democratic organizations. In turn, these outspoken organizations would come right back and object to the American money used to grow the military. It was a vicious, vicious cycle. [...] However, it astounded me that many of the Islamists parties went to these organizations to get training in election management and campaigning. Many of those made it into the parliament *because* of the training they received.
>
> *(87–90, original emphasis)*

Highlighting political aspects satirically but without undermining their complexity and global interconnectedness, Youssef is able to address the shortcomings of Egypt's political elite and mainstream media. The Anglophone imaginary, in this sense, serves as a heuristic device to expose the vested interests of global powers vis-à-vis their implicatedness in the vernacular. Much like Rasa's translational resistance in *Guapa*, Youssef's chief weapon of choice, as it were, remains language itself. He turns language on its head to expose the *manipulative* nature of the vernacular rhetoric of Egypt's ruling elite by *manipulating* the language of another order:

> Satire is a great antidote to that fear mentality. When you laugh, you are not afraid anymore. Dictators are afraid of jokers. Laughing in the face of tyranny and fear disarms them in front of their supporters. Ridiculing them, making fun of them, and questioning their empty rhetoric exposes them and sends them running naked through the streets.
>
> *(272)*

Although Arabic has its own tradition of satire and humour, Youssef's influences are admittedly American, and necessarily Anglophone media products: Jon Stewart, the 24 hours news media, sitcoms, Facebook, 140-character tweets, TV host shows, and stand-up comedies – all of which, as it were, make English "a criminal language."

Conclusion

In "criticizing both American and Arab society and political systems,"[38] the two Arab Anglophone authors discussed in this chapter do not merely write back to neo-imperialist influences of US foreign/Western politics. Rather their work becomes an expression of "writing back to themselves" in what is a critique of internal hegemonic practices.[39] To do so, both Haddad and Youssef employ what Hayward calls "polycentric writing" which points towards the "temporary positions or pivots on which to stand while in search of the next place from which a sense of being may flow forth."[40] English and its attendant Anglophone imaginary become one such act of polycentric writing, a pivot from which the local and vernacular hierarchies can be critiqued while simultaneously exposing its hegemonic tendencies. English, in that sense, becomes both a boon and a curse. It exposes Rasa and Youssef's danger of being suspected as foreign agents infiltrating the vernacular tradition while simultaneously enabling the language required for critiquing nativism and vernacular purism. In tune with the literary history of Arab Anglophone writing since the turn of the 20th century, the two texts follow the trajectory of post-9/11 and post-Iraq War literatures which cast an "inward gaze" on the local power structures and hierarchies. In the process, they both move away from the hyphenated, arms-length relationship to the English language of earlier generations and recast the Anglophone cultural capital of their protagonists to lend deeper insights into vernacular populism than the vernacular texts could possibly yield. By putting the vernacular hierarchies in their place, the texts ennoble the spirit of the Arab Spring: its subaltern and civic origins, and the dissent and discontent which were hijacked by the competing narratives of vernacular purism which are deeply immersed in, if not naturalized by, the historical trajectories of Egyptian nationalism.

Notes

1 Parts of this chapter have previously been published in a chapter on "Contemporary Arab Novels in English: Political Resistance in the City Spaces of Arab Spring Novels by Saleem Haddad and Omar Robert Hamilton" in Nadia Butt, Alexander Scherr and Ansgar Nünning, eds., *The Anglophone Novel in the Twenty-First Century: Cultural Contexts – Literary Developments – Model Interpretations* (Trier: Wissenschaftlicher Verlag Trier, 2023) and are reproduced by friendly permission of the publisher.
2 Bassem Youssef, *Revolution for Dummies* (New York: Dey Street Books, 2017): 25.
3 Personal communication with Ajay Gudavarthy, Associate Professor of Political Science, Jawaharlal Nehru University, Delhi.
4 Dipesh Chakrabarty, *Provincializing Europe* (Princeton: Princeton University Press, 2008): 5.
5 Arundhati Roy, "What is the Morally Appropriate Language in Which to Think and Write," *Literary Hub*, 25 July 2018, https://lithub.com/what-is-the-morally-appropriate-language-in-which-to-think-and-write/.
6 Saleem Haddad, *Guapa* (New York: Europa Editions, 2017).
7 Maggie Jonas, "An Interview with Nuruddin Farah," *Journal of Refugee Studies* 1.1 (1988): 75.
8 Jonas, "An Interview with Nuruddin Farah."
9 Roy, "Morally Appropriate Language."

10 Ahdaf Soueif, *In the Eye of the Sun* (New York: Pantheon Books, 1993).
11 Rajaa Alsanea, *The Girls of Riyadh* (New York: The Penguin Press, 2007).
12 Geoffrey Nash, "Arab Voices in Western Writing: The Politics of the Arabic Novel in English and the Anglophone Arab Novel," *Commonwealth Essays and Studies* 39.2 (2017): 27–37.
13 Edward W. Said, "Living in Arabic," *Raritan* 21.4 (2002): 220–236.
14 Said, "Living in Arabic," 230.
15 Nouri Gana, "Introduction: The Intellectual History and Contemporary Significance of the Arab Novel in English," in *The Edinburgh Companion to the Arab Novel in English: The Politics of Anglo Arab and Arab American Literature and Culture*, edited by Nouri Gana (Edinburgh: Edinburgh University Press, 2013): 13.
16 Gana, "Introduction," 6.
17 Evan M. Mwangi, *Africa Writes Back to Self: Metafiction, Gender, Sexuality* (New York: SUNY Press, 2017): 27–29.
18 See Waïl S. Hassan, "The Rise of Arab-American Literature: Orientalism and Cultural Translation in the Work of Ameen Rihani," *American Literary History* 20.1–2 (2008): 245.
19 Lisa Suhair Majaj, "New Directions: Arab American Writing Today," in *Arab-Americas: Literary Entanglements of the American Hemisphère and the Arab World*, edited by Ottmar Ette and Friederike Pannewick (Frankfurt: Vervuert, 2006): 124.
20 Layla Al-Maleh, "Anglophone Arab Writing: An Overview," in *Arab Voices in Diaspora: Critical Perspectives on Anglophone Arab Writing*, edited by Layla Al Maleh (Amsterdam and New York: Rodopi, 2009): 4–5.
21 Hassan, "The Rise of Arab-American Literature," 271.
22 Al-Maleh, "Anglophone Arab Writing," 11.
23 Fadia Faqir, *Pillars of Salt* (London: Quartet, 1996); Samia Seralgedine, *The Cairo House* (Syracuse: Syracuse University Press, 2000).
24 Maysa Abou-Youssef Hayward, "Identity, Transformation and the Arab Anglophone Novel," in *The Edinburgh Companion to the Arab Novel in English: The Politics of Anglo Arab and Arab American Literature and Culture*, edited by Nouri Gana (Edinburgh: Edinburgh University Press, 2013): 336.
25 Al-Maleh, "Anglophone Arab Writing," 1–2.
26 Majed Shadaid Alenezi, *Shifting Paradigms of Postcolonial Theory: Internal Concerns of Post-2000 Anglophone Arab Fiction* (Dissertation. Middle Tennessee State University, 2019): 203.
27 Layla Halabi, *Once in a Promised Land: A Novel* (Boston: Beacon, 2008); Rabih Alameddine: *The Hakawati* (New York: Alfred A. Knop, 2008); Alia Yunis, *The Night Counter* (New York: Crown, 2009).
28 Fadia Faqir, *Willow Trees Don't Weep* (London: Heron Books, 2014); Rabih Alameddine, *An Unnecessary Woman* (New York: Grove, 2014).
29 Hisham Matar, *In the Country of Men* (New York: Viking Books, 2006); *Anatomy of a Disappearance* (New York: Viking, 2011); *The Return* (New York: Viking, 2016).
30 Haytham Bahoora, "Writing the Dismembered Nation: The Aesthetics of Horror in Iraqi Narratives of War," *The Arab Studies Journal* 23.1 (2015): 188.
31 Haddad Saleem, *Guapa* (New York: Europa Editions, 2017): 27–28. Further page references are in the main text.
32 See Michael C. Frank and Pavan Kumar Malreddy, *Narratives of the War on Terror: Global Perspectives* (Abingdon: Routledge, 2020).
33 Suzanne Enzerink, "Arab Archipelagoes: Revolutionary Formations and a Queer Undercommons in Saleem Haddad's *Guapa*," *Feminist Formations* 33.1 (2021): 260.

34 Ngũgĩ wa Thiong'o, "Decolonizing the Mind: State of the Art," *Présence Afric-aine* 197 (2018/1): 97–102.
35 Abou-Youssef Hayward, "Identity, Transformation and the Arab Anglophone Novel," 323.
36 Youssef, *Revolution for Dummies*, x. Further page references are in the main text.
37 Ngũgĩ wa Thiong'o, *Globalectics: Theory and the Politics of Knowing* (New York: Columbia University Press, 2014).
38 Al-Maleh, "Anglophone Arab Writing," 25.
39 Mwangi, *Africa Writes Back to Self*, 2–3.
40 Abou-Youssef Hayward, "Identity, Transformation and the Arab Anglophone Novel," 323.

Bibliography

Abou-Youssef Hayward, Maysa. "Identity, Transformation and the Arab Anglophone Novel." In *The Edinburgh Companion to the Arab Novel in English: The Politics of Anglo Arab and Arab American Literature and Culture*, edited by Nouri Gana. Edinburgh: Edinburgh University Press, 2013: 321–338.

Alameddine, Rabih. *The Hakawati*. New York: Alfred A. Knopf, 2008.

———. *An Unnecessary Woman*. New York: Grove Press, 2014.

Alenezi, Majed Shadaid. *Shifting Paradigms of Postcolonial Theory: Internal Concerns of Post-2000 Anglophone Arab Fiction*. Dissertation. Middle Tennessee State University, 2019.

Al-Maleh, Layla. "Anglophone Arab Writing: An Overview." In *Arab Voices in Diaspora: Critical Perspectives on Anglophone Arab Writing*, edited by Layla Al Maleh. Amsterdam and New York: Rodopi, 2009: 1–59.

Alsanea, Rajaa. *The Girls of Riyadh*. New York: The Penguin Press, 2007.

Bahoora, Haytham. "Writing the Dismembered Nation: The Aesthetics of Horror in Iraqi Narratives of War." *The Arab Studies Journal* 23.1 (2015): 184–208.

Chakrabarty, Dipesh. *Provincializing Europe*. Princeton: Princeton University Press, 2008.

Enzerink, Suzanne. "Arab Archipelagoes: Revolutionary Formations and a Queer Undercommons in Saleem Haddad's *Guapa*." *Feminist Formations* 33.1 (2021): 245–274.

Faqir, Fadia. *Pillars of Salt*. London: Quartet, 1996.

———. *Willow Trees Don't Weep*. London: Heron, 2014.

Frank, Michael C. and Pavan Kumar Malreddy. *Narratives of the War on Terror: Global Perspectives*. Abingdon: Routledge, 2020.

Gana, Nouri. "Introduction: The Intellectual History and Contemporary Significance of the Arab Novel in English." In *The Edinburgh Companion to the Arab Novel in English: The Politics of Anglo Arab and Arab American Literature and Culture*, edited by Nouri Gana. Edinburgh: Edinburgh University Press, 2013: 1–35.

Haddad, Saleem. *Guapa*. New York: Europa Editions, 2017.

Halabi, Layla. *Once in a Promised Land. A Novel*. Boston: Beacon, 2008.

Hassan, Waïl S. "The Rise of Arab-American Literature: Orientalism and Cultural Translation in the Work of Ameen Rihani." *American Literary History* 20.1–2 (2008): 245–275.

Jonas, Maggie. "An Interview with Nuruddin Farah." *Journal of Refugee Studies* 1.1 (1988): 74–77.

Majaj, Lisa Suhair. "New Directions: Arab American Writing Today." In *ArabAmericas: Literary Entanglements of the American Hemisphere and the Arab World*, edited by Ottmar Ette and Friederike Pannewick. Frankfurt: Vervuert, 2006: 123–136.

Malreddy, Pavan Kumar and Stefanie Kemmerer. "Contemporary Arab Novels in English: Political Resistance in the City Spaces of Arab Spring Novels by Saleem Haddad and Omar Robert Hamilton." In *The Anglophone Novel in the Twenty-First Century: Cultural Contexts – Literary Developments – Model Interpretations*, edited by Nadia Butt, Alexander Scherr and Ansgar Nünning. Trier: Wissenschaftlicher Verlag Trier, 2023.

Matar, Hisham. *Anatomy of a Disappearance.* New York: Viking, 2011.

———. *In the Country of Men.* New York: Viking, 2006.

———. *The Return.* New York: Viking, 2016.

Mwangi, Evan M. *Africa Writes Back to Self: Metafiction, Gender, Sexuality.* New York: SUNY Press, 2017.

Nash, Geoffrey. "Arab Voices in Western Writing: The Politics of the Arabic Novel in English and the Anglophone Arab Novel." *Commonwealth Essays and Studies* 39.2 (2017): 27–37.

Roy, Arundhati. "What is the Morally Appropriate Language in which to Think and Write." *Literary Hub,* 25 July 2018. https://lithub.com/what-is-the-morally-appropriate-language-in-which-to-think-and-write/ (last accessed 15 April 2023).

Said, Edward W. "Living in Arabic." *Raritan* 21.4 (2002): 220–236.

Seralgedine, Samia. *The Cairo House.* Syracuse: Syracuse University Press, 2000.

Soueif, Ahdaf. *In the Eye of the Sun.* New York: Pantheon Books, 1993.

wa Thiong'o, Ngũgĩ. "Decolonizing the Mind: State of the Art." *Présence Africaine* 197 (2018/1): 97–102.

———. *Globalectics: Theory and the Politics of Knowing.* New York: Columbia University Press, 2014.

Youssef, Bassem. *Revolution for Dummies.* New York: Dey Street Books, 2017.

Yunis, Alia. *The Night Counter.* New York: Crown, 2009.

6

"BILINGUAL SILENCE"? NEW ANGLOPHONE LITERATURE FROM THE BALKANS AND ITS MIGRATIONAL METAMULTILINGUAL MODE

Miriam Wallraven

Introduction: "Migration Necessitates Narration"

"Migration necessitates narration," Aleksandar Hemon, the US-Bosnian author of numerous texts that have been defined as new world literature,[1] states in an interview.[2] New world literature, Sigrid Löffler claims, is indeed a literature of non-native authors, a literature written by language-changers.[3] So how and in which language/s is it possible to narrate migration? Over the last decades, the term new Anglophone literatures has primarily been utilised to define English writing emerging from a postcolonial context. However, there are numerous other bestselling and award-winning texts that contribute to the cosmos of new Anglophone literatures – for instance those by English-speaking authors from the non-Anglophone Balkans who have migrated to Anglophone countries and thematise migration especially after the Yugoslav Wars in the 1990s. If, as Hemon contends, "migration necessitates narration" and English is employed as a non-native language, how is the contact zone caused by migration created in literature?

This analysis focuses on two texts by authors from former Yugoslavia who have migrated to Anglophone countries and write in English: In Aleksandar Hemon's short story "Blind Jozef Pronek and Dead Souls" (2000), Bosnia meets the US, which results in complex negotiations of culture clashes, misunderstandings, and ultimately "bilingual silence." In A.S. Patrić's novel *Black Rock White City* (2015), the contact of former Yugoslavia and Australia leads to multilayered reflections on the silence and the bilingualism of the migrant.

DOI: 10.4324/9781003464037-9
This chapter has been made available under a CC-BY-NC-ND 4.0 license.

In their study of modernist authors in exile, Englund and Olsson investigate the situation of writing between languages, and their argument proves to be illuminating for displacement and writing in general:

> Literary writing, in other words, becomes the point of intersection between native and acquired language, between the indigenous and the alien, between self and other, in a complex bi- or multilingual dynamic specific to the situations of exile and migration. To be an expatriate writer is to be constantly faced with a gap in one's language and identity, to exist in a state of in-between, which, as the phenomenon of exile literature has come to prove time and again, is often as aesthetically fertile as it is bewildering and difficult.[4]

These central concepts such as "point of intersection," "gap," and "state of in-between" have to be located on intratextual levels where characters negotiate difficult language issues in the process of migration and on the extratextual level where authors use English to mediate these issues for an Anglophone audience. How can these tensions, complexities, and dynamics of a writing in-between cultures and languages be conceptionalised? How can migration be narrated? In the following, it will be shown how such Anglophone texts from the Balkans are characterised by what I call the *migrational metamultilingual mode*. Literary strategies characteristic of this mode elucidate the complex negotiations of language, identity, and migration in contact zones in a globalised world in general.

Balkan Spaces and Anglophone Literature From the Balkans

Numerous English-speaking texts with Balkan origins have received international attention. Already in 1998, Goldsworthy mentions "the burgeoning of a new Balkan literature in English, produced by a growing body of Balkan writers who have migrated westwards since the 1980s" and states that "[a]lthough such books now dominate Anglophone Balkan manufacture, responses to them have been patchy. [...] Thus far, the books fall under the radar of English studies."[5]

As a geographic signifier, Balkan[6] was first used in Anglophone travel literature, and the disagreement about where the Balkans begin crucially depends on the contested definitions that became charged with largely negative meanings. The complex status as non-postcolonial as concerns the Anglophone world is juxtaposed first with the complicated history of being occupied by the Ottoman and Austro-Hungarian/Habsburg Empires and second with the status of being subject to an ongoing British "narrative colonialisation"[7] as a "discursively and historically imagined location."[8]

106 Miriam Wallraven

Since most scholars agree that Edward Said's model of Orientalism cannot be applied to the Balkans, Todorova has advanced the term "Balkanism." Especially the "historical and geographical concreteness of the Balkans as opposed to the intangible nature of the Orient" sets the two discourses apart.[9] Instead of being associated with sensuality and luxury as the imagined Orient, the Balkans "with their unimaginative concreteness, and almost total lack of wealth, induced a straightforward attitude, usually negative, but rarely nuanced."[10] Therefore, Balkanism serves as "shorthand for the tropes of backwardness, savagery, discord and obfuscation,"[11] as Hammond succinctly puts it. He shows how Great Britain's "persistent interference through diplomacy, militarism and venture capitalism has had a profound and lasting impact, and has produced extensive literary engagement with the region."[12] Furthermore, he argues that the American tradition of representing the Balkans influenced British perceptions after the Balkan Wars of 1912–1913.[13] This Anglophone influence on the Balkans becomes salient as soon as literature from the Balkans becomes an effective vehicle of dealing with migration to Anglophone countries.

"So Balkan is always the Other," Žižek states and elaborates that "it lies somewhere else, always a little bit more to the southeast."[14] With that, he reveals how the processes of Othering in the form of deferring the border of "civilisation" function in the case of the Balkans, which then become "the terrain of ethnic savagery and intolerance, of the primitive irrational warrior passions."[15]

As a space "in-between," the Balkans have been described as a bridge between East and West,[16] a liminal space which is at the same time marked by its very centrality in Europe due to the "position at the crossroads."[17] Addressing the Balkans as such a space in-between, the strategies employed in Anglophone literature emerging from this space foreground the complex negotiations of language and migration in the contact zone. Conceiving of contact zones as "social spaces where disparate cultures meet, clash, grapple with each other, often in highly asymmetrical relations of domination and subordination,"[18] according to Pratt's seminal approach, can shed light on processes of migration in this context.

Literature of Migration and Metamultilingualism

The liminal status of the Balkans is further reinforced by the liminal status of migrant authors, which makes it necessary to explore metamultilingualism as a mode comprising various strategies of writing in such a contact zone – an increasingly important paradigm of New Anglophone literature not only from the Balkans. In his work on the functions of language, Roman Jacobson distinguishes between two levels of language: "A distinction has been made in modern logic between two levels of language, 'object language' speaking of objects and 'metalanguage' speaking of language."[19] In contrast

New Anglophone Literature from the Balkans **107**

to the focus on contents, what Jacobson calls the "metalingual function" focuses on the use of language to describe and discuss itself: "Whenever the addresser and/or addressee need to check up on whether they use the same code, speech is focused on the CODE: it performs a METALINGUAL (i.e. glossing) function."[20] In fact, this metalingual function is of particular significance in the context of writing about migration that involves various contact zones and several languages coming into contact. However, multilingualism "has been and continues to be refracted through the monolingual paradigm," as Yasemin Yildiz argues.[21] Hence, in order to expose the assumed dominance of the monolingual as well as "multilingual attempts to overcome it,"[22] she employs the term "postmonolingual"[23] which refers to a "field of tension in which the monolingual paradigm continues to assert itself and multilingual practices persist or reemerge."[24] It is precisely this "field of tension" dominating the contact zone in the novels that raises various issues of language, narration, and migration.

Many texts dealing with migration, such as Hemon's and Patrić's, are less characterised by linguistic forms of multilingualism such as interferences and code-switching than by reflections about multilingualism, as "[m]etamultilingualism denotes speaking about languages in the broadest sense."[25] Crucial metalingual issues coming into existence in the context zone in the process of migration are negotiated in what I want to propose as the migrational metamultilingual mode. This mode comprises more than just related topics and shows itself particularly in the metareflections thus affecting the textual structure as a whole. Which are the literary strategies created by and in turn productive of this mode? The first criterion is the accumulation of misunderstandings and communication problems that govern the contact zones in the novel. Second, a loss of language crucially affects the identity of the migrant characters and is thus the main plot trigger. The third factor becomes visible in the explicit metareflections, a permanent "speaking about languages"[26] that structures the texts and complicates them by another layer. A fourth point relates to the metareflections extending beyond the characters in the story to the thematisation of authorship. In this way, this mode can elucidate the complex processes of a writing in migrational contact zones, a writing in-between languages that is fundamental for new world literature in English.

New Anglophone Literature of Migration From the Balkans: Hemon and Patrić

English, it has often been argued, appears as a particularly "democratic" language that can be joined from everywhere.[27] Joining it, however, is not necessarily an easy and straightforward venture. Belonging to two different generations of immigrant authors from Yugoslavia to Anglophone countries, Hemon and Patrić both "join English" as their literary language and deal with migration in their writing.

108 Miriam Wallraven

Aleksandar Hemon was born in Sarajevo in 1964 and took a degree in English at the University of Sarajevo. While working as a journalist for the Sarajevan youth press, Hemon was invited to Chicago in 1992 with a scholarship. During his stay, Sarajevo came under siege, and being unable to return, Hemon stayed in Chicago. Hemon still visits Sarajevo often and also writes for Bosnian newspapers. A.S. Patrić was born in Zemun, Serbia, and migrated to Melbourne with his family when he was one year old. Patrić himself is thus a second-generation migrant who emphasises the importance of immigrant stories for Australian culture in his writing. The following analysis shows how both authors utilise the migrational metamultilingual mode in order to thematise the silence and multilingualism in the process of migration via the fictional characters, while the authors themselves write in English to mediate these issues of migration and language for an Anglophone audience.

"Bilingual Silence" and the Migrant: Bosnia Meets the US in Aleksandar Hemon's "Blind Jozef Pronek and Dead Souls" (2000)

In interviews, Hemon describes how he was stuck between languages after arriving in the US, a situation which elicited his differentiated reflections on writing between languages in both his theoretical and fictional writings. Thus, he repeatedly discusses the effects of two languages on writing and identity and explains that to "be bilingual is to enjoy various aspects of yourself and your personality. Everyone is more than one person and more than one thing. But if you're bilingual or multilingual then you have various languages for those personalities."[28] The characters in his stories, for example in "Blind Jozef Pronek and Dead Souls," however, embody a sharp contrast to the author's bilingualism.

In this story, the protagonist Pronek, a young man from Sarajevo, is invited to the US as a journalist when tensions begin to arise in Bosnia. Staying in Chicago, he experiences various forms of discrimination while being confronted with the outbreak of the Bosnian War back home on TV. He works in several underpaid jobs, and wherever he goes he is confronted with the American ignorance of Bosnia and world politics as a whole.

Pronek's arrival in the US begins with communication problems that govern the plot from the outset: "There was a man holding a sign with Pronek's name misspelled on it (Proniek)" (139).[29] Already when Pronek leaves the plane he is interpellated wrongly and as a consequence helplessly agrees to this "misspelled" identity which follows him wherever he goes in the US: "Pronek walked up to him and said, 'I am that person.'" (139). After the connecting flight to Washington, Pronek encounters a similar situation: "Behind a frail, long, black ribbon, there stood a man with Pronek's name (misspelled as 'Pronak'), followed by a question mark" (145). While the protagonist is thus reduced to a question mark, the subtle and ironic dislocation of Pronek

New Anglophone Literature from the Balkans **109**

by the repeated misspelling of his name indicates how issues of language are intertwined with unequal power relations for migrants in the contact zone. It is striking that initially it is not the migrant who encounters language problems, but the Americans do not make any effort to address Pronek correctly.

The American ignorance of world politics is presented in a satirical form as communication problems throughout the plot. American speculations about the war in Bosnia fuelled by prejudices make it impossible for Pronek to share anything about his country:

"I didn't know you could watch American movies there [in Sarajevo]," Reg Buttler said. "We could." "So what's gonna happen there?" Milius asked. "I don't know," Pronek said. "Thousands of years of hatred," Reg Buttler said and shook his head compassionately. "I can't understand a damn thing." Pronek didn't know what to say. "Hell, I'll call General Schwarzkopf to see what we can do there. Maybe we can go there and kick some ass," Milius said. "Like we kicked Saddam's ass," said Reg Buttler.

(153)

Pronek's inability to provide an explanation of the Bosnian War testifies both to the complexity of the political situation and to Pronek's inability to express himself. The claim that " 'They just hate each other over there'" (173) reveals how the Western conception of the Balkans as irrevocably Other functions and testifies to the stereotypical tropes of Balkanism which particularly denote backwardness and barbarism, savagery and hatred. Language misunderstandings are continually paired with ignorance and a racist form of Othering, hence actualising Žižek's provocative statement "So Balkan is always the Other."[30] In particular, seemingly funny misunderstandings govern the plot:

"So what's going on in Czechoslovakia?" Andrea's mother asked. "Yugoslavia, Mom, Yugoslavia," Andrea said. "I read about it, I tried to understand it, but I simply can't," Andrea's father said. "Thousands of years of hatred, I guess." "It's a sad saga," Andrea's mother said. "It's hard for us to understand, because we're so safe here." "It's mind-boggling," Andrea's father said. "I hope it is over before we have to get involved."

(177)

This dialogue, which leaves Pronek out, is significant for the construction of a space of Othering and projection based on ignorance and a sense of American superiority. Dialogues – or rather monologues – along those lines admit to ignorance based on a predefined set of opinions: Instead of a political reality, the Yugoslav Wars are a far away "saga" in which the Balkans are once

110 Miriam Wallraven

again regarded as characterised by barbarism and hatred. Repeatedly confronted with language problems and wilful ignorance, Pronek is condemned to silence.

Apart from misunderstandings that prove fundamental for the deployment of the narrative, the migrational metamultilingual mode also encompasses the exploration of how the loss of language affects identity. Through watching TV and reading newspaper coverages about the war in Bosnia, Pronek develops an estranged relationship to his home country, while at the same time remaining a mute stranger in the US. The narrator hints at the signs of trauma, such as survivor's guilt and dissociation (193–4), whereas Pronek himself remains silent; hence, the "unspeakable" of trauma[31] is intensified by the repeated "culture shocks" (142).

A central situation in the story highlights the migrant's position in-between, when two realities come into conflict: While faced with traumatising images in the media of "a man in a Serbian concentration camp" (188) which he is unable to process by speaking about them, an American customer complains that someone has put the wrong kind of lettuce on his sandwich:

> "Excuse me, but this is not romain lettuce. This is iceberg lettuce. What do you have to say about that?" [...] "Nothing." "I'd like my Turkey Dijon with romain lettuce, please," the man said. "What's difference?" Pronek said. "Excuse me?" the man raised his voice, his double chin doubly corrugated in disbelief. "Romaine lettuce, iceberg lettuce, what's difference?" with a sudden vision of stuffing the lettuce leaf into the man's mouth. "May I talk to someone who can speak English, please?" [...] He [Pronek] wanted to say something, something clever that would smash the man, but could not think of any English words that could convey the magnitude of the absurdity, other than: "Romaine lettuce, iceberg lettuce, what's difference?" He kept mumbling it to himself, like a magic word that would make him fly, and wobbled away in a vain hope that the man might just give up.
>
> *(189)*

The absurdity of the situation based – once again – on a misunderstanding at once highlights the power difference between Americans and migrants; it underscores Pronek's position between cultures as well as his speechlessness. Two questions are indicative of the deeper layers of the contact zone characterised by "highly asymmetrical relations of domination and subordination."[32] The question "What do you have to say about that?" reaches further than this particular instance: All that he might have to say about discrimination and the American sense of entitlement which clashes with the war in Bosnia is expressed by one question and then by silence. Pronek's question: "What's difference?" likewise gains a deeper significance as a fundamental question about cultural and linguistic difference that he, perceived as the

Other, constantly has to face. The fact that Americans can distinguish between two similar kinds of lettuce but not between countries underscores a stance that is not interested in anything than convenient consumption. Pronek's repetition of the grammatically wrong phrase emphasises his speechlessness; he is reduced to "mumbling" and the crucial question fails to act as a "magic word" to save him from being fired.

Several instances of miscommunication that punctuate the plot amount to metareflections on language, which is the main feature of the migrational metamultilingual mode. At one point, the author writes himself into the text as an alter ego, as a migrant co-worker with the name Hemon from the Dominican Republic. This funny figure can be read as an instance of highlighting the common fate of migrants, such as the exploitation in menial jobs and once again language problems, since "[a]t their lunch breaks, Pronek and Hemon would sit in bilingual silence" (185). The "bilingual silence" hence unites the migrants and becomes significant for texts governed by the migrational metamultilingual mode.

In this way, this mode is not only characterised by severe misunderstandings and communication problems, a loss of language leading to silence and a struggle for identity, as well as constant metareflections about language, but one final criterion of this mode is the struggle for language that extends to writing in the contact zone: "'Andrea told us you were a writer,' Andrea's mother said. [...] 'I was,' Pronek said." (176). Pronek's simple answer shows that he does not write any longer since having migrated. The struggle for a language evokes further metareflections about writing in English that transcend the textual level of the characters and includes the extratextual level of the author and the genesis of the text itself: "Discussion so far would suggest that the multilingual world at least *seems* to be a blessing for Hemon. His fictional characters are, however, rarely equally fortunate,"[33] Miočević states. The migrational metamultilingual mode is based on this tension which turns out to be productive for many authors of what has been described as new world literature who as language-changers[34] expand the Anglophone literary canon.

"The Familiar Silence" and Defamiliarisation in Exile: Yugoslavia Meets Australia in A. S. Patrić's Black Rock White City *(2015)*

In contrast to Aleksandar Hemon, A. S. Patrić is a second-generation immigrant who explains that "[m]y parents immigrated in the early seventies and I met refugees from the Bosnian war in the late nineties. [...] *Black Rock White City* is a Melbourne novel and I'd worry if readers picked it up expecting a story about Bosnia."[35] For him, a "Melbourne novel" does not preclude but include migrant experience. For the main characters in *Black Rock White City*, however, Australian life governed by a monolingual paradigm and their previous lives in Yugoslavia together with their mother tongue are presented as irreconcilable until they undergo a process that can be read

112 Miriam Wallraven

with the parameters of the migrational metamultilingual mode. Jovan and Suzana's Brakočević are academics (he is also a former poet and she an aspiring novelist) who come from Belgrade but who lived in Sarajevo when the Balkan Wars began. In the war, they lost their children; Suzana was raped and Jovan tortured. After migrating to Melbourne, both are forced to take on menial jobs, while their marriage, characterised by mutual silence triggered by trauma and the difficult immigrant experience, is on the verge of breaking apart. The novel's realism, however, is interrupted by a mysterious thriller element that pivots on language. Disturbing poetic graffiti keep appearing in the hospital where Jovan works as a janitor: sprayed on the wall, written in blood, or carved into a mutilated corpse. Jovan has to clean the place, and feeling more and more threatened by the graffiti and the mysterious sprayer, he is roused from his resignation by being forced to reflect on his life. In the meantime, Suzana is likewise triggered to break the silence and begins to write in both Serbian and English.

The initial silence of the characters in-between cultures is once again caused by communication problems that govern the contact zone in the novel and eventually make real contact impossible. Not only does Jovan encounter problems to express himself in English, but the communication problems on the Australian side already begin – as in "Blind Jozef Pronek and Dead Souls" – with the pronunciation of Jovan's name:

> Many of the hospital's employees speak to Jovan as though his slow, thick words are the result of brain damage. When attempting to pronounce his name they become retarded themselves – "Jo ... Ja ... Joh-von. Ja-va. Ah, fuck, we'll call you Joe." "What is hard to speak Yo-vahn? Jovan. The sounds all in English." [...] "It matters. I hate the fucking 'Joe'."
>
> (3)[36]

Here, the negative perception of Jovan clashes with the Australians' inability to even attempt to pronounce his name correctly. Being multilingual – Jovan also speaks German and Russian – does not prevent discrimination; as Suzana remarks: "It could almost make her laugh to think how useless all his languages were to him here in Australia" (169).

Apart from that, prejudices flanked by an ignorance of the political situation in Yugoslavia characterise the Australians similar to the Americans in Hemon's story. Hence, dialogue is marked as impossible from the beginning:

> There's no conversation. Nothing can change a mind made in ignorance, but Jovan wishes he could speak anyway. To explain that there had been lots of ordinary people with ordinary religion, who started killing each other, for reasons less and less clear as more and more people died.
>
> (114)

New Anglophone Literature from the Balkans **113**

Although "Jovan wishes he could speak anyway," he remains silent. Ultimately, this combination of communication problems and a discrimination of migrants constitutes the first characteristic of the migrational metamultilingual mode for foregrounding the dynamics between silence and multilingualism.

The novel exhibits the division of the two languages and two worlds of past and present, of Yugoslavia and Australia, and for much of the plot for Jovan "[t]he two worlds drift further and further apart" (125). This seeming irreconcilability caused by migration and trauma results in silence: "The familiar silence goes on now" (71). Only when Jovan is confronted with the graffiti he has to wash away is he forced to face his memories which he cannot erase:

> **The dead will not bother you. The dead have left you a world.**
> **The dead will welcome you. The dead have slept here. The dead have**
> **been born here. The dead look like you. The dead have the same**
> **names. The dead already own your father. The dead have**
> **already fucked your mother.**

(9)

This text is sprayed on the hospital wall in an empty room for children and can be connected to the death of Jovan's and Suzana's children that forms the roots of their trauma. It seems to refer to the world left after experiencing the trauma, particularly the process of emigrating from Yugoslavia but also to imply that the two protagonists already appear dead due to their silence.

More graffiti cut into a dead body is presented as a cruel as well as a displaced message:

> The hospital discovers a body on a trolley in the lobby on the weekend.
> Cut into the flesh with a scalpel, from throat to navel, is the word

> I
> N
> S
> P
> I
> R
> A
> T
> I
> O
> N.

(11)

114 Miriam Wallraven

This "strangely inappropriate word" (11) testifies to the defamiliarisation: Message and medium do not fit. In Russian formalism, according to Shklovsky, "[t]he purpose of art is to impart the sensation of things as they are perceived and not as they are known."[37] This conceptual framework of defamiliarisation is conceived as presenting the common and familiar in an unfamiliar way, so the world can be seen differently and in turn effect a change in perception.

More graffiti appears to refer to identity and hence highlights Jovan's alienation from his past and indeed his present life:

Do You know Me
Do You know
Do You
Do
I.

(25)

The fact that this graffiti is placed on an optometrist's eye chart indicates how Jovan is forced to open his eyes to the past and to the future. In the process, Jovan thus moves from a feeling of alienation and displacement to reflections on himself, which is actualised in the end: The perpetrator turns out to be one of the surgeons who only briefly features as a character and whose trajectories are not explored. Merely employed as a catalyst, the graffiti sprayer can be read as a deus ex machina in a twisted sense. The whole detective plot in this way pivots on metareflections on language and writing in different forms. They are triggered by defamiliarisation since "[t]he technique of art is to make objects 'unfamiliar'."[38] Here, the object is language itself which entails the defamiliarisation of everything connected with it, particularly the past and experiences of migration in the contact zone. By such instances of defamiliarisation, the "familiar silence" (71) is ended.

Asserting the importance of writing and language, the novel also explores the position of the migrant author: "Jovan had been a poet in Yugoslavia when that was still a country. [...] In Australia, he never commits a word to paper. He finds himself recalling phrases, some old, some new, playing them over and again in his mind" (3). When Jovan remains silent and has stopped writing, the graffiti sprayer's expression comes to substitute Jovan's, which forces Jovan to recover what he has lost, since in the beginning it appears as if "[e]verything that he has been serious about, all his work, [was] left behind with his native tongue" (95). From this point onwards, "Obliteration. Oblivion" (183), as one piece of graffiti says, is no longer an option.

In contrast to Jovan, Suzana begins to write in English and admits that "[t]he truth is that she's falling deeper in love with the English language. Her native Serbian is tied into everything she was and everything she had already thought and done" (89). Her very act of taking up her writing in Serbian alongside writing in English signifies her readiness to connect the two places and phases of her life. With that, she becomes truly bilingual. Significantly, the confrontation of her traumatic past in Yugoslavia is expressed by her beginning to write a historical novel set in Belgrade: "All of these new pages in Serbian. She will translate them into English for her second draft" (163). Not only is writing in one's native language presented as a powerful agent in the formation of memory in a situation of displacement, but by the act of translating her Serbian historical novel into English, she eventually translates her past into her present and Belgrade, the White City, into the space of Black Rock in Melbourne.

Such metareflections on writing in several languages that are characteristic of the migrational metamultilingual mode are intensified by intertextuality on different levels. Not only is Suzana's writing triggered by a historical novel in Serbian – Milosh Tsernianski's *Migrations* – but a quotation by Ivo Andrić before the beginning of the novel on the one hand prefigures the interweaving of the pain of migration and trauma with writing:

> "*Wherever I look there are poems –*
> *whatever I touch is pain.*
> IVO ANDRIĆ."
> (n. pag.)

On the other hand, this reference as well as the numerous other references to Andrić – winner of the Nobel Prize in Literature in 1961 – are deployed for creating a bridge between Serbian literature and world literature. Only after the intrusion of the metareflections on language triggered by the graffiti sprayer is this bridge accessible to Suzana, who thus moves from silence to bilingualism.

The migrational metamultilingual mode, then, furnishes an effective vehicle for structuring this process as a journey of migration into silence and out of it. Therefore, the novel moves from the exploration of misunderstandings and communication problems to a negotiation of a state in-between (which results in silence) to metareflections about language and writing that are reinforced by intertextual connections. In the end, the text depicts how the characters move from a "familiar silence" to a yet unfamiliar future with bilingual means of expression and ultimately located between the places of the title, between Melbourne and Belgrade. Understood in this sense, the "Melbourne novel" is a novel of Yugoslavia, too, and in essence a novel of migration.

Conclusion: A Balkan Turn and Metamultilingual Writing in World Anglophone Studies

In German literary studies, a "Balkan Turn"[39] and an "Eastern Turn"[40] have already been discussed, since German-speaking literature with a Balkan origin has turned out to have a significant impact on German literature as a whole. An analysis of English-speaking authors with a Balkan background such as Hemon or Patrić demonstrates why an exploration of such a turn is also necessary in order to gain a more comprehensive view of Anglophone literature from non-postcolonial areas influenced by worldwide processes of migration.

Discussions about new conceptualisations of Anglophone studies have led to a closer examination of the advantages of a movement from postcolonial to World Anglophone. In this context, Walkowitz maintains that the concept of World Anglophone "can be an important catalyst for fresh questions about the organization of our intellectual work, in particular the organization of our work around the unit of the single language."[41] Including World Anglophone to a greater extent in the discussion would definitely widen the scope to include Anglophone literature from a non-postcolonial and instead from a more ambiguous context such as the in-between space of the Balkans. Such a "potential mode of inquiry"[42] requires differentiated parameters in order to address the literary strategies this kind of literature exhibits. "The emergent literature of deterriorialized peoples and literary studies beyond the confines of national literatures have as yet no name or configuration," Seyhan stated in 2001.[43] Since then, many studies have attempted to address this kind of writing as migrant literature, new world literature, or transcultural literature. In this context, exploring the migrational metamultilingual mode as structuring such Anglophone texts written by multilingual authors in-between cultural affiliations can serve an important purpose, namely that of identifying the interplay of the communication problems governing the contact zones, the (temporary) loss of language leading to silence as the main plot trigger, and the explicit metareflections, the "speaking about languages"[44] culminating in the thematisation of authorship between languages. Paying attention to this mode can contribute to highlighting the literary strategies resulting from and dealing with migration in a globalised world, since "[m]igration is [...] a key concept in understanding an important and unavoidable aspect of world literature and world culture: world literature is literature (and people) on the move."[45] Questions of how to narrate migration and of the role of literature are particularly salient in the contemporary political context in which an estimated 82 million people in the world are forcibly displaced.[46] The near future will present us with more stories reconfiguring the experience of migration, particularly for readers in English as the global language.

Notes

1 See for example Sigrid Löffler, *Die neue Weltliteratur und ihre großen Erzähler* (München: C. H. Beck, 2014): 321–335, and Anne Cornelia Kenneweg, "Im Niemandsland: Poetik der Zugehörigkeit bei Aleksandar Hemon," in *Jugoslawien – Libanon: Verhandlung von Zugehörigkeit in den Künsten fragmentierter Kulturen*, edited by Miranda Jakisa and Andreas Pflitsch (Berlin: Kadmos, 2012): 185.

2 Seila Rizvic, "'Migration Necessitates Narration': An Interview with Aleksandar Hemon," *Hazlitt*, 17 June 2019, https://hazlitt.net/feature/migration-necessitates-narration-interview-aleksandar-hemon.

3 See Löffler, *Weltliteratur*, 15.

4 Axel Englund and Anders Olsson, "Introduction: Twentieth-Century Ruptures of Location and Locution," in *Languages of Exile: Migration and Multilingualism in Twentieth-Century Literature*, edited by Axel Englund and Anders Olsson (Oxford: Peter Lang, 1994): 1.

5 Vesna Goldsworthy, *Inventing Ruritania: The Imperialism of the Imagination* (New Haven: Yale University Press, 1998): xxii–xxiii.

6 Since Maria Todorova in her seminal study *Imagining the Balkans* (Oxford: Oxford University Press, 1997) includes Albania, Romania, Greece as well as most of former Yugoslavia (31), I also work with this designation which takes into account the historical definitions and self-definitions.

7 Goldsworthy, *Inventing Ruritania*, xxvi.

8 Dragana Obradović, *Writing the Yugoslav Wars: Literature, Postmodernism, and the Ethics of Representation* (Toronto: U of Toronto P, 2016): 136.

9 Todorova, *Imagining*, 13.

10 Todorova, *Imagining*, 14.

11 Andrew Hammond, *The Debated Lands: British and American Representations of the Balkans* (Cardiff: U of Wales P, 2007): 8.

12 Hammond, *The Debated Lands*, 3.

13 Hammond, *The Debated Lands*, 3.

14 Slavoj Žižek, "The Spectre of Balkan," *The Journal of the International Institute* 6.2 (1999), https://quod.lib.umich.edu/j/jii/4750978.0006.202?view=text;rgn=main.

15 Žižek, "The Spectre."

16 See Goldsworthy, *Inventing*, 9. Also compare Obradović, *Writing the Yugoslav Wars*, 136.

17 Goldsworthy, *Inventing*, 9.

18 Mary Louise Pratt, *Imperial Eyes: Travel Writing and Transculturation* (London: Routledge, 1992): 4.

19 Roman Jacobson, "Closing Statement: Linguistics and Poetics," in *Style in Language*, edited by Thomas A. Sebeok (Cambridge, MA: M.I.T. Press, 1964): 356.

20 Jacobson, "Closing Statement," 356.

21 Yasemin Yildiz, *Beyond the Mother Tongue: The Postmonolingual* Condition (New York: Fordham University Press, 2012): 3–4.

22 Yildiz, *Beyond the Mother Tongue*, 4.

23 Yildiz, *Beyond the Mother Tongue*, 4.

24 Yildiz, *Beyond the Mother Tongue*, 5.

25 Elke Sturm-Trigonakis, *Comparative Cultural Studies and the New Weltliteratur* (West Lafayette: Purdue University Press, 2013): 85.

26 Sturm-Trigonakis, *Comparative Cultural Studies*, 85.

27 Löffler, *Weltliteratur*, 16.

28 Rizvic, "Migration."

118 Miriam Wallraven

29 All otherwise unmarked references in this chapter refer to Aleksandar Hemon, "Blind Jozef Pronek and Dead Souls," in *The Question of Bruno* (London: Picador, 2000): 137–213.
30 Žižek, "Spectre."
31 For a conception of trauma as unspeakable due to its inaccessibility compare for example Cathy Caruth, "Introduction," in *Trauma: Explorations in* Memory, edited by Cathy Caruth (Baltimore: Johns Hopkins University Press, 1995): 10.
32 Pratt, *Imperial Eyes*, 4.
33 Ljubica Miočević, "'What's Difference?': On Language and Identity in the Writings of Aleksandar Hemon," in *Languages of Exile: Migration and Multilingualism in Twentieth-Century Literature*, edited by Axel Englund and Anders Olsson (Oxford: Peter Lang, 1994): 67.
34 Löffler, *Weltliteratur*, 15.
35 Gerard Elson, "Dissolving into Humanity: An interview with A.S. Patrić," *KYD*, 4 May 2015, www.killyourdarlings.com.au/2015/05/dissolving-into-humanity-an-interview-with-a-s-Patrić/
36 All otherwise unmarked references in this chapter refer to A. S. Patrić, *Black Rock White City* (Brooklyn: Melville House, 2017).
37 Viktor Shklovsky, "Art as Technique," in *Literary Theory: An Anthology*, edited by Julie Rivkin and Michael Ryan (Oxford: Blackwell, 1998): 18.
38 Shklovsky, "Art as Technique," 18.
39 Boris Previšić, "Poetik der Marginalität: Balkan Turn gefällig?" in *Von der nationalen zur internationalen Literatur: Transkulturelle deutschsprachige Literatur und Kultur im Zeitalter globaler Migration*, edited by Helmut Schmitz (Amsterdam: Rodopi, 2009): 189–203.
40 Brigid Haines, "Introduction: The Eastern European Turn in Contemporary German-Language Literature," *German Life and Letters* 68:2 (2015): 145–153.
41 Rebecca L. Walkowitz, *"Response: World Anglophone is a Theory,"* *Interventions* 20.3 (2018): 363.
42 Akshya Saxena,"A Worldly Anglophony: Empire and Englishes," *Interventions* 20.3 (2018): 317.
43 Azade Seyhan, *Writing Outside the Nation* (Princeton: Princeton University Press, 2001): 9.
44 Sturm-Trigonakis, *Comparative Cultural Studies*, 85.
45 Karen-Margrethe Simonsen and Jakob Stougaard-Nielsen, "Introduction: World Literature and World Culture," in *World Literature World Culture*, edited by Karen-Margrethe Simonsen and Jakob Stougaard-Nielsen (Aarhus: Aarhus University Press, 2008): 17.
46 Compare the data provided by the World Health Organisation: https://www.who.int/health-topics/refugee-and-migrant-health

Bibliography

Caruth, Cathy. "Introduction." In *Trauma: Explorations in Memory*, edited by Cathy Caruth. Baltimore: Johns Hopkins University Press, 1995: 3–12.
Elson, Gerard. "Dissolving into Humanity: An Interview with A.S. Patrić." *KYD*, 4 May 2015. www.killyourdarlings.com.au/2015/05/dissolving-into-humanity-an-interview-with-a-s-patric/ (last accessed 10 April 2024).
Englund, Axel and Anders Olsson. "Introduction: Twentieth-Century Ruptures of Location and Locution." In *Languages of Exile: Migration and Multilingualism in Twentieth-Century Literature*, edited by Axel Englund and Anders Olsson. Oxford: Peter Lang, 1994: 1–18.

Goldsworthy, Vesna. *Inventing Ruritania: The Imperialism of the Imagination.* New Haven: Yale University Press, 1998.

Haines, Brigid. "Introduction: The Eastern European Turn in Contemporary German-Language Literature." *German Life and Letters* 68.2 (2015): 145–153.

Hammond, Andrew. *The Debated Lands: British and American Representations of the Balkans.* Cardiff: U of Wales P, 2007.

Hemon, Aleksandar. "Blind Jozef Pronek and Dead Souls." In *The Question of Bruno.* London: Picador, 2000: 137–213.

Jacobson, Roman. "Closing Statement: Linguistics and Poetics." In *Style in Language*, edited by Thomas A. Sebeok. Cambridge, MA: M.I.T. Press, 1964: 350–377.

Kenneweg, Anne Cornelia. "Im Niemandsland: Poetik der Zugehörigkeit bei Aleksandar Hemon." In *Jugoslawien – Libanon: Verhandlung von Zugehörigkeit in den Künsten fragmentierter Kulturen*, edited by Miranda Jakisa and Andreas Pflitsch. Berlin: Kadmos, 2012: 185–203.

Löffler, Sigrid. *Die neue Weltliteratur und ihre großen Erzähler.* München: C. H. Beck, 2014.

Miočević, Ljubica. " 'What's Difference?': On Language and Identity in the Writings of Aleksandar Hemon." In *Languages of Exile: Migration and Multilingualism in Twentieth-Century Literature*, edited by Axel Englund and Anders Olsson. Oxford: Peter Lang, 1994: 55–79.

Obradović, Dragana. *Writing the Yugoslav Wars: Literature, Postmodernism, and the Ethics of Representation.* Toronto: U of Toronto P, 2016.

Patrić, A. S. *Black Rock White City.* Brooklyn: Melville House, 2017.

Pratt, Mary Louise. *Imperial Eyes: Travel Writing and Transculturation.* London: Routledge, 1992.

Previšić, Boris. "Poetik der Marginalität: Balkan Turn gefällig?" In *Von der nationalen zur internationalen Literatur: Transkulturelle deutschsprachige Literatur und Kultur im Zeitalter globaler Migration*, edited by Helmut Schmitz. Amsterdam: Rodopi, 2009: 189–203.

Rizvic, Seila. " 'Migration Necessitates Narration': An Interview with Aleksandar Hemon." *Hazlitt*, 17 June 2019. https://hazlitt.net/feature/migration-necessitates-narration-interview-aleksandar-hemon (last accessed 10 April 2024).

Saxena, Akshya. "A Worldly Anglophony: Empire and Englishes." *Interventions* 20.3 (2018): 317–324.

Seyhan, Azade. *Writing Outside the Nation.* Princeton: Princeton University Press, 2001.

Shklovsky, Viktor. "Art as Technique." In *Literary Theory: An Anthology*, edited by Julie Rivkin and Michael Ryan. Oxford: Blackwell, 1998: 17–23.

Simonsen, Karen-Margrethe and Jakob Stougaard-Nielsen. "Introduction: World Literature and World Culture." In *World Literature World Culture*, edited by Karen-Margrethe Simonsen and Jakob Stougaard-Nielsen. Aarhus: Aarhus University Press, 2008: 9–21.

Sturm-Trigonakis, Elke. *Comparative Cultural Studies and the New Weltliteratur.* West Lafayette: Purdue University Press, 2013.

Todorova, Maria. *Imagining the Balkans.* Oxford: Oxford University Press, 1997.

Walkowitz, Rebecca L. "Response: World Anglophone is a Theory." *Interventions* 20.3 (2018): 361–365.

Yildiz, Yasemin. *Beyond the Mother Tongue: The Postmonolingual Condition.* New York: Fordham University Press, 2012.

Žižek, Slavoj. "The Spectre of Balkan." *The Journal of the International Institute* (University of Michigan) 6/2 (1999). https://quod.lib.umich.edu/j/jii/4750978.0006.202?view=text;rgn=main (last accessed 10 April 2024).

7

INVISIBILISING FEMINISM IN TRANSLATION

Representation of Women in *Dreaming in Cuban* and *Soñar en cubano*[1]

María Escobar-Aguiar

Introduction

Over the last decades, special attention has been granted in translation studies to the relationship between gender and the discursive practice of translation, and, more specifically, to how social and cultural conceptions of the former affect the latter.[2] As a movement seeking to subvert unfair and oppressive social structures, feminism has evolved through the years in order to address new and varied materialisations of patriarchy in different socio-cultural, geo-political, and discursive contexts.[3] Translation, understood as a privileged space to critically analyse power structures and asymmetries bred by and between languages, plays a key role in feminism[4] – it has the capacity not only of contesting patriarchal norms and values but also of forging "cross-border feminist alliances."[5]

It is therefore relevant to analyse the role played by translation in the pro-duction of women narratives, so as to nourish a feminist translation histori-ography that challenges the hegemonic patriarchal literary and translational canon, weaves bonds of solidarity between marginalised subjects, and creates a theoretical space for feminist empowerment.[6] The analysis of the transla-tion of authors like Cristina García, a one-and-a-half generation[7] Cuban-U.S. American woman writer, allows us to explore the negotiation of the identities of women in Latinx communities within the United States both in English and Spanish. In this chapter, I will analyse selected extracts that deal with long-naturalised gender patterns in the first novel of Cristina García, *Dream-ing in Cuban*,[8] and its translation into Spanish, *Soñar en cubano*.[9] This first novel addresses different violences, demands, and gender expectations, mate-rialised in discourse, that contribute to the discursive configuration of female

DOI: 10.4324/9781003464037-10
This chapter has been made available under a CC-BY-NC-ND 4.0 license.

characters who are settled in conflict and tension, torn apart by two opposing forces – the Cuban and the U.S. American cultures and their associated languages. My central objective is, therefore, to ponder on the effect that the different textual and discursive materialisations of these conflicts in each language have on the disruptive force of the texts and the overall construction of a feminist literary and translational canon in the Anglophone and Hispanophone spheres.

Cristina García, A One-and-a-Half Generation Writer

Cristina García is, as she describes herself, a U.S. American, but with an accent.[10] Born in La Habana, Cuba, on 4 July 1958, she moved to New York in 1961, when her family fled Cuba and the Revolución with the first Cuban migratory wave. Her father was Guatemalan and her mother was Cuban, so her childhood was flooded with the Spanish language and stories about the island they had left. This childhood places the writer in the 1.5 generation,[11] that of children born on the island but raised and educated in the United States. The members of this generation are therefore marginal to both the old generation (that of people who migrated as adults) and the new one (that of children born in the new country). This in-betweenness,[12] this space between generations and cultures, left a deep mark on García, which materialises in her writing.

In 1984, García visited Cuba for the first time after having migrated in 1961. Eight years later, in 1992, she published her first novel, *Dreaming in Cuban*, with the renowned U.S. American publishing house Ballantine Books (Random House). She declared in an interview with Elinor Burkett, "I surprised myself by how Cuban the book turned out to be. [...] I don't remember growing up with a longing for Cuba, so I didn't realize how Cuban I was, how deep a sense I had of exile and longing."[13] With this first novel, García attempts to show that Cuba is more than just a polarity between revolutionaries and anti-revolutionaries, Castrists and anti-Castrists. Rather, she features a story that shows that there are as many ways to be Cuban as Cubans in a world in which cultural borders are ever more difficult to mark.

The English text was quickly translated into Spanish: *Soñar en cubano*, translated by Marisol Palés Castro, was published a year later by Espasa Calpe (Grupo Planeta). Cristina García herself has declared that the translation of her novels into Spanish, one of the languages of her childhood, is a necessary step towards the completion of her work, since that language is a part of her identity.[14] The translation of her work into Spanish has therefore a special importance, yet the translation of her work into Spanish has received almost no attention from academia so far, which has tended to focus on the literary analysis of her work. Thus, I seek to make a first contribution to the analysis of her translated work.

Writing Caribbean Women's Identity

Following Hall,[15] identity is not an essentialist concept but rather a positional and strategic one. Identities are multiple, and they change through context-specific discursive practices, rendering identity construction a process that comprises many instances of negotiation and translation.[16] Judith Butler asserts that gender identities are built in discourse by means of associations and reiterations of certain features that constitute regulatory fictions of sex and gender while disqualifying those features that subvert hegemonically established categories.[17] Moreover, following Alejo López, migratory processes reformulate the national identity patterns of migrants and of the societies to where they migrate, so that new transnational and hybrid identities are forged.[18] These new identities offer fresh and innovative aesthetic productions which account for their unique situation, and the construction and performance of gender identities is particularly significant in the discursive production of subjects that undergo migratory processes.

Silenced and oppressed by men in Western cultures, women have historically produced writings using hegemonic languages to account for their marginalisation and to claim access to public spheres.[19] Indeed, the struggle of women for the negotiation of their identity and their own image is a recurring topic among Caribbean women writers living in the United States.[20] Their women characters are fragmented by the effects of patriarchal societies of the Caribbean, on the one hand, and of the consumption culture and sexism of the United States, on the other. In this context, the identification with the beauty canon of Western cultures with which women are expected to comply implies the neglect of the African heritage of Caribbean cultures. Western patriarchal beauty standards are ruthless: bodies perceived as deviant are forced either to conform to an accepted body image, or they are neglected into non-existence.[21] As a consequence of these fragmentations and demands, women's bodies become "sites where violence and racism converge."[22] By means of their writing, Caribbean women aim at criticising the beauty conventions determined by the physical features of the dominant group[23] – the so-called "white" – which reject the image of Afro-American women. By denouncing the desire for "whiteness" and Western standards, they also attempt to reclaim and vindicate their Afro-Caribbean cultural inheritance. Their work is strong and feminist in that, by means of their writing, Caribbean women protect and keep their bodies safe from the objectification, domestication, and depersonalisation inherent to the U.S. and Caribbean – and, in fact, global – patriarchal systems.[24]

Very much like the works of her peers, the narrative of Cristina García does challenge, from within the Anglophone literary system, these harmful Western beauty standards and the patriarchal demands that go beyond any geopolitical border. The novel analysed in this chapter features women characters engaged in politics, art, religion, and the economy by means of a narrative that renders Cuban women's experiences historically and culturally significant.[25] Acknowledging the importance of these topics in the works of Caribbean women writers such as García, the analysis of *Dreaming in Cuban* and *Soñar en cubano* in this chapter focuses specifically on the construction of the image and representation of these women.

Translation and Feminism

Following Venuti, I understand translation as a political, cultural, and discursive practice which serves to support, transgress, rethink, or question the values of the target culture.[26] Both source text and translation advance aesthetic and cultural values that result from established hierarchies materialised in discourse.[27] From their social and professional contexts, translators assume the responsibility of socially and culturally reconstructing the author and their work, (ideally) conscious of the exercise of power that recreating the other's subjectivity implies.[28] Translation is, therefore, a political activity with rhetoric and ideological implications[29] that demands a repositioning derived from the affirmation of writers' and translators' linguistic and cultural identities.[30] If we see translation not as an instrument for interlinguistic communication but as a kind of literary activism in which "[t]ranslators are necessarily involved in a politics of transmission, in perpetuating or contesting the values which sustain our literary culture,"[31] it then becomes a rich field for the creation of new meanings and the performance and negotiation of cultural identities.

Over the last decades, the articulation of translation and feminisms under the light shed by these premises has remained a strong point on the translation studies agenda.[32] As a "substantial force and form of social justice activism against intersecting regimes of domination, both locally and transnationally,"[33] feminist translation plays a key role in challenging the "already existing directives" of gender – that socio-political construct that limits an individual's behaviour by deeming what is and what is not appropriate of their gender.[34] Feminist translation has, therefore, aimed at recovering women writers and translators invisibilised in dominant discourses, questioning feminist theories and practices, reflecting upon feminist translators' ethics and responsibility, examining linguistic gender representation in translation, analysing feminist and sexist translations, and promoting metaphors and myths around translation that challenge the traditional androcentric translation discourse.[35]

Acknowledging the need to address these issues from an intersectional perspective, transnational feminisms developed, comprising a set of situated theories and practices that approach gender oppression from many different angles. In this way, they aim at unveiling colonialist, neo-colonialist, and imperialist approaches and at decolonising the Western universal-intended character of hegemonic feminisms. From this perspective, translation is understood as a privileged space to critically analyse power structures and asymmetries,[36] challenge patriarchal norms and values, and forge transnational alliances.[37] Due to its potential for solidarity, the analysis and retrieval of women's writings and translations raises the interest of many feminist translators and scholars.[38]

The importance of doing research on translation studies as a means of unveiling the ways in which identities are constructed and of studying the performance and affirmation of these identities is thus evident. The literary production of women as a minority group[39] awakes a special interest, since for these groups, writing and translation are tools for remembering, re-historicising memory, and re-writing identities.[40] For the analysis of the selected fragments and their translations in this chapter, I will draw on the classification advanced by Marc Démont[41] for the different modes of translating so-called queer literature. Misrecognising translations ignore the queer features of the source text while producing a target text that is written from a hegemonic perspective, suppressing the disruptive force of the source text.[42] Minoritising translations seek to find strict word-for-word equivalences, rendering translations that are unidimensional, monosemic, and superficial in nature and ultimately assimilating the disruptive force of the source text. Last, queer translations acknowledge the potentially subversive text in all its queerness and seek to enhance it in the target text, allowing for multiple readings.

Drawing on Démont's classification, I will analyse the disruptive force of the narrative discursively built in these fragments and their translation, focusing on the creation and negotiation of women's identities, and I will reflect on their impact on the overall text in order to determine whether the translation of the source text has hindered, ignored, or enhanced its disruptive and feminist components.

Dreaming in Cuban and *Soñar en cubano*

Dreaming in Cuban features the stories of several generations of Cuban families, crossed by the history of Cuba, the Revolución, the migratory waves; the longings of exile; and the norms and demands of different countries, cultures, languages, and traditions. The novel leads readers into the intimate worlds of women characters through internal monologues and non-verbal resources such as art, telepathic communication, and *santería*, one of the greatest heritages of Afro-Caribbean cultures. The relationships between all these women are fractured by national, geographic, and economic borders. Bearing restraints and demands of both U.S. American and Cuban cultures, framed in larger Anglophone and Hispanophone spheres, these *mestizas*[43] build their personal and community identities through different discursive practices which in turn reflect what is expected from women in each culture.

García's characters inhabit public and private, central and peripheral spaces, and their stories shed light on the many aspects of the process of women's transnational identity construction. If the Caribbean is a linguistically and culturally fluid space, García extends its hybridity to the U.S. by presenting the point of view of several women characters of different ages and opposing opinions and the cross-cultural, cross-border, and cross-linguistic solidarity bonds between them, thus building a new transnational and multilingual gynocentric homeland.[44] Just as Cuba is depicted as a mythic and changing hybrid space which challenges male dominant conceptions of the nation, the bodies of women are presented as hybrid, fluid, mythic, too – a rich field to dispute the dominant patriarchal standards.

This first novel of Cristina García is feminist in that it explicitly addresses and denounces multiple materialisations of patriarchy in both Cuba and the United States at different stages of their history. It brings to the spotlight women as subjects who have traditionally been silenced and excluded from history and denounces and criticises the violence inflicted upon them in different political and economic systems.[45] *Dreaming in Cuban* is also transnational in that it recognises the power threads interwoven between these two countries by women at discursive, economic, sociocultural and geopolitical levels.

The following subsections offer some fragments of the novel that challenge cultural demands on women and, therefore, play a key role in constructing a new gynocentric, transnational, multilingual landscape.

Example A: Determination

After marrying the son of a Cuban wealthy family, Lourdes started working hard to refurbish the old and abandoned ranch of her husband's family. These fragments depict the scene (emphasis added):

After her honeymoon, she got right to work on the Puente ranch. She reviewed the ledgers, fired the cheating accountant, and took over the books herself.	*Al regresar de su luna de miel, consideró que tenía el derecho de inmiscuirse en la hacienda de los Puente.* Revisó las cuentas, echó al contable tramposo, y tomó las riendas de los libros. (177)

The English text shows the determination with which Lourdes started working to improve her husband's patrimony, which is now hers, too. However, a completely different view of the scene is favoured in the translated text

126 María Escobar-Aguiar

by means of two textual procedures. First, the comparative reading shows that the translation performs two additions, one implicit and one explicit. Where the English text features the phrase "get right to" (that is, do something immediately), the text in Spanish, by means of an implicit addition of a definite article, features a translation of "get *the* right to" (that is, "*tener el derecho*"), rendering a completely different meaning. This is accompanied by the addition in the Spanish text of the verb "*consideró*" ("judged"), absent in the English text. Second, the word "work" that allows for a discursive image of Lourdes as an active, hands-on woman is rendered as "*inmiscuirse*" ("to intrude").

These additions and alterations open up a different chain of signifiers that create in Spanish a discursive image of Lourdes as an intrusive and abusive woman who unrightfully takes control over her husband's – a man's – patrimony. Whereas the character in the English text is depicted as a woman who, breaking with patriarchal expectations, does not obediently follow her husband nor abides by his wishes, the result of these two procedures is a text that favours a judgemental view of Lourdes's independence and proactive attitude and a sexist stance in implying that even when she has ownership rights over the ranch, it is improper of her – a woman – to exercise them.

The determination of a strong female character is, thus, not only invisibilised but even condemned in the Spanish text, eradicating the potentially disruptive force of translation. The fragments that follow exemplify the violence of the discursive materiality of the English text that characterises this novel.

Example B: Sexual Violence

At one station there was a little girl, about six, who wore only a dirty rag that didn't cover her private parts. She stretched out her hands as the passengers left the train, and in the bustle I saw a man *stick his finger in her*.	En una estación había una niña como de seis años que llevaba puesto tan sólo un sucio trapo que apenas le cubría siquiera sus partes privadas. Tendía las manos a medida que los pasajeros iban saliendo del tren, y en medio del ajetreo alcancé a ver a un hombre que *le puso encima sus repugnantes manazas*. (84, emphasis added in both versions)

As the comparative reading shows, the act of rape featured in this scene is almost completely left out in the translation. While the English text shows how an adult man can carry out an act of paedophilia in the middle of a public and crowded place and go unpunished, this denouncement is largely mitigated in the translation, and only a faint and rather vague trace of this act of sexual violence remains. The complete verbal phrase is transformed by

Invisibilising Feminism in Translation **127**

means of two main modifications: generalisation, for the finger becomes the man's "disgusting hands," and inversion, for the direction and movement of the hands in Spanish are opposite to those described in the English text. It is only from the comparative reading of these fragments that the reader is able to unveil an instance of mitigation of the sexual violence present in the English text.

In this sense, we could argue that this translation into Spanish responds to alleged cultural sensitivities in the target culture to the point of invisibilising the disruptive force of the narrative regarding sexual violence against women. The last set of examples refers to another recurring topic in Caribbean women's writings – the discursive construction of a non-hegemonic female body.

Example C: Bodies

The following fragments deal with the description of Lourdes's gaze regarding her strabismus (emphasis added):

Suddenly Lourdes's *wandering eye*, like a wary spy, fixes on the quarters sliding across the counter to Maribel.	De repente, el *ojo observador* de Lourdes, cual espía cauteloso, se fija en las monedas de 25 centavos que se deslizan sobre el mostrador en dirección a Maribel. (98)
Her *wandering eye* would transform the stalagmites and stalactites into sculptures of hanging alligators, witches' claws, or the face of her hated history teacher.	Sus *ojos errantes* sabían transformar las estalagmitas y las estalactitas en esculturas de lagartos colgantes, en garras de brujas, o en la cara de su maestro de historia más odiado. (297)
"May I help you?" she asks, startled by Lourdes's *drifting eye*.	– ¿La puedo ayudar en algo? – pregunta asustada al ver los *ojos desorbitados* de Lourdes. (301)

In the translated text, this feature of Lourdes's body, for whom complying with Western beauty standards and being accepted by others are of crucial importance, is absent. While the adjectives of the English text accompanying the noun "eye" clearly indicate Lourdes's strabismus, the adjectives of the Spanish text portray her gaze as observing and anxious. Lourdes's body is therefore made to conform to these standards, resulting in the misrecognition of the disruptivity of a body that is deviant from U.S. cultural expectations and, ultimately, its invisibilisation.

By opening a completely different set of semantic associations, the subversive content of the text is transformed in translation by means of a conservative strategy to hide not only what is thought of as a deviant body but also

128 María Escobar-Aguiar

the challenge to unbearable demands imposed on the bodies of women itself. That is, a body that does not conform to Western standards is written into existence in the novel, while it is erased into non-existence in the translation.

Conclusion

The misrecognition and mitigation of the disruptive force of the narrative in the selected fragments in Spanish are representative of the overall translation of the novel. The textual operations analysed here favour the mitigation and even invisibilisation of the discursive violence of the English text, the bodies that do not adjust to the established Western beauty standards, and the attitudes deemed improper for a woman in patriarchal cultures. In this sense, this translation is misrecognising in that the potentially subversive content of the text is conservatively invisibilised.

Just as the complexity of Cubanness questions binary approaches to the history of the island, the plurality of women's voices, characters, and bodies calls into question the essentialism of hegemonic patriarchal discourses. However, not only could no textual operations to highlight the transnational feminist content of the novel be found, but also the potentially subversive discursive content is dismantled, enhancing a conservative and sexist ideology that is detrimental to both feminist movements and women in general.

As has been argued throughout these pages, translation is potentially a powerful and rich form of activism. Transnational feminist translation, in particular, highlights the cruciality of nourishing local feminist movements with the experiences, writings, and theories of fellow movements developed and developing in other parts of the globe. Unfortunately, in the translated text of this feminist novel we could not reconstruct an engagement in a gender or feminist agenda. On the contrary, the translation into Spanish of *Dreaming in Cuban* dampens the feminist alliances forged in the English text. Even more, the images of women who clash with the reigning hegemonic imaginary are suppressed into an image that not only adjusts to this imaginary but also strengthens it. In consequence, the literary genealogy of feminist translated works in Spanish suffers from an important missing link in its development over the years. The Spanish-speaking audience, therefore, is deprived of a literary piece of writing that contributes to the construction, performance, and negotiation of transnational and feminist identities in an ever-more culturally and linguistically hybrid world.

Given the importance assigned by the author to the Spanish language in her life and in her narrative, the disruptive, transnational, and feminist nature of her work suffers a setback due to the sexism advanced in the Spanish translation of her first novel. By curtailing the polysemy of the English text, the cross-border feminist bonds created by Cristina García's writing are cut off, dividing, once again, the cultures and languages associated

Invisibilising Feminism in Translation **129**

with the nationalities that constitute her identity. The Anglophone literary world, therefore, receives a transnational feminist text that challenges Western androcentric narratives and nourishes Anglophone feminist movements while the Hispanophone world is deprived of such literary influence, encountering, rather, an obstacle in the transnational construction of a gynocentric land.

Notes

1 This research was conducted as a junior member of the research project "Escritura de minorías, ethos y (auto)traducción" [Minor literatures, ethos and (auto)translation], accredited by Universidad Nacional de La Plata (UNLP) and directed by Dr María Laura Spoturno. This research was supported by the Consejo Interuniversitario Nacional, Argentina.
2 See, for example, Lori Chamberlain, "Gender and the Metaphorics of Translation," *Signs: Journal of Women in Culture and Society* XIII.3 (1988): 454–472; Sherry Simon, *Gender in Translation* (London and New York: Routledge, 1996); Luise von Flotow, *Translation and Gender: Translating in the Era of Feminism* (Manchester and Ottawa: St. Jerome Publishing and University of Ottawa, 1997); Sonia Alvarez, Claudia de Lima Costa, Verónica Feliu, Rebecca Hester, Norma Klahn and Millie Thayer, eds., *Translocalities/translocalidades: Feminist Politics of Translation in the Latin/a Americas* (Durham: Duke University Press, 2014); Luise von Flotow and Farzaneh Farahzad, eds., *Translating Women: Different Voices and New Horizons* (London and New York: Routledge, 2017); Cibele de Guadalupe Sousa Araújo, Luciana de Mesquita Silva and Dennys Silva-Reis, "Translation Studies and Black Women in the Light of Feminism," *Revista Ártemis* 27.1 (2019): 14–24; Olga Castro, Emek Ergun, Luise von Flotow and María Laura Spoturno, "Towards Transnational Feminist Translation Studies," *Mutatis Mutandis: Revista Latinoamericana de Traducción* 13.1 (2020): 2–10; Pilar Godayol, *Feminismos y traducción (1965–1990)* (Granada: Comares, 2021).
3 Olga Castro and María Laura Spoturno, "Feminismos y traducción: apuntes conceptuales y metodológicos para una traductología feminista transnacional," *Mutatis Mutandis. Revista Latinoamericana de traducción* 13.1 (January–June 2020): 15, https://revistas.udea.edu.co/index.php/mutatismutandis/article/view/340988/20795805.
4 Alvarez et al., *Translocalities*, 557.
5 Olga Castro and Emek Ergun, "Translation and Feminism," in *The Routledge Handbook of Translation and Politics*, edited by Jonathan Evans and Fruela Fernández (London and New York: Routledge, 2018): 132, 133.
6 Godayol, *Feminismos*, XX.
7 Rubén G. Rumbaut, "Generation 1.5, Educational Experiences of," in *Encyclopedia of Diversity in Education*, edited by James A. Banks (Washington, DC: Sage Publications, 2012): 982.
8 Cristina García, *Dreaming in Cuban* (New York: Ballantine Books, Random House, 1992).
9 Cristina García, *Soñar en cubano*, translated by Marisol Palés (Madrid: Espasa Calpe, Grupo Planeta, 1993).
10 In this chapter, I have deliberately avoided the use of the demonym "American" as an equivalent of "U.S. American." This use of the word is abusive in that it excludes American peoples from their own continent in favour of the people of just one country. Cristina García, however, did use the term "American" in

130 María Escobar-Aguiar

the following interview: Cristina García, "The Nature of Inheritance," interview by Jessica Murphy, *The Atlantic*, April 2003, www.theatlantic.com/magazine/archive/2003/04/the-nature-of-inheritance/303087/.

11 Rumbaut, "Generation 1.5," 982.

12 Homi K. Bhabha, *El lugar de la cultura*, translated by César Aira (Buenos Aires: Manantial, 2002 [1994]): 18.

13 Cristina García, "Author Focuses on Cuban Nostalgia," interview by Knight Elinor Burkett, *Chicago Tribune*, 9 April 1992.

14 Cristina García, "Translation as Restoration," in *Voice-Overs: Translation and Latin American Literature*, edited by Daniel Balderston and Marcy Schwartz (Albany: State University of New York Press, 2012): 45.

15 Stuart Hall, "Who Needs 'Identity'?" in *Questions of Cultural Identity*, edited by Stuart Hall and Paul Du Gay (London: Sage Publications Ltd, 1996): 1.

16 María Laura Spoturno, "La construcción discursivo-enunciativa de las identidades culturales en *When I was Puerto Rican* y *Cuando era puertorriqueña* de Esmeralda Santiago," in *Escrituras de minorías, heterogeneidad y traducción*, coordinated by María Laura Spoturno (La Plata: Universidad de La Plata. Facultad de Humanidades y Ciencias de la Educación, 2018): 170.

17 Judith Butler, *Gender Trouble: Feminism and the Subversion of Identity* (New York: Routledge, 1990): 12, 43–46.

18 Alejo López, "Nueva York como enclave caribeño: extraterritorialidad y caribenización en la literatura nuyorican," *CELEHIS: Revista del Centro de Letras Hispanoamericanas* 37 (2019): 69.

19 Andrea O'Reilly Herrera, "Women and the Revolution in Cristina García's *Dreaming in Cuban*," *Modern Language Studies* 27.3/4 (Autumn–Winter 1997): 70.

20 Yolanda Pampín Martínez, "Mutilation, Politics and Aesthetics: Writing the Female Body in Cristina García's 'Dreaming in Cuban' and 'The Agüero Sisters,'" *Letras Femeninas* (Asociación Internacional de Literatura y Cultura Femenina Hispánica) 30.1 (2004): 51.

21 Paloma Fernández Sánchez, "Imágenes corporales: construcciones del cuerpo femenino en *Las hermanas Agüero* de Cristina García," *Diálogos, Revista Electrónica de Historia*, Volumen especial (2015): 167.

22 Martínez, "Mutilation," 56.

23 Richard L. Jackson, as cited in Martínez, "Mutilation," 52.

24 von Flotow, *Translation and Gender*, 17.

25 Herrera, "Women," 79.

26 Lawrence Venuti, *The Translator's Invisibility: A History of Translation* (London and New York: Routledge, 1995): 19.

27 Pilar Godayol, "Metaphors, Women and Translation: From *les belles infidèles* to *la frontera*," *Gender and Language* 7.1 (2013): 102.

28 Pilar Godayol, "Escriure (a) la frontera: autores bilingües, traductors culturals," *Quaderns* 3 (1999): 36.

29 José Santaemilia, "Sexuality and Translation as Intimate Partners? Toward a Queer Turn in Rewriting Identities and Desires," in *Queering Translation, Translating the Queer: Theory, Practice, Activism*, edited by Brian James Baer and Klaus Kaindl (New York: Routledge, 2018): 12.

30 Spoturno, "La construcción discursivo-enunciativa," 165.

31 Simon, *Gender in Translation*, ix.

32 See, for example, Samia Mehrez, "Translating Gender," *Journal of Middle East Women's Studies* 3.1 (2007): 106–127; Luise von Flotow, ed., *Translating Women* (Ottawa: University of Ottawa Press, 2011); Flotow and Farahzad, *Translating Women*; Claudia de Lima Costa, "Gender and Equivocation: Notes on Decolonial Feminist Translations," in *The Palgrave Handbook of Gender and Development Critical Engagements in Feminist Theory and Practice*, edited by Wendy Harcourt

Invisibilising Feminism in Translation **131**

(Hampshire: Palgrave Macmillan, 2016): 48–61; María Laura Spoturno, "Subjetividad, identidades de género y autotraducción. *America's Dream* y *El sueño de América* de Esmeralda Santiago," *Revista académica Liletrad* 2 (2016): 825–836; Castro and Ergun, "Translation and feminism"; Pilar Godayol, *Tres escritoras censuradas: Simone de Beauvoir, Betty Friedan y Mary McCarthy* (Granada: Comares, 2017); Luciana Carvalho Fonseca, Liliam Ramos da Silva and Dennys Silva-Reis, "Consideraciones fundamentales de los Estudios de la Traducción Feminista en América Latina," *Mutatis Mutandis. Revista Latinoamericana De Traducción* 13.2 (2020): 210–227.

33 Castro and Ergun, "Translation and Feminism," 125.
34 Judith Butler, "Performative Acts and Gender Constitution: An Essay in Phenomenology and Feminist Theory," *Theatre Journal* 40.4 (1988): 526.
35 Pilar Godayol, " 'Un espacio de trabajo en relación': el ensayo feminista traducido de laSal, edicions de les dones," *Transfer* XV.1–2 (2020): 116.
36 Claudia de Lima Costa, "Introduction to Debates about Translation/Lost (and Found?) in Translation/Feminisms in Hemispheric Dialogue," in *Translocalities/Translocalidades: Feminist Politics of Translation in the Latin/a Americas*, edited by Sonia E. Alvarez, Claudia de Lima Costa, Verónica Feliu, Rebecca Hester, Norma Klahn and Millie Thayer (Durham: Duke University Press, 2014): 20; Ovidi Carbonell i Cortés and Esther Monzó-Nebot, "Introduction: Translation and Interpreting Mediating Asymmetries," in *Translating Asymmetry – Rewriting Power*, edited by Ovidi Carbonell and Esther Monzó (Amsterdam: John Benjamins, 2021): 1, 2.
37 Castro and Ergun, "Translation and Feminism," 132–133.
38 Godayol, "Un espacio," 116–117.
39 Gilles Deleuze and Félix Guattari, *Kafka: Toward a Minor Literature*, translated by Dana Polan (Minneapolis: University of Minnesota Press, 1986 [1975]): 16.
40 Spoturno, "La construcción discursivo-enunciativa," 170.
41 Marc Démont, "On Three Modes of Translating Queer Literary Texts," in *Queering Translation, Translating the Queer: Theory, Practice, Activism*, edited by B. J. Baer and K. Kaindl (New York: Routledge, 2018): 157–171.
42 Démont, "On Three Modes," 157, 159, 163.
43 Gloria Anzaldúa, *Borderlands/La Frontera: The New Mestiza* (San Francisco: Aunt Lute Books, 1987).
44 Maite Zubiaurre, "Hacia Una Nueva Geografía Feminista: Nación, Identidad y Construcción Imaginaria en 'Dreaming in Cuban' (Cristina García) y en 'Memory Mambo' (Achy Obejas)," *Chasqui* 28.1 (May 1999): 3.
45 Martínez, "Mutilation," 57.

Bibliography

Alvarez, Sonia E., Claudia de Lima Costa, Verónica Feliu, Rebecca Hester, Norma Klahn and Millie Thayer, eds. *Translocalities/Translocalidades: Feminist Politics of Translation in the Latin/a Americas*. Durham: Duke University Press, 2014.

Anzaldúa, Gloria. *Borderlands/La Frontera: The New Mestiza*. San Francisco: Aunt Lute Books, 1987.

Araújo, Cibele de Guadalupe Sousa, Luciana de Mesquita Silva and Dennys Silva-Reis. "Translation Studies and Black Women in the Light of Feminism." *Revista Ártemis* 27.1 (2019): 14–24.

Bhabha, Homi K. *El lugar de la cultura*, translated by César Aira. Buenos Aires: Manantial, 2002 [1994].

Butler, Judith. *Gender Trouble: Feminism and the Subversion of Identity*. New York: Routledge, 1990.

———. "Performative Acts and Gender Constitution: An Essay in Phenomenology and Feminist Theory." *Theatre Journal* 40.4 (1988): 519–531.

Carbonell, Ovidi and Esther Monzó. "Introduction. Translation and Interpreting Mediating Asymmetries." In *Translating Asymmetry – Rewriting Power*, edited by Ovidi Carbonell and Esther Monzó. Amsterdam: John Benjamins, 2021: 1–12.

Carvalho Fonseca, Luciana, Liliam Ramos da Silva and Dennys Silva-Reis. "Consideraciones fundamentales de los Estudios de la Traducción Feminista en América Latina." *Mutatis Mutandis. Revista Latinoamericana De Traducción* 13.2 (2020): 210–227.

Castro, Olga and Emek Ergun. "Translation and Feminism." In *The Routledge Handbook of Translation and Politics*, edited by Jonathan Evans and Fruela Fernández. London and New York: Routledge, 2018: 125–153.

Castro, Olga, Emek Ergun, Luise von Flotow and María Laura Spoturno. "Towards Transnational Feminist Translation Studies." *Mutatis Mutandis: Revista Latinoamericana de Traducción* 13.1 (2020): 2–10.

Castro, Olga and María Laura Spoturno. "Feminismos y traducción: apuntes conceptuales y metodológicos para una traductología feminista transnacional." *Mutatis Mutandis. Revista Latinoamericana de traducción* 13.1 (January–June 2020): 11–44.

Chamberlain, Lori. "Gender and the Metaphorics of Translation." *Signs: Journal of Women in Culture and Society* XIII.3 (1988): 454–472.

Costa, Claudia de Lima. "Gender and Equivocation: Notes on Decolonial Feminist Translations." In *The Palgrave Handbook of Gender and Development Critical Engagements in Feminist Theory and Practice*, edited by Wendy Harcourt. Hampshire: Palgrave Macmillan, 2016: 48–61.

———. "Introduction to Debates about Translation/Lost (and Found?) in Translation/Feminisms in Hemispheric Dialogue." In *Translocalities/Translocalidades: Feminist Politics of Translation in the Latin/a Americas*, edited by Sonia E. Alvarez, Claudia de Lima Costa, Verónica Feliu, Rebecca Hester, Norma Klahn and Millie Thayer. Durham: Duke University Press, 2014: 19–36.

Deleuze, Gilles and Félix Guattari. *Kafka: Toward a Minor Literature*, translated by Dana Polan. Minneapolis: University of Minnesota Press, 1986 [1975].

Démont, Marc. "On Three Modes of Translating Queer Literary Texts." In *Queering Translation, Translating the Queer: Theory, Practice, Activism*, edited by Brian James Baer and Klaus Kaindl. New York: Routledge, 2018: 157–171.

Fernández Sánchez, Paloma. "Imágenes corporales: construcciones del cuerpo femenino en *Las hermanas Agüero* de Cristina García." *Diálogos, Revista Electrónica de Historia*, Volumen especial 16 (2015): 163–181.

Flotow, Luise von. *Translating Women*. Ottawa: University of Ottawa Press, 2011.

———. *Translation and Gender: Translating in the Era of Feminism*. Manchester and Ottawa: St. Jerome Publishing and University of Ottawa, 1997.

Flotow, Luise von and Farzaneh Farahzad. *Translating Women: Different Voices and New Horizons*. London and New York: Routledge, 2017.

García, Cristina. "Author Focuses on Cuban Nostalgia." Interview by Knight Elinor Burkett. *Chicago Tribune*, 9 April 1992.

———. *Dreaming in Cuban*. New York: Ballantine Books (Random House), 1992.

———. "The Nature of Inheritance." Interview by Jessica Murphy. *The Atlantic*, April 2003. www.theatlantic.com/magazine/archive/2003/04/the-nature-of-inheritance/303087/ (last accessed 10 April 2024).

———. *Soñar en cubano*, translated by Marisol Palés. Madrid: Espasa Calpe (Grupo Planeta), 1993.

Invisibilising Feminism in Translation **133**

———. "Translation as Restoration." In *Voice-Overs: Translation and Latin American Literature*, edited by Daniel Balderston and Marcy Schwartz. Albany: State University of New York Press, 2012: 45–48.

Godayol, Pilar. "Escriure (a) la frontera: autores bilingües, traductores culturals." *Quaderns* 3 (1999): 29–37.

———. *Feminismos y traducción (1965–1990)*. Granada: Comares, 2021.

———. "Metaphors, Women and Translation: From les belles infidèles to la frontera." *Gender and Language* 7.1 (2013): 97–116.

———. *Tres escritoras censuradas: Simone de Beauvoir, Betty Friedan y Mary McCarthy*. Granada: Comares, 2017.

———. " 'Un espacio de trabajo en relación': el ensayo feminista traducido de laSal, edicions de les dones." *Transfer* XV.1–2 (2020): 115–141.

Hall, Stuart. "Who Needs 'Identity'?" In *Questions of Cultural Identity*, edited by Stuart Hall and Paul Du Gay. London: Sage Publications Ltd., 1996: 1–17.

López, Alejo. "Nueva York como enclave caribeño: extraterritorialidad y caribenización en la literatura nuyorican." *CELEHIS: Revista del Centro de Letras Hispanoamericanas* 37 (2019): 68–86.

Mehrez, Samia. "Translating Gender." *Journal of Middle East Women's Studies* 3.1 (2007): 106–127.

O'Reilly Herrera, Andrea. "Women and the Revolution in Cristina García's *Dreaming in Cuban*." *Modern Language Studies* 27.3/4 (Autumn–Winter 1997): 69–91.

Pampín Martínez, Yolanda. "Mutilation, Politics and Aesthetics: Writing the Female Body in Cristina García's 'Dreaming in Cuban' and 'The Agüero Sisters.'" *Letras Femeninas (Asociación Internacional de Literatura y Cultura Femenina Hispánica)* 30.1 (2004): 51–63.

Rumbaut, Rubén G. "Generation 1.5, Educational Experiences of." In *Encyclopedia of Diversity in Education*, edited by James A. Banks. Washington, DC: Sage Publications, 2012: 982.

Santaemilia, José. "Sexuality and Translation as Intimate Partners? Toward a Queer Turn in Rewriting Identities and Desires." In *Queering Translation, Translating the Queer: Theory, Practice, Activism*, edited by Brian James Baer and Klaus Kaindl. New York: Routledge, 2018: 11–25.

Simon, Sherry. *Gender in Translation*. London and New York: Routledge, 1996.

Spoturno, María Laura. "La construcción discursivo-enunciativa de las identidades culturales en *When I Was Puerto Rican* y *Cuando era puertorriqueña* de Esmeralda Santiago." In *Escrituras de minorías, heterogeneidad y traducción*, coordinated by María Laura Spoturno. La Plata: Universidad de La Plata. Facultad de Humanidades y Ciencias de la Educación, 2018: 165–188.

———. "Subjetividad, identidades de género y autotraducción. America's Dream y El sueño de América de Esmeralda Santiago." *Revista académica Liletrad* 2 (2016): 825–836.

Venuti, Lawrence. *The Translator's Invisibility: A History of Translation*. London and New York: Routledge, 1995.

Zubiaurre, Maite. "Hacia Una Nueva Geografía Feminista: Nación, Identidad y Construcción Imaginaria en 'Dreaming in Cuban' (Cristina García) y en 'Memory Mambo' (Achey Obejas)." *Chasqui* 28.1 (May 1999): 3–15.

8

DECOLONISATION, AUTHENTICITY, AND THE OTHER

Talking in and About Englishes in Algeria[1]

Camille Jacob and Leonald Kazibwe

Introduction

Large-scale protests took place across Algeria between 2018 and 2020, sparked by the announcement that President Bouteflika, despite not having been seen in public since his stroke in 2013, would seek re-election. A large cross-section of the population took part, from students and families to moudjahidat,[2] demanding a radical change from the group of elites who had been gravitating around the centres of power since 1962. In July 2019, three months after Bouteflika's resignation after twenty years at the helm of state, Tayeb Bouzib, minister of higher education and scientific research, suggested in a televised speech that the use of English should be "consolidated" in universities and that French, the current medium of instruction in the most prestigious disciplines, "led nowhere." The announcements were widely covered in the news and on social media and sparked debates over the place, function, and symbolic roles of languages in Algeria. Questionnaires were sent by the Ministry to university staff to garner opinions regarding increasing the use of English, and unofficial polls circulated on Facebook, widely relayed by the press and social media. However, talking about language is never just about which code to use in a specific situation. Debates over the place of French within the Algerian higher education system and Algerian society more widely are not new or even confined to the post-independence period, as language was one of the battlegrounds of anticolonial movements. Tayeb Bouzid's speech is embedded within debates whose meaning have transformed over decades, from the importance of Arabisation in the 1960s and 1970s to equating language with political values during the 'dark decade' of the 1990s.[3] The weight of the latter interpretation continues to

DOI: 10.4324/9781003464037-11
This chapter has been made available under a CC-BY-NC-ND 4.0 license.

loom large in current discussions, with ministers who speak French occasionally accused of being a 'fifth column' representing the interests of the former coloniser instead of those of Algeria. Calls for more English and statements that English is replacing French therefore need to be understood within the Algerian context and not just as an uncritical acceptance of the wider global context of dominance of English.

While the announcements by the then-minister of higher education were made in response to the specific current political situation in Algeria and within the wider historical and social context of the country, the way they were formulated, read, and understood is also embedded within wider discourses of a competition between two former colonial languages at the global level. They echoed narratives of 'French' being in competition with 'English,' especially in former French colonies in Africa, and claims of English as the 'universal language' and 'language of science,' offering opportunities for social mobility, economic development, and democratisation. The increasing visibility of English in the political and education landscapes across African countries labelled as 'Francophone,' encompassing situations as diverse as Morocco, Rwanda, and Cameroon, has often been analysed as the result of the promises of a language that is 'decolonised' and linked to globalisation and human capital. However, there is very little understanding of what this 'replacement' looks like, what political and social impact this post-colonial linguistic competition has, and how language users themselves make sense of it.

In Algeria, as in other countries, discourses sometimes appear contradictory, with English touted as both the means for national liberation from French neo-colonialism and as creating trilingual illiterates; as something crucial for the national interest but irrelevant to people's lives; as opening opportunities to all but only affordable by some. Throughout our fieldwork, participants talked about English as being simultaneously neutral and against French, everywhere and nowhere, the path to (re)claiming an authentic national and self-identity, and a mark of Otherness. In this chapter we argue that these contradictory discourses need to be taken into account, as they allow us to understand how narratives of decolonisation and identity at the national and individual level are being relocalised into English. Relocalising entails questioning the very tenet that English has been adapted (which still starts from the assumption that it had a core or point of origin) and posits instead that existing sociolinguistic practices have a new name.[4] If the focus is on the user and on practices rather than on explaining the object called 'English,' the 'contradictions' which emerge from participants' responses can be explored not by selecting a 'truer' overarching narrative but by taking participants' explanatory frameworks seriously. We therefore argue that explaining the interactions between discourses and practices around English and their entanglements within existing social structures and political forces requires accounting for the complex ways in which 'English' and Englishes are used to index decolonisation, authenticity, and Otherness in specific settings.

The first section of this chapter presents a brief overview of how the explanatory frameworks for English and French in the world and the exclusive focus on language competition shapes understandings of local discourses and practices of English. The following section underlines the importance of taking participants as co-theorists rather than data points or naive informants, drawing on the work of political anthropologists such as Michel-Rolph Trouillot and Yarimar Bonilla, in order to re-entangle methodology, methods, and ethics both 'in the field' and after and to make sense of discourses *in* and *about* Englishes.

World Englishes in the f/Francophonie: Talking About Englishes in Countries Labelled 'French-Speaking'

Several frameworks have been elaborated to make sense of the use of English and French in the world, from the concept of 'spread' to that of World Englishes. Dominant frames of understanding are important not just in academic terms but also for the ways in which they are (re)produced by participants in their explanations of their own practices and what they deem priorities for their country.

A first set of explanations describe English as having 'spread' due to socio-cultural and linguistic factors, combining a monolingual bias towards the necessity of a common language with theories of cultural superiority and universality. The 'global' status of English is conceived as inherently positive in these accounts, as "the convenience of having a lingua franca available to serve global human relations and needs has come to be appreciated by millions," with English supposedly providing "a 'glue' which brought people together and a medium which gave them common access to opportunities."[5] Nonetheless, the idea that a common language is necessary for communication and automatically equates a "common access to opportunities" is not neutral but rests on an implicit monolingual bias and belief in the possibility and desirability of a 'universal language.' It facilitates readings of the world through a Eurocentric lens, privileging the study of European languages above others. Whether in suggesting that multilingualism is a problem that should be 'solved' by monolingualism, in labelling all non-European languages as 'local,' or in focusing research on linguistic repertoires which include European languages (as highlighted by Kubota),[6] academic discourses of spread and lingua franca systematically foreground some practices and erase others.

"World Englishes," developed by Braj Kachru in the 1980s, is the main explanatory model used to theorise the notion of 'spread' without erasing the colonial experience. This approach focuses on the diversity and creativity of English users, beyond what had traditionally been termed "native speakers."[7] It is based on the idea of three concentric circles which categorise different forms and functions of English and therefore separate Englishes in their own right. It thereby helps researchers question the notion of a unique 'centre,' where a standard code is produced and passed down to the rest of the world, contending instead with local linguistic and social dynamics to investigate how English is appropriated and adapted. In the third circle (the Expanding Circle), parts of the world where English was not the colonial language, English functions as a marker of prestige, indexing Western consumerism but also creativity and wealth, thereby explaining its omnipresence in the semiotic landscape beyond immediately apparent communicative needs. The idea that individuals learn a lingua franca as a way to improve their current socioeconomic status, in the belief that adding the language to their repertoire will have beneficial effects, needs to be explored further in a context where English is not the national or even regional lingua franca, and other languages (here Arabic and French) already play this role.

The main paradigm used to investigate French outside of France is that of the 'francophonie,' used for both the political and cultural organisation (Organisation Internationale de la Francophonie – OIF, often shortened to Francophonie with a capital "F") and the concept to denote speaking French ('francophonie'). The similarity between the two terms has led to confusions in their usage, with the actions and pronouncements of the institution being equated to practices across the globe. None of the conceptual frameworks developed within Francophone regional languages studies, creolistics, or critical sociolinguistics, such as polynomie, pluricentrisme, and passeurs linguistiques,[8] have received much coverage in Anglophone academic circles, with understandings of 'French' largely unproblematised or reduced to political pronouncements. French in the world is nearly systematically understood through the prism of conflict with English, both in French- and English-language publications. English is seen as a 'threat' to the global presence (and importance) of French, and therefore both discourses and practices around the language are described as a response to the perceived domination of English. For instance, English is seen as threatening the place of French as the 'language of modernity' or 'the language of science,' especially in Africa, as governments and higher education institutions shift their medium of instruction, scholars publish in English, or the latter becomes more visible online. Language change is described as a shift and a zero-sum game, with English 'replacing' French rather than adding to it, compounded by French political pronouncements pleading to "save our language while there is still time."[9] Together with the growing equation of the institutional Francophonie with France, the close attention paid to the quotes and reports from language institutions such as the *Académie Française* leads many scholars to the conclusion that a key way of understanding the French language in the world is through discourses of conquest and conflict, and narratives of the world being threatened by "l'anglo-américain."[10]

The focus on linguistic competition erases users and dissimulates the differences between policies and practices. As Wright notes, despite narratives of 'France' being opposed to 'English,' the realities on the ground show a much more complex expansion of people's linguistic repertoire and inclusion of English as a medium of instruction and symbol of cultural capital.[11] Moreover, this explanatory framework reproduces a colonial outlook where the speeches and actions of a handful of administrators in 'mother countries' are necessary and sufficient to understand language dynamics in their former colonies.

In the literature on North Africa and on Algeria especially, conflict and competition are presented as the main lenses through which contemporary language dynamics can be understood. In this sense, there is a fractal recursivity of discourses of conflict, with wider discourses of competition between the francophonie and English in the world, or between the two ex-colonial powers, being applied to the Algerian context. Studies of actual language use as opposed to discourses about languages remain relatively few. This has repeatedly led to a gap between findings pointing to additive multilingualism and apparent daily mixing of languages on the one hand and overarching discourses of hierarchy and competition on the other.[12]

Beyond a focus on languages as labels and objects which have an existence outside users (and therefore can be 'spread'), other approaches focus on a broader concept of linguistic repertoires and the notion that practices are being relocalised into differently named languages. Makoni and Pennycook, in their critique of discourses about 'English,' deconstruct the idea that understanding English in the world requires mapping how the language is spreading and how this neatly bounded entity might be modified in different settings.[13] Instead, they suggest focusing on what people do with language or, to use Bakhtin's terminology, how people 'language.' This chapter thus analyses how existing practices of identity-making in Algeria are relocalised into discourses *about* English, much more than discourses *in* English.

Entangling Methodology, Methods, and Ethics

The research for this chapter was conducted between 2015 and 2021 in different locations across Algeria. This included eleven months of ethnographic fieldwork conducted by the first author between 2016 and 2017 in Algiers, with shorter contrasting visits undertaken in cities of the south and west in 2017 and interviews conducted both in-person and remotely between 2015 and 2020 across the country. Discussions and interviews were conducted in English and French, with a small amount of Derja.[14] The second author also conducted interviews with Anglophone African students at four different universities in Algeria between 2020 and 2021. Observations and interviews, and the repeated and ongoing presentation of preliminary conclusions to participants for their feedback, were all crucial in developing a more complex picture of what claims of 'English is replacing French' mean in practice.

Discussions of methodology are often corralled into discussing research methods only, and the process of turning field notes into academic publications, although discussed in specialist literature, is rarely explicit. One of the biggest issues with research into Englishes, language change, or the relation between discourses and practices is how to make sense of the 'contradictions' which emerge from the data and the resulting tensions between ethical responsibility towards participants and expected codes of academic writing.

Some of the prevalent narratives about what 'English' was and what people were doing with it were similar to other contexts, with the language seen as a marker or catalyst of development, as a gateway to opportunities for individuals and for the country, and as a symbol of the hope for change. But many of these narratives were presented and explained in decidedly localised forms and responded to existing Algerian debates rather than simply reproducing global tropes. In addition, throughout our fieldwork, participants emphasised different aspects of their own journey and that of others, their own practices and that of others, depending on which aspects of our identity as researchers they were responding to.[15] It would be easy to dismiss claims of English as empowering, transformative, or decolonising as simply a sign of successful PR campaigns by foreign actors such as the UK and the US and that therefore Algerians must be naive victims of neo-colonialism. However, this would in fact be reproducing both the colonial trappings of Western research paradigms and the exploitative positioning of the researcher as above their research participants and the only arbiter (if not creator) of truth.

These questions have enriched our own understanding of what it means to 'do' ethnography as well as of ethical responsibilities during the research itself and in the publication process. Even interpretive methods can "construct that [epistemological] passivity [of the participants] by silencing the competency effect of the native voice in their commentary."[16] As Kim TallBear highlights:

> If what we want is democratic knowledge production that serves not only those who inquire and their institutions, but also those who are inquired upon (and appeals to 'knowledge for the good of all' do not cut it), we must soften that boundary erected long ago between those who know versus those from whom the raw materials of knowledge production are extracted.[17]

Yarimar Bonilla suggests engaging with participants as co-theorists throughout the process of ethnography:

> In the field, this involves not reading over the natives' shoulders, so to speak, but standing alongside them, facing the action, and collectively reflecting on matters of mutual concern. On the page, it requires careful attention to the place of our informants' voices in both the narrated and the narrative frame, not by simply 'giving them a voice' (itself a treacherous endeavor), but by taking seriously their arguments and their native categories: elaborating on them, theorizing with them, and questioning and departing from them as necessary – as one does with all theorists.[18]

This also means moving away from the coloniality of dominant research practices, where the research is "conducted away from the researcher's primary context, with data being 'extracted' and taken back to this primary context to be analysed and disseminated. Those in the context where the data is generated usually never see the researcher again or learn about the findings."[19] Rather than a frame of 'giving back,' which embeds a colonial and developmental mindset into research practices, we sought a continuous and repeated engagement with the people we were working with, presenting ongoing findings, sharing plans for publications, and inviting feedback throughout,[20] in addition to taking their analytical insights seriously.

Relocalisation in Practice: Decolonisation, Authenticity, and the 'Other'

In Algeria, what qualifies as 'English' is mediated by understandings of the existing linguistic context of Algeria and especially the place of French. Understanding language practices and linguistic situations requires taking into account "the perspectives, the language ideologies, the local ways of knowing, through which language is viewed," in the sense that language is both the choices we make but also the retrospective creation of these choices.[21] When presenting our research at different universities, students and staff from English departments nearly always told us that we 'need to look at French.' Similarly, when learners and teachers complained about the absence of English in Algeria and the impossibility of practising, what they also (or mostly) referred to was the comparatively high presence of French. When we mentioned to students and teachers in language schools that their situation was not dissimilar to that of most learners around the world, several participants explicitly stated that the only way to learn was for English to become as present as French currently is in Algiers. The low presence of English in comparison to French was thus qualified as 'absence.' When it was included within multilingual practices, it was read as an instance of 'Algerian

French,' or simply a decorative form of language use, rather than an example of Algerian English.

The question of what users of English do within a society where actual daily use is limited is intimately connected to discourses. A language perceived as 'absent' can help construct personal and group identity, not mainly through communicative or purely decorative use but also through highly ritualised phrases, as it becomes "a way of inscribing not only the speaker but also the audience as part of a group."[22] In fact, whether or not our participants were learning English, the idea that the language was a tool of resistance against French and its colonial and neo-colonial interference remained a prevalent explanatory framework. French was equated to colonial destruction, existing elites, and, by extension, closed political and economic systems as well as exclusionary language ideologies of purity and mastery. Constructions of English as 'neutral' and 'international' (or even 'universal' for some participants) are appropriated across all groups within the Algerian context to signal a competition with French, hopes of political change (in various guises depending on the group), and the (re)creation of a newly (re)found authentic Algerian identity. Pennycook contends that understanding the place of Englishes in the world is not so much a question of a centre/periphery dichotomy but rather a "constant tension between the global flow of an ideology and the local fixity of what authenticity means and how it should be realised."[23] Importantly, in the Algerian context, who is saying what does not follow neatly delineated identity-through-language categories, with self-defined 'Francophones' being just as likely as 'Arabophones' to refer to the supposed neutrality of English and competition with French.

The strategic use of English indexes both new connections within Algeria and to the outside, performing a certain Algerian-ness for 'new' audiences through social media, community work, and self-development. For the Algiers-based creators of an online radio, one of the aims of using English was both to discuss sensitive topics with the additional distance that the language brings and "show that we speak English in Algeria." One of the universities the first author visited had been taking part in a US-organised online cultural exchange programme, which was designed to "develop the spirit of tolerance" and give students "experience with foreigners," in the words of the manager running the programme. The criteria used to select the students were not linguistic knowledge but mostly cultural knowledge (of Algeria and the wider world) and "interpersonal behaviour," as they were expected to behave as ambassadors of the nation. The idea of English as facilitating the presentation of worthy representatives of the nation is not specific to just one region of the country. Participants repeatedly explained the indexicality of English as 'foreign' and 'international' and how this enabled the relocalisation of practices in this language to be read as a way of inserting Algerian knowledge and events within a 'new' (because not limited to France) global frame. The 'new generation' was to be both filled with civic and national pride and fully integrated and connected with the world through their linguistic repertoires.

As discussed in detail elsewhere,[24] Arabic already had the function of an anti-colonial language, and in many ways English is presented as a seemingly 'decolonial' option, allowing for the reinvention of society and state and the dismantling of coloniality in knowledge production, economic relations, and political organisation.[25] However, and despite their prevalence across our fieldwork and in academic and news coverage, describing these discourses in such a disembodied way (as 'discourses' without speakers) erases the complex ways in which these discourses are produced, appropriated, and enacted. In fact, discourses of decolonisation were mostly present in informal group settings and only came up in individual interviews when participants were talking about other people. Discourses at the individual level, found in one-to-one interviews about the participants' own journey with English, replicate more closely global discourses about English as 'international' and the 'language of development,' which also obscures the ways in which existing hierarchies are reproduced rather than challenged.[26] Learning and using English was closely connected discursively to hopes of spatial and social mobility, with linguistic competence equated to a form of symbolic capital. 'English' was seen as offering opportunities to build one's network beyond established social connections and reinvent a group identity that was self-focused, proudly Algerian and connected to the world, sometimes as a way to truly decolonise Algeria, and sometimes as a personal journey of self-development. The discourses and practices of 'new identities' bridged the personal and the professional, physical and online, and often the university and the world of work. The articulation between individual and collective identity is complex and rests on the idea that the search for an 'authentic' Algerian identity goes through language and the erasure of the damage of French colonisation,[27] and that contemporary economic, social, and political challenges are due to the dislocation in individuals' understanding of themselves.[28] However, while English seemingly allows for the reinvention of a more authentic – because decolonised – Algerian identity, in practice not everyone can gain equal access to these claims of a new identity, and existing socio-economic hierarchies continued to determine who is rewarded for their linguistic repertoires.

When learning about our research topics, people would often follow a similar structure of answers: first talking about French, then about English as the international language, followed by a comment about a certain category of people speaking more English than French. For instance, one recruiter from the West of the country suggested that English was mostly spoken amongst young people as "ils parlent beaucoup l'anglais"[29] and have not learnt French 'properly' at school. However, when asked about how old they are, where they use English, or what they do with it, participants mostly responded in general terms, repeating ideas of the international language, social media, or not liking French. When discussing their own family's and friends' linguistic repertoire, participants were often the only ones within their circle to speak and use English. This not only demonstrates the importance of English-language spaces in their socialisation practices but also exemplifies how English is both constructed as 'everywhere' and 'nowhere,' as 'foreign' and a way of talking about Algerian issues.

The first 'Other' we encountered was 'the young generation,' a group seen as key to the increasing interest in and visibility of English in Algeria but also always refracted to those younger than oneself, even by university students. Earlier concerns about the psychological repercussions of French-Arabic bilingualism on 'personality'[30] are re-purposed within discourses about English and the threatening nature of the 'new generation.' Globalisation (and its associated language, English) is also perceived as a destabilising threat, although this discourse was mostly reproduced in academic circles and by older professionals. Amongst younger participants, the idea of English-mediated technology (and especially social media) as a threat to traditional values was a common discussion topic in classes, both in universities and in language schools. Although the fears about the 'young generation' are not directly related to English, the strong symbolic links between the language and the concept of the 'new generation' as well as social media means it plays a role in constructing this 'Other' who does things differently, even when the speakers themselves are speaking in English.

Another 'Other,' prevalent especially in participants from Algiers but also found in Tlemcen, is 'the South,' which is viewed as more English-speaking because less French-speaking. However, fieldwork highlighted that conceptions of the Sahara as a monolithic more English-speaking space than the North were simplistic, as the differences between cities were much greater than between 'South' and 'North.' Economic, geographical, and social factors play a role in making 'the South' a diverse space, from the proximity of the Tunisian border and its trade opportunities in one city, to the class make-up of engineering students in another university and its links to the oil and gas multinationals less than 100 kilometres away. While the North/South dichotomy was being reinforced through talking about English, these discourses are not new. Administered by the army rather than integrated into the settler colony during French colonisation, these 'Southern' spaces continue to be thought of as in opposition to 'the North' and suffer from a lack of infrastructure and access to employment, despite the presence of oil and gas fields. The last twenty years have seen several localised and more large-scale protests centred around demands for equality and equity in terms of resources. While the protesters' demands are couched in class rather than racial terms, inhabitants of the Sahara are themselves described in racial and racist terms, as the North's 'Other.'[31]

144 Camille Jacob and Leonald Kazibwe

Last, 'native speakers' are also constructed as an 'Other,' with the category following racial lines. In Algiers, as a white European with a British accent, participants all explicitly labelled the first author as a 'native speaker' and modified their definitions of the term to continue including her once she explained that she had not been raised in an English-speaking environment. This was not the case for the second author, even though he does come from an English-speaking country. Similarly, teachers of colour from the US were uneasily accommodated within the native speaker category, and rankings of 'authenticity' based on whiteness appeared between the foreign teachers working at the same institution. Repeated visits to language schools between 2015 and 2020 and interviews with owners and Algerian teachers have shown that native speakerism is on the rise, encouraged by British and North American organisations and fuelled by wider discourses of 'native speaker saviourism,'[32] replicating the coloniality of expertise rather than challenging it. Interviews with Black Anglophone students in four different universities also highlighted the complex intersection of the desirability of English and the negative portrayal of people from sub-Saharan Africa, amplified by European discourses of North Africa as 'transit states,' the delocalisation of EU border operations ever further South, and an increasingly racialised framing of debates on migration and belonging.[33]

Constructions of English as new, foreign, and neutral therefore also serve to invisibilise existing practices: if English is new and foreign, it cannot already be 'Algerian.' Because 'English' is embedded within discourses of novelty and absence, and therefore supposedly 'outside' existing identity frameworks, talking about who speaks and uses English also becomes a way of relocalising narratives of regional identities, privilege, and exclusion. In turn, 'the South,' 'the capital,' and 'the West' are seen as places where there is 'more English' by participants who are not there and serve to emphasise differences. Constructed as 'foreign' and therefore not Algerian, the idea that it is always others who speak more English is constructed both as a complaint and grounds for suspicion, especially towards 'the new generation,' also by people who could be considered part of the elite themselves. The presence of English in the semiotic landscape is erased or ignored, recognising only the practices of English users within already prestigious spaces: companies (especially multinationals), universities, foreign NGOs. Far from enabling more inclusive language ideologies, 'English' often promotes the foregrounding of the white Western 'expert' and racialised understandings of the 'native speaker' at the expense of African and Asian users.

Conclusion

The first section highlighted how dominant frameworks of understanding English(es) in the world and the prevalence of conflict as an analytical lens are reproduced and appropriated by participants to explain language dynamics in Algeria. The second section focused more specifically on a dialogue between different conceptualisations of 'English in Algeria,' bringing together participants' explanatory frames in conversation with each other and with our own commentary. These frames could appear at first to contain 'contradictory' elements such as the idea that English is both universal and foreign, a way towards a more authentic decolonised Algerian identity and a marker of otherness. We argue that the apparent contradictions stem from the fact that wider discourses regarding identities, political and social equality, relations to others and the world, and race, are partly relocalised into discourses about English (rather than into English). Talking about English thus needs to be read alongside and within existing debates on history, belonging, and political priorities rather than simply taken as straightforward assessments of language change.

Notes

1 This work was supported by the Arts & Humanities Research Council (grant reference AH/L012006/1) in a collaboration between the University of Portsmouth and the British Council in Algiers, the Leverhulme Trust (grant reference SAS-2018–088\1), and the Economic & Social Research Council (grant reference ES/V010077/1). The funders have not been involved in the study design, collection, analysis and interpretation of data, nor in the writing of the chapter. Although we cannot name them, we are indebted to our participants for sharing their time and insights with us and for their constructive feedback throughout. Thank you also to Natalya Vince, Mario Saraceni, Olivia Rutazibwa, Hayat Messekher, and Li Wei for their thoughtful comments and feedback on earlier drafts of this chapter. All remaining shortcomings and errors are our own. This chapter includes extracts from the first author's unpublished thesis, *English and Social Worlds in Contemporary Algeria* (University of Portsmouth, 2019), https://researchportal. port.ac.uk/en/studentTheses/english-and-social-worlds-in-contemporary-algeria.
2 Female war veterans, here specifically of the Algerian Revolution (1954–1962).
3 Lardjane, Omar, M. Madi, K. Taleb Ibrahimi, M. Haddab, H. Remaoun and M.-L. Maougal, eds., *Elites et questions identitaires en Algérie* (Algiers: Casbah Editions, 1997); Yassine Temlali, "Language Policies in Algeria since 1962: Identity Renewal in Light of Realpolitik Imperatives," in *Routledge Handbook of Francophone Africa*, edited by Natalya Vince and Tony Chafer (Milton Park, Abingdon: Routledge, 2024): 197–225.
4 Alastair Pennycook, *Language as a Local Practice* (Milton Park, Abingdon: Routledge, 2010).
5 David Crystal, *English as a Global Language* (Cambridge: Cambridge University Press, 2003).
6 Ryuko Kubota, "Inequalities of Englishes, English Speakers, and Languages: A Critical Perspective on Pluralist Approaches to English," in *Unequal Englishes: The Politics of Englishes Today*, edited by Ruanni Tupas (Basingstoke: Palgrave Macmillan, 2015): 21–41.
7 Brach Kachru, "World Englishes: Approaches, Issues and Resources," *Language Teaching* 25.1 (1992): 1–14.
8 See, for instance, Myriam Achour-Kallel, ed., *Le social par le langage. La parole au quotidien* (Tunis, Paris: IRMC, Karthala, 2015); Ibtissem Chachou and Meriem Stambouli, eds., *Pour un plurilinguisme algérien intégré – Approches critiques et*

renouvellement épistémique (Paris: Riveneuve, 2016); Jean-Baptiste Marcellesi, Thierry Bulot and Philippe Blanchet, *Sociolinguistique: Epistémologie, Langues régionales, Polynomie* (Paris: L'Harmattan, 2003).

9 Hélène Carrère d'Encausse, quoted in Sue Wright, "French as a Lingua Franca," *Annual Review of Applied Linguistics* 26 (2006): 49.

10 See the special issue of *Hermès* 2004/3, for instance.

11 Wright, "French as a Lingua Franca," 50–54.

12 For instance Mohamed Benrabah, *Language Conflict in Algeria: From Colonialism to Post-Independence* (Bristol: Multilingual Matters, 2013).

13 Sinfree Makoni and Alastair Pennycook, eds., *Disinventing and Reconstituting Languages* (Bristol: Multilingual Matters, 2007).

14 Sometimes also called "Algerian Arabic" and also spelt Darja or Darija, Derja is the shared language of the vast majority of Algerians.

15 Discussions of our own linguistic, cultural, and administrative identities ended up forming part of our research, as people explicitly related to us in different ways and foregrounded different socio- and politico-linguistic explanations, for example, depending on whether they saw the first author as an English-speaker from France, a French-speaker from the UK, a sociolinguistics PhD student, a former languages teacher, or a shifting combination of these various facets.

16 Michel-Rolph Trouillot, *Global Transformations: Anthropology and the Modern World* (New York: Palgrave Macmillan US, 2003): 132.

17 Kim TallBear, "Standing With and Speaking as Faith: A Feminist-Indigenous Approach to Inquiry," *Journal of Research Practice* 10.2 (2014), http://jrp.icaap.org/index.php/jrp/article/view/405/371.

18 Yarimar Bonilla, *Non-Sovereign Futures: French Caribbean Politics in the Wake of Disenchantment* (Chicago: University of Chicago Press, 2015): xvii.

19 Bukola Oyinloye, "Towards an Ọmọlúàbí Code of Research Ethics: Applying a Situated, Participant-Centred Virtue Ethics Framework to Fieldwork with Disadvantaged Populations in Diverse Cultural Settings," *Research Ethics* 17.4 (2021): 418–419.

20 See also Max Liboiron, *Pollution is Colonialism* (Durham: Duke University Press, 2021): 25.

21 Pennycook, *Language as a Local Practice*, 128, 137–138.

22 Jocelyn C. Ahlers, "Framing Discourse," *Journal of Linguistic Anthropology* 16.1 (2006): 68.

23 Alastair Pennycook, *Global Englishes and Transcultural Flows* (Milton Park, Abingdon: Routledge, 2007): 112.

24 Camille Jacob, "English as a Decolonial Language: Academic Frames, Popular Discourses and Language Practices in Algeria," *The Journal of North African Studies* 25.6 (2020): 1013–1032.

25 For more on coloniality and decolonial approaches see, for instance, Gurminder K. Bhambra, "Postcolonial and Decolonial Dialogues," *Postcolonial Studies* 17.2 (2014): 115–121.

26 See also Camille Jacob, " 'Back to the "Futur"': Mobility and Immobility through English in Algeria," *Language & Communication* 68 (2019): 6–16.

27 Chafia Yamina Benmayouf, *Renouvellement social, renouvellement langagier dans l'Algérie d'aujourd'hui* (Paris: L'Harmattan, 2008): 16, 18–25.

28 Foudil Cheriguen, ed., *Les enjeux de la nomination des langues dans l'Algérie contemporaine* (Paris: L'Harmattan, 2007).

29 This could translate as "they speak a lot of English," "they often speak English," and "a lot of them speak English."

30 Cf. Khaoula Taleb-Ibrahimi, *Les Algériens et leur(s) langue(s): éléments pour une approche sociolinguistique de la société algérienne* (Algiers: Editions el Hikma, 1995).

31 Naoual Belakhdar, "« L'éveil du Sud » ou quand la contestation vient de la marge: Une analyse du mouvement des chômeurs algériens," *Politique Africaine* 137.1 (2015): 27–48; Naoual Belakhdar, "When Unemployment Meets Environment: The Case of the Anti-Fracking Coalition in Ouargla," *Mediterranean Politics* 24.4 (2019): 420–442; Yaël Kouzmine, *Le Sahara algérien: Intégration nationale et développement regional* (Paris: L'Harmattan, 2012).
32 Christopher Joseph Jenks and Jerry Won Lee, "Native Speaker Saviorism: A Racialized Teaching Ideology," *Critical Inquiry in Language Studies* 17.3 (2019): 186–205.
33 Isabella Alexander-Nathani, "Trapped on the Island: The Politics of Race and Belonging in *Jazīrat al-Maghrib*," *The Journal of North African Studies* 24.5 (2019): 786–806; Salim Chena, *Les traversées migratoires dans l'Algérie contemporaine: Africains subsahariens et Algériens vers l'exil* (Paris: Karthala, 2016); Massika Lanane, "La migration africaine en Algérie: une éventuelle intégration ou un passage à l'autre rive de la Méditerranée?" in *Polarisation et enjeux des mouvements migratoires entre les deux rives de la Méditerranée*, edited by Gilles Ferréol and Abdel-Halim Berretima (Fernelmont: EME Editions, 2013): 199–218.

Bibliography

Achour-Kallel, Myriam, ed. *Le social par le langage. La parole au quotidien.* Tunis, Paris: IRMC, Karthala, 2015.
Ahlers, Jocelyn C. "Framing Discourse." *Journal of Linguistic Anthropology* 16.1 (2006): 58–75.
Alexander-Nathani, Isabella. "Trapped on the Island: The Politics of Race and Belonging in *Jazīrat al-Maghrib*." *The Journal of North African Studies* 24.5 (2019): 786–806.
Belakhdar, Naoual. "'L'éveil du Sud' ou quand la contestation vient de la marge: Une analyse du mouvement des chômeurs algériens." *Politique Africaine* 137.1 (2015): 27–48.
———. "When Unemployment Meets Environment: The Case of the Anti-Fracking Coalition in Ouargla." *Mediterranean Politics* 24.4 (2019): 420–442.
Benmayouf, Chafia Yamina. *Renouvellement social, renouvellement langagier dans l'Algérie d'aujourd'hui.* Paris: L'Harmattan, 2008.
Benrabah, Mohamed. *Language Conflict in Algeria: From Colonialism to Post-Independence.* Bristol: Multilingual Matters, 2013.
Bhambra, Gurminder K. "Postcolonial and Decolonial Dialogues." *Postcolonial Studies* 17.2 (2014): 115–121.
Bonilla, Yarimar. *Non-Sovereign Futures: French Caribbean Politics in the Wake of Disenchantment.* Chicago: University of Chicago Press, 2015.
Chachou, Ibtissem and Meriem Stambouli, eds. *Pour un plurilinguisme algérien intégré – Approches critiques et renouvellement épistémique.* Paris: Riveneuve, 2016.
Chena, Salim. *Les traversées migratoires dans l'Algérie contemporaine: Africains subsahariens et Algériens vers l'exil.* Paris: Karthala, 2016.
Cheriguen, Foudil, ed. *Les enjeux de la nomination des langues dans l'Algérie contemporaine.* Paris: L'Harmattan, 2007.
Crystal, David. *English as a Global Language.* Cambridge: Cambridge University Press, 2003.
Jacob, Camille. "'Back to the "Futur"': Mobility and Immobility through English in Algeria." *Language & Communication* 68 (2019): 6–16.
———. "English as a Decolonial Language: Academic Frames, Popular Discourses and Language Practices in Algeria." *The Journal of North African Studies* 25.6 (2020): 1013–1032.

———. *English and Social Worlds in Contemporary Algeria*. Unpublished PhD thesis. University of Portsmouth, 2019. https://researchportal.port.ac.uk/en/studentTheses/english-and-social-worlds-in-contemporary-algeria.

Jenks, Christopher Joseph and Jerry Won Lee. "Native Speaker Saviorism: A Racialized Teaching Ideology." *Critical Inquiry in Language Studies* 17.3 (2019): 186–205.

Kachru, Brach. "World Englishes: Approaches, Issues and Resources." *Language Teaching* 25.1 (1992): 1–14.

Kouzmine, Yaël. *Le Sahara algérien: Intégration nationale et développement regional*. Paris: L'Harmattan, 2012.

Kubota, Ryuko. "Inequalities of Englishes, English Speakers, and Languages: A Critical Perspective on Pluralist Approaches to English." In *Unequal Englishes: The Politics of Englishes Today*, edited by Ruanni Tupas. Basingstoke: Palgrave Macmillan, 2015: 21–41.

Lanane, Massika. "La migration africaine en Algérie: une éventuelle intégration ou un passage à l'autre rive de la Méditerranée?" In *Polarisation et enjeux des mouvements migratoires entre les deux rives de la Méditerranée*, edited by Gilles Ferréol and Abdel-Halim Berretima. Fernelmont: EME Editions, 2013: 199–218.

Lardjane, Omar, M. Madi, K. Taleb Ibrahimi, M. Haddab, H. Remaoun and M.-L. Maougal, eds. *Elites et questions identitaires en Algérie*. Algiers: Casbah Editions, 1997.

Liboiron, Max. *Pollution is Colonialism*. Durham: Duke University Press, 2021.

Makoni, Sinfree and Alastair Pennycook, eds. *Disinventing and Reconstituting Languages*. Bristol: Multilingual Matters, 2007.

Marcellesi, Jean-Baptiste, Thierry Bulot and Philippe Blanchet. *Sociolinguistique: Epistémologie, Langues régionales, Polynomie*. Paris: L'Harmattan, 2003.

Oyinloye, Bukola. "Towards an Ọmọlúàbí Code of Research Ethics: Applying a Situated, Participant-Centred Virtue Ethics Framework to Fieldwork with Disadvantaged Populations in Diverse Cultural Settings." *Research Ethics* 17.4 (2021): 401–422.

Pennycook, Alastair. *Global Englishes and Transcultural Flows*. Milton Park, Abingdon: Routledge, 2007.

———. *Language as a Local Practice*. Milton Park, Abingdon: Routledge, 2010.

Taleb-Ibrahimi, Khaoula. *Les Algériens et leur(s) langue(s): éléments pour une approche sociolinguistique de la société algérienne*. Algiers: Editions el Hikma, 1995.

TallBear, Kim. "Standing with and Speaking as Faith: A Feminist-Indigenous Approach to Inquiry [Research Note]." *Journal of Research Practice* 10.2 (2014). http://jrp.icaap.org/index.php/jrp/article/view/405/371.

Temlali, Yassine. "Language Policies in Algeria since 1962: Identity Renewal in Light of Realpolitik Imperatives." In *Routledge Handbook of Francophone Africa*, edited by Natalya Vince and Tony Chafer. Milton Park, Abingdon: Routledge, 2024: 197–225.

Trouillot, Michel-Rolph. *Global Transformations: Anthropology and the Modern World*. New York: Palgrave Macmillan US, 2003.

Wright, Sue. "French as a Lingua Franca." *Annual Review of Applied Linguistics* 26 (2006): 35–60.

III

Contact, Crossover, and Creolization

9

PERFORMING MASCULINITIES USING SHENG IN KENYAN POPULAR CULTURE

The Billingsgate Genres

Alex Nelungo Wanjala

Introduction

Sheng is a linguistic phenomenon in which Swahili is mixed with words drawn from English and other local Kenyan languages. It has been in existence for several years and has been defined as follows:

> Sheng is a mixed language that emerged from the complex multilingual situation of Nairobi City. It is mainly spoken by young people – preadolescents to young adults – and dominates the discourse of primary and secondary school children outside their formal classroom setting. Its syntax is basically Swahili, but through ingenious code switching, it draws from the phonology, morphology and lexicon of Kenyan languages spoken in the city, such as, but not restricted to Luo, Gikuyu, Maasai, Luhya and coastal languages such as Giriama and Taita.[1]

Its development has been documented in articles by linguists such as David Parkin, Abdulaziz and Osinde, Mary Spyropolous, Alamin Mazrui, Chege Githiora, and Frederick Kang'ethe-Iraki, among others.[2]

Sheng is a marker of social identity that originated in colonial times as a para-code of the "underclass."[3] Mazrui demonstrates how Sheng has the peculiarity of possessing the socio-psychological function of differentiating those who use it from others. He traces the origins of the code to the 1930s in Nairobi, when it was used by pickpockets and other members of the underworld. Mazrui describes how the use of this jargon then spread from these professionals of the underworld to young men in Nairobi's Eastlands who popularised it. Eastlands was at the time a unique melting pot in Nairobi inhabited by families drawn from all over Kenya, in what was then a new urban setting. It provided a new home for a large group of people in a city that was defined by its colour bar. Eastlands was the preserve of Africans, while other parts of the city such as Parklands and Westlands were populated by Asians and Europeans, respectively. The youth in Nairobi's Eastlands used the code in order to distinguish their speech from the local languages that were used at home by their parents and elders. Through the use of Sheng, the lower-class urban youth of Nairobi created an in-group as a marker of their social identity that created a social distance between themselves and mainstream urban culture (outgroup). The use of the mixed code was a means of expressing their solidarity in informal social settings.

It may be added that in the post-independence period, the colonial contours of the city of Nairobi were retained, and Nairobi's Eastlands remained the most densely populated part of the city, mainly inhabited by Africans with a relatively low income, and the parts of the city that had been settled by Asians and Europeans remained the same, albeit with an influx of well-heeled Africans. There thus developed a divide in the city that is based on class rather than racial categories. With a large inflow of people from the rural areas into the formal and informal settlements of Eastlands, Sheng continued its expansion in terms of numbers of speakers, as the populations in informal settlements are more mobile in terms of maintaining contact with their rural kin. It has thus in more recent years been continuously absorbed by the outgroup Kenyan population, while the ingroup continuously modifies the code further. A variant based on the grammatical structures of English that draws upon Sheng and English slang called Engsh has also developed and is now increasingly used by middle-class youth in the more affluent parts of the city.

Due to its origins, the use of Sheng has been more pronounced among men and has over time become an arena for the performance of masculinity outside the confines of the institutionalised forms of "traditional masculinity"[4] that have been interpellated through the cultural norms of ethnic societies as well as the institutionalisation of Western culture in colonial and post-colonial times.

The Critical Reception of the Use of Sheng in Mainstream Kenyan Society

The existence and the development of this mixed code has not been received kindly within circles that deal with the evaluation and teaching of languages in Kenya and are thus the institutions in charge of the interpellation of normative masculinity in modern Kenyan society. Most educationists and sociolinguists pinpoint the informal use of the code as being responsible for the deteriorating standards in the performance of learners of English as well as Kiswahili. Articles relating to the subject abound in print media as well as journal publications. An example is Clara Momanyi's article "The Effects of

"Sheng" in the Teaching of Kiswahili in Kenyan Schools."[5] Momanyi reports in her article on the hostility with which a suggestion made by the Kenya Publishers Association in 2006 that they publish some books in Sheng targeted towards a school readership was met by Kenyan parents. The proposal led to a huge debate conducted through Kenyan media in which it was argued that such efforts to mainstream the use of Sheng should be done away with. Parents argued for the formulation of a stronger language policy that would ensure that Sheng is kept out of schools, as the use of the mixed code should be left to "touts, drug pushers, hip hop musicians and school dropouts."[6] The use of Sheng is therefore perceived in mainstream culture as being marked by a class and age difference that locks it out of "normative" language use in Kenyan society, thus the tags given to its users connoting "social deviants" whom "responsible" youth should not emulate.

Thus, we can perceive a cleavage in society between the institutional stigmatisation of the use of Sheng, and its continued proliferation in informal language use, leading to an official/unofficial opposition in language use in Kenyan society. Sheng thus joins other "African Urban Youth Languages" that have been stigmatised in contemporary African society, as indicated in an article by Philip W. Rudd.[7]

Articulating Kenya's Transnation

Despite the official attitude towards the use of Sheng in Kenya, it would be useful to capture this language while it is still in its process of formation and to document its existence as part of Kenya's contemporary cultural artefacts that play a major role in questions of identity formation among the youth in the country today. This requires a form of openness by ourselves as literary critics that allows us to accommodate the divergent cultural experiences of these youth in a manner that privileges their perspective rather than imposing our own standards and ethics upon their worldview. In other words, a certain level of ethics of cosmopolitanism[8] would be expected from the literary critic addressing the study of Sheng and its cultural artefacts.

To do so, it would be helpful for the purposes of this chapter to recognise the collectivity that speaks Sheng as forming part of Kenya's transnation. Bill Ashcroft defines transnation as follows:

> Transnation is the fluid migrating *outside* of the state that begins *within* the nation. This 'outside' is geographical, cultural and conceptual, and is possibly most obvious in India, where the 'nation' is the perpetual scene of *translation*, but translation is but one example of the movement, the 'betweenness' by which the subjects of the transnation are constituted. The transnation is a way of talking about subjects in their ordinary lives, subjects who live in between the categories by which subjectivity is normally constituted.[9]

154 Alex Nelungo Wanjala

One of the distinguishing features of the collectivity that uses Sheng is that its subjects experience a sense of exile, even while being located within their own national borders. This is because with their parents' geographical dislocation from their original rural homes to an urban setting, the subsequent generation experienced loss in their collective identity as members of specific ethnic communities and are now trying to form a new community domiciled in postcolonial urban space. They use the mixed code as a means of expressing conviviality among themselves as subjects, eschewing the categorisation imposed on them by the nation-state of Kenya, in which they are supposed to identify themselves as members of a particular ethnic group and communicate either in one of the local languages, Kiswahili, or English. In so doing, they represent localised subjects who have worked through the structures of the nation-state in order to express a difference without necessarily crossing any state-defined geographical border. They thus occupy a certain in-between space within the nation, through which they articulate[10] their agency as subjects, endorse a utopian potentiality of the transformation of Kenya through their language use, and challenge the status quo and official authorities.

It is thus the intent of this chapter to demonstrate how members of this collectivity articulate their masculinities through literary texts. As I have argued elsewhere,[11] there is a lot of creativity in texts that are exchanged by Sheng speakers that exploit social media platforms such as WhatsApp, Twitter, TikTok, and Instagram for their dissemination. Issues affecting Kenyans are discussed through such platforms in a very creative manner that exploits the use of Sheng. Stories and memes are created by individuals and disseminated on these platforms. Such texts actualise Arjun Appadurai's assertion that the imagination has, over the past century or so, become a collective fact due to technological changes that have led to the existence of mass medialisation of the world. As he opines, "the imagination has broken out of the special expressive space of art, myth, and ritual and has now become a part of the quotidian mental work of ordinary people in many societies."[12]

The Billingsgate Genres

The texts that I have chosen to present in this study are selected from memes that are predominant on social media platforms and are sometimes generated randomly but are mostly created in response to a topical issue, an event, or a festival. They are interesting in their attempt to elicit humour in their reworking of a normative masculinity by debasing the female gender in a manner that would reveal and celebrate the gender identities of the authors of the text. In other words, they are texts that reveal male bonding by members of the Sheng ethne who are performing their own types of masculinities as a transgression of the hegemonic masculinities perpetuated in the official strata of society.

Performing Masculinities Using Sheng in Kenyan Culture **155**

These texts arguably can be considered contemporary versions of what the translators of Mikhaïl Bakhtin's *Rabelais and His World* have termed the "Billingsgate" genres, as depicted in the novels of François Rabelais. Bakhtin examines popular humour and folk culture in the Middle Ages and Renaissance period in an effort to understand how similar cultural aspects were represented in François Rabelais's novels while at the same time indicating how in the classical and the romantic period that follows the Renaissance period, "the wholeness of the world's comic aspect is destroyed, and that which appears comic becomes a private reaction,"[13] leading to some loss in meaning in the study of literature in modern times due to the rendering of some aspects of folk culture as being vulgar and not worthy of study.

In my analysis of the texts that are shared on digital platforms using Sheng, I will demonstrate how their depiction of humour is somewhat akin to the function of popular humour in the Billingsgate genres as studied by Bakhtin and how by extension an understanding of the meaning of these texts is arrived at through discerning intertextual masculinities by contrasting the hegemonic masculinity prevalent in Kenyan society with the depictions of society conjured up creatively by young men who feel disempowered and marginalised by the socio-economic set up of the society and are thus performing a transgressive type of masculinity as a way of bonding with their counterparts.

One such text is a meme which was created anonymously and has been disseminated through social media platforms since 2016. It is a photograph of a scene that could be a marketplace, as in the background of the photo is a small group of people, and in the foreground, there is a tray containing a large quantity of avocadoes that could be interpreted to be some of the merchandise that is available for sale at this market. The main focus of the photograph is two individuals, one a well-dressed young man who is crouching in order to properly address his interlocuter, a young lady, who is seated. The young man is holding one of the avocadoes that is offered for sale in the palm of his hands. The two seem to be in an intimate conversation, as the young lady is captured laughing while explaining something, whereas the young man is listening keenly to what is being said.

The meme has a caption containing the words: "*Ushawai bargain avocado for 30 minutes*," which is supposed to elicit humour from the reader due to a play on words in the sentence that – when contrasted with the visual imagery presented in the photo to those words – brings out a clear demonstration of the use of innuendo in the text. Through a study in semiotics, one can call attention to the way language is being used by the author of the caption in a manner that is of interest to practitioners of literary and cultural studies.

In the caption of the image, there is clear evidence of the use of code mixing in the sentence "*Ushawai bargain avocado for 30 minutes*," as the first word, "*ushawai*," is a word that is derived from Swahili, although its use

156 Alex Nelungo Wanjala

in a contracted form and the tone in which the word would be pronounced indicate that it has already been transformed into Sheng. In standard Swahili, it would be proper to say "*umesha wahi*" rather than "*ushawai*." However, the words both connote "have you ever?" The rest of the sentence would be understandable to any English speaker, as all the words "bargain avocado for 30 minutes" are in that language. However, the syntactic organisation of that part of the sentence remains that of Kiswahili. The sentence would therefore translate to "Have you ever spent 30 minutes haggling over the price of an avocado?" What elicits humour in the caption is the ambivalent use of the word *avocado*, which through the evidence provided in the photograph not only refers to the material object of avocado as a fruit but as a play on words suggesting that it may also denote breasts, which are clearly captured in the image with attention being drawn to how they bear some resemblance to the fruits on display. The innuendo in the meme is that the young man captured in the photograph is not only interested in the fruits per se but is also attracted to the young girl, which is hinted at through the play on significance in the use of the word avocado, thus connoting sexual desire using food imagery.

A literary examination of the caption thus provides evidence of the death of the word "avocado" as an English word that connotes fruit and an attempt to transform its meaning into a new Sheng usage. We thus capture the process through which the word has been made to become ambivalent, because it now refers not only to the fruit but also to a body part. The semiotics of the imagery used thus reflects a grotesque realism, as the word "Avocado," when relexified from its connotation as a fruit to instead indicate a female body part, demonstrates degradation and the death of a word through humiliation and derision. At the same time, it highlights an aspect of birth and renewal, however, because we observe the probability of a new Sheng word being coined, while the entire phrase plays on the mixing of English, Kiswahili, and local languages to provide new meaning through the use of grotesque humour.

The intertext in this text is arrived at by understanding how the "turning upside-down" of the meaning of the word avocado requires the reader to be familiar with the mainstream connotation of the word and its meaning in English that have been taught through the formal use of English. The reader must then display complicity with the marginalised groups for whom a transgressive reading of the text would elicit humour through an understanding of the new connotation for the word arrived at through its being debased. The debasing of the word avocado thus plays into gender politics through semiotics in its representation of lack of the phallus, thus complementing the image of the woman in the photograph while depicting the man in the photograph as being present and as being the voice in the caption by virtue of being closer to the transcendental signifier. The function of this meme is to counter hegemonic masculinity by transgressing the norms of politeness in mainstream society. The humour it elicits in its readers through this is a form of male bonding for Kenya's transnation. The meme is thus an example of a modern form of the Billingsgate genres that is disseminated through social media platforms. As Bakhtin states, "the genres [...] [have] great powers of travesty, of debasement and materialization which render the world more carnal [...] bringing an atmosphere of freedom, frankness and familiarity."[14]

Another example of such a text is as follows.

FIGURE 9.1   Mpenda kuni hali nauli.

The above meme illustrates a more finished product regarding the aspiration for the death of a word in the sense it is used in an existing language and its rebirth in Sheng through the use of grotesque humour. Using festival laughter, this sentence, which is a parody of a traditional African proverb, renews language by providing it with new meanings. In this case, the meaning of the Swahili word "kuni" has been altered from its original connotation of "firewood," which at the material level means wood that is used for cooking and heating, and been relexified in Sheng to refer to a bodily part of the lower stratum, which is the penis. The word in its new sense is already a popular expression used by Sheng speakers. Hence "kuni," used in the parody of proverb, elicits humour while at the same time providing a commentary on a contemporary cultural phenomenon.

Indeed, the last two words of the phrase "hali nauli" are in reference to a transaction that has become commonplace in courtship among youth in contemporary Kenyan society, in that it is expected that when a young man invites a young lady to come over to his house for a visit, he would facilitate her movement by providing money for her transport, usually through mobile money transfer services such as the popular Mpesa, so that the expression "tuma fare" (send me transport money) that is exchanged in SMS conversations among the youth is now commonly seen as an expression of the willingness on the part of the girl being courted to enter into the next phase of the relationship. Social commentary on such interactions indicates that there are some ladies who go against the expected norm by receiving the transport money but then simply fail to show up – an act which is known in popular parlance as "kukula fare" or "eating the transport money." In the context of the previous meme, the phrase "kukula fare," which contains the Kiswahili word "kukula" and the English word "fare" to connote a commonly used phrase, has been made exotic through transforming the word "fare" into "nauli" so as to wink towards the possibility of it sounding like an authentic Kiswahili proverb. This parody of a proverb translates into "She who loves the penis does not eat transport money" and seemingly provides an explanation on the nature of people who are not likely to use the fare sent to them for other purposes, thus demonstrating the moral attitude of the community towards the "kukula fare" phenomenon in a humorous manner. One could also read the fears of the persona (or speaker) in this proverb, which represents the male voice as a cuckold in contemporary times, as those of a man who is worried that the financial transaction he has engaged in is not binding and who is thus trying to project his fears as the fault of the woman but then tries to assuage himself (and his male counterparts) that the symbol of the phallus will surmount financial inadequacies. This is paradoxical because the same phallus that the text consciously presents as a compensation mechanism is really a representation of the castration anxiety suffered by the author of the text. Through an understanding of the intertext, one can read how the humour in the text provides male bonding for the members of Kenya's transnation while at the same time revealing their anxieties.

This parody of a proverb, while ushering in a new meaning of the word "kuni," also retains the traditional functions of a proverb and is thus a good text for literary analysis. Its exposition demonstrates that the study of the Billingsgate genres not only captures the evolution of language through word play, but, at a higher level, these genres can be tackled as valuable tools of analysis in addressing "serious" issues related to culture and society. This is because, as Bakhtin points out, carnival culture "belongs to the borderline between art and life. In reality, it is life itself, but shaped according to a

Performing Masculinities Using Sheng in Kenyan Culture **159**

certain pattern of play."[15] We thus interrogate how Kenyan urban youth use humour that is ambivalent in its nature not only to give birth to an idiom that depicts the horizonal reality of their ethne (as opposed to the vertical reality of official culture, as has been demonstrated in the memes depicted previously) but also in order to attain a certain visibility through the depiction of their own worldview in opposition to certain aspects of official culture, which is depicted in the ongoings in homogenous culture.

Festival Humour in Sheng

As we highlighted previously, through the focus on memes in social media, popular culture in Kenya has developed a corpus of humorous texts that are non-official in nature and are generated in opposition to the hegemonic masculinity displayed in the official state apparatus as well as in the serious tone of various cultural events that take place in the country from time to time. The memes also provide a parody of serious topical events that are receiving increased public attention. When such topics receive prolonged attention on social media, they are said to be "trending."

One of the public festivities that has been parodied on social media in Kenya is the Valentine's Day celebration. With the rapid urbanisation of Africa as well as the adoption of Western practices, Valentine's Day has achieved tremendous commercial success in Kenya, and marketing companies use it as an opportunity to push for the purchase of their products, including offers for couples to dine at various restaurants, accommodation packages in hotels, bouquets of flowers, chocolates, and other gifts that society expects men to offer their partners in commemoration of the occasion. Such offers are quite lavish and far out of reach of the average urban youth. The hyper-marketing of such offers that has come with increased media visibility in the digital age has been a source of financial pressure on young men in urban society, who are expected to conform and adapt to the current cultural trends in regard to the observation of Valentine's Day, despite the harsh economic realities that they experience in their day-to-day lives. The marketing agencies that come up with such campaigns could be said to be promoting hegemonic masculinity through informing the public that men must spend money over the Valentine's Day period in order to demonstrate their love for their partner, which then would strain relationships within couples, as the man is expected to conform to these expectations.

It is due to the pressure that comes with the celebration of the occasion that an imaginary event came up as a countermeasure to Valentine's Day. It originated in South Africa but due to its online presence was quickly picked up by Kenyan youth through social media platforms. The event is known as the Men's Conference. In an effort to "disappear" from the scene during the period of festivities around Valentine's Day, men are provided with the opportunity to attend a "conference" exclusively reserved for them. It is always scheduled to begin around the eve of Valentine's Day and to continue until the day after Valentine's. The venue of the conference is supposedly secret, thus giving men an imagined opportunity to be incommunicado from their partners over the duration of the Valentine's period. A hashtag #Mens Conference trends over the Valentine's period, expounding on the nature and exclusivity of the event, with suggested activities being creatively enumerated by anonymous individuals. Celebrities and marketers have also begun to tap into the carnival mood created by the hashtag to market their products.

Over the period around St. Valentine's Day, memes are disseminated through the hashtag #Men'sConference, with the most humorous ones gaining a lot of traction and being shared widely by the public.

FIGURE 9.2 Men's conference.

The above is an example. It is not clear what the origins of the photograph are. It depicts a young man in agony as he is under attack by five other men who have surrounded him, one of them holding him by the scruff of the neck. The men in the photograph are all well dressed and thus would seem to have been attending an official ceremony when the incident took place. It is not clear why they are attacking the young man, but it could be surmised from the situation that the young man did something that interfered with a formal event and that his aggressors are in the process of ejecting him from the event. The violent nature of the photograph is however made light of using captions that suggest the reason the young man has found himself in such a situation. The captions have the resulting effect of making light of the serious situation through injecting humour into it, thus depicting grotesque imagery.

In relation to the Men's Conference, the photograph is usually captioned with comments that capture the nature of the offence he committed in order

Performing Masculinities Using Sheng in Kenyan Culture **161**

to arouse the anger of the security officials, such as "Kevo amepatikana hapa Men's conference akitext wife" ("Kevin was caught texting his wife at the Men's conference"), or "Mr.Otieno being ejected out of the Men's conference after our security team was notified that he sent fare to one Mwende yesterday."

It is evident from the imagined festivities around the Men's Conference, as depicted creatively through the use of memes, that the members of Kenya's transnation use popular art forms in order to express their difference from the official structures of the nation-state. The official structures require that men effectively participate in the Valentine's Day festivities. However, this collectivity, while displaying an understanding of what is expected officially, instead creates a parody of the acknowledged official day, through which, as opposed to the formal requirements of Valentine's Day celebrations, they come up with informal activities that are organised on the basis of laughter, including comic rituals and spectacles that are externally linked to the official day but, most importantly, devoid of its commercial interests. The use of parody and the humour that arises from the grotesque realism of the memes that are swapped regarding the Men's Conference indicate a sense of the carnivalesque. The social function in this case is that because of the borderline nature of art and reality, through the means of such texts, young men can find solace and an imaginary means of escape from the harsh economic demands surrounding Valentine's Days festivities.

Another illustration of the use of festival humour using memes on social media in Kenya was evident during the relaunch of the Safari Rally Championship in Kenya as a World Rally Championship event in June 2021. The Safari Rally has been part and parcel of Kenya's cultural celebrations since the colonial period and was something that all families looked forward to around the Easter Period. However, the event was dropped from the World Rally Championship calendar in 2002, leading to its disappearance from Kenya's social calendar.

It was revived, however, as a World Rally Championship event in 2021, which was quite a significant achievement for the country, considering that at the time the entire world was experiencing the ravages of the COVID-19 pandemic. As a result of the protocols in place due to the pandemic, most of the stages of the Safari Rally took place near Naivasha town, which is located some 90 kilometres to the northwest of Nairobi. In popular lore, Naivasha has always been known as part of the hunting grounds of a group of aristocratic British socialites that had settled in what were then known as the White Highlands of Kenya during the colonial period. They were famous for their hedonistic lifestyle that earned the area the appellation "Happy Valley." The exploits of the aristocrats in their adherence to what is popularly referred to as "the three A's – alcohol, altitude, adultery" are well documented by such writers as James Fox,[16] Nicholas Best,[17] and Juliet Barnes.[18]

In the contemporary Kenyan imagination, the kind of hedonistic lifestyle practiced by the Happy Valley set of the colonial period is represented by a group of young men referred to as "Subaru boys," commonly seen driving their noisy vehicles at breakneck speeds down the highway leading to and from Naivasha, in total disregard of road safety rules as they go on weekend escapades involving decadence and irresponsibility. They display the fast life that is a social phenomenon in hegemonic masculinities. Naivasha town is therefore perceived by youth from Nairobi as a place to go to when they want to escape from the vagaries of city life, and thus most young men in Nairobi aspire towards the lifestyle of the "Subaru boys." Indeed, according to the director of Kenya's National Transport and Safety Authority, Mr. George Njao, speaking in 2020, these "Subaru boys" are responsible for the spike in road accidents on Kenyan roads in recent times. The "Subaru boys" have also created an online presence over the years by forming a Subaru Owners Club on Facebook and creating WhatsApp groups through which they organise out-of-town events.

Over the week before the rally event therefore, a combination of the popular lore around the "Happy Valley" area, a love for fast motor vehicles by the youth, and the images that abound about the hedonistic lifestyle of the "Subaru boys" contributed to the generation of memes in popular media. These memes were running concurrently to the official news of the plans that were underway in preparation for the event. There was an abundance of humorous memes that focused on how the "Subaru boys" were poised to take over the highways the coming weekend and would drive down from Nairobi to "Vasha" in a long procession of Subaru vehicles, each in the company of somebody else's girlfriend. A tweep, Zero Gravity, summarised this view using a text written in Sheng: "sai nairobi subaru legends wamejaa pale waiyaki way wakielekea safari rally pale naivasha this weekend. Hapo kwa backseat madem wenu watakua wametulia na 6 pack za Savanna cider wakisupply fake laughter alafu warudi online Tuesday. Stay Strong Champions."[19] The meme was completed with a laughter emoji to indicate that this is just a joke. It translates into "From Thursday onwards, Nairobi Subaru legends will be spotted on Waiyaki Way headed towards Naivasha for the Safari Rally that takes place this weekend. On the back seat of their cars will be your girlfriends who will be relaxing next to a 6-pack supply of Savanna cider and providing fake laughter. They will only reappear online as from Tuesday next week. Stay Strong Champions." Similar memes started trending on Twitter using hashtags such as #Vashatings, #Subaruboys, and #Vasha. They mostly focused on warning young men in a humorous manner to watch out, as that weekend they were bound to lose their girlfriends to the "Subaru boys" who would have convinced their girls to drive down to Naivasha with them, ostensibly to watch the rally event but in reality to engage in adulterous activities.

Performing Masculinities Using Sheng in Kenyan Culture   **163**

It is thus evident that youth in Kenyan society used memes to take the focus away from the Safari Rally Championship that was an official function that had been programmed to occur over a certain weekend and was receiving good publicity in mainstream media. The youth instead chose to focus on imagined social activities that would take place on the periphery of the main event. The members of the transnation were vicariously participating in an activity that they knew they could not physically attend through their male bonding online. Thus, the memes they shared indicate a parody of the official rally through focusing upon activities that would be more appealing to the youth that form Kenya's transnation had they been able to afford getting to the venue.

One could thus interpret them as expressing aspirations by the youth towards social mobility, so that in the future they may be like their more well-heeled counterparts, whom they depict as having taken advantage of their privileged economic circumstances to snatch away their girlfriends. The flurry created by the youth in their exchange of messages on digital platforms over the week preceding the event generated even more publicity about the event than the official messages, and given the borderline between life and art, may have encouraged even more youth to travel to Naivasha than would have been the case otherwise. The Billingsgate genres in this case served the social function of allowing the youth to imagine themselves as participants in functions that would run parallel to the state-functioned popular event of the June 2021 Safari Rally World Championship.

Conclusion

This chapter has illustrated how in Kenya, the mixed code of Sheng, which is a marker of social identity, has led to the production of literary texts that are modern manifestations of popular folk culture, albeit disseminated through social media platforms thanks to the proliferation of digital media in Kenyan society due to the rise in the use of Internet communications technology. It has also shown how these texts serve as a platform for male bonding. The chapter has identified such texts as being worthy of consideration in serious literary scholarship alongside other texts studied in the canon of contemporary Kenyan literature. The chapter examined the literary features of the texts in an effort to point out how the language used demonstrates that there exists in Kenya a collectivity that articulates the intertext between traditional Africa, the modern nation-state of Kenya, and the marginalised in society and that these texts are thus a representation of Kenya's transnation, who through reworking English and Kiswahili into the future language of Sheng are defining their place as a new ethne in global society on their own terms.

164 Alex Nelungo Wanjala

Notes

1 Chege Githiora, "Sheng: Peer Languages, Swahili Dialect or Emerging Creole?" *Journal of African Cultural Studies* 15.2 (2002): 159.
2 See David Parkin, "Language Switching in Nairobi," in *Language in Kenya*, edited by W. H. Whiteley (Oxford: Oxford University Press, 1974): 189–216; Mohamed H. Abdulaziz and Ken Osinde, "Sheng and English: Development of Mixed Codes among the Urban Youth in Kenya," *International Journal of the Sociology of Language* 125 (1997): 45–53; Mary Spyropolous, "Sheng: Some Preliminary Investigations into a Recently Emerged Nairobi Street Language," *Journal of the Anthropological Society of Oxford* 18.2 (1987): 125–136; Alamin Mazrui, "Slang and Code-Switching: The Case of Sheng in Kenya," *Afrikanistische Arbeitspapiere* 42 (1995): 168–179; Githiora, "Sheng"; Kang'ethe Frederick Iraki, "Cognitive Efficiency: The Sheng Phenomenon in Kenya," *Pragmatics: Quarterly Journal of the International Pragmatics Association* 14.1 (2004): 55–68.
3 Mazrui, "Slang and Code-Switching," 172.
4 By 'traditional masculinities,' I refer to the social description of persons describes as male in different cultural groupings interpellating people according to their sexes as 'men' and 'women.' See Judith Gardiner, "Men, Masculinities, and Feminist Theory," in *Handbook of Studies on Men & Masculinities*, edited by Michael S. Kimmel, Jeff Hearn and R. W. Connell (Thousand Oaks: Sage, 2005): 35–50.
5 Clara Momanyi, "The Effects of 'Sheng' in the Teaching of Kiswahili in Kenyan Schools," *The Journal of Pan-African Studies* 2.8 (March 2009): 127–138.
6 Momanyi, "The Effects of 'Sheng'," 134.
7 Philip W. Rudd, "A Case Study of the Stigmatized Code Sheng: The AUYL Syndrome," *Ufahamu: A Journal of African Studies* 40.1 (2018): 155–174.
8 We are guided in this quest by Kwame Anthony Appiah's *Cosmopolitanism: Ethics in a World of Strangers* (New York: Norton, 2007).
9 Bill Ashcroft, "Transnation," in *Rerouting the Postcolonial: New Directions for the New Millennium*, edited by Janet Wilson, Cristina Şandru and Sarah Lawson Wel (New York: Routledge, 2010): 73.
10 Ashcroft prefers the use of the term 'articulation' rather than 'hybridity' in order to refer to the action of subjects in their interstitial subjectivity rather than simply suggesting location.
11 See Alex Wanjala, "From Swahili to Sheng: Documenting the Emergence of a New Ethne in Kenyan Society," *Phoenix: Sri Lanka Journal of English in the Commonwealth* 15 and 16 (2018/2019): 81–89.
12 Arjun Appadurai, *Modernity at Large: Cultural Dimensions of Globalization* (Minneapolis: Minnesota University Press, 1996): 87.
13 Mikhail Bakhtin, *Rabelais and His World*, translated by Hélène Iswolsky (Indiana University Press, 1984): 12.
14 Bakhtin, *Rabelais*, 195.
15 Bakhtin, *Rabelais*, 7.
16 James Fox, *White Mischief: The Murder of Lord Errol* (New York: Random House, 1983).
17 Nicholas Best, *Happy Valley: The Story of the English in Kenya* (London: Martin Secker & Warburg, 1979).
18 Juliet Barnes, *The Ghosts of Happy Valley: Searching for the Lost World of Africa's Infamous Aristocrats* (London: Aurum Press, 2013).
19 Zero Gravity [@iconic_gravity], 22 June 2021.

Bibliography

Abdulaziz, Mohamed H. and Ken Osinde, "Sheng and English: Development of Mixed Codes among the Urban Youth in Kenya." *International Journal of the Sociology of Language* 125 (1997): 45–53.

Appadurai, Arjun. *Modernity at Large: Cultural Dimensions of Globalization*. Minneapolis: Minnesota University Press, 1996.

Appiah, Kwame. *Cosmopolitanism: Ethics in a World of Strangers*. New York: Norton, 2007.

Ashcroft, Bill: "Transnation." In *Rerouting the Postcolonial: New Directions for the New Millennium*, edited by Janet Wilson, Cristina Şandru and Sarah Lawson Welsh. New York: Routledge, 2010: 72–85.

Bakhtin, Mikhail, *Rabelais and His World*, translated by Hélène Iswolsky. Bloomington: Indiana University Press, 1984.

Barnes, Juliet. *The Ghosts of Happy Valley: Searching for the Lost World of Africa's Infamous Aristocrats*. London: Aurum Press, 2013.

Best, Nicholas. *Happy Valley: The Story of the English in Kenya*. London: Martin Secker & Warburg, 1979.

Bosire, Stella. "Ezekiel Mutua's Woes Were Painfully Predictable." 10 August 2021. https://nation.africa/kenya/life-and-style/culture/dr-bosire-ezekiel-mutua-s-woes-were-painfully-predictable–3506260?fbclid=IwAR0i1H1tsvXEat-WTKpv JQWIZEJSNzwWvo7u6DfjhAIzyMufKv3YWARXOEo (last accessed 27 March 2024).

Connell, R. W. *Masculinities*. Cambridge: Polity Press, 1995.

Fox, James. *White Mischief: The Murder of Lord Erroll*. New York: Random House, 1983.

Gardiner, Judith, Kegan. "Men, Masculinities, and Feminist Theory." In *Handbook of Studies on Men & Masculinities*, edited by Michael S. Kimmel, Jeff Hearn and R. W. Connell. Thousand Oaks: Sage, 2005: 35–50.

Githiora, Chege. "Sheng: Peer Languages, Swahili Dialect or Emerging Creole? *Journal of African Cultural Studies* 15.2 (2002): 159–181.

Iraki, Kang'ethe Frederick. "Cognitive Efficiency: The *Sheng* Phenomenon in Kenya." *Pragmatics: Quarterly Journal of the International Pragmatics Association* 14.1 (2004): 55–68.

Kahiu, W. (Director). *Rafiki* (Film). Big World Cinema, MPM Film, Shortcut Films, 2018.

LaGuardia, David P. *Intertextual Masculinity in French Renaissance Literature: Rabelais, Brantôme and the cent nouvelles nouvelles*. Burlington: Ashgate, 2008.

Mazrui, Alamin. "Slang and Code-Switching: the Case of Sheng in Kenya." *Afrikanistische Arbeitspapiere* 42 (1995): 168–179.

Mokua, K. M. [@KevinProVOKE]. "Subaru Boys Going Through the List of Girlfriends Booked for the Vasha Rally # Vasha." [Tweet]. 24 June 2021.

Momanyi, Clara, "The Effects of 'Sheng' in the Teaching of Kiswahili in Kenyan Schools." *The Journal of Pan-African Studies* 2.8 (March 2009): 127–138.

Parkin, David. "Language Switching in Nairobi." In *Language in Kenya*, edited by W. H. Whiteley. Oxford: Oxford University Press, 1974: 189–216.

Rudd, Philip W. "A Case Study of the Stigmatized Code Sheng: The AUYL Syndrome." *Ufahamu: A Journal of African Studies* 40.1 (2018): 155–174.

Spyropolous, Mary. "Sheng: Some Preliminary Investigations into a Recently Emerged Nairobi Street Language." *Journal of the Anthropological Society of Oxford* 18.2 (1987): 125–136.

Wako, Amina. "Subaru Boys Fingered by NTSA in Road Accident Spike." 29 October 2020. https://nairobinews.nation.co.ke/subaru-boys-fingered-by-ntsa-in-road-accident-spike-video/ (last accessed 27 March 2024).

Wanjala, Alex. "From Swahili to Sheng: Documenting the Emergence of a New Ethne in Kenyan Society." *Phoenix: Sri Lanka Journal of English in the Commonwealth* 15 and 16 (2018/2019): 81–89.

Zero Gravity [@iconic_gravity]. "sai nairobi subaru legends wamejaa pale waiyaki way wakielekea safari rally pale naivasha this weekend. Hapo kwa backseat madem wenu watakua wametulia na 6 pack za Savanna Cider wakisupply fake laughter alafu warudi online Tuesday. Stay Strong Champions." 22 June 2021. https://x.com/KenyanTraffic/status/1540186424418631680 (last accessed 22 January 2024).

10

SITUATING CHICK LIT OF THE GLOBAL SOUTH IN PRINT AND ONLINE

Nicklas Hållén and Delphine Munos

Although it has non-white precursors such as *Waiting to Exhale* (1992) by African American writer Terry McMillan, chick lit is often traced back to a British and/or a US import, namely Helen Fielding's *Bridget Jones's Diary* (1996) and Candace Bushnell's *Sex and the City* (1997) which "began as newspaper columns and went on to become bestsellers."[1] Unsurprisingly in this context, the genre, which emerged from the very centre of the late capitalist world system, is generally seen as an expression of a 'big-city' Western subjectivity while being typically associated with a 'post-feminist' culture and sensibility, that is, a "practice, ideology, and way of being"[2] where female agency is predicated on consumption, individualism, and freedom of choice.

However, critics working within the fields of popular cultures of the Global South have suggested that there might be more to the chick lit genre than just Bridget Jones's (or Carrie Bradshaw's) 'post-feminist' Anglo-American narrative. Two major developments troubling assumptions about the "white-normative"[3] and western-centric aspect of the chick lit genre are of special interest to us in this chapter. The first development relates to the creation of chick lit imprints situated outside the Anglo-American literary market with local and/or trans-regional audiences in mind, notably in India and in the English and French speaking part of sub-Saharan Africa.[4] For instance, in Nigeria, Ankara Press established a local chick lit imprint in 2014,[5] while Penguin India launched Metro Reads in 2010, a series offering "racy quickies"[6] to big-city commuters. In South Africa alone, 2010 saw the creation of Nollybooks and Sapphire Press, both imprints targeting Black 'born-frees' using different storylines and various formats. Equally importantly, the multiplication of 'local' chick lit imprints in contemporary sub-Saharan Africa now goes hand in hand with the popularisation of social media and digital

DOI: 10.4324/9781003464037-14
This chapter has been made available under a CC-BY-NC-ND 4.0 license.

technologies, which is "radically changing the composition, size and power of the African reading public" and has led to a "second wave of African literary production on social media platforms."[7] This is exemplified, for instance, by the recent creation of the Kenyan Drumbeat-Romance-series, which publishes chick lit in eBook format, or the phenomenal success of Mike Maphoto's serialised Facebook chick lit blog, *Diary of a Zulu Girl* (2013), whose digital format allowed Maphoto to interact with his readers,[8] even to take on board some of their comments and tailor his storyline according to the real-life experiences of the 'born-free' generation.[9]

In the emerging ecologies of chick lit in Nigeria and India, social mobility and aspiration are key themes that are also inscribed into the form itself, which is often tackled by aspiring authors who are very active in building an audience, not least on social media. The question remains, though, as to what extent Global South iterations of chick lit can accommodate the cracks inherent in the tension between, on the one hand, a genre with roots in the urban metropolis and in the English language, and on the other, narratives based in globalising cities of the Global South where "jumbled up" and "palimpsestic cultural times" are made to co-exist.[10] Needless to say, these projects are not always successful or even coherent literarily speaking. Yet they open new windows onto the ways in which the key theme of aspiration – which is itself framed by local contexts of production – plays out on the thematic and linguistic levels. More specifically, in this chapter, we want to study the role of englishes in Indian and Nigerian chick lit, where strategic uses of different forms of englishes are interrelated with the protagonists' as well as the authors' aspirational projects.

In the context of post-liberalisation India, Rashmi Sadana notes that English is both "a language of aspiration and a curse for those [who are] not in a position to master it."[11] The cultural anthropologist indeed reminds us that "English is spoken fluently by close to 5 percent of Indians and is 'known' by as much as 10 percent of the population (i.e., about 50 million to 100 million people of a population of just over one billion)."[12] Sadana emphasises a significant shift in perception of English in post-liberalisation India – from a "language of colonization" to a "language of aspiration" (6). In fact, she continues, English is now "integral to middle-class identity" (3) in the subcontinent, so much so that "people speak not of 'knowing' English but of 'having' it" (14). Alluding to the "disparate thought-worlds" that are associated with the daily practice of multilingualism in India and transposing them to Indian fiction in English, Sadana notes that English might be "part of the social scene" but that "the bulk of conversations and sentiments of fictional characters would in reality take place not in English but in one or more of the other Indian languages" (4). Sadana's remarks about English as a language of aspiration and the "disparate thought-worlds" at play in multilingual societies apply equally well to the Nigerian context. In fact, in self-published Nigerian Anglophone chick lit, the authors' balancing act of faithfulness to the genre on the one hand and need to reshape it on the other is reflected in their sometimes creative use of non-local dialects and idioms. A reason for this is arguably that certain kinds of non-Nigerian language practices and codes are associated with metropolitan urban culture and a materially comfortable life, while more local and traditional ways of naming and speaking are connected with social immobility. Romanus Aboh argues for the existence of a literary idiom – "Nigerian Literary English" – that is associated with creative writing and that is perceived by readers as distinctly Nigerian.[13] We hesitate to assume the existence of a definable literary idiom with its own linguistic properties that is found only in literary works and is distinct from Standard Nigerian English. However, we want to underscore Aboh's point that it is possible to conceptualise the English in some forms of Nigerian literature as a literary construct and "a variety of English that many Nigerians can identify with."[14] Rather than *a* literary English, we see the use of English in self-published Nigerian genre-fiction as a mix of eng-lishes for rhetorical and aesthetic purposes. In other words, particularly in self-published 'popular' literature, there is often a polyglossic shifting (rather than switching) between Nigerian and non-Nigerian englishes, sociolects, dialects, ethnolects, gendered registers, and so on. Nuances between different forms of English (and Pidgin), we argue, take on more than superficial mean-ing in the narrative.

This chapter looks at how englishes are used strategically in selected Indian and Nigerian chick lit texts, particularly in relation to narratives about social mobility, to signal rootedness in the local but also connectedness with life-styles and identity constructions that are associated with spaces located beyond the 'here and now' – what Myambo calls "first-world cultural time zones."[15] In what follows, we endorse Sandra Ponzanesi's remarks that if, on the one hand "the genre reveals common patterns of denomination, linked to consumerism, female upward mobility and rapid urbanization," on the other, chick lit from countries in Africa, Latin America and Asia "presents inherent features linked to the country-specific economic development, particular his-tories of feminism and locally inflected responses to commoditized patterns of behaviour."[16] We also take as a point of departure the position that Lynda Gichanda Spencer defines when, taking on board Stephanie Newell's sugges-tion that dominant genres can also "signify resistance, reassertion, renewal and rethinking"[17] whenever they are taken up by writers who are "situated geographically and economically outside the centres of mass production," she describes chick lit from the Global South as an "uprising form," one that is "capable of conveying potentially radical challenges to (dominant) gender ideologies."[18]

Looking at selected Indian and Nigerian commercial fiction (both born-digital and in print), this chapter opens new vistas on how 'local' chick

Situating Chick Lit of the Global South in Print and Online **169**

lit from the Global South "registers its situated-ness"[19] by both adopting ideologies and genre conventions central to "mainstream" Western chick lit and "rethinking" them.[20] More specifically, we are interested in studying chick lit as a form that "works in tandem with the economic policies of global neoliberal capitalism to construct a desirable world order where the values of materialistic individualism reigns supreme"[21] but that moves across an economic world system that is uneven, multi-polar, and multilingual, including within the postcolony.

India: Having English

The paradox of chick lit as a potentially "uprising form"[22] that can convey radical challenges to gender conservatism and yet continues to "wor[k] in tandem with the economic policies of global neoliberal capitalism,"[23] to return to Myambo's words, is nowhere more evident than in contemporary Indian commercial fiction. In fact, as we will show in this section, writers such as Chetan Bhagat, Anuja Chauhan, Durjoy Datta, and Sudeep Nagarkar appear to be hyper-conscious of the fact that English stands at the heart of many social changes in post-liberalisation India, and Bhagat even goes as far as self-reflexively (and strategically) alluding to his own work as a means of entering the social scene associated with this "language of aspiration" (Sadana).

Bhavya Tiwari notes that in the last two decades, new writings in English have emerged that are "independent from the literary and publishing connections" that South Asian diasporic 'star' authors of the past, such as Salman Rushdie and Amitav Ghosh, often "enjoyed in the UK and North America."[24] As Abhijit Gupta remarks, the liberalisation of the Indian economy in the 1990s went hand in hand with the coming of satellite television and new English-language print and electronic media, all of which have "generated a set of new narrative protocols that found their ways into fiction"[25] and conjured up "a new regime of English-language publishing in India."[26] Mostly falling within the commercial categories of "chick lit, lad lit, and Bharati fantasy"[27] or confusingly more than one or two of these categories,[28] these new writings are not marked for export and are "distributed outside the metropolitan bookstore circuit, in gas stations and traffic stops, convenience stores and footpaths."[29]

Designed to appeal to the lower- and middle-class Indian youth, post-millennial 'tween lit,' which Basu associates with a "third phase in the realm of Indian writing in English"[30] sells at INR 100 (USD 1.20) and sometimes lower in pirated versions. This is about six times cheaper than 'literary' Indian writing in English à la Ghosh and Rushdie, whose "second-phase" elitist texts are much feted abroad but are perceived to boil down, at home, "to a short extract in textbooks meant for select Indian high schools."[31]

FIGURE 10.1   Bookstalls close to Churchgate, one of Mumbai's main inner-city train hubs, December 2022. Photograph by Delphine Munos.

Disregarded as they may be by cultural commentators who call them "lo-cal literati,"[32] writers such as Chetan Bhagat, Anuja Chauhan, Durjoy Datta, and Sudeep Nagarkar, among others, have vibrantly captured the lives of a contemporary Indian youth who navigate "exam culture, family expectations, professional anxieties, and often stifling horizons"[33] but embrace new forms of aspiration such as "entrepreneurialism, social mobility, financial independence (and) individual success"[34] in the context of postmillennial India. This is a context within which the liberalisation of the Indian economy in the early 1990s has overlapped with new developments such as the rise of Hindu nationalism (especially in the wake of the election of Narendra Modi in 2014); the framing of Muslim Indians as second-class citizens by the dominant discourse of Hindutva; the ever-growing influence of the middle classes;[35] and "a flourishing of cultural production outside the erstwhile elite centres of artistic and literary value," which also includes films and born-digital products such as "interactive media, music, podcasts, webzines, stand-up comedy, spoken word, satire, journalism, blogs, web series, spoofs, remakes and countless others."[36]

Looking at local tween lit and genre fiction from the vantage point of 2019, Ulka Anjaria contends that the new face of Indian literature goes hand

Situating Chick Lit of the Global South in Print and Online **171**

in hand with what she calls "new provincialism," that is, a shift away from a 'Western-friendly' postcolonial and/or diasporic 'big-city' vocabulary of loss, exile, migrancy, melancholy, and trauma, to a determination to give visibility to "the long-ignored Tier 2 and 3 cities"[37] in the subcontinent, "locating livable [sic] futures not only in India's megalopolises that more easily exemplify capitalist aspiration but also in India's less fashionable regions and provincial towns."[38] In the introduction to *Reading India Today*, Anjaria remarks that Bhagat's *Half Girlfriend* (2014)[39] is a case in point, as the protagonist refuses to stay in the USA after the end of his internship with the Gates Foundation in New York, returns home, and finally makes it in Bihar (of all places!)[40] instead, in a move that combines "enterprise, romance, and return."[41] Remarking that postcolonial fiction is obsessed with history while "the new English-language commercial fictions" are firmly anchored in the contemporary and "seek alternatives both to the secular cosmopolitanism of the Rushdie generation and to a statist nationalism,"[42] the critic emphasises that the latter category broaches "new themes" such as "aspiration, everyday life, sexuality and desire, dreams for better selves, dreams for a better India, provincialism, and new futures."[43]

Clearly, Bhagat's very successful writings mark a watershed moment for the emergence of Anjaria's "new provincialism," since the writer, who "claims 'blockbuster' status"[44] for his work, directly addresses his Indian readers with "endearing intimacy" in his books, especially those living in small towns, "where the newest and hungriest generation of Indian readers proliferate."[45] No wonder, then, that Bhagat moved from dedicating his first novel, *One Night @ the Call Centre* (2007; 2005), to his "twin baby boys" and his wife,[46] to dedicating *Half Girlfriend* (2014), which was published about a decade afterwards, to "his mother, rural India, and the non-English types."[47] As Tiwari, Anjaria, and Viswamohan[48] suggest, Bhagat's increasing use of reader addresses to what he calls the "non-English types" in *Half Girlfriend* constructs his ideal readership as small-town ordinary young men who aspire to "the Indian Dream" but are "plagued with the regular insecurities of an average misfit."[49] As Bhagat's dedication to rural India and "the non-English types" makes clear, these insecurities centre on the English language, which indirectly emphasises "a connection between class and language."[50]

In *Half Girlfriend*, Madhav Jha, the protagonist from Dumraon, Bihar, initially feels insecure about his English, which he describes as being "90 per cent Bihari Hindi mixed with 10 per cent really bad English" (section 1). As he declares at the start of the novel, his "really bad English" of yore is the reason why he will spare his readers "a headache" and "say everything in [proper] English" instead, even if he asks them, too, to resuscitate his past self and "imagine [his] words in Bhojpuri-laced Hindi, with the worst possible English thrown in" (section 1). In a later passage, as Madhav is

172 Nicklas Hållén and Delphine Munos

still insecure about his English and conscientiously prepares for an interview, he lists ten "tools" through which he will improve his speaking skills, which range from forcing himself to spend "English-only days – no Hindi conversation allowed," through "working on speech content in Hindi first," to "reading *simple* English novels,"[51] which his love interest, that is, the "half girlfriend" of the title, instantly translates as "reading simple English novels, like, the one by that writer, what's his name, Chetan Bhagat" (section 25).

In keeping with other writers of 'tween lit' such as Anuja Chauhan,[52] Bhagat thus makes it clear that English always exists alongside Hindi and other Indian languages (or 'bhashas') in today's India, and his brand of "stripped-down English" reflects a "provincialist imaginary" through which the language of aspiration is not celebrated for its "literary beauty – for what it represents" but boils down to a "practical vehicle for self-transformation," that is, a "means to an end."[53] In many ways, *Half Girlfriend* offers fascinating insights into the hierarchies of language and linguistic divides at play in today's India, which get replayed too, within Madhav's own subjectivity. In fact, the inner split generated by Madhav's aspirational subjectivity (which intersects with his obsession with "having" English, to return to Sadana's remark, and having sex with Riya, his upper-class "half girlfriend") is nowhere more evident than in his Hindi-medium gut reaction to what he perceives to be physical rejection from his love interest. As he comes to visit the one that his class-obsessed friends have nicknamed "the BMW 5-series Riya Somani" (section 7), she insists on them being platonic lovers, and Madhav uses physical force to try to kiss her. In a last-ditch attempt to make out with her, Madhav switches from English to Hindi, which is left untranslated in the novel. He then blurts out "deti hai to de, varna kat le" in "coarse Bhojpuri-accented Hindi," which he first sugarcoats as "make love to me or leave" and then moves on to translate more accurately as "fuck me or fuck off" (section 11). This code-switching suggests that what Madhav retroactively reads as the shameful expression of his "combined state of horniness, bravado and stupidity" (section 12) could only take place in Hindi (and "coarse Bhojpuri-accented Hindi" at that), which implicitly creates a linguistic hierarchy between English, Hindi, and Bhojpuri. Moreover, Madhav's embattled subjectivity is reflected in the different translations he offers in the novel, which illuminates Madhav's desire to aspire to "English-type" respectability while residually identifying, on the gut level, with "a crass Bihari from Dumraon" (section 11), as he later acknowledges.

To return to Basu's terminology about the different phases of Indian writing in English, even if the "second" and "third" phases appear to share a common language, namely English, and a similar desire to "provincialize" English by bringing it "into intimate proximity"[54] with national and regional vernaculars (such as Hindi), it is perhaps clear by now that Rushdie's famed indigenisation (or "chutnification") of English is markedly different from the

Situating Chick Lit of the Global South in Print and Online **173**

"Hinglish" wielded by third-phase writers, who do not lead "a hyphenated existence."[55] Relying on Gayatri Spivak's remark that writers who divide their time between the Indian subcontinent and the Western world abrogate Standard English and claim the vernacular so as to make a "public declaration of ethnic identity in metropolitan space,"[56] Basu notes that, by contrast, the use of code-switching by writers of the Bhagat generation is emphatically "homegrown."[57] As we have previously discussed, Bhagat code-switches between Hindi and English. Similarly, Durjoy Datta incorporates Gujarati into his English,[58] and Chauhan's chick lit deploys a "mixed Hindi-English vocabulary that is less interested in translating itself for an international readership [...] than in making visible the richness and nuance of Indian English itself as a variably accented language."[59] Because he writes columns in both the English and Hindi presses, Bhagat also further develops his readership via Hindi-language newspapers, a presence across languages that allows him to bridge the gap between India's reading and book cultures and to appeal to Hindi-medium readers who might find it easier, in turn, to switch back and forth between his journalistic pieces in Hindi and in English and his easy-to-read English fiction.[60] For Suman Gupta, Indian commercial fiction in English thus traces "a circuit of Indians talking to Indians in a closed space, a national space, albeit in the most international of languages."[61]

Nigerian Chick Lit: Plural Englishes, Aspiration, and Economic Unevenness

As in Western chick lit, a central dilemma in Nigerian chick lit is the balance between career, love, and independence. The protagonist is typically in her early thirties and stuck in what Alcinda Honwana (2012) has called "wait-hood" – a prolonged period of waiting for an opportunity to get established enough to leave social adolescence behind and become an adult in the eyes of the community.[62] From a normative perspective, for many Nigerian women this typically means getting married and having children. From the perspective of the texts discussed in the following, this requires that the protagonist's future husband be wealthy enough to provide the material security deemed necessary to start a family.

There is, in other words, an aspirational narrative at the heart of the text. The protagonist's hopes and dreams are at the centre of the text and at the same time projected onto an uncertain future that likely will be revealed at the end of the story. However, in the works discussed, aspiration for a better future for the individual is not only thematised in the narrative, but is also inscribed in the text itself, since these works are written by self-published, non-professional but aspiring authors. The texts can be seen as the result of the authors' largely unaided attempts to create a textual product that appeals to as large an audience as possible. Therefore, their authorial decisions can

174 Nicklas Hållén and Delphine Munos

be interpreted not only as discursive, rhetorical, or aesthetic but as part of the authors' audience-building. This perspective can be applied to traditionally published texts as well, but these non-professional authors are also editors, publishers, and marketers, and it is therefore difficult to separate the commercial, ideological, and aesthetic aspects of the work. As we will see in a moment, the authors' strategic use of englishes is one way in which these aspects of the text are interconnected.

Notions of what is and is not proper for unmarried women are often a component in Nigerian chick lit, particularly when these ideas are negotiable. In Olayemi Oyinkansola's self-published chick lit novella *Finding Mr. Right* (2020), the relation between wealth and religious faith is a central topic.[63] The female main characters discuss their relation to God and the important role religion plays in their lives, and they expect it to be important also to the men they consider as their future husbands. The protagonist Kiki, who is older than her friends and flatmates Ify and Pelz/Pearls, often questions their choices in men and brings them back down to earth when they become excited about receiving the attention of men, asking what they really know about their commitment to God. However, as a Christian woman, she has a hard time justifying the fact that what she considers a worthy future husband is a man who is wealthy, since what she should look for in a man is faith. At one point in the story Kiki explicitly points out the problem in her philosophy about what qualities a husband should have and says to her friend Ify that according to her Christian beliefs, a poor but spiritual man should make a good husband. The issue is resolved when the friends agree that wanting a wealthy husband is not in itself the problem, but the fact that some women, like their friend Pearls, are moved by "money and looks" and forget about spirituality. A key problem in the narrative, then, is how the African urban everyday can be brought into contact with life-worlds characterised by economic affluence without disturbing the moral codes that the text relies on. While this problem is central also to Western metropolitan chick lit, the Nigerian chick lit author deals with particular limitations and possibilities generated by the unevenness of an economy that is characterised by the simultaneous proximity and distance of abject poverty and extreme wealth.

In Joy Eju'ojo's chick lit novella *The Reunion*, which is currently serialised on the Nigerian literary platform *Ebonystory*,[64] the everyday is represented in the beginning of the story, where the protagonist Mariah is working as a cashier in a supermarket and has to deal with rude costumers. She gets an opportunity to get out of this life when she is invited to a school reunion at a luxury hotel in an unnamed Nigerian city. The reunion is organised and paid for by Stevie, a former classmate who now is an internationally successful musician and celebrity. The men at the party have all achieved economic success since they finished school and are now professional basketball players, businessmen, and celebrities, and so Mariah and her quirky friend Lisa spend

Situating Chick Lit of the Global South in Print and Online **175**

their time at the party trying to figure out who of these men are real gentlemen with a good heart, and thus eligible for marriage. The problem with the abstract distance between precarity and wealth is solved by the author's invention of a relatively unlikely but interesting scenario: it later turns out that the class reunion is an orchestrated media stunt designed to boost Stevie's celebrity status. The former classmates who attend the party, and between whom a romantic drama immediately develops, are filmed around the clock. The outcome for the less affluent former classmates, who pursue those whose fortunes have been better, in other words, does not only depend on their attractiveness to their love interests. There is also the chance that they will make their success by charming the future audience of the media spectacle and that this will offer a way into a better future.

The unevenness on which the Nigerian chick lit text stands is to an extent smoothed out, so to speak, through the application of a language in which a specific kind of euphemism is the main rhetorical trope. As has been indicated, the type of Nigerian chick lit text discussed here finds its way around the problem of connecting the worlds of precarity and wealth by focalising places, situations, and language that are associated with the latter by erasing the former. This happens on a linguistic level, by shifting the English used toward Western idioms, but also on the level of literary invention, thorough placing the heroines in unusual scenarios that take them away from everyday life.

Englishes, Nicknames, and De-Familiarisation

One example of the strategic use of a form of English that is conspicuously non-Nigerian is expressions and nicknames borrowed from Black American English. In *The Reunion*, the main characters Mariah and Lisa not only have Western names, like the men they flirt with; they also speak with "duh voices," "squeal like high school girls," give each other "goofy smiles," call each other "babe," and are "shopaholics" in search of "potential boos" whom they address as "dude." However, although the two heroines sometimes talk like US chick lit and rom-com protagonists and find themselves in situations that are common in American romantic comedies, they are at other times unmistakably Nigerian. They use "abeg," "oo," and other expressions and interjections that are associated with Nigerian Pidgin and Nigerian English. The language used in dialogues is in other words both familiarising and defamiliarising. Like the unlikely reunion party scenario that Mariah and Lisa find themselves in, the Westernised English they sometimes speak emphasises their (temporary) distance from the everyday. However, the use of phrases in Nigerian Pidgin here and there reminds us that Mariah and Lisa are less exceptional than Mariah's male ex-classmates, who due to careers overseas have become extremely wealthy and whose English is markedly non-Nigerian.

In Olayemi Oyinkansola's *Finding Mr. Right*, the protagonist and narrator's name is central in the opening of the narrative. Her name is Kikelomo ("pampered child" in Yoruba), but she is called Kiki by her friends Ifeoma and Pelumi, the narrator explains, whom she calls Ify and Pelz or Pearls in return. They are the only ones brave enough to call her Kiki, however, because her father has since her childhood insisted that she be referred to by her full name. This foreshadows plot events that can be seen as typical in the genre. The reader learns early on that Kiki is twenty-nine and some months. She says that by this age, she is "supposed to be married with one and a half kids (if you understand), in [her] own house, having a car of [her] own, a fat bank account and a good job." Instead, she does not have much going for her. However, the reader knows from the prologue, which takes place months after the beginning of the story, that she will be interviewed on a talk show in Washington, DC. There, she is welcomed on stage to the crowd's cheers as Kiki, which is the name by which she has reached success and become famous and adored.

The first comic scene in the story sees Kiki enter her home, tired and beaten down because she feels that her life is at a standstill. She is welcomed home by her flatmates, and Pelz announces that she will from now on go by "Pearls." Kiki refuses to call her friend by this name, and it becomes clear why when Ify and Pelz trick her to try to pronounce the name, which makes her lips look like "a sagging wire abi na oversucked orange." What makes the word difficult for Kiki to pronounce is presumably the vowel (and semi-vowel), which in Nigerian English would be more open (the semi-vowel would not be pronounced) than in Standard American and British English.

As a narrator, Kiki, like the omniscient narrator in Eju'ojo's *The Reunion*, uses an English with very few obvious Nigerianisms, and this frequently leads to ambiguity and semantic slippage. When one of the girls, Ify, brings her future fiancé home for the first time and it turns out he has helped her "ma" out of a bind some days before the meeting, the mother and the boyfriend stand up and hug, and Ify and her father exclaim "So you guys know each other?!" In this particular context, it would have been reasonable to assume that they speak Igbo even though the dialogue is in English, but since the boyfriend is Yoruba, they must actually speak English, which makes the very American and very informal use of the genderless "guys" stand out even more. The women in the text exclaim "yass!," call each other "babe" and "girl" and their love interests "boo," which might seem out of place but semantically correct, but an unfaithful husband is described as an "infidel."

In *The Reunion*, linguistic confusion is caused through non-typical use of idiomatic expressions. Having arrived at the hotel where the reunion takes place, Mariah and Lisa immediately split up as they approach different romantic interests. The morning after their arrival, Mariah therefore wakes up to find that Lisa has snuck into her room to sleep. She throws a pillow at Lisa and yells at her "in her bedroom voice," while Lisa tries to calm her down with a "pillow talk voice." The sexual connotations of the idiomatic use of the metonyms *bedroom* and *pillow* do not seem to be evoked consciously in this passage, since this would imply a sexual tension between the two friends in a text that is otherwise staunchly heteronormative. Instead, the passage can be read as an attempt at a neutral joke, based on the repetition of terms belonging to the same semantic domain: bedroom voice, in this context, means an explicitly frustrated voice, while pillow-talk means to speak softly.

Our point here is not that the texts contain a number of awkward linguistic choices but that the instances of linguistic instability are a sign that the authors use non-Standard codes and idioms because of their perceived distance from the ordinary and familiar. The texts are self-published online, on platforms whose users are predominantly Nigerian, so the reason for this choice of code is arguably not to reach a global audience primarily, since this would not explain the frequent use of local expressions and interjections and the use of Nigerian Pidgin. Instead, the non-standard Nigerian English used by the narrators and the markedly American nicknames and expressions used in dialogue might be meant to be associated with "socioeconomic advancement" and a lifestyle that exists *elsewhere*,[65] far away in socio-economic terms from spaces of economic precarity. In both of the texts, men who show a command of European or American English are not only also described as wealthy or as having prospects in life but are considered possible future husbands. What is intended to be interpreted as the protagonists' command of non-Nigerian English, therefore, might be seen as signalling preparedness for a prosperous future even when they struggle to find a way forward in life. If this is so, however, the linguistic instability in the texts must in turn be read as anchoring the text on one side of the economic unevenness: the side of relative precarity and waithood.

Social Mobility, Aspiration, and Formal Transformations in the Global South

As we hope to have shown in this chapter, aspiration and upward social mobility are at the centre of the chick lit text, not least in Global South iterations of the genre. As Srijanai Ghosh argues, commodities, consumption, and identity construction are "triangulat[ed]" in the chick lit genre,[66] in that the consumption of actual products and objects of desire but also social connections lays the foundation for the emergence of a sense of self. Anglophone Global South chick lit might use a formerly colonial language and rely on the Anglo-American 'chick-lit formula' – what Suman Gupta calls a "global commercial fiction publishing template."[67] Still, the fact that this brand of popular literature is "saturated with local content"[68] and is aimed at local and/or regional audiences often makes it a perfect vehicle for engaging with context-specific gender politics and for offering fascinating insights into the palimpsestic language hierarchies and disparate thought-worlds at play in India and Nigeria. Unsurprisingly in this context, Melissa Tandiwe Myambo has theorised chick lit's journey from Europe/North America to Africa and Asia as a form of "frontier migration."[69] The term refers to the moving "of people, capital, ideas and technology from a more 'developed' economy to a less 'developed' one," and the phenomenon is "deeply influenced by the hierarchies inherent in geopolitical power relations."[70] Again, this means that the rhetoric, style, and focus of the chick-lit novel inevitably must be negotiated as it is adopted by writers in the Global South. As we have discussed in selected Indian and Nigerian chick lit, linguistic strategies are also employed by writers and characters to negotiate these relations between identity, social mobility, and the futures worth aspiring to, and these negotiations are made partly through strategic uses of a variety of englishes that reflect the entanglement of the local and the global within the postcolony.

Notes

1 Lynda Gichanda Spencer, " 'In Defence of Chick-Lit': Refashioning Feminine Subjectivities in Ugandan and South African Contemporary Women's Writing," *Feminist Theory* 20.2 (2019): 156.
2 Pamila Gupta and Ronit Frenkel, "Chick-Lit in a Time of African Cosmopolitanism," *Feminist Theory* 20.2 (2019): 124.
3 Pamela Butler and Jigna Desai, "Manolos, Marriage and Mantras: Chick-Lit Criticism and Transnational Feminism," *Meridians: Feminisms, Race, Transnationalism* 8.2 (2008): 3.
4 See Susanne Gehrmann, "Varieties of Romance in Contemporary Popular Togolese Literature," in *Routledge Handbook of African Popular Culture*, edited by Grace A. Musila and Karin Barber (Basingstoke: Routledge, 2022): 74–91; Lynda Gichanda Spencer, "In Defence of Chick-Lit"; Rebecca Fasselt, "Chick Lit Politics in a Post-Truth Era: Tricksters, Blessees and Postfeminist Girlpower in Angela Makholwa's *The Blessed Girl*," *Safundi* 19.4 (2018): 375–397; and Suman Gupta, "Contemporary Indian Commercial Fiction in English," in *South Asian Fiction in English: Contemporary Transformations*, edited by Alex Tickell (London: Palgrave Macmillan London, 2016): 139–161.
5 See Gehrmann, "Varieties of Romance," 84.
6 See Sangeeta Barooah Pisharoty, "A Novel Idea," *The Hindu Online*, 17 February 2010.
7 Shola Adenekan, Rhonda Cobham-Sander, Stephanie Bosch Santana, and Kwabena Opoku-Agyemang, "Introduction to the Guest Issue," in *Digital Africas*, edited by Shola Adenekan, Rhonda Cobham-Sander, Stephanie Bosch Santana, and Kwabena Opoku-Agyemang. Spec. issue of *Postcolonial Text* 15.3/4 (2020): 3, www.postcolonial.org/index.php/pct/article/view/2702.
8 See Stephanie Bosh Santana, "From Nation to Network: Blog and Facebook Fiction from Southern Africa," *Research in African Literatures* 49.1 (Spring 2018): 197–208.
9 See Mike Maphoto's "The South African Story is a Universal Story: Mike Maphoto at TEDxSoweto," 29 November 2019. www.youtube.com/watch?v=AGhvGhAmrpg (last accessed 21 April 2024).

10 Melissa Tandiwe Myambo, "The Spatial Politics of Chick Lit in Africa and Asia: Sidestepping Tradition and Fem-Washing Global Capitalism?" *Feminist Theory* 21.1 (2020): 116.

11 Rashmi Sadana, *English Heart, Hindi Heartland: The Political Life of Literature in India* (Berkeley: University of California Press, 2012): 5.

12 Sadana, *English Heart*, 14. Further page references are in the main text.

13 Romanus Aboh, *Language and the Construction of Multiple Identities in the Nigerian Novel* (Makhanda: NISC, 2018): 81.

14 Aboh, *Language*, 81.

15 See Myambo, "The Spatial Politics of Chick Lit."

16 Sandra Ponzanesi, *The Postcolonial Cultural Industry: Icons, Markets, Mythologies* (Basingstoke: Palgrave Macmillan, 2014): 176.

17 Stephanie Newell, *Ghanaian Popular Fiction: Thrilling Discoveries in Conjugal Life and Other Tales* (Oxford: James Currey, 2000): 144.

18 Spencer, "In Defence of Chick-Lit," 158.

19 Ashleigh Harris and Nicklas Hållén, "African Street Literature: A Method for an Emergent Form Beyond World Literature," *Research in African Literatures* 51.2 (2020): 22.

20 Spencer, "In Defence of Chick-Lit," 159.

21 Eva Chen, "Shanghai(ed) Babies: Geopolitics, Biopolitics and the Global Chick Lit," *Feminist Media Studies* 12.2 (2012): 217.

22 See Spencer, "In Defence of Chick-Lit."

23 Myambo, "The Spatial Politics of Chick Lit," 115.

24 Bhavya Tiwari, "The Multilingual Anglophone: World Literature and Post-Millennial Literature in Postcolonial India," *Interventions* 23.4 (2021): 624–625.

25 Abhijit Gupta, "Popular Writing in India," in *The Cambridge History of Post-colonial Literature*, edited by Ato Quayson (Cambridge: Cambridge University Press): 1032.

26 Gupta, "Popular Writing in India," 1033.

27 Tiwari, "The Multilingual Anglophone," 625.

28 For instance, Anuja Chauhan's *The Zoya Factor* is both marketed as 'cricket lit' and 'chick lit,' and Sudeep Nagarkar's commercial fiction mixes the conventions of both chick lit and lad lit. See Anuja Chauhan, *The Zoya Factor* (New Delhi: HarperCollins Publishers, 2008) and Sudeep Nagarkar, *You're Trending in My Dreams* (London: Ebury Press, 2017).

29 Priya Joshi, "Chetan Bhagat: Remaking the Novel in India," in *A History of the Indian Novel in English*, edited by Ulka Anjaria (Cambridge: Cambridge University Press, 2015): 311.

30 Manisha Basu, *The Rhetoric of Hindu India* (Cambridge: Cambridge University Press, 2017): 167.

31 Basu, *The Rhetoric of Hindu India*, 166.

32 Sheela Reddy cited in Joshi, "Chetan Bhagat," 315. Joshi argues that in Reddy's hyphenated moniker, the prefix 'lo' emphasises both their "lowbrow status" and the "local nature of their popularity."

33 Joshi, "Chetan Bhagat," 311.

34 Ulka Anjaria, *Reading India Now: Contemporary Formations in Literature and Popular Culture* (Philadelphia: Temple University Press, 2019): 29.

35 See Rupa Oza, *The Making of Neoliberal India: Nationalism, Gender, and the Paradoxes of Globalization* (New York: Routledge, 2006).

36 Anjaria, *Reading India Now*, 10.

37 Joshi, "Chetan Bhagat," 317.

38 Anjaria, *Reading India Now*, 29.

39 Chetan Bhagat, *Half Girlfriend* (New Delhi: Rupa, 2014).

40 Bihar is one of the most deprived Indian states and is described as the "poorest of the poor" in *Half Girlfriend* (see section 1).
41 Anjaria, *Reading India Now*, 27.
42 Anjaria, *Reading India Now*, 29.
43 Anjaria, *Reading India Now*, 13.
44 Joshi, "Chetan Bhagat," 314.
45 Joshi, "Chetan Bhagat," 315.
46 See Chetan Bhagat, *One Night @ The Call Centre* (New Delhi: Rupa, 2007 [2005]): np. Tiwari notes that *One Night* is dedicated to Bhagat's "alma mater" and "his mother," which contradicts the dedication made in the edition of the book used for this chapter.
47 Tiwari, "The Multilingual Anglophone," 626.
48 Aysha Iqbal Viswamohan, "Marketing Lad Lit, Creating Bestsellers: The Importance of Being Chetan Bhagat," in *Postliberalization Indian Novels in English*, edited by Aysha Iqbal Viswamohan (London: Anthem Press, 2013): 19–29.
49 Viswamohan, "Marketing Lad Lit," 27.
50 Tiwari, "The Multilingual Anglophone," 626.
51 Our emphasis.
52 See Charmaine Carvalho, "National Romances: Singleton Desire and the Discovery of India in Chick Lit Narratives," *South Asia: Journal of South Asian Studies* 44.5 (2021): 834–850.
53 Anjaria, *Reading India Now*, 49.
54 Basu, *The Rhetoric of Hindu India*, 171.
55 Viswamohan, "Marketing Lad Lit," 21.
56 Spivak cited in Basu, *The Rhetoric of Hindu India*, 171.
57 Basu, *The Rhetoric of Hindu India*, 172.
58 See Joshi, "Chetan Bhagat," 315.
59 Anjaria, *Reading India Now*, 53.
60 See Joshi, "Chetan Bhagat," 318.
61 Gupta, "Contemporary Indian Commercial Fiction in English," 150.
62 See Alcinda M. Honwana, *The Time of Youth: Work, Social Change, and Politics in Africa* (West Hartford: Kumarian Press, 2012).
63 Olayemi Oyinkansola, *Finding Mr. Right*, Okadabooks.com, 2022. The primary texts discussed in this section have no page numbers.
64 Joy Eju'ojó, *The Reunion: A Novel*, Ebonystory.com, no date.
65 Bashir Muhammad Sambo, "Factors Governing Language Choice in Mairi Ward of Maiduguri," in *Convergence: English and Nigerian Languages. A Festschrift for Munzali A. Jibril*, edited by Ozo-mekuri Ndimele (Port Harcourt: M & J Grand Orbit Communications, 2016): 193.
66 Srijani Gosh, "Spectacular Selves: Fashion and Identity in Lee Tulloch's Fabulous Nobodies," *The Journal of Popular Culture* 55.2 (2022): 333.
67 Gupta, "Contemporary Indian Commercial Fiction," 150.
68 Spencer, "In Defence of Chick-Lit," 159.
69 Myambo, "The Spatial Politics of Chick Lit," 112.
70 Myambo, "The Spatial Politics of Chick Lit," 112.

Bibliography

Aboh, Romanus. *Language and the Construction of Multiple Identities in the Nigerian Novel*. Makhanda: NISC, 2018.
Adenekan, Shola, Cobham-Sander Rhonda, Santana Stephanie Bosch and Opoku-Agyemang Kwabena. "Introduction." *Digital Africas*, Spec. issue of *Postco-*

lonial Text 15.3/4 (2020). www.postcolonial.org/index.php/pct/article/view/2702 (last accessed 21 April 2023).

Anjaria, Ulka. *Reading India Now: Contemporary Formations in Literature and Popular Culture*. Philadelphia: Temple University Press, 2019.

Basu, Manisha. *The Rhetoric of Hindu India*. Cambridge: Cambridge University Press, 2017.

Bhagat, Chetan. *Half Girlfriend*. New Delhi: Rupa, 2014.

———. *One Night @ The Call Centre*. New Delhi: Rupa, 2007 [2005].

Bosh Santana, Stephanie. "From Nation to Network: Blog and Facebook Fiction from Southern Africa." *Research in African Literatures* 49.1 (Spring 2018): 197–208.

Butler, Pamela and Jigna Desai. "Manolos, Marriage and Mantras: Chick-Lit Criticism and Transnational Feminism." *Meridians: Feminisms, Race, Transnationalism* 8.2 (2008): 1–31.

Carvalho, Charmaine. "National Romances: Singleton Desire and the Discovery of India in Chick Lit Narratives." *South Asia: Journal of South Asian Studies* 44.5 (2021): 834–850.

Chauhan, Anuja. *The Zoya Factor*. New Delhi: HarperCollins Publishers, 2008.

Chen, Eva. "Shanghai(ed) Babies: Geopolitics, Biopolitics and the Global Chick Lit." *Feminist Media Studies* 12.2 (2012): 214–228.

Eju'ojó, Joy. *The Reunion: A Novel*. Ebonystory.com, no date.

Fasselt, Rebecca. "Chick Lit Politics in a Post-Truth Era: Tricksters, Blessees, and Postfeminist Girlpower in Angela Makholwa's *The Blessed Girl*." *Safundi* 19.4 (2018): 375–397.

Gehrmann, Susanne. "Varieties of Romance in Contemporary Popular Togolese Literature." In *Routledge Handbook of African Popular Culture*, edited by Grace A. Musila. Basingstoke: Routledge, 2022: 74–91.

Ghosh, Srijani. "Spectacular Selves: Fashion and Identity in Lee Tulloch's Fabulous Nobodies." *The Journal of Popular Culture* 55.2 (2022): 333–349.

Gupta, Abhijit. "Popular Writing in India." In *The Cambridge History of Postcolonial Literature*, Vol. 2, edited by Ato Quayson. Cambridge: Cambridge University Press, 2012: 1023–1038.

Gupta, Pamila and Ronit Frenkel. "Chick-Lit in a Time of African Cosmopolitanism." *Feminist Theory* 20.2 (2019): 123–132.

Gupta, Suman. "Contemporary Indian Commercial Fiction in English." In *South Asian Fiction in English: Contemporary Transformations*, edited by Alex Tickell. London: Palgrave Macmillan London, 2016: 139–161.

Harris, Ashleigh and Nicklas Hållén. "African Street Literature: A Method for an Emergent Form beyond World Literature." *Research in African Literatures* 51.2 (Summer 2020): 1–26.

Honwana, Alcinda. *The Time of Youth: Work, Social Change, and Politics in Africa*. West Hartford: Kumarian Press, 2012.

Joshi, Priya. "Chetan Bhagat: Remaking the Novel in India." In *A History of the Indian Novel in English*, edited by Ulka Anjaria. Cambridge: Cambridge University Press, 2015: 310–323.

Maphoto, Mike. "Diary of a Zulu Girl: From Mud Huts, Umqomboti and Straight Back to Penthouses, Expensive Weaves and Moët." 29 November 2023. https://diaryofazulugirl.co.za (last accessed 21 April 2024).

Myambo, Melissa Tandiwe. "The Spatial Politics of Chick Lit in Africa and Asia: Sidestepping Tradition and Fem-Washing Global Capitalism?" *Feminist Theory* 21.1 (2020): 111–129.

Nagarkar, Sudeep. *You're Trending in My Dreams*. London: Ebury Press, 2017.

Newell, Stephanie. *Ghanaian Popular Fiction: Thrilling Discoveries in Conjugal Life and Other Tales*. Oxford: James Currey: 2000.

Oyinkansola, Olayemi. *Finding Mr. Right*. Okadabooks.com, 2022.

Oza, Rupa. *The Making of Neoliberal India: Nationalism, Gender, and the Paradoxes of Globalization*. New York: Routledge, 2006.

Pisharoty, Sangeeta Barooah. "A Novel Idea." *The Hindu Online*, 17 February 2010. https://www.thehindu.com/books/A-novel-idea/article16815187.ece (last accessed 21 April 2023).

Ponzanesi, Sandra. *The Postcolonial Cultural Industry: Icons, Markets, Mythologies*. Basingstoke: Palgrave Macmillan, 2014.

Sadana, Rashmi. *English Heart, Hindi Heartland: The Political Life of Literature in India* Berkeley: University of California Press, 2012.

Sambo, Bashir Muhammad. "Factors Governing Language Choice in Mairi Ward of Maiduguri." In *Convergence: English and Nigerian Languages. A Festschrift for Munzali A. Jibril*, edited by Ozo-mekuri Ndimele. Port Harcourt: M & J Grand Orbit Communications, 2016: 183–194.

Spencer, Lynda Gichanda. " 'In Defence of Chick-Lit': Refashioning Feminine Subjectivities in Ugandan and South African Contemporary Women's Writing." *Feminist Theory* 20.2 (2019): 155–169.

Tiwari, Bhavya. "The Multilingual Anglophone: World Literature and Post-Millennial Literature in Postcolonial India." *Interventions* 23.4 (2021): 621–635.

Viswamohan, Aysha Iqbal. "Marketing Lad Lit, Creating Bestsellers: The Importance of Being Chetan Bhagat." In *Postliberalization Indian Novels in English*, edited by Aysha Iqbal Viswamohan. London: Anthem Press, 2013: 19–29.

11

"TOO MUCH JOY, I SWEAR, IS LOST"

Ambiguity in Ocean Vuong's *On Earth We're Briefly Gorgeous*

Elena Furlanetto

Ocean Vuong's 2019 debut novel, *On Earth We're Briefly Gorgeous*, is a sweeping reflection on language.[1] The protagonist spots elements of the written page in unexpected places: feet are flecked with quotation marks, necks have scars like commas, the small bones along his mother's spine are an untranslatable "row of ellipses" (84). Nature is inhabited by syntax and lexicons. Within the protagonist's lived environment, dense with language phenomena, ambiguity emerges as a mode of paramount importance. Semantic or rhetorical ambiguity has mostly been defined as a multiplicity of meaning or plurisignation[2] but also appears in the shape of amphiboly or vagueness, puns, or contradictions within a text, narrative unreliability, and silence. Zygmunt Bauman argues that ambiguous textual phenomena disrupt the language's dedication to clarity, classification, segregation, naming, and setting apart, all of which *On Earth We're Briefly Gorgeous* systematically defies.[3] By contrast, ambiguity emerges when "the linguistic tools of structuration prove inadequate; either the situation belongs to none of the linguistically distinguished classes, or it falls into several classes at the same time."[4]

Bauman is far from believing ambiguous language to be "inadequate" or "flawed," he rather speaks of ambivalence as language's "permanent companion" and "normal condition."[5] However, in the classic oratory tradition, ambiguity was in fact understood as language malfunctioning leading to undesirable interpretive dilemmas, until New Criticism and especially William Empson reconfigured it into a deliberate aesthetics capable of significantly enriching literary language.[6] The New Critics' ambiguity research, however, participates in what has been abundantly critiqued as the movement's general indifference towards history, and the junctures between literature and historical phenomena such as enslavement, exile, erasures, and

DOI: 10.4324/9781003464037-15
This chapter has been made available under a CC-BY-NC-ND 4.0 license.

184 Elena Furlanetto

oppression.[7] There is ample evidence of how white Western authors have made use of ambiguity in their writing, but ambiguity's potential as a means of expression of the interstitial identities of migrants, mixed-race individuals, and fluid sexualities remains largely unexplored. In what follows, I will attempt an ambiguity reading of Vuong's *On Earth We're Briefly Gorgeous* and isolate important textual patterns I recognize as manifestation of an ambiguity aesthetics in the novel. The first part of the chapter will explore phenomena of language scarcity, while the second part will turn to language excess, with particular emphasis on what I term "transparency."[8] Through his use of ambiguity, Ocean Vuong's migrant and queer voice "rip[s] the page of literary history"[9] as it strives to materialize the hesitations, stutters, silences, and slippages that happen in the blank spaces between languages, in the distance between the mother('s) tongue, and the language of the everyday.

In *On Earth We're Briefly Gorgeous*, ambiguity is present from the first sentence onwards. The novel begins on a precipice of things unsaid: "Let me begin again" (3), and gestures at the accumulation of failed writings on which the novel is built. The present chapter is mostly concerned with the kind of ambiguity that emerges from the convergence of the protagonist's two languages, Vietnamese and English, and with textual places where both languages are either too little or too much. Although these language slippages trigger anxiety and melancholia in the characters involved, and can be read as "communication failure[s],"[10] they are not only a marker of Vuong's unique craft, but also shed powerful light on interstitial identities such as the protagonist's, Little Dog, who grows up Vietnamese, mixed-race, migrant, and gay in the US. When Little Dog writes his mother that "to speak in our mother tongue is to speak only partially in Vietnamese, but entirely in war" (32), he revises the contingency of mother tongue and national identity in terms of ambiguity: if their mother tongue is only part Vietnamese, the other part remains undecipherable, and both parts – wordless or not – participate in the articulation of trauma. In the same way, the American War in Vietnam haunts the characters' lives and selves beyond the point where they become only "part" Vietnamese: past their escape and arrival in the US, when Vietnamese must make room for English, and their Vietnamese selves for American selves.

Little Dog is the son of a half-Vietnamese, half-American mother, Hong/ Rose, and the grandson of Lan, who fled Saigon with her daughter at the end of the war. This family of three lives in Hartford, Massachusetts, where Little Dog starts school without yet speaking English and grows up amidst the dilemmas of migrancy, the traumatic legacy of the war, and the joys and hardships of queer sexuality. The novel is written in epistolary form: a paradoxical letter to a mother who cannot read English, haunted and hollowed by an impossible addressee. Hong is employed in a nail salon which relentlessly chips away at her physical and mental health; she is sometimes

"Too Much Joy, I Swear, Is Lost" **185**

affectionate, sometimes violent, but also the lens through which Little Dog experiences life: so much so that in several moments in the text Little Dog's self merges beyond recognition with hers. *On Earth We're Briefly Gorgeous* is also a homosexual bildungsroman, mediated through the figure of Trevor, a working-class white boy Little Dog meets through a summer job at a tobacco farm. Trevor initiates Little Dog to love, sex, and ultimately mourning when he dies from overdose. Little Dog writes this letter from a future where he is an established poet living in New York: the coordinates of his life are almost indistinguishable from those of Ocean Vuong himself, suggesting we are in the presence of what Sandeep Bakshi calls "a work of auto-ethnographic worldmaking reinforced by the first-person narrative."[11]

Dynamics of excess and defect pervade the texture of the plot and sediment in all textual areas, not only those that show a direct connection with Little Dog's bilingualism. The image of his sleeping grandmother contains both stillness and alarm, a binomial that culminates in an oxymoronic "twitching quiet" (16). Hong, too, is a creature of silence and deafening noise: "My family, I thought, was this silent arctic landscape, placid at last after a night of artillery fire" (20). In the remainder of this chapter, I will linger on two ambiguity phenomena. First, language scarcity, when words are inadequate to describe the interstitial realities of bilingual and bicultural individuals struggling with intergenerational trauma; second, language excess, when different languages cross-pollinate and multiply, producing a sequence of unexpected semantics. The first ambiguity is closely related to the existential condition of being *neither-nor*, the second to being *both-and*. The choice of arranging these two ambiguities across a binary and in two different sections is dictated by practical reasons but is highly misleading: every example of scarcity can be read in terms of excess, and vice versa.

Blanks, Silences, Stutters: Language Scarcity

> But what if the mother tongue is stunted? What if the tongue is cut out? Can one take pleasure in loss without losing oneself entirely? The Vietnamese I own is the one you gave me, the one whose diction and syntax reach only the second-grade level.[12]

Birgit Neumann underscores the centrality of this passage in Vuong's poetics. The "language insufficiency" determined by the void where the mother tongue should be is felt not only in terms of semantic lack, Neumann argues, but also signals other, vaster absences that imply dispossession, deprivation, and loss.[13] Although Little Dog writes off his Vietnamese as stunted, what burns deeper marks and excruciating memories is the perceived insufficiency of his mother's and grandmother's English.

The first episode of language scarcity happens ten pages into the novel when Little Dog, riding a train to New York, has a panic attack and calls his mother, who "hum[s] the melody to 'Happy Birthday'" on the phone (10); it is not Little Dog's birthday, but that is the only song Hong knows in English. Her wordless response is slanted, inadequate, painfully revealing her partial knowledge of English and disregard of cultural context. Yet, her choice is also indicative of her profound knowledge of her son's inner world. "I was having a panic attack," Little Dog writes, "and you knew it" (10). By humming an English song instead of a Vietnamese one, Hong leaves her familiar universe and home culture to enter her son's. Through the gentle melody of "Happy Birthday," Hong vanquishes the resurfacing of trauma. In this case language scarcity, in the shape of a wordless song out of context, results in comfort and closeness: Little Dog listens, "the phone pressed so hard to my ear that, hours later, a pink rectangle was still imprinted on my cheek" (10).

The American and the Vietnamese grate against each other in a similar way when Hong tries to assess the unfamiliar American materialities around her. Everything from hummingbirds, flowers, and Walmart lace curtains are "đẹp quá" (beautiful). Little Dog suggests that Hong's Vietnamese is as limited as her English: "When it comes to words," in either language, "you possess fewer than the coins you saved from your nail salon tips" (29). What Little Dog labels as Hong's shortcoming signals in fact a melancholic dismissal of the variety of her present natural and material environment. To the narrator, Hong's limited vocabulary seems inadequate to describe the excess of American stimuli around her. The reverse, however, is also true, as American objects and life forms are incompatible with or unworthy of the semantic variety of Vietnamese; two general words, "đẹp quá," will suffice to describe an indecipherable reality that seems to drive Hong to a state of melancholic exhaustion. As Hong and Little Dog observe a hummingbird hovering above an orchid, Hong asks her son "what it was called and I answered in English – the only language I had for it. You nodded blankly. The next day, you had already forgotten the name, the syllables slipping right from your tongue" (29). The hummingbird becomes an expression of an overpowering American alienness for which Hong has no words, or wants to find none.

Little Dog's relation to his mother and grandmother is defined by more nameless animals and flowers and through the two women's language scarcity. A nameless purple flower Lan asks her grandson to pick for her in a stranger's garden not only becomes identical with all purple flowers and with the memory of Lan, but also with Lan's feet which turn purple and bloodless a few moments before her death. "I would never know those flowers by name. Because Lan never had one for them" (209), Little Dog explains, but this lacuna comes to encompass all purple flowers the protagonist ever sees: "To this day, every time I see small, purple flowers, I swear they're the flowers I had picked that day" (209). "But without a name, things get lost," he

"Too Much Joy, I Swear, Is Lost"   **187**

continues, as the colour spills from flowers to Lan's toes on her deathbed, from plenitude to absence, from the loss of a name to a vaster loss.

In one of the reverse instances where Little Dog's English falters, he goes back to his school days when bullies target him on the bus and pressure him to speak English. " 'Don't you ever say nothin'? Don't you speak English? [...] Say something. [...] Can't you say even one thing?" (24). In this instance, silence is first and foremost a marker of Otherness: the language of victimization and strategic alterity, as Achino-Loeb suggests, is "silence-laden."[14] Little Dog's conspicuous inaction and "communication failure"[15] enrages Hong, who equates lack of language with lack of manliness. "What kind of boy would let them do that?" (26), she taunts him, foreshadowing the juncture of Little Dog's migrant and queer identity. Replicating a pattern that radiates throughout Vuong's prose, this moment of language scarcity triggers one of language plenitude: as Hong urges her son to take action by talking back, she reminds him he has "a bellyful of English" (26). Little Dog's metaphorically full belly flows into his belly literally filling up in the following passage, when Hong feeds him glasses upon glasses of "American milk" in the hope he would grow taller and stronger (27). Little Dog trustingly "drink[s] it down, gulping, [...] hoping that the whiteness vanishing into me would make me more of a yellow boy" (27). English, whiteness, and masculinity cascade into Little Dog's belly, colonizing his body on the sheer level of colour and bones.

The infamous oxtail incident, often quoted in reviews of the novel,[16] is a watershed moment in Little Dog's understanding of his own agency as an authoritative English-speaker, when he finally accepts his role as mediator between his family's Vietnamese-speaking universe and the American every-day. At the butcher, Hong does not know the word for oxtail. At first, she asks in Vietnamese, "Anh có đuôi bò không?", and is met with bewilderment. She then ventures into an unfortunate pantomime of a cow. She tries French, "Derriere de vache!" and the butcher calls for a Spanish-speaking assistant. The flurry of languages vortexing around an absent centre[17] once more combine scarcity and excess. Shocked by the commotion caused by the lack of a single word and mortified be the spectacle of parental ridicule, Little Dog promises to "never be wordless when you needed me to speak for you [his mother]. [...] From then on, I would fill in our blanks, our silences, stutters, whenever I could" (32).[18]

Vietnamese American novelist Viet Thanh Nguyen writes that the language of first-generation migrants in the US is one of stutters and hesitations: "Outside those ethnic walls, facing an indifferent America, the other clears her or his throat, hesitates, struggles to speak, and, most often, waits for the next generation raised or born on American soil to speak for them."[19] Vuong completes the picture drawn by Nguyen and writes from the perspective of a second generation that hesitates and stutters in the language of the first.

188 Elena Furlanetto

While Hong's and Little Dog's English may be faulty, Vietnamese – being a "stunted," interrupted, unmotherly mother tongue (31) – does not offer any immediate comfort. To the contrary, Vietnamese, perhaps even more so than English, signifies loss, non-belonging, and trauma. Hong's limited Vietnamese vocabulary, as Little Dog describes it, is a constant reminder of the way the war impacted her education, as she watched her school collapse after a napalm raid, stopping her education in its tracks, and blocking her language at "the second-grade level" (31). Instead of being a place of belonging, writes Little Dog, their mother tongue points at a void, marking "where your education ended, ashed" (32).

By the same token, most of the language scarcity episodes in *On Earth We're Briefly Gorgeous* are placeholders for vaster absences: primarily the identitarian vacuum in which Hong's and Little Dog's mixed-race bodies dwell in both home and host countries. Little Dog gives the example of a trial for the murder of an unnamed Chinese man in 1884, where the case was dismissed because it did not involve a human being, as only white, African American, or Mexican bodies were considered human. There is an implicit but obvious "slippage"[20] between "the nameless yellow body," who was "not considered a man because it did not fit in a slot on a piece of paper" (63) and Little Dog's own queer Vietnamese American body, both perceived and dismissed as constant sites of ambiguity. Manifestations of language scarcity in *On Earth We're Briefly Gorgeous* are intimately connected with the identitarian predicament of being neither/nor. Namelessness, intended as the incapacity of words to stick to plants, animals, and bodies marks a mode of impermanence that defines the migrant's experience, caught in a gap between culture of birth and culture of adoption. Little Dog remains nameless in Vietnamese. His real name is only given in English translation, "patriotic leader of the nation," and he is known to the reader only as "Little Dog." His queerness cannot find expression in Vietnamese either, as "before the French occupation, our Vietnamese did not have a name for queer bodies" (130). As he comes out to his mother, Little Dog can choose between a French word that misrepresents and criminalizes his sexuality "pê-đê – from the French pédé, short for pédéraste" – or a periphrasis that describes him ex negativo, "I don't like girls" (130).

Language abundance turns into scarcity in the face of Lan's death, a vaster absence that disables all chances of articulation. "Despite my vocabulary, my books, knowledge, I find myself against the wall, bereft. [...] I sit, with all my theories, metaphors, equations, Shakespeare and Milton, Barthes, Du Fu, and Homer, masters of death who can't, at last, teach me how to touch my dead" (210). This profusion of written texts, proof of Little Dog's ultimate conquest of literacy and fluency, leaves him motionless and wordless in the face of death. But there is also a cultural dimension emerging from these lines. The overwhelming whiteness of the authors who (with

"Too Much Joy, I Swear, Is Lost" **189**

the exception of Du Fu) do not come to Little Dog's rescue suggests that Western literature and philosophy may have alienated Little Dog from Vietnamese mourning practices. In fact, while Hong and her sister Mai "care for their own with an inertia equal to gravity," Little Dog "sit[s]" (210), unable to move, unable to touch his grandmother's body, and to connect with his ancestors.

Spirals, Cycles, Transparencies: Language Excess

"If you knock English enough, it becomes a door to another language," Cathy Park Hong writes in her autobiography *Minor Feelings: An Asian American Reckoning*.[21] The first part of this chapter has elaborated on the ability of language scarcity to express an interstitial identity straddling migrant, queer, Vietnamese, and American. The following pages, instead, will follow Vuong's "knocking" at English until it becomes a door to Vietnamese. In other words, I will look at phenomena of language excess.

"Silence both maintains a presence and refers to the physicality of absence," Chris P. Miller writes in his definition of silence. Ellipses, in particular, "serve as both indices for meaning and loss, in that they can signify an absence functioning as a metaphor or commentary on relationships of empowerment and voice."[22] In the nail salon where Hong works, what one hears the most is "sorry," a word that functions in this context as an ellipse of the body. Employees apologize "dozens of times," over and over, with or without reason. "Sorry" is, therefore, a word used in excess because of quantity, but also because of the word's manifold meanings and uses.

> In the nail salon, sorry is a tool one uses to pander until the word itself becomes currency. It no longer merely *apologizes*, but insists, reminds: *I'm here, right here, beneath you.* It is the lowering of oneself so that the client feels right, superior, and charitable. In the nail salon, one's definition of sorry is deranged into a new word entirely, one that's charged and reused as both power and defacement at once.
>
> *(53)*[23]

"Sorry" is a site of ambiguity, because, first, it explodes into a variety of functions: it is a "tool," a "currency," a means to an end, a "passport to remain" (92) for the Vietnamese migrant workers in the nail salon. Second, "sorry" is a synthesis of the apparent opposites of "power and defacement"; by erasing themselves, or making themselves scarce through speech redundancy, the workers remind the client of their presence, they "insist" by withdrawing into contrition. In this sense, the semantic space of the apology "mark[s] the experience of presence disguised as absence":[24] even the suppression of experience inherent in a groundless apology, Vuong suggests, can be weaponized

190 Elena Furlanetto

into resistance. "Sorry" is not only a quotidian word that, through its endless repetition, synthesizes both redundance and minimalism, it is also one of what Bakshi calls the "quotidian acts" through which Vuong articulates the migratory experience, acknowledges the colonial wound, and highlights the importance to resist it.[25]

The burden and power of the word "sorry," initially contextualized in the nail salon, trickles onto Little Dog's identity. "And because I am your son," he writes later, when the boy working next to him in the field introduces himself as Trevor, "I said, 'Sorry.' Because I am your son, my apology had become, by then, an extension of myself" (94). While ambiguities related to language scarcity were articulations of *neither/nor* identities, ambiguities related to excess lay emphasis on *both/and* plenitude. In this case, Little Dog's identities as a son and a son of migrants intersect with his (homo)sexuality, foreshadowing the interwoven languages of power and vulnerability that will inform his sexual relationship with Trevor.

Familial and romantic love is itself interlocked with dynamics of semantic excess: "love, at its best, repeats itself, shouldn't it?" wonders Little Dog, it "should say *Yes* over and over, in cycles, in spirals, with no other reason but to hear itself exist" (34). Spirals, cycles, and redundancies as articulations of semantic excess and love reappear in the expanding circles of Lan's storytelling: "Mostly, [...] she rambled, the tales cycling one after another. They spiraled out from her mind only to return the next week with the same introduction" (22).[26] Although the use of the word "rambling" and Little Dog's occasional bouts of impatience seem to at least partially attribute Lan's redundant speech patterns to senility, the narrative also illuminates the symbolic strength of her circular storytelling. By endlessly retelling family stories and the stories behind family names, Lan contrasts the memoricidal impact of displacement and assimilation. While "the street below glowed white, erasing everything that had a name" (191), Lan goes on to repeat that her daughter's name was Rose four times in five lines, as in an effort to exorcise American winds of erasure.

Dynamics of excess also extend to textual places where "two languages [...] become a third" (33). English and Vietnamese compenetrate to build semantic bridges between them, each culture being present and permanent within the other, and visible in transparency. *Transparency* is a somewhat paradoxical term for an ambiguity phenomenon: hegemonic language, Bauman argues, leads "a fight of determination against ambiguity, of semantic precision against ambivalence, of *transparency* against obscurity."[27] I do, however, reconcile transparency with ambiguity by speaking of transparency as the presence of a barely legible something below the surface of a text. The surface text becomes as transparent as water to reveal shapes and movement beneath. Walter Benjamin's theorization of the concept of *superimposition* in

"Too Much Joy, I Swear, Is Lost" **191**

the context of urban studies may be of use in the description of transparencies across two languages:

> When we say that one face is similar to another, we mean that certain features of this second face appear to us in the first, without the latter's ceasing to be what it has been. [...] Under these conditions even a sentence (to say nothing of the single word) puts on a face, and this face resembles that of the sentence standing opposed to it.[28]

Instead of a sentence standing opposed to another, transparencies reveal another language flowing beneath the one on the page,[29] a language that remains implicit, covert, dormant. In this sense, transparency has much in common with Éduard Glissant's concept of "opacity," the right of Selves and their language to remain partially illegible to their interlocutor, who, in turn, has to "give up [...] discovering what lies at the bottom of natures" (190). Like Glissant's opacity, the language appearing below the surface of Vuong's text operates in the "texture and weave" of language and not in its "components."[30] These last pages will explore three textual places where covert processes[31] of translation between English and Vietnamese appear in transparency.

When Hong says "I'm not a monster. I'm a mother" (13), Little Dog disagrees:

> a monster is not such a terrible thing to be. From the Latin root *monstrum*, a divine messenger of catastrophe, then adapted by the Old French to mean an animal of myriad origins: centaur, griffin, satyr. To be a monster is to be a hybrid signal, a lighthouse: both shelter and warning at once.
>
> *(13)*

Little Dog tells his mother she is not a monster, but immediately admits to his reader that he lied. He initially does Other his mother as a monster, a "hybrid signal" of affection and abuse. Yet, he later reports an incident involving him wearing one of Hong's dresses in the front yard, which earns him the reputation of "freak, fairy, fag" among the neighbourhood kids. "Those words," Little Dog concludes, "were also iterations of *monster*. [...] You're a mother, Ma. You're also a monster. But so am I" (14). Both Hong and Little Dog are, in the logic of the metaphor, iterations of monstrosity, as they both are creatures of two bodies and two races, like centaurs, griffins, and satyrs. Eventually the word *mother* coalesces, in content but also in form, with the similar word *monster*; as the son of a monster, he is a monster himself, a creature with a hybrid body.

Monster's excess derives from the word's capacity to subsume issues of motherhood, migrant identities, and queer sexualities, but it also becomes

192 Elena Furlanetto

a door to Vietnamese, visible in transparency. When Hong claims to be not a monster but a mother, the reader inevitably wonders if this sentence was originally spoken in Vietnamese, and if so, what it would look like, and if the lexical proximity of *monster* and *mother* was a product of Little Dog's prose, or of his mother's speech. Is Little Dog's transformative command of English something he absorbed from Hong's equally nimble Vietnamese? In fact, the phonetic similarity of *mother* and *monster* is strongly reminiscent of the Vietnamese *má*[32]/mother and *con ma* or *ma quái*/ghost or monster. The hypothetical use of this binomial would complicate the equation between mother and monster by engaging the ghost and its metaphorical poignancy for stories of intergenerational trauma, particularly in Asian contexts.[33] This hypothesis, however, as is often the case with ambiguity readings, has to remain on the level of speculation.

These transparencies, a recurrent feature of the novel, remain covert but nevertheless knock gently at the prose's English surface until it becomes a door to Vietnamese. These phenomena appear in clusters and can be observed in a less speculative manner when Little Dog reflects on the polysemy of *nhớ*, "the word for missing someone and remembering them" (186). "When you ask me over the phone, *Con nhớ mẹ không?*" I flinch, thinking you meant, *Do you remember me?*" (186). Read in terms of language scarcity, the ambiguity of the term in Vietnamese leads to misunderstanding and heartache in English, but the word also generates other semantic multiplications later on, when Little Dog's free associations bring him from *nhớ*/to miss, to remember to *nhỏ*/small.

As a rule, be more.
As a rule, I miss you. [nhớ]
As a rule, "little" is always smaller than "small." [*nhỏ*]
(192)

The lyrical associations of part three, which blurs the border of prose and poetry through its sparse disposition of lines on the page, continue to create another transparency: "I'm sorry I don't call enough. [...] I'm sorry I keep saying *How are you?* When I really mean *Are you happy?*" (192). The difference between these two formulations can be discussed at length. The happiness reference brings back a previous exchange between Little Dog and his mother, who shows him her mood ring – that, too, a *đẹp quá* object – and asks "Am I happy?" (33). However, it can also be read through the prism of transparency, as Vietnamese does not ask how one is, but whether one is healthy, *anh/chị có khỏe không?*/are you healthy? Little Dog's apology for symbolically not prioritizing his mother's happiness runs parallel to his apology for not prioritizing Vietnamese above English, or for not inquiring after her health and happiness through the Vietnamese formulation she could more easily relate to, *are you healthy/happy* instead of *how are you*.

By circumventing Vietnamese, Little Dog relinquishes the possibility to access what Amy Tan, in her essay "Mother Tongue," calls her mother's "internal language," and with it "her intent, her passion, her imagery, the rhythms of her speech and the nature of her thoughts."[34] In *Minor Feelings*, Cathy Park Hong aligns with Tan and Vuong when she reflects on a fellow artist's use of English: "English was not her language, [...] English could never be a true reflection of her consciousness, [...] it was as much an imposition on her consciousness as it was a form of expression."[35] By operating a bilingual layering of the text, however, Little Dog opens the possibility of Vietnamese within English: he signals that he comprehends and treasures "the difference in language systems despite his lacunas"[36] and begins closing the gap between the rhythms of his mother's speech and his own.

Conclusion

What is, then, the dissenting impetus of Vuong's aesthetics of bilingual ambiguity? Phenomena of transparency contradict the truism that "the unspoken is nonexistent," but Vietnamese, although unspoken and "made obsolete by gunfire" (38), has not disappeared from Vuong's English prose; "rather it is glossed differently."[37] The voices that have guided and directed this analysis – Maria-Luisa Achino-Loeb, Zygmunt Bauman, Cathy Park Hong, Amy Tan, and Vuong himself, among others – unanimously agree that there is power in ambiguity, and that ambiguity can be close-read. "If we want to understand how power works," writes Achino-Loeb, "we must look at the interstitial spaces where meaning is ambiguous; the spaces beyond the margins of meaning, where significance is up for grabs."[38] Along similar lines, Tony Morrison notes that "one has to work very carefully with what is in between the words. What is not said. Which is measure, which is rhythm, and so on. So, it is what you don't write that frequently gives what you write its power."[39] The unsaid and the in-between, which Morrison locates in measure and rhythm, lingers in Vuong's alchemies of in-excess and in-defect writing, but also in the polysemous and cryptic quality of some metaphors ("what is a country but a life sentence?" 9), the silences, the blank spaces between lines, the punctuation signs which are present but unspoken and which the reader keeps finding ingrained in the bodies of the characters, and in the insistent knocking of Vietnamese below the surface of English.[40]

Notes

1 Ocean Vuong, *On Earth We're Briefly Gorgeous* (London: Penguin, 2019).
2 M. H. Abrahams, *A Glossary of Literary Terms* (Boston: Cengage Learning, 1998): 10.
3 See Birgit Neumann, " 'Our Mother Tongue, then, is No Mother at All – but an Orphan': The Mother Tongue and Translation in Ocean Vuong's *On Earth We're Briefly Gorgeous*," *Anglia* 138.2 (2020): 277–298.

4 Zygmunt Bauman, *Modernity and Ambivalence* (Cambridge: Polity Press, 1991): 2.
5 Bauman, *Modernity and Ambivalence*, 1.
6 See Abrahams, *A Glossary of Literary Terms*, 10–11.
7 See Cleanth Brooks, "The New Criticism," *The Sewanee Review* 87.4 (1979): 592–607.
8 The volume *Voices and Silence in the Contemporary Novel in English*, edited by Vanessa Guignery, gathers numerous studies on the co-presence of scarcity and excess in the work of Graham Swift (reticence and excess), John Fowles (silence and logorrhoea), Kazuo Ishiguro (wordless voice), Salman Rushdie (sentencing the excess), Jamaica Kincaid and Zadie Smith (the erotics of silence and excess), Ryhaan Shah (silent screams), and others. For an essay on silence as a collective mother tongue, see Ihab Hassan, "Frontiers of Criticism: Metaphors of Silence," *The Virginia Quarterly Review* 46.1 (1970): 81–95.
9 Cathy Park Hong, *Minor Feelings: An Asian American Reckoning* (London: One World, 2020): 139.
10 Neumann, "The Mother Tongue and Translation," 1.
11 Sandeep Bakshi, "The Decolonial Eye/I: Decolonial Enunciations of Queer Diasporic Practices," *Interventions* 22.4 (2020): 538.
12 Vuong, *On Earth We're Briefly Gorgeous*, 31.
13 See, for example, Neumann, "The Mother Tongue and Translation," 2, 3, 5.
14 Maria-Luisa Achino-Loeb, ed., *Silence: The Currency of Power* (Oxford and New York: Berghahn Books, 2006): 4.
15 Neumann, "The Mother Tongue and Translation," 1.
16 See reviews by Ella Johnson, "A Dog's World," *Oxford Review of Books*, 10 June 2021, www.the-orb.org/post/a-dog-s-world; and Jia Tolentino, "Ocean Vuong's Life Sentences," *The New Yorker*, 3 June 2019, www.newyorker.com/magazine/2019/06/10/ocean-vuongs-life-sentences.
17 A term used in the context of Gothic fiction by Owen Robinson, "City of Exiles: Unstable Narratives of New Orleans in George Washington Cable's *Old Creole Days*," in *Transatlantic Exchanges: The American South in Europe, Europe in the American South*, edited by Richard Gray and Waldemar Zacharasiewicz (Los Angeles: OAW, 2007): 293–308. The idea of an ambiguous narration revolving around a centre that is silent, erased, and impossible to locate is indebted to Jaques Deridda's argument in "Structure, Sign, and Play in the Discourse of the Human Sciences," *Writing and Difference* 278 (1978): 278–294, http://www2.csudh.edu/ccauthen/576f13/DrrdaSSP.pdf.
18 This passage resonates strongly with Amy Tan, "Mother Tongue," in *Dreams and Inward Journeys: A Rhetoric and Reader for Writers*, edited by Marjorie Ford and Jon Ford. (London: Pearson, 2010): 34–44, where the author reflects on the difference between her own highly polished, academic English and her mother's "expressive" English. "My mother's 'limited' English," Tan observes, "limited my perception of her. I was ashamed of her English. I believed that her English reflected the quality of what she had to say. That is, because she expressed them imperfectly her thoughts were imperfect." In Little Dog's case, it is the narrator's own 'limited' or 'scarce' Vietnamese that limits the perception of his mother's consciousness, which will be discussed later.
19 Viet Thanh Nguyen, "What is Vietnamese American Literature?" in *Looking Back on the Vietnam War*, edited by Brenda M. Boyle and Jeehyun Lim (New Brunswick: Rutgers University Press, 2016): 50–63, 50.
20 Summer Kim Lee, "Staying In: Mitski, Ocean Vuong, and Asian American Asociality," *Social Text* 37.1 (2019): 28.
21 Hong, *Minor Feelings*, 140.

"Too Much Joy, I Swear, Is Lost" **195**

22 Chris Miller, "Silence," 2007. https://csmt.uchicago.edu/glossary2004/silence.htm.
23 Unless otherwise indicated, emphases are in the original.
24 Achino-Loeb, *Silence*, 3–4.
25 Bakshi, "The Decolonial Eye/I," 543.
26 For studies of verbosity in elderly adults and how it bears on intergenerational contact see Pushkar Gold, Tannis Y. Arbuckle and David Andres, "Verbosity in Older Adults," in *Interpersonal Communication in Older Adulthood: Interdisciplinary Theory and Research*, edited by Mary Lee Hummert, John M. Wiemann and John F. Nussbaum (Thousand Oaks: Sage, 1994): 107–129; see also Robert M. McCann, Aaron C. Cargile, Howard Giles and Cuong T. Bui, "Communication Ambivalence toward Elders: Data from North Vietnam, South Vietnam, and the USA," *Journal of Cross-Cultural Gerontology* 19.4 (2004): 275–297.
27 Bauman, *Modernity and Ambivalence*, 6 (emph. added).
28 Walter Benjamin, *The Arcades Project* (Cambridge, MA: Harvard College, 1999): 418. See also Lena Mattheis and Jens Gurr, "Superpositions," *Literary Geographies* 71 (2021): 5–22; and Lena Mattheis, *Translocality in Contemporary City Novels* (Berlin: Springer, 2021), esp. 60.
29 This approach is also indebted to David Punter's spectral readings, where words are haunted by "a text that lies beneath the text." David Punter, *The Gothic Condition: Terror, History and the Psyche* (Cardiff: University of Wales Press, 2016): 263.
30 Édouard Glissant, *Poetics of Relation* (Ann Arbor: The University of Michigan Press, 1997): 190.
31 See Neumann, "The Mother Tongue and Translation," 10.
32 It is legitimate to assume that Hong, being from Hồ Chí Minh City (Saigon in the novel) and therefore from South Vietnam, would say *má*, instead of the North Vietnamese variant *mẹ*. In another sentence I will turn to later, however, she refers to herself as *mẹ*. In a *Late Night* interview with Seth Meyers, Ocean Vuong addresses his mother as *mẹ* ("Ocean Vuong Wrote His Debut Novel in a Closet," interview by Seth Meyers, *Late Night with Seth Meyers*, *YouTube*, 13 June 2019, video, 6:51, www.youtube.com/watch?v=cQl_qbWwCwU.
33 See, for example, Jung Ha Kim's "What's with the Ghosts? Portrayals of Spirituality in Asian American Literature," *Spiritus: A Journal of Christian Spirituality* 6.2 (2006): 241–248; and the work of Janna Odabas, especially *The Ghosts Within: Literary Imaginations of Asian America* (Bielefeld: transcript Verlag, 2018).
34 Tan, "Mother Tongue."
35 Hong, *Minor Feelings*, 155.
36 Bakshi, "The Decolonial Eye/I," 547.
37 Achino-Loeb, *Silence*, 11.
38 Achino-Loeb, *Silence*, 16.
39 Toni Morrison, *Toni Morrison: Conversations*, edited by Caroline C. Denard (Jackson: University Press of Mississippi, 2008): 67.
40 The author would like to thank Thanh Tùng Nguyễn for the language support and for considering my arguments from the critically important perspective of a diasporic Vietnamese native speaker. The results presented in this article originate from a project funded by the Deutsche Forschungsgemeinschaft (DFG, German Research Foundation), project number 322729370.

Bibliography

Abrahams, Meyer Howard. *A Glossary of Literary Terms*. Boston: Cengage Learning, 1998.
Achino-Loeb, Maria-Luisa, ed. *Silence: The Currency of Power*. Oxford and New York: Berghahn Books, 2006.

Bakshi, Sandeep. "The Decolonial Eye/I: Decolonial Enunciations of Queer Diasporic Practices." *Interventions* 22.4 (2020): 533–551.

Bauman, Zygmunt. *Modernity and Ambivalence*. Cambridge: Polity Press, 1991.

Benjamin, Walter. *The Arcades Project*. Cambridge, MA: Harvard College, 1999.

Brooks, Cleanth. "The New Criticism." *The Sewanee Review* 87.4 (1979): 592–607.

Derrida, Jacques. "Structure, Sign, and Play in the Discourse of the Human Sciences." *Writing and Difference* 278 (1978): 278–294. http://www2.csudh.edu/ccauthen/576f13/DrrdaSSP.pdf.

Glissant, Édouard. *Poetics of Relation*. Ann Arbor: The University of Michigan Press, 1997.

Gold, Pushkar Dolores, Tannis Y. Arbuckle and David Andres. "Verbosity in Older Adults." In *Interpersonal Communication in Older Adulthood: Interdisciplinary Theory and Research*, edited by Mary Lee Hummert, John M. Wiemann and John F. Nussbaum. Thousand Oaks: Sage, 1994: 107–129.

Guignery, Vanessa, ed. *Voices and Silence in the Contemporary Novel in English*. Newcastle upon Tyne: Cambridge Scholars, 2009.

Hassan, Ihab. "Frontiers of Criticism: Metaphors of Silence." *The Virginia Quarterly Review* 46.1 (1970): 81–95.

Hong, Cathy Park. *Minor Feelings: An Asian American Reckoning*. London: One World, 2020.

Kim, Jung Ha. "What's with the Ghosts? Portrayals of Spirituality in Asian American Literature." *Spiritus: A Journal of Christian Spirituality* 6.2 (2006): 241–248.

Lee, Summer Kim. "Staying In: Mitski, Ocean Vuong, and Asian American Asociality." *Social Text* 37.1 (2019): 27–50.

Mattheis, Lena. *Translocality in Contemporary City Novels*. Berlin: Springer, 2021.

Mattheis, Lena and Jens Gurr. "Superpositions." *Literary Geographies* 7.1 (2021): 5–22.

McCann, Robert M., Aaron C. Cargile, Howard Giles and Cuong T. Bui. "Communication Ambivalence toward Elders: Data from North Vietnam, South Vietnam, and the USA." *Journal of Cross-Cultural Gerontology* 19.4 (2004): 275–297.

Miller, Chris. "Silence." 2007. https://csmt.uchicago.edu/glossary2004/silence.htm.

Morrison, Toni. *Toni Morrison: Conversations*, edited by Caroline C. Denard. Jackson: University Press of Mississippi, 2008.

Neumann, Birgit. " 'Our Mother Tongue, then, is No Mother at All – but an Orphan': The Mother Tongue and Translation in Ocean Vuong's *On Earth We're Briefly Gorgeous*." *Anglia* 138.2 (2020): 277–298.

Nguyen, Viet Thanh. "What is Vietnamese American Literature?" In *Looking Back on the Vietnam War*, edited by Brenda M. Boyle and Jeehyun Lim. New Brunswick: Rutgers University Press, 2016: 50–63.

Odabas, Janna. *The Ghosts Within: Literary Imaginations of Asian America*. Bielefeld: transcript Verlag, 2018.

Punter, David. *The Gothic Condition: Terror, History and the Psyche*. Cardiff: University of Wales Press, 2016.

Robinson, Owen. "City of Exiles: Unstable Narratives of New Orleans in George Washington Cable's *Old Creole Days*." In *Transatlantic Exchanges: The American South in Europe, Europe in the American South*, edited by Richard Gray and Waldemar Zacharasiewicz. Los Angeles: OAW, 2007: 293–308.

Tan, Amy. "Mother Tongue." In *Dreams and Inward Journeys: A Rhetoric and Reader for Writers*, edited by Marjorie Ford and Jon Ford. London: Pearson, 2010: 34–44.

Tolentino, Jia. "Ocean Vuong's Life Sentences." *The New Yorker*, 3 June 2019. www.newyorker.com/magazine/2019/06/10/ocean-vuongs-life-sentences (last accessed 30 March 2024).

Vuong, Ocean. "Ocean Vuong Wrote His Debut Novel in a Closet." Interview by Seth Meyers, *Late Night with Seth Meyers*. YouTube, 13 June 2019. Video, 6:51, www.youtube.com/watch?v=cQl_qbWwCwU (last accessed 30 March 2024).

———. *On Earth We're Briefly Gorgeous*. London: Penguin, 2019.

12

TOWARDS SHONGLISH?

An Analysis of Chenjerai Hove's *Ancestors*

Tanaka Chidora

Introduction

The argument of which language to use when writing what is referred to as African literature is a very old debate but still finds ways of coming back into contemporary controversies of what African literature is and how we arrive at the label of African literature.[1] Contemporary debates have shown how unimaginative it is to speak of African literature as if it were one homogenous thing, as if it emerged from a homogenous cultural unit. Taiye Selasie's "African Literature Doesn't Exist" is probably emerging from the discomfort of lumping all of the continent's literatures under one taxonomy, as if each author represents a single continental sensibility.[2] The literatures of the African continent emerge from various biogeographical and cultural settings that communicate various experiences that should not be regarded as unitary representations of what Africa looks like. Thus, in my analysis of Hove's novel, I have deliberately avoided speaking of the novel as a representation of something 'African.' Even my use of the word 'Shona' should not be misconstrued to mean something unified. The sensibility I have outlined here is also related to the arguments concerning World literatures and Afropolitanism. Both are oriented towards a view of Africa and what is 'African' that has an outward orientation rather than an inward-looking one. Thus, instead of the cultural nationalist whose definition of Africa is inward-looking, or the 'outsider' whose view of what is 'African' ticks the flagpole list of African stereotypes, the view of African literatures as World literatures, and the Afropolitan view of the African as a being of the world both liberate African literatures from the limitations of classification. What is called African literature, therefore, becomes World literature in that it participates, together with the rest of the

DOI: 10.4324/9781003464037-16

This chapter has been made available under a CC-BY-NC-ND 4.0 license.

198 Tanaka Chidora

literatures of the world, in creating a picture of what the world looks like. In the same vein, English is not a unitary language, nor do we have a World English. What we have are World Englishes. These include Shonglish.

Shonglish is simply direct translation from Shona to English. In Zimbabwe, it is so common and ingrained that it is difficult to notice if something is 'wrong' with the English, that is, judging by the British English that was introduced to Zimbabwe by colonialism. It is not uncommon to hear a respectable professor introducing a lecture thus: "Today we want to discuss *about* the implications of this and that." This is an example of direct translation from Shona to English. The result is what is called Shonglish. It is a version of English that borrows from the Shona Language. Shona is the most dominant non-English language in Zimbabwe and is spoken in most parts of Zimbabwe with minor variations in dialect here and there. Writers like Charles Mungoshi, Memory Chirere, Chenjerai Hove, and Brian Chikwava are popular for using Shonglish. However, Hove's *Ancestors* is the most sustained experiment in translation.[3]

Other levels of Shonglish involve using Shona words and not providing a glossary or explaining what they mean. The assumption is that the words have become part of the English vocabulary and there is no need to explain or translate them. In the past, any word from non-English languages would be defined under the "Glossary of terms," highlighting that it was important to use the word although it is not an English word. The fact that in a predominantly English novel that was written following the rules of British English one would find these 'indigenous' words which would later be defined under a glossary had implications on the value of the indigenous language, especially given the fact that the indigenous words were merely called upon to add some kind of light-heartedness and discarded when the writer wanted to communicate deeply philosophical thoughts beyond the names of trees, food, animals, and children's games.

Shonglish may also manifest in a writer using the 'cultural eye' and cadence of the Shona language in English. Language is a carrier of culture. Shona culture can manifest in English through how a writer controls the rhythm of his/her sentences, giving them the baseline of Shona speech patterns. This is especially prominent in the use of orality. Shona orature includes Shona proverbs, riddles, children's games, folk songs, rituals, and banalities. Instead of finding an English equivalent, the writer either writes any of those oral art forms through direct translation or in the original Shona language. For instance, the proverb, "*Imbwa nyoro ndidzo tsengi dzamatovo*" has an English equivalent in "Still waters run deep." Instead of using that English version, a writer may choose, "Dogs that look reserved are the ones that eat the hides that we leave to dry in the sun." Again, the cultural eye is apparent in that the proverb is emanating from the forms of life of Shona people as keepers of cattle. It is therefore my argument in this chapter that Hove tries to retain the oral culture of the Shona people in his experimental novel, *Ancestors*.

Situating Hove's Art in a National and Global Context

The late Chenjerai Hove, who died in exile in 2015, was one of the most prolific and anthologised poets from Zimbabwe alongside Musaemura Zimunya. While Zimunya was more of Hove's predecessor, prolifically writing poetry during the Rhodesian period, Hove's watershed period came after independence. In 1981, he contributed fourteen poems in the first black Zimbabwean anthology, *And Now the Poets Speak*, edited by Musaemura Zimunya and Mudereri Kadhani.[4] The poems carried the trademark that would characterise Hove's poetic delivery in *Up in Arms*,[5] *Red Hills of Home*,[6] *Rainbow in the Dust*,[7] and *Blind Moon*:[8] simplicity that came from his version of English that carried everyday experiences of the Shona people. This is not to say the ideas he communicated were simple; the idea is that the transition from Shona to English did not mutilate the seamlessness with which the ideas were supposed to be assimilated by one whose first language was Shona.

This trademark is more visible in *Bones*,[9] reaching its most experimental level in *Ancestors*. Like in most of his poems, Hove uses female narrators in *Bones*, as if to subtly suggest that he was communicating in the mother tongue. Storytelling in the oral history of the Shona was the domain of women, especially grandmothers. In *Ancestors*, this is captured when the narrator says, "In the folktales, old women whisper the story of a maiden who refused to enrich her people."[10] The children would gather around the old woman while shelling groundnuts or roasting maize cobs and listen to stories that usually started with, "*Paivapo*" (in the beginning) and ended with "*Ndipo pakaperera sarungano*" (this is where the storyteller ends). Sarungano also means "the owner of the story." Hove's novels also have a mother tongue aesthetic that appropriates the rhythms and patterns of Shona speech to communicate what it means to be a Shona woman and to be peripheralised.

By extending the myth of Charwe,[11] which he uses in *Bones*, to *Ancestors*, where Miriro silences Mucha in order for Mucha to speak on her behalf, Hove is performing his own bit in the struggle of women the world over and reclaiming their agency, especially in a world where "only the story of the men, our fathers, were told."[12] According to L.M. Hove,

> Miriro, in her vocal deformity, is a prototype of Zimbabwean and – by extension – third-world women. She is at once a different being and a symbol that offers an analytical and political framework for the exploration of women's histories and struggles against sexism and postcolonial marginalisation. Her socio-cultural location as a voiceless woman allows for her interpellation into pervasive and systemic Zimbabwean discourses on patriarchal domination.[13]

200 Tanaka Chidora

In doing what L.M. Hove observes previously, Hove is extending his subversive challenge to patriarchy as seen in *Bones* when he challenges the patriarchal mythologisation of Charwe. Thus, *Ancestors* can be read as "an artistic and architectural design [...] that re-genders both the political and social space through the figure of Miriro."[14] By highlighting this interpretation of *Ancestors* early into my chapter, I am attempting to discourage any thinking that Hove's use of Shonglish is based on an inward-looking aesthetic that is common among many cultural nationalists.

Hove also seemed to be a follower of Achebe's paradigm from the great Makerere debate. Achebe's paradigm seeks to accept the logic of the presence of English in the African writer's creative process. The relationship is not easy at first, and Marechera's narrator in *House of Hunger* expresses it thus:

> It was like this: English is my second language, Shona my first. When I talked it was in the form of an interminable argument, one side of which was always expressed in English and the other side always in Shona. At the same time, I would be aware of myself as something indistinct but separate from both cultures. I felt gagged by this absurd contest between Shona and English.[15]

Because of this contest between Shona and English, the narrator feels gagged. In many ways, the narrator is Marechera himself, because in a self-interview he says it never occurred to him to write in Shona, because it appeared to him like the ghetto demon he was trying to exorcise from himself. Conquering English by using it seemed to be the way towards this redemption: "for a black writer, the language is very racist; you have to have harrowing fights and hair-raising panga duels before you can make it do all that you want it to do."[16] These hair-raising panga duels resulted in something that Marechera was always accused of by African cultural nationalists: a Joycean stream of consciousness characterised by a fragmented plot, flashbacks, disjointed syntax, and imagery forcefully hammered into place. Instead of the linear approach that one finds in Shona orature, where the story moves from point A to B without any stylistic hiccups, Marechera's style requires more concentration and re-readings in order to grasp the essence of the story.

Hove, however, does not seem to experience these limitations caused by the duel between Shona and English. This is not to say his narratives are linear and simplistic. There are flashbacks and fragmentations, too. In fact, *Ancestors* is regarded as the most difficult of all of Hove's novels.[17] Rather, the simplicity lies in the fact that Marechera's hair-raising panga duels between Shona and English do not seem to bother Hove, allowing him to seamlessly move from Shona to English and integrate some Shona words and phrases into his canon of English words. This sets Hove apart from scholars who

Towards Shonglish? **201**

advocate for Ngugi's approach of completely rejecting English. Hove aligns himself with Achebe for whom the choice to use English is a deliberate one: "Is it right that a man should abandon his mother tongue for someone else's? It looks like a dreadful betrayal and produces a guilty feeling. But for me there is no other choice. I have been given the language and I intend to use it."[18] Achebe thought that it was still possible to capture those African experiences using English in an Africanised way. Thus, *Things Fall Apart* appears to be "a masterful rendition of African proverbs and riddles in English [which] made it possible for readers from all across the globe to appreciate the wisdom and the universal appeal of African proverbs and riddles which were integral parts of African culture."[19]

Ken Saro Wiwas's *Sozaboy*,[20] Hove's *Ancestors*, and, of late, Brian Chikwava's *Harare North*[21] are deliberate experiments that seek to take Achebe's thesis to another level. All these novels use a form of English whose cadence is localised while at the same time connecting it to a global audience. Thus, one can say that the novels' use of English is not as inward-looking as Ngugi would have wanted African literatures to be. Their uses of English expose their characters to a global audience, but without in any way altering their characters for the sake of making them speak English. Rather, it is the English that is altered.

The Shonglish of the Ancestors

The immediate and major narrator of *Ancestors* is a male character called Mucha who tells his own story through the pronoun 'you.' However, Mucha is also a ventriloquist through whom a female ancestor, Miriro, predominantly speaks, although there is a Tariro here and there. Through Mucha, Miriro narrates the history of the family spanning many decades. The female ancestor was deaf and dumb during her lifetime, although she claims that what she is narrating is what she heard: people's conversations, songs and the sounds of birds and animals. Miriro hanged herself at a young age after being forced to marry a drunkard. Her death transmogrifies her into a female ancestor who speaks through Mucha via dreams and trances that look like spirit possession. This is one of Hove's narrative techniques seen also in *Bones*. In *Bones*, the voice of the mythical ancestor, Charwe, speaks through Marita, who in turn speaks through Janifa and the Unknown Woman. In an interview, Hove speaks of this narrative mode thus:

> I use a different narrative mode. [...] But it is also very Zimbabwean. [...] Because it is like a dream. And I use the Shona belief in spirit mediums. The woman who died, the woman who is actually the story-teller, died when she was young [...] so now I resurrect her in the book.[22]

202 Tanaka Chidora

In all these cases, the dead are women, lending credence to the argument that Hove's version of a 'mother' tongue involves female characters who, in Shona culture, are invariably regarded as mothers. Motherhood, in Shona culture, is not conferred by birthing. One's mother is not only the woman from whom one was birthed, but every other woman in the community.

Mucha cements his position as a ventriloquist when he says:

> They are the words I have shared with this woman who is a mere dream, the storyteller who tells female stories to so many deaf ears. They are stories about the female blood in me, blood that has been neglected by so many tales which father has hidden away from me. [...] I hear them in her voice, Miriro's, the one who is awaited, the one yet to arrive, the one who departed before she arrived.[23]

What is apparent is that Miriro is aggrieved. According to Chirere,

> [a]s she manifests herself to Mucha, Miriro is seemingly aggrieved, most probably for being forced by her father into a loveless marriage during her times in the land of the living. It is not clear how she intends to settle her score, if at all. But at some point there are suggestions that she intends to do harm to Mucha's father.[24]

The idea that is being communicated here is that of *Ngozi*, the avenging spirit of someone who died an aggrieved person. The ngozi spirit manifests through a living person in order to air out its grievances so that the living can find a way of appeasing it. Like Miriro, Tariro was also given away in marriage in 1958, and Miriro gives Mucha information to the effect that wherever she is, Tariro is dead, a 'bare grave.' The phrase 'bare grave' is usually used in Shona to denote someone who is as good as dead. Thus, Mucha becomes the conduit through which aggrieved women in the family manifest to incriminate the male line for forcing them into marriages. The Shona belief system that undergirds Hove's narrative in *Ancestors* is what enables him to Shonalise his English in order to make it carry the weight of Mucha's and Miriro's experiences in a Shona setting.

Hove's Shonalised English, sometimes referred to as a rural idiom,[25] can be read for the mere lyricism of the Shona language peeping from beneath the veneer of English.[26] In the following dreamy memory, Hove's Shona lyricism is very apparent:

> Your father and mother sit, on opposite sides of the fireplace. [...] Words burn also: they cannot cross the fire zone. Words are spilled in the air, then the smoke catches them. [...] You want to cry to both, to say to them:

Father, words are burning! Mother, words are burning in the fire!. [...] Mother's head is bowed, like one praying [...] with a tiny twig in her hand, fingering it, scratching the hard cement floor with the stick as young maidens do when young men frighten them with words of love. I lose sleep whenever I think of you. I cannot eat. And when the young maidens hear those burning words, their supple eyes glitter with amusement. Lose sleep? Cannot eat? What sort of man is this who lies for the sake of touching the grass where the king's cattle graze?[27]

In this scene, Mucha is transported to the scene where his parents argue concerning giving away their daughter in marriage, yet there is also another piece of memory where Mucha's mother thinks of their courtship days. The descriptions are pregnant with Shona pastoral courtship scenes, involving the girl bashfully breaking twigs and the boy lying that when the girl is not around, he does not sleep.

Another instance is where Hove translates Shona relationships into English: "Son of my sister [...], come let us work the rich soils of these new lands together."[28] 'Son of my sister' is a direct translation of "*Mwana wehanzvadzi yangu.*" According to Kadenge, "the use of kinship terms such as 'sister,' 'son,' 'brother,' 'mother,' 'father,' 'senior wife' and 'junior wife' represents an area where semantic extension contributes to the indigenisation of the English language in Zimbabwe."[29] As I have pointed out in the case of 'mother,' these terms are not used in the context of one's immediate (biological/nucleus) family only. They extend to the whole community. And this communal nature of these kinship terms even extends to the ancestors who, in many respects, are not limited by biological affiliations: "In drink, your ancestors and mine shake hands and say: see, our children know how to share the earth."[30] Thus, terms that denote kinship have a wider application, as is the case in the Shona language. Hove translates them directly in a way that maintains the nuances of the relationships. Even the spirit that is possessing Mucha is not referred to as a demon or in such psychological terms as are used to describe madness. The spirit is an ancestor, hence the title of the novel.

Further, when talking about children born of the same father but from different mothers, Hove's second-person narrator, for instance, avoids such English words like 'step-sister' and 'step-brothers':

You see these children from your father's homestead. They are not children from the neighbours. Only children of the same blood. The songs you have left in far-away places are born again in the voices of children of your own mothers. Many mothers, young and old. Young brothers and sisters, elder brothers and sisters.[31]

204 Tanaka Chidora

The phrase, "Only children of the same blood" is a direct translation of *"vana veropa rimwe"* to denote children who share the same father. The children are from a polygamous father, hence the phrase, "many mothers." Where children share the same mother, they are said to be from the same womb (*"vana vemudumbu rimwe"*).[32] Kandege goes further to give an inventory of other kinship terms that are used in an Shonalised way in *Ancestors* to communicate a polygamous marriage. These include 'senior wife' to refer to *"mukadzi mukuru"* (first wife) in a polygamous marriage;[33] and 'young wife' to refer to *"mukadzi mudiki"* (junior/second/third/fourth wife) in a polygamous marriage.[34] Even the term 'polygamous' here is being used in an 'English' way and does not capture the nuance of the arrangement, because the word carries derogatory elements. In a Shona setting the word that means 'polygamy' is *barika*. When speaking of a man who is in a polygamous marriage, Shona people do not say, "He is polygamous." Rather, they say, "He has many wives." The second translation of *barika* captures it as a union that has a communal nuance to it. Thus, women in a *barika* are regarded as 'mothers' by all the children. The child of a senior wife cannot regard his/her father's junior wife as 'Father's wife.' She is Mother. Also, even when marrying, a man is said to be marrying for the whole clan: "Musindo [knew] that a man who marries a young wife also marries for those of his blood who are not yet born."[35] In Shona, this translates as *"Waroora mukadzi aroorera dzinza."* This points even to possibilities of inheriting the wife in the event that Musindo dies. Thus, the language Hove uses here speaks of kinship ties whose nuances are best captured through direct translation. These ties show us the place of women in such a patriarchal setting.

Hove also directly translates proverbs and idioms from Shona culture without looking for their English equivalents. The proverbs are made to retain their cultural essence for the sake of capturing the nuances of the culture that produced them. Sometimes, the translation uses an equivalent scenario in Shona culture to arrive at the same meaning that is being communicated by the proverb. For instance, the statement, "When a calabash of water is carried on the head of a small girl, we can only thank the ancestors after we have drunk some water,"[36] used to communicate uncertainty, is an equivalent of *"Totenda dzamwa dzaswera nebenzi."*[37] However, the Shona proverb cited here does not talk about calabashes. In fact, directly translated, the proverb is supposed to say, "We can only heave a sigh of relief if a madman herding our cattle allows them to drink some water." Hove created a version of the proverb in English but using the same nuances of the Shona setting. However, most of the proverbs do not look for an equivalent scenario in Shona culture; they are directly translated in order to retain the nuances of Shona culture. The following is a brief inventory of these proverbs in English and the original proverbs in Shona in Hove's *Ancestors*.

Towards Shonglish? **205**

Proverb in Shonglish	Proverb in Shona
1. To rush is not to arrive (11)	*Kumhanya hakusiko kusvika*
2. The little beast gets fat by eating another little beast (59)	*Kakara kununa hudya kamwe*
3. This is food for the eyes only, the tongue may rest (98)	*Ndezvemeso muromo zvinyarare*
4. You cannot put spices in a gourd of milk – you spoil it (109)	*Chakanaka chakanaka mukaka haurungwi munyu*
5. An old woman is a wife. It is not the same as sleeping on a cold mat (146)	*Chembere mukadzi hazvienzani nekurara mugota*
6. In a fight, a man can be said to be dead only when flies perch on his intestines (152)	*Kufa kwemurume kubuda ura*
7. It is the soil which knows that a tortoise's baby is ill (153)	*Chinoziva ivhu kuti mwana wembeva anorwara*
8. The person who walks along the footpath across the rock without faltering has surely walked there before (178)	*Muzivi wenzira yeparuware ndiye mufambi wayo*

Meanings of the Proverbs
1. Sometimes one needs to take one's time when doing something, because rushing does not mean one will be able to complete the task at hand.
2. There are some people whose success is based on oppressing others.
3. Some things are only meant to be seen and not commented on.
4. Certain levels of perfection need no alterations or additions. There are certain things that we must accept as they are because that is where their goodness lies.
5. Sometimes we may receive little, but it is better than not having anything.
6. A real man can only be stopped by death.
7. He who feels it knows it.
8. A person who does a difficult thing repeatedly becomes an expert in doing it.

From the oral culture of the Shona, Hove also borrows names of children's games and communal dances. He does not translate them but uses them as direct loan words. These include *mahumbwe* (69), *dudu muduri* (93), and *jerusarema* (126). He does the same with the names of trees like *muroro* (62), *mupani* (167), *munhanzva* (171), and many others. There is no glossary list to explain these terms. The assumption by the author is that they are as English as any other word in the novel.

The names of trees and children's games also enable us to appreciate Hove's use of the rural idiom in *Ancestors*. It should be understood that *Ancestors* is the closest Hove came to writing an autobiography of himself to the extent that it is possible to see bits and pieces of Hove in Mucha, including Mucha's dreams of flying. "I used to dream that I was flying. And my father used to think that I needed a traditional healer to cure me of that. I refused the

206 Tanaka Chidora

attention of the healer. Young as I was, I said, 'Why should I not dream like that? It is so beautiful to fly.'"[38] And like Mucha, Hove's family migrated to an equivalent of Fanwell's place (in *Ancestors*) when they moved to a Native Purchase Area in Gokwe from the Mazvihwa Tribal Trust Lands in Zvishavane in search of better soils. Mucha's father who eventually receives a Master Farmer's certificate in *Ancestors* can easily be read as Hove's father. Therefore, Hove is working with very familiar people, places, and cultures, and this enables him, even as he is using English, to stay close to the trees, grass, soil, and cultural nuances that characterised his upbringing. That he is close to his upbringing is captured when he says about his poetry, "It is in the songs and dances of my birth that I drink the waters of poetry [...] in poetry I am part of other voices in other hearts, but I am also part of the voices that are ignored."[39] Yet what is apparent in this statement, in being 'part of other voices,' is a globalist vision that makes him more outward looking than a cultural nationalist who is only interested in defending his/her culture.

Hove also resorts to Shona in naming his characters. In Shona, names are potent carriers of histories, grievances, supplications to ancestors, and many other social statements. Thus, Musindo, to whom Tariro is forcibly married off (before she runs away), means a noisemaker, "the derelict whose explosive cough sent the children running for their lives and silenced the whole court."[40] Tariro means hope and captures the young girl's longing for freedom. Marunda is a poor, sickly looking man who at one point drank until he soiled his trousers. Nyarai, Tariro's mother, who speaks against the erasure of her daughter (the ancestor) from memory through libation, "is not like a drunkard who wakes up the following morning and claims he does not know a thing of what happened yesterday. She has pain in her heart [...] the pain of childbirth."[41] Her name is also associated with the verb, *Tinyarei*, which means 'Give us space.' Thus, her character of speaking against men, of telling them to give women space to speak, agrees with her name.

Criticism of Hove's Shonglish

Hove's audacious experiment has not gone without being criticised. One of the most immediate criticisms, perhaps, comes from a cultural nationalist belonging to Ngugi's camp in the language debate. As one of the strongest critics of English, Ngugi observes: "The domination of a people's language by the languages of the colonizing natives was crucial to the domination of the mental universe of the colonized."[42] Thus, Ngugi does not believe that when English is made to carry the weight of African experiences the mental domination occasioned by English is over; he believes that localising English actually enriches it at the expense of local languages.

However, one may want to follow an argument that treats English not just as the language of the former coloniser, but as a language that has become

Towards Shonglish? **207**

indigenous to, in this context, the Shona. In this, Achebe's argument becomes relevant:

> Those African writers who have chosen to write in English and French [...] are by-products of the same processes that made the new nation-states of Africa. [...] Those of us who might have inherited the English language may not be in a position to appreciate the value of the inheritance. Or we may go on resenting it, because it came as a part of a package deal that included many other items of doubtful value, especially the atrocities of racial arrogance and prejudice which may yet set the world on fire. But let us not, in rejecting the evil, throw out the good with it.[43]

The good in English, in Achebe's case, includes the fact that he used it to subvert Eurocentric stereotypes of Africa. Thus, if English is political in the sense that it is a language of subjugation, it is, in the same vein, political, because it is a language of freedom. In the case of Hove, Shonalising English was not done in order to defend the Shona people as a group being wiped away in a world that is Anglicising; he uses English in *Ancestors* in order to communicate the oppressions that Shona women face. He communicates those oppressions in their natural cultural and linguistic settings in order to capture their nuances. So, when Hove writes about "[t]he young girl with breasts like the small tips of a young man's thumbs [who] is led by the women to a place she does not know"[44] (literally translated from "*kasikana kane mazamo akamira kuti twi*"), he is highlighting the importance of marrying young, sometimes under-aged girls, in the patriarchal Shona society where "hushed virginal girls" are forms of gifts. But the importance of this practice can only be well-captured in its linguistic and cultural setting, hence the translation. By doing so, Hove is assuming a globalist vision that seeks the emancipation of women. Emancipation begins with understanding what is going on.

Besides, the Shonalisation of English, if we are to talk about politics, is itself a political act that begins with the refusal to use standardised English to write. The use of Shonalised English enables the stories of those who speak Shona to be told on the world stage while retaining the nuances of the Shona language. This English is familiar on the global stage, yet it contains traces of Shona. This makes Hove a world writer and his novel a world text. In fact, that ability to use it interchangeably or simultaneously with Shona also means that English has become as indigenous as Shona. This agrees with Achebe's argument that "a language spoken by Africans on African soil, a language in which Africans write, justifies itself."[45] The politics in this approach lies in the subversion of binaries that reduce literature to either nativist or globalist, African or Worldist. According to Mukherjee, "[t]hese oppositional arguments are losing their relevance in the current world scenario where transnationalism is the new form of global connectedness."[46]

208 Tanaka Chidora

Unlike Achebe and Ngugi, Hove is not trying to set the record straight. It is therefore not unusual for Hove to want to enjoy the luxuries of this linguistic ambivalence that he resolves through Shonglish, especially given the fact that English is also spoken well in his country and among the Shona.

Another piece of criticism that can be levelled against Hove's *Ancestors* is that of Hove imposing his idiom on every character in the novel as if all the characters, regardless of age, speak in the same way. In her criticism of Hove's *Bones*, Flora Veit-Wild thinks that Hove's characters use a language that makes it difficult to distinguish "between facts and fiction, feelings and intellect."[47] Hove's experiment in *Ancestors* allows him to move seamlessly between "characterisation, confession, protest, hybridism, feminism, spiritualism, magic realism. [...] He also borrows very heavily from dream, hallucination, memory and the Shona concepts of ancestry, mamhepo (negative influences from the spiritual world) and ngozi, sometimes called 'the avenging spirit.'"[48] All of this is done without altering Hove's idiom. This creates a lot of confusion for readers, so much confusion that Gibbs complains: "I am tired of the shifts (in this novel), wearied of the elegiac and apocalyptic. Even the episodes about the grandfather's grave are allowed to become maudlin!"[49] For that reason, *Ancestors* is regarded as the most difficult book Hove has ever written. Chirere, however, bids us – and understandably so – to understand what Hove was trying to do because "*Ancestors* is Hove's biggest experiment to date. It is a very deliberate way of writing, and more work must have gone into deciding how to tell the story than the invention of the story itself."[50] Thus, besides telling the story of Shona women to a global audience, *Ancestors* is also a piece of the author's personal indulgence in the methods of telling a story and using two languages simultaneously.

Conclusion

This chapter demonstrated that Hove's *Ancestors* is an experimental novel. One of the experiments includes the use of Shonglish which involves direct translation from Shona to English, the use of Shona words (names of trees, dances, food, and so on) without providing definitions or a glossary of terms, direct translations of proverbs into English without opting for the standardised English equivalents, and constant borrowing from Shona oral history. In doing this, Hove is not in any way waging a war against English like the cultural nationalists but is, in fact, communicating the oppression of Shona women by using the linguistic idiom of the culture that oppresses them. The idea is to capture the nuances of that culture and its language. In doing so, Hove creates a text whose vision is globalist, making *Ancestors* a world text that communicates using one of the many Englishes available in the world. Also, because he is writing about women, it is important for the 'mother' tongue and its lyricism to be heard under the surface of the English.

Notes

1 The Makerere Language Debate of 1963 remains, to this day, an iconic one in terms of definitions of what African literature is, who should write it, and the language that is supposed to be used in writing it. On one side is Ngũgĩ wa Thiong'o whose approach is that of completely rejecting European languages (in his case, English) and using languages that were in existence before colonialism. In his case, the language is Gikuyu. It should be noted, however, that even though he wrote *Devil on the Cross* (1980), *I Will Marry When I Want* (1982), *Matigari* (1986), *Wizard of the Crow* (2006), and *The Perfect Nine* (2020) in Gikuyu, the works were all translated into English. On the other side is Achebe whose approach involves localising English in ways that capture African experiences in their cultural settings. This entails localising English. *Things Fall Apart* (1958) is an experiment in that regard.
2 Taiye Selasie, "African Literature Doesn't Exist," 2013, https://literaturfestival. com/wp-content/uploads/ilb-OpeningSpeech-2013-en.pdf.
3 Chenjerai Hove, *Ancestors* (Harare: College Press, 1996).
4 Musaemura B. Zimunya and Mudereri Kadhani, eds., *And Now the Poets Speak* (Gweru: Mambo Press, 1981).
5 Chenjerai Hove, *Up in Arms* (Harare: ZPH, 1982).
6 Chenjerai Hove, *Red Hills of Home* (Gweru: Mambo Press, 1985).
7 Chenjerai Hove, *Rainbow in the Dust* (Harare: Baobab Books, 1998).
8 Chenjerai Hove, *Blind Moon* (Harare: Weaver Press, 2003).
9 Chenjerai Hove, *Bones* (London: Heinemann, 1988).
10 Hove, *Ancestors*, 113.
11 Charwe, the medium of Nehanda (popularly known as Nehanda Nyakasikana), was a religious figure reputed to have led an uprising against European settlers in the Mazowe area of modern-day Zimbabwe. She is regarded as a heroine in Zimbabwe to the extent that her statue was unveiled at the centre of Harare in 2021. The irony, though, is that the mythologisation and hagiographisation of Nehanda is usually done to endorse the male politics of Zimbabwe, so that Hove's *Bones* can be read as a subversion of those (ab)uses of Nehanda.
12 Hove, *Ancestors*, 12.
13 Muchativugwa L. Hove, "Reversions and Revisions: Displacement, Heritage and History in Chenjerai Hove's *Ancestors* (1996)," *Current Writing: Text and Reception in Southern Africa* 26.1 (2014): 84, https://doi.org/10.1080/10139 29X.2014.897820.
14 Hove, "Reversions and Revisions," 84.
15 Dambudzo Marechera, *The House of Hunger* (London: Heinemann, 1978): 43.
16 Flora Veit-Wild and Ernst Schade, eds., *Dambudzo Marechera, 1952–1987* (Harare: Baobab Books, 1988): 7–8.
17 Hove's novel *Shadows* is written in such a way that there are no page numbers and one can begin reading the story from anywhere and still understand it; see Chenjerai Hove, *Shadows* (Harare: Baobab Books, 1991).
18 Ngugi wa Thiong'o, *Decolonising the Mind* (London: James Currey, 1986): 7.
19 Sheikh Zobaer, "The Language Debate: Thiong'o and Achebe on English in Africa," *Crossings* 9 (2018): 135.
20 Ken Saro-Wiwa, *Sozaboy* (Harlow: Longman, 1985).
21 Brian Chikwava, *Harare North* (London: Jonathan Cape, 2009).
22 Hove, "Interview with Daly Thompson," Unpublished, 23 May 1996.
23 Hove, *Ancestors*, 45–46.
24 Memory Chirere, "'In My Work There Is a Constant Conversation between the Earth, Nature and the Sky:' Conversations Inside and Outside of Conversations in Chenjerai Hove's *Ancestors*," *Journal for Studies in Humanities and Social Sciences* 2.2 (December 2013): 133.

210 Tanaka Chidora

25 James Gibbs, "Book Review of Chenjerai Hove's *Ancestors*," *World Literature Today* 71.4 (1997): 856, www.thefreelibrary.com/Ancestors.-a020417874"> Ancestors.
26 Chirere, "Conversations".
27 Hove, *Ancestors*, 122.
28 Hove, *Ancestors*, 61.
29 Maxwell Kadenge, "The Indigenisation of English in Chenjerai Hove's Novels *Bones* and *Ancestors*: A Case of Lexical and Semantic Features of chiShona-English," *South African Journal of African Languages* 32.1 (2012): 13, https://doi.org/10.2989/SAJAL.2012.32.1.3.1126.
30 Hove, *Ancestors*, 64.
31 Hove, *Ancestors*, 94.
32 Kadenge, "The Indigenisation of English".
33 Hove, *Ancestors*, 116.
34 Hove, *Ancestors*, 99; 176.
35 Hove, *Ancestors*, 103.
36 Hove, *Ancestors*, 8.
37 Kadenge, "The Indigenisation," 15.
38 Memory Chirere, "Reading Chenjerai Hove's *Ancestors*," University of Zimbabwe Institutional Repository, 1: Microsoft Word – Chenjerai Hove.doc (uz. ac.zw).
39 Chirere, "Reading Chenjerai Hove's Ancestors," 3.
40 Hove, *Ancestors*, 109.
41 Hove, *Ancestors*, 125.
42 Wa Thiong'o, *Decolonising*, 16.
43 Chinua Achebe, "English and the African Writer," *Transition* 18 (1965): 28.
44 Hove, *Ancestors*, 104.
45 Chinua Achebe, "Thoughts on the African Novel," *The Dalhousie Review* 53.4 (1974): 632.
46 Rituparna Mukherjee, "Determining Chimamanda Ngozi Adichie's Position in the African Literary-Language Debate," *The Indian Review of World Literature in English* 18.2 (July–December 2020): 4.
47 Flora Veit-Wild, *Teachers, Preachers and Non-Believers: A Social History of Zimbabwean Literature* (London, Melbourne, Munich and New York: Hans Zell Publishers, 1992): 318.
48 Chirere, "Conversations," 137.
49 Gibbs, "Book Review," 856.
50 Chirere, "Conversations," 137.

Bibliography

Achebe, Achebe. "English and the African Writer." *Transition* 18 (1965): 27–30.
———. *Things Fall Apart*. London: Heinemann, 1958.
———. "Thoughts on the African Novel." *The Dalhousie Review* 53.4 (1974): 631–637.
Chikwava, Brian. *Harare North*. London: Jonathan Cape, 2009.
Chirere, Memory. "'In My Work there is a Constant Conversation Between the Earth, Nature and the Sky': Conversations Inside and Outside of Conversations in Chenjerai Hove's *Ancestors*." *Journal for Studies in Humanities and Social Sciences* 2.2 (December 2013): 131–140.
———. "Reading Chenjerai Hove's *Ancestors*." University of Zimbabwe Institutional Repository. 2005. https://ir.uz.ac.zw/handle/10646/600 (last accessed 27 April 2024).

Gibbs, James. "Book Review of Chenjerai Hove's *Ancestors*." *World Literature Today* 71.4 (1997): 856.

Hove, Chenjerai. *Ancestors*. Harare: College Press, 1996.

———. *Blind Moon*. Harare: Weaver Press, 2003.

———. *Bones*. London: Heinemann, 1988.

———. Interview with Daly Thompson (Unpublished), 23 May 1996.

———. *Rainbow in the Dust*. Harare: Baobab Books, 1998.

———. *Red Hills of Home*. Gweru: Mambo Press, 1985.

———. *Shadows*. Harare: Baobab Books, 1991.

———. *Up in Arms*. Harare: ZPH, 1982.

Hove, Muchativugwa L. "Reversions and Revisions: Displacement, Heritage and History in Chenjerai Hove's *Ancestors* (1996)." *Current Writing: Text and Reception in Southern Africa* 26.1 (2014): 82–90.

Kadenge, Maxwell. "The Indigenisation of English in Chenjerai Hove's Novels *Bones* and *Ancestors*: A Case of Lexical and Semantic Features of chiShona-English." *South African Journal of African Languages* 32.1 (2012): 11–16.

Marechera, Dambudzo. *The House of Hunger*. London: Heinemann, 1978.

Mukherjee, Rituparna. "Determining Chimamanda Ngozi Adichie's Position in the African Literary-Language Debate." *The Indian Review of World Literature in English* 18.2 (July–December 2020): 1–8.

Mungoshi, Charles. *Waiting for the Rain*. London: Heinemann, 1975.

Saro-Wiwa, Ken. *Sozaboy*. Harlow: Longman, 1985.

Selasie, Taiye. "African Literature Doesn't Exist." 2013. https://literaturfestival.com/wp-content/uploads/ilb-OpeningSpeech-2013-en.pdf (last accessed 28 April 2024).

Veit-Wild, Flora. *Teachers, Preachers, Non-Believers: A Social History of Zimbabwean Literature*. London, Melbourne, Munich and New York: Hans Zell Publishers, 1992.

Veit-Wild, Flora and Ernst Schade, eds. *Dambudzo Marechera, 1952–1987*. Harare: Baobab Books, 1988.

wa Thiong'o, Ngũgĩ. *Decolonising the Mind*. London: James Currey, 1986.

———. *Devil on the Cross*. London: Heinemann, 1980.

———. *I Will Marry When I Want*. London: Heinemann, 1982.

———. *Matigari*. London: Heinemann, 1986.

———. *The Perfect Nine*. New York: New Press, 2020.

———. *Wizard of the Crow*. New York: Pantheon, 2006.

Zimunya, Musaemura B. and Mudereri Kadhani, eds. *And Now the Poets Speak*. Gweru: Mambo Press, 1981.

Zobaer, Sheikh. "The Language Debate: Thiong'o and Achebe on English in Africa." *Crossings* 9 (2018): 132–138.

13

THE MIGRANT CHILD

Doing the Puzzle of Home in Suneeta Peres da Costa's Novella *Saudade*

Jean Page

According to cultural theorist Eva Hoffmann, "we live in a world in which various kinds of cross-national movements – migrations, travel, various kinds of both enforced and voluntary nomadism – are ever on the rise."[1] Such movements are at the heart of Suneeta Peres da Costa's novella *Saudade*.[2] Already the title sets in train themes of home and belonging central to the English-language novella published in Australia in 2018. 'Saudade,' the Portuguese word often deemed untranslatable, describes a mix between homesickness and longing considered essential to Portuguese identity. *Saudade* is set neither in Portugal nor Australia but in an initially unidentified location which the reader learns is Benguela on the south-west coast of the then–Portuguese African colony, Angola. The events surrounding the domestic life of this immigrant family occur in the 1960s and early 1970s during the last years of Angola's colonisation.

Saudade can be considered a post-colonial Bildungsroman. It is told in the first person by its young female protagonist, Maria Cristina, whose name the reader does not learn until later in the novel. It is related chronologically, but retrospectively, from the age of three until seventeen. Peres da Costa, a writer of Goan ancestry born in Sydney in 1976, makes tribute in an end note to the experience of her aunt Livia de Abreu Noronha, who, like many Goan nationals, lived in the then–Portuguese colony of Angola, following the Indian annexation of Goa in 1961. Rochelle Almeida describes Peres da Costa's work as falling within the category of "immigrant postcolonial Indo-English literature,"[3] part of a wider body of contemporary Australian immigrant writing.

Peres da Costa's English-language novella is richly and naturally scattered with the untranslated languages of Portuguese, suggested by its title; the West

DOI: 10.4324/9781003464037-17
This chapter has been made available under a CC-BY-NC-ND 4.0 license.

African Bantu variant, Kimbundu, associated with the location in which the novella is set; and what we learn is the Goan Konkani language of its protagonist family. A novella of diaspora, it engages with the post-colonial themes of dislocation, questions about home, and belonging, complicated by the particular context of colonial disruptions and discontinuities, of imperial identities, and by other, not-necessarily territorial, homes of language and culture. At the personal level of the narrative it engages in successive chronological segments of a changing present constructed through what the reader learns are the accrued memories of the late adolescent at the novella's conclusion.

Diaspora involves "the sense of being a 'people' with historical roots and destinies outside the time/space of the host nation."[4] Bill Ashcroft et al. have described how the diasporic subject looks in two directions towards a historical cultural identity on the one hand and the society of relocation on the other.[5] Stuart Hall refers to "ruptures and discontinuities [...] subject to the continued 'play' of history, culture and power."[6] Nonetheless, as a first-generation migrant child, Maria-Cristina has not, in Vijay Mishra's words, been "wrenched [as such] from [her] mother(father) land":[7] as the young daughter of voluntary economic migrants from Goa to Angola, her diasporic consciousness and its accompanying intuitions of "absence" and "loss"[8] are only understood gradually as the migrant child protagonist comes to learn the nature of her cultural and ethnic history.

Peres da Costa uses the Bildungsroman genre to depict the child's personal awakening, her journey to understanding an identity obscured by her dysfunctional immigrant family. I argue that the plot unfolds as a puzzle in which the protagonist assembles, from what is at hand, pieces or clues that trace her own uncertain identity. At the same time the text constructs an evolving interrogating sketch of a changing Portuguese colonial society. This chapter traces the accreted assembly of cultural motifs through which the young girl learns about her identity by exploring the parameters of her expanding world, and her personal awakening, from an initial domestic focus on the kitchen and food, domestic helpers, and, notably, their different local languages and cultures, to the wider world of school, the city, and unfolding contemporary political and sociological events in colonial Angola. It addresses how the cultural tropes of food (including the incumbent metaphor of hunger) but also clothing and language in its oral, vernacular, and higher literary forms help construct the protagonist's awakening.

Synthesis and Summary

The protagonist's self-portrait related in a first-person narrative over fourteen years from infancy (c 1961) to late adolescence (1975) reflects a journey from a more domestic inside to outside worlds shifting between the binaries of innocence and awareness, from a muteness, associated with naïveté

214 Jean Page

or a reluctance to judge, tó acts of speaking bordering on outspokenness, between satisfaction or passive acceptance and a more assertive hunger. The narrative introduces the trope of inscription (acculturation) and its opposite – erasure. It is constructed over 114 pages, each chapter depicting a telling consecutive episode which leaves its mark on the growing child who very early in the novella is described as a "*tabula rasa*" – the philosopher's empty slate (4). Its backdrop is growing local resistance to the colonial Portuguese regime in Angola, dated by key historical events intersecting with the personal narrative.

The novella opens in an early childhood present, set in a middle-class family home with garden in Benguela. This comfortable, seemingly harmonious, Portuguese colonial household consists of a diasporic professional Goan family with a local servant class: it is richly multilingual with the common imperial Portuguese, also spoken by their adopted mestiço Mozambiquan orphan houseboy, Caetano, as well as the Kimbundu of the local housemaid Ifigênia. The young protagonist – "three years old, perhaps four" (3) – lives in a state of "hungerlessness that might well be called paradise" (3). However, that peaceful environment has already been disturbed in the opening sentence by the mother's warning to her daughter about "bruxas" [witches, in Portuguese] and the "dead walk[ing] backwards" leading the unsuspecting to "their world" (2–3), foreshadowing how the mother's "words could come to have a dangerous sway" (3).

As the girl grows up, the wider world increasingly impinges directly on domestic and personal life. These start with radio reports of the 1961 "Santa Maria" mutiny of naval officers plotting an alternative to Salazar's colonial regime in Angola and continue with reports of increasing social unrest and violence (an expatriate cotton farmer killed is her father's client) and independentist insurrections in the early 1970s (with food shortages in Luanda and the servants leaving for their homelands). The later chapters are marked by the murder of the Guinea Bissau independence leader Amilcar Cabral (hero of the now adolescent girl's boyfriend) by the Portuguese intelligence service in 1973, factory closures, and at the novella's conclusion the fall of the Portuguese colonial regime to the independentist MPLA (Movimento Popular de Libertaçâo de Angola) in November 1975.

A growing postcolonial awareness is central to the girl's emerging consciousness. With the family move to the capital Luanda she notes how the street names, including Rua da Camôes, are "set out on the same grid as Lisbon, being a mirror of the colonial imaginary" (29), something she would later discover in the streets of Goa, another palimpsest of Portuguese imperial nomenclature. As a more aware and articulate primary student she is scolded for repeating independentist criticism of early Portuguese navigator Bartholomeu Dias. A school boat excursion to the Ilha de Luanda causes her to muse on the Portuguese voyaging and its "discoveries," unleashing

The Migrant Child **215**

her speculation on the theme of "unmoorings" or dislocations central to this diasporic novella. These musings would be reinforced by her later encounter, together with her boyfriend, with the Portuguese voyage literature of Luis de Camões and Fernando Pessoa.

At a more personal level, it is only two-thirds of the way through this Bildungsroman that the reader learns the (Catholic) name of the protagonist (Maria Cristina) when, at age 13, with her inquiry into identity in full swing, she prepares for *Crisma*, the Catholic rite of confirmation, and begins to reflect on the possibility of Hinduism as an alternative belief system, and part of her own birth-rite.

The construction of identity, though presented chronologically, is done in hindsight, largely from memory, and the text is punctuated with indications of retrospectivity – "I did not yet know" (4), "I came to see" (20), "I understood the implications only later" (20) – and with other prophetic pointings forward and rememberings.

Triggered by broader political occurrences, the personal events accruing to the girl's awakening – her father's suicide, the school closing, her evacuation to her grandfather in Goa ("going home," 109) – constitute huge disruptions, thus filling in the clue ("when everything shattered," 21) foreshadowed in Chapter 3. Unlike many narratives of dislocation, the "rupture" experienced by Maria Cristina occurs in reverse, at the end of the narration, when she is returned to her ancestral home in Goa and a new-found identity, though this knowledge has been gradually unfolding under the surface. Parallel to this forward-moving narrative of significant external events in the lead-up to Angolan independence, the text is interspersed and enriched with cultural motifs and tropes by which the growing child assembles a notion of her own identity otherwise obscured by her uncommunicative, diasporic family, themselves insecure about their own place in the Angolan colonial cultural hierarchy. It is in this way that the girl pieces together the puzzle of her own cultural home as well as those of the other characters of the diverse ethnic community within and surrounding her household in 1960s Benguela and Luanda.

The Trope of Food

Literary food studies offer intimate perspectives on the human condition – on cultural and ethnographic identity, history, relationships, and communities (seen in meal-sharing) and social hierarchies (visible in food preparation and consumption); they can be illuminating in postcolonial critical studies. The food trope vivifies affective life: food preparation and food sharing as love, or hunger, food's absence, signifying a wider deprivation. Food is one of the main tropes through which Maria-Cristina learns about her personal history and cultural identity and the wider social hierarchy: the motif is strongly

216   Jean Page

linked to the home and its varied cultures. While her protected infant state is initially associated with a "hungerlessness that might well be called paradise" (3), the appearance of food introduces moments of communion in the mixed community of the colonial household. The narrative begins with the Angolan Portuguese and Kimbundu-speaking maid Ifigênia grinding "coconut and chillies for the *recheado*" (7) [Portuguese for "filling"].[9] She makes the local Kimbundu "*funje* [Angolan cassava porridge] sweetened with molasses, one of my favourite things to eat" (38) and also the rich syrupy Portuguese egg cakes "*papos de anjos*" [angels' jowls] offered, in the front room, to the visiting Madeiran expatriate friend of her mother – "devour[ed] one after the other" (11), as if signalling Dona Angela's homesickness.

Repasts and snacks of hybrid origin thread through the narrative in the comforting ritual of the everyday, the "*frango* [chicken in Portuguese] with *piri-piri* [chilli] and bread" (60) of the school picnic at Ilha de Luanda, the local snack "*pé de moleque*" [peanut brittle of Brazilian origin] (62) as relief to the increasingly gathering tensions, both in the family and society. Food also reflects the child's growing knowledge and rejection of the colonial social hierarchy. The breath of the bullying Portuguese nun-teacher "smells stale – as of onions and salt pork sitting in a pot too long" (49). The ritual of eating is associated with interludes of truce, as when the increasingly irritable father returns for the evening meal with news of farm strikes: "Ifigênia had prepared *calulu de peixe* [Angolan fish stew with okra] and we ate without speaking" (67). The meal also sets the scene for new levels of understanding. The increasingly self-aware adolescent, back from seeing friends, joins her parents and the adopted Mozambiquan house-boy Caetano for a sensually described meal of "*cafrael*" [Goan spicy chicken curry] prepared by her mother, as Ifigênia has left the household for her village. The act of eating – with the *cafrael* "tart and the green chilli intensely hot, and the flesh of the chicken [falling] away from the bone" (89) – drives her to a kind of epiphany: "here we are across the table, orphans of Empire" (89–90).

Eating is the natural metaphor, more generally, for acculturation within the post-colonial domain, but notably so in the narrative of the Bildungsroman, as the emancipating six-year-old comes to realise: "For so many years, I had been like a little bird, gobbling the food, words and ideas, that she put directly into my mouth, already half-masticated" (40). She concludes with another statement of awakening consciousness: "Now I began to consider what was real and what was not, what pleased me and what did not" (41).

From the paradisical hungerlessness of her early, amorphous childhood she has become driven to enquire about her own identity. After the independence of Angola in 1975 and her sudden return to Goa, now known as her family home, she meets her elderly grandparents for the first time at the age of seventeen and is told to wash and get ready for table, marking a moment in her new beginning. Her closure with her difficult father occurs through the motif of food as cultural remembering:

> I now remembered how, in a rare and tender moment, my father had told me [...] he would like nothing other than to get up in the morning and wait in the kitchen as [the family servant] heated up the left-over *kulchi codi* [left-over curry] so he could mop it up with the freshly baked *pão* [bread].
> *(114)*

The closing lines of the novella signal Maria-Cristina's arrival at cultural self-knowledge, with eating as its consummation: "I began to eat then, with a hunger I had not known, and in the same manner" (114).

Dress and Ethnicity

The accumulating motifs of dress and skin-tone also feed the child's dawning understanding of cultural differentiation as she grows up, illuminating the colonial social hierarchy in which the Portuguese-speaking Goan migrant family found itself in Angola. Cultural historian Rochelle Pinto has characterised the Goan settlers in the following manner:

> The Catholic Goan elite [...] saw itself as a participant in the European Enlightenment and in the extension of Portuguese imperialism. The predominantly upper-class Catholic Goan intelligentsia was accustomed to a fair degree of mobility within Portugal and its colonies, [...] accustomed to seeing themselves as prominent, if not equal, citizens of the expansive cultural milieu that constituted the Portuguese empire.[10]

They were not seen as "crioulos" [creoles].[11] This profile is evident in the studiously cautious behaviour of the ambitious father, doing his best to mimic the culture and values of the Portuguese elite. After the visit of the mother's Madeiran friend Dona Angela, the pre-school child stays in the front room to examine the "array of family portraits, distant strangers, with dark skin like my own dressed up in dresses and suits like good men and women of the Empire" (13). In this ironic note her family, as in Rochelle Almeida's words, are "becoming mottled – [...] like the [Lacanian] technique of camouflage."[12] There is, however, an insistent notation of the "dark skin," a sense of difference in her family's identity. The mother points out, possibly reflecting caste hierarchies, that "with my darker complexion I took after Papá's people [...] the solemn faces of the portraits hanging in the living room" (25). The impression remains of a nervous self-erasure among the second-ranking subalterns of the Portuguese colonial administration.

218 Jean Page

The most telling, if conflicting, revelation about the child's ethnic history is her witnessing of the mother happily winding herself into her Indian *sari*, in readiness for an important work party, and applying to her forehead the married woman's *bindi* (third eye) marker taken from her Goan jewellery box (24). The mother's vesting of traditional robe, while humming a song in Konkani, is subsequently violently harangued by the husband: "did she want to make a spectacle wearing a *sari* among the people who might promote him in the Administration?" (26). Thus, Goan identity is something the socially ambitious father prefers to mask, making Maria-Cristina's puzzle harder to complete. The father is acutely conscious of the precarity of the Goan family's place in the Angolan colonial hierarchy. He admonishes his daughter for playing outside on the ground ("it was not good for the servants to see me sitting in the dirt like that. Do you know whose daughter you are?" 17), ironically acknowledging his daughter's very lack of self-knowledge.

By the time they have moved to Luanda with her father's promotion, the daughter at about age six is aware of her ethnic difference from the Portuguese ruling-class, but this offers a sense of intrigue rather than inferiority: "My face, belonging to another landscape, one I did not know, gave me the thrill of unexpected discovery" (45–46). After her innocent repetition in class of independentist criticism of the iconic Portuguese explorer-navigator Bartolmeu Dias as an invader, such ethnic difference becomes a target for attack by the patriotic Portuguese nun-teacher: "Bartholomeu Dias [...] was responsible for civilising the people of Angola and was part of the long line of *fidalgos* [nobles] who had cultivated my own loinclothed and mud-thatched and blue-godded people" (49). In Stuart Hall's words, the young girl is effectively being "positioned [by the European teacher] as the Other."[13] Her most satisfactory moment of cultural self-discovery comes at age eleven, in an act of rejection while she is preparing for *Crisma*, the Catholic rite of confirmation for children. Symbolically, the almost bridal, white *Crisma* dress is already too tight for the young adolescent. The protagonist's Portuguese Catholic name is first mentioned here already two-thirds into the novella: "My own name, Maria-Cristina, in fact said everything and nothing about who I was or my origins" (72). As with mapping, naming performs the function of cultural palimpsest. Recalling the legendary "Shakuntala" from her early reading of the Sanskrit epic poem the *Mahabharata*, the young adolescent indicates her wish to shuck the imposed for the rediscovered culture: "I should like to take that name rather than that of Saint Teresa. [...] For I should feel more kinship with such a woman, born among the birds, who escaped to a forest to raise her child" (73).

Like Shakuntala, the baby abandoned in the forest, Maria-Cristina can be seen as a cultural orphan, a Cinderella step-child with an ambitious self-deluded father and a weak, self-effacing mother, both guilty of cultural negligence. She can only appreciate a sense of exile and dislocation when she fully understands her cultural and ethnic origins. As social unrest moves the Angolan colony towards Portuguese withdrawal and independence, the father shifts into bitterness and the mother into the past, now talking to her daughter about her early life in Goa, showing photos of the old house in Goa, and revealing the hybrid Goan colonial world of coconut-lined rice paddies and her convent school where the nuns taught "Latin, maths [...] Portuguese stitches" (80). Already well through the novella the adolescent girl is now aware of her Goan ethnic and cultural origins, but she has spent most of her life-narrative since infancy assembling this story from fragments – photos, food, clothing – and pieces of domestic life such as the *devanagari* [Brahman] engraving on her mother's *Crisma* crucifix (69), all of which bear powerful phenomenological significance. As Rita Felski has written: "words may also speak of the secret lives of things, reveal[ing] something of the mute matter to which they gesture."[14]

Quite early in the novella the young child, hearing of rural worker unrest, foreshadows the coming crisis "when everything shattered" (21), noting how she "glimpsed it clearly, albeit through the shards of memory" (21). Such "shards" offer vital details that help piece together, like beads in a necklace, orderly episodes in the retrospectively understood personal narrative. Salman Rushdie has written similarly on challenges to the diasporic writer's recovery of the past and strategies for doing so, through such "shards of memory," notwithstanding their "partial nature [...] their fragmentation."[15] Rushdie underlines how the "broken glass," a significant modernist symbol, "is not merely a mirror of nostalgia [but] also [...] a useful tool with which to work in the present."[16] In understanding the significance of these fragments, the protagonist has come "to see how the past, like some ancient *karma*, inscribes itself on the body as much as the mind" (21).

Language: Oral, Vernacular, Literary

As indicated in its title, *Saudade* is distinctive for its use of languages other than English, or code-switching, implanting in the basic English text – and not translating – the languages of European and non-European derivation spoken in the hybrid linguistic community of the Goan household in late colonial Angola. This adds the rich oral sphere of communication, and later its written, literary variants, to the phenomenological domestic world in Maria-Cristina's childhood identity puzzle. The base-language of English has been accepted by many post-colonial writers, including Salman Rushdie and Chinua Achebe, as a "cultural vehicle to [reach] a world audience."[17] To this Peres da Costa adds fragments of at least three non-English languages – mainly words for objects, food, dress, music, and household things difficult or unnecessary to translate. Portuguese, the official common language of the colony, is spoken fluently by the Goan parents and to a much

220 Jean Page

lesser degree by the growing girl, by the Angolan housemaid-cook Ifigênia and by the adopted Mozambiquan houseboy Caetano as well as more widely in the community. Ifigênia and Caetano also speak the local Bantu dialect of Kimbundu. The Goan family speak their own regional language Konkani – "a language inherited from some other place."[18] In the opening pages the infant points to a lost clue: "I did not yet know that Konkani was a tongue that might have belonged to the people from whom I was also descended" (4). Other languages or dialects from colonial Portugal are in evidence, the creole of the postboy from Cabo Verde singing a *morna* [folk-song] and the Sao Tome and Principe dialect of the accordionist performing the [Portuguese] fado "The Boat." The infant naively accepts this sea of hybrid orality, of voices barely understood, hearing but not heeding her mother's criticism of the Bantu language: "I did not yet have cause to identify with the confused souls of Babel" (7).

Bill Ashcroft has observed how, as far back as Shakespeare's proto post-colonial play *The Tempest*, "Language has power [providing] the terms by which reality may be constituted, [...] the names by which the world may be known."[19] Language thus creates social hierarchies in diasporic communities. Maria-Cristina is ordered by her mother not to speak to the Cabo Verde postboy, ostensibly because "she was sure [he] was a communist" (15), but also because he spoke a lowly Creole dialect of Portuguese. The Kimbundu-speaking maid Ifigênia "had been told to speak Portuguese in my company but she often forgot and spoke Kimbundu anyway" (15–16). Seeking to allay the mother's concerns about the young child's apparent muteness, their doctor counsels that the parents should make sure "they spoke Portuguese not Konkani to me at home" (42). In terms of the imposed Portuguese imperial monoglossia the household members are "speaker[s] in the borderlands,"[20] even within their own country.

For their part the other local languages can be the vehicles of subversion, especially if not well understood by the colonial class: "Kimbundu might be the language, as I might be the source, of some of their plaints and grievances" (16). The language trope underpins the binary themes of communication and understanding that drive the process of Maria-Cristina's journey to knowledge and also illuminate the tensions and misunderstandings arising in a linguistically hybrid society. These binaries are accentuated by the young child's disinclination to speak, deemed muteness by her anxious mother, but also reflecting the child's natural wish to observe and reserve judgment. The young Maria-Cristina is not only mute, but also deaf or blind to the social hierarchies of language, a 'knowledge' still to be obtained. *Saudade* effectively depicts a youthful innocent receptivity to orality: the girl enjoys, while not understanding, the Cabo Verdean postboy's language: "I was happy to hear him speaking, to hear this other voice with its unusual cadences" (15).

The Migrant Child **221**

She responds similarly to the housemaid Ifigênia's native language: "Though I could only understand a smattering I found Kimbundu, with its spirited rhythms, beautiful" (16).

The untranslated non-English language in *Saudade* mainly relates to things heard in an oral realm, household words corresponding to objects (food, dress, the sensory world, songs, music) representing a kind of authentic originary naming in the language of the culture to which those objects belong, a cultural differentiation. Such linguistic use suggests the functioning of oral cultures in which "words [...] have the *power* of the things they signify, because they are imputed to *be* the things they signify."[21] As the narrative unfolds, the girl retains her youthful delight in the orality not only of language but also song. This can be linked to Kenyan writer Ngũgĩ wa Thiong'o's defence of the "suggestive magical power" of his homeland Gikuyu, "the music of our language."[22] Peres da Costa's text is sprinkled with references to popular song encountered in everyday settings: the popular song of Portuguese Sergio Godinho's "Falling in Love" on the radio (65), or her mother humming a Konkani song while putting on her *sari* (23) or nostalgically singing a traditional Konkani *manso* [Catholic popular song] before going to bed (67). When older, the girl hears in a café the lyrics of the Angolan folk-singer Rui Mingas: "It is the sweat of my face which waters the plantations" (87). These aural fragments, mostly translated into English, accentuate the protagonist's emotional engagement in the narrative, a sensorial being in a precise moment and a specific locale.

In contrast with the homeliness of local languages, the encounter with Portuguese high literary culture, the literature of Camões and Pessoa, introduces tropes of dislocation and longing (*saudade*). Maria-Cristina's soon-to-be boyfriend Miguel recites from the poem "Lisbon Revisited" by Pessoa's shipping engineer heteronym Alvaro de Campos ("Once more I see you, City of my own horrifyingly lost childhood," 88) in words underlining the girl's intuition of an important absence. She becomes increasingly aware of the Portuguese empire's deep implication in the production of diaspora, which she calls an "unmooring" (62). A school trip to the Ilha de Luanda launches a reflection on the human impact of the Portuguese voyages which had passed by the Sao Miguel Fort:

I wondered whether de Novães [the first Portuguese governor of Luanda] and the sailors of the Discoveries sometimes saw humpbacks, and how, taken from their native towns in the Alentejo, they might have trembled to be out on the sea alone with them; how at night, with the sea dark and vast and only the light of the southern stars to orient them, the sky itself different to the sky of home, they must have prayed that their own seasickness might end.

(61)

222 Jean Page

She contemplates the slaves being pressed into ships for Brazil and the dispersion of the Indians in the forest there, but her thoughts shift from the historical to a more personally implicating present: "I wondered what home may mean and what different routes one might take to get there. [...] I was wondering whether life itself was a terrible unmooring" (62). "Unmooring" is a potent, culturally apt metaphor for the physical dislocations occasioned though oceanic voyaging, a haphazard loosening of ties, connecting with and intensifying *Saudade*'s other recurring trope of disconnection, that of the orphan ("Orphans of Empire," 90) and its attendant emotion of unbelonging and longing.

Even as an adolescent in the café, seeing the sepia photos of Angolan independentist writers, the girl expresses doubt about the reliability of the written word: "for all their eloquence would they ever close the growing distance between words and things?" (88). As she matures, the protagonist confirms her greater trust, and even delight, in the phenomenological world of objects, the demotic spoken word, and people of her everyday life.

Relexification

George Steiner, author of *After Babel*, has spoken of modern writers as "wanderers across language."[23] Eva Hoffmann has asked: "What kind of knowledge is needed to feed meaningful cross-cultural contact?"[24] It is also pertinent to ask how such knowledge might be represented respectfully in the languages of diasporic (extraterritorial) cultures, including the difficult question of translation. Hoffmann tentatively outlines a formula if not a practice: "Like literal translation, cross-cultural back and forth requires a simultaneous reception to the other's subjective language [...] a cross-checking between the two [or more] 'languages' or forms of sensibility [...] maintaining empathy for its tonalities and textures, its expressive palette."[25]

Much has been written on the challenges arising in the use of language in the post-colonial domain. Salman Rushdie, reflecting on challenges in the use of English for the "out-of-country" and "out-of-language" Indian writer has advocated "remaking [English] for our purposes."[26] Achebe writes of a "new English [...] altered to suit new African surroundings."[27] Bill Ashcroft has argued that "a global language, such as English, inflected with locally produced variations, can become a key mode of empowerment."[28] Linguist Loreto Todd proposed the "relexification of one's mother tongue, using English vocabulary but indigenous structures and rhythms" as an alternative for translation, in which the non-English language is simulated into the Europhone text.[29] Taking Todd's idea forward, Chantal Zabus has written about "a new register of communication, which is neither the European target language nor the indigenous source language, [and] functions as an 'interlanguage' or 'third register.'"[30] By this she means the operation of one language

The Migrant Child **223**

onto the other within the same text. Relexification thus seeks to "decolonise the language of early colonial literature and to affirm a revised, non-atavistic orality via the imposed medium."[31] Nineteenth-century linguist Max Müller stressed the revitalising force of the vernacular: "the real and natural life of language is in its dialects."[32] This can increasingly be seen in the dialects or idioms of transnational language and literature.[33] Ngũgĩ considered that Karl Marx had identified the first element of communication in the "language of real life" among "the human community" notably related to "food, clothing, houses."[34] Such more sensory language is closely bound to the phenomenological world of objects and their names. Apart from the things it depicts language itself can be considered home, especially for people of the diaspora, as expressed recently by Lebanese poet Zeina Hashem Beck in her poem "Naming Things (For refugees, September, 2015)": "Kiss me, for where else/ do we carry home now, habibi,/if not on our lips?"[35]

Conclusion

The option to include fragments of non-English everyday language, but not to translate them, followed by the author throughout *Saudade* offers a deft tribute to cultural otherness or difference. Ashcroft considers such strategy of language variance, or "performative use,"[36] as capable of signifying cultural difference rather than cultural essence,[37] bringing about a post-colonial transformation. The refusal to translate is a device Australian novelist David Malouf used sensitively in concluding his short story on the challenges of anthropological etymology, "The Only Speaker of his Tongue."[38] Suneeta Peres da Costa's novella constructs, in discreet measure, an emblematic code-switching heteroglossia that succeeds in bringing to life, empathetically and naturalistically, the diverse, strongly vernacular, cultural and linguistic matrix of Maria-Cristina's diasporic household world. It thus imparts the richly mixed fabric of the everyday "here" that matches the reality of increasingly transnational, and hybrid, diasporic worlds. The naturalistic use of language variance in *Saudade*, within a fundamentally English language text, also brings to mind the proposition for a multicultural, multi-ethnic consciousness explored by Chicana cultural theorist Gloria Anzaldúa. Taking further Mexican philosopher José Vasconcelas's idea of a *"raza cosmica,"* Anzaldúa proposes the concept of a "new *mestiza* consciousness" as a product of the "Borderlands" [involving] the transfer of cultural and spiritual values from one group to another."[39] By remaining flexible, Anzaldúa argues, the *"mestiza"* is able to "stretch the psyche horizontally and vertically," shifting from "convergent thinking to divergent thinking [...] that includes rather than excludes."[40]

While *Saudade* doesn't directly broach questions of a *"mestiza"* ethnicity, in its very inclusive use of what might be considered the local vernacular and

224 Jean Page

its plurality of vision it might be seen as constructing the diverse linguistic foundation for representing such a multi-lingual *"mestiza* consciousness" through its new syncretic, macaronic forms. As an infant Maria-Cristina is either too ignorant, too innocent, or too uncannily wise to be perturbed by the prospect of "identify[ing] with the confused souls of Babel" (7) of her multicultural childhood world, perhaps agreeing intuitively with Indian linguistic scholar Pratap Bhanu Mehta that "[t]here was no sin of Babel."[41] By the age of seventeen, on her return to her ancestral home of Goa where, as a *"tabula rasa* all over again" (111) she encounters a culture, history, and languages barely known to her, it would seem she is even less fazed about extending her consciousness to the domain of the Other which is her own unfamiliar family.

Notes

1 Eva Hoffman, "Introduction," in *The Inner Lives of Cultures*, edited by Eva Hoffman (London: Counterpoint, 2011): 5.
2 Suneeta Peres da Costa, *Saudade* (Artarmon NSW: Giramondo, 2018).
3 Rochelle Almeida, "Anglo-Indian Migrants: Children of Colonialism and the Cultural Geographies of Encounter," in *Experiences of Freedom in Postcolonial Literatures and Cultures*, edited by Annalisa Oboe and Shaul Bassi (London and New York: Routledge, 2011): 155.
4 James Clifford, "Diasporas," in *The Post-Colonial Studies Reader*, 2nd ed., edited by Bill Ashcroft, Gareth Griffiths and Helen Tiffin (London and New York: Routledge, 2006): 453.
5 Bill Ashcroft, Gareth Griffith and Helen Tiffin, "Introduction to Part Sixteen: Diaspora," in *The Post-Colonial Studies Reader*, 2nd ed., edited by Bill Ashcroft, Gareth Griffiths and Helen Tiffin (London and New York: Routledge, 2006): 425.
6 Stuart Hall, "Cultural Identity and Diaspora," in *The Post-Colonial Studies Reader*, 2nd ed., edited by Bill Ashcroft, Gareth Griffiths and Helen Tiffin (London and New York: Routledge, 2006): 435.
7 Vijay Mishra, "The Diasporic Imaginary: Theorizing the Indian Diaspora," in *The Post-Colonial Studies Reader*, 2nd ed., edited by Bill Ashcroft, Gareth Griffiths and Helen Tiffin (London and New York: Routledge, 2006): 448.
8 Mishra, "The Diasporic Imaginary," 449.
9 Translations indicated in brackets are by the author of this chapter.
10 Rochelle Pinto, *Between Empires: Print and Politics in Goa* (Oxford: Oxford University Press, 2007): 16.
11 Pinto, *Between Empires*, 18.
12 Almeida, "Anglo-Indian Migrants," 158.
13 Hall, "Cultural Identity and Diaspora," 436 FN 13.
14 Rita Felski, *The Uses of Literature* (Oxford: Blackwell, 2008): 98.
15 Salman Rushdie, "Imaginary Homelands," in *The Post-Colonial Studies Reader*, 2nd ed., edited by Bill Ashcroft, Gareth Griffiths and Helen Tiffin (London and New York: Routledge, 2006): 429.
16 Rushdie, "Imaginary Homelands," 429.
17 Bill Ashcroft, "Language and Transformation," in *The Post-Colonial Studies Reader*, 2nd ed., edited by Bill Ashcroft, Gareth Griffiths and Helen Tiffin (London and New York: Routledge, 2006): 277.
18 Bill Ashcroft, *Caliban's Voice: The Transformation of English in Post-Colonial Literatures* (London and New York: Routledge, 2009): 99.

The Migrant Child **225**

19 Ashcroft, *Caliban's Voice*, 1.
20 Ashcroft, *Caliban's Voice*, 98.
21 Ashcroft, *Caliban's Voice*, 126.
22 Ngũgĩ wa Thiong'o, *Decolonizing the Mind: The Politics of Language in African Literature* (London: James Currey, 1981): 11.
23 George Steiner, *Extraterritorial: Papers on Literature and the Language Revolution* (New York: Atheneum, 1971): 11.
24 Hoffmann, *The Inner Lives of Cultures*, 6.
25 Hoffmann, *The Inner Lives of Cultures*, 8.
26 Rushdie, "Imaginary Homelands," 432.
27 Chinua Achebe, *Morning Yet on Creation Day* (Garden City, New York: Doubleday, 1975): 62.
28 Ashcroft, *Caliban's Voice*, 6.
29 Loreto Todd, "The English Language in West Africa," in *English as a World Language*, edited by Richard W. Bailey and Manfred Görlach (Ann Arbor: University of Michigan Press, 1982): 303.
30 Chantal Zabus, "Relexification," in *The Post-Colonial Studies Reader*, 2nd ed., edited by Bill Ashcroft, Gareth Griffiths and Helen Tiffin (London and New York: Routledge, 2006): 286.
31 Zabus, "Relexification," 288.
32 Max Müller, *Lectures on the Science of Language* (London: Longmans Green and Co., 1882): 52.
33 Linguist Henri Gobard has proposed a tetraglossic hierarchy for language in which the first level, the vernacular, deals with the "here." Cited by Rainier Grutman, "Migration and Territoriality in Deleuze and Steiner," in *Migrancy and Multilingualism in World Literature*, edited by K. Alfons Knauth and Ping-hui Liao (Berlin and Zurich: LIT, 2016): 173.
34 Ngũgĩ wa Thiong'o, "The Language of African Literature," in *The Post-Colonial Studies Reader*, 2nd ed., edited by Bill Ashcroft, Gareth Griffiths and Helen Tiffin (London and New York: Routledge, 2006): 266.
35 Zeina Hashem Beck, "Naming Things (For Refugees, September, 2015)," *The Rialto* 84 (Winter 2015): 9.
36 Ashcroft, *Caliban's Voice*, 97.
37 Ashcroft, "Language and Transformation," 279.
38 David Malouf, "The Only Speaker of His Tongue," in *Antipodes* (London: Vintage, 1999 [1985]): 70–74.
39 Gloria Anzaldúa, "Towards a New Consciousness," in *The Post-Colonial Studies Reader*, 2nd ed., edited by Bill Ashcroft, Gareth Griffiths and Helen Tiffin (London and New York: Routledge, 2006): 208.
40 Anzaldúa, "Towards a New Consciousness," 209.
41 Pratap Bhanu Mehta, "Culture in Modern India: The Anxiety and the Promise," in *The Inner Lives of Cultures*, edited by Eva Hoffmann (London: Counterpoint, 2001): 107, eprints.kingston.ac.uk.

Bibliography

Achebe, Chinua. *Morning Yet on Creation Day*. New York: Doubleday, 1975.
Almeida, Rochelle. "Anglo-Indian Migrants: Children of Colonialism and the Cultural Geographies of Encounter." In *Experiences of Freedom in Postcolonial Literatures and Cultures*, edited by Annalisa Oboe and Shaul Bassi. London and New York: Routledge, 2011: 151–162.
Anzaldúa, Gloria. "Towards a New Consciousness." In *The Post-Colonial Studies Reader*, 2nd ed., edited by Bill Ashcroft, Gareth Griffiths and Helen Tiffin. London and New York: Routledge, 2006: 208–210.

226 Jean Page

Ashcroft, Bill. *Caliban's Voice: The Transformation of English in Post-Colonial Literatures*. London and New York: Routledge: 2009.

————. "Language and Transformation." In *The Post-Colonial Studies Reader*, 2nd ed., edited by Bill Ashcroft, Gareth Griffiths and Helen Tiffin. London and New York: Routledge, 2006: 277–280.

Ashcroft, Bill, Gareth Griffiths and Helen Tiffin. "Introduction to Part Sixteen: Diaspora." In *The Post-Colonial Studies Reader*, 2nd ed., edited by Bill Ashcroft, Gareth Griffiths and Helen Tiffin. London and New York: Routledge, 2006: 425–427.

Bhanu Mehta, Pratap. "Culture in Modern India: The Anxiety and the Promise." In *The Inner Lives of Cultures*, edited by Eva Hoffmann. London: Counterpoint, 2001: 86–119. eprints.kingston.ac.uk.

Clifford, James. "Diasporas." In *The Post-Colonial Studies Reader*, 2nd ed., edited by Bill Ashcroft, Gareth Griffiths and Helen Tiffin. London and New York: Routledge, 2006: 451–454.

Felski, Rita. *The Uses of Literature*. Oxford: Blackwell, 2008.

Grutman, Rainier. "Migration and Territoriality in Deleuze and Steiner." In *Migrancy and Multilingualism in World Literature*, edited by K. Alfons Knauth and Ping-hui Liao. Berlin and Zurich: LIT Verlag, 2016: 171–185.

Hall, Stuart. "Cultural Identity and Diaspora." In *The Post-Colonial Studies Reader*, 2nd ed., edited by Bill Ashcroft, Gareth Griffiths and Helen Tiffin. London and New York: Routledge, 2006: 435–438.

Hashem Beck, Zeina. "Naming Things" (For Refugees, September, 2015). *The Rialto* 84 (Winter 2015): 7–9.

Hoffman, Eva. "Introduction." In *The Inner Lives of Cultures*, edited by Eva Hoffman. London: Counterpoint, 2011: 5–13. eprints.kingston.ac.uk.

Malouf, David. "The Only Speaker of his Tongue." In *Antipodes*. London: Vintage, 1999 [1985]: 70–74.

Mishra, Vijay. "The Diasporic Imaginary: Theorizing the Indian Diaspora." In *The Post-Colonial Studies Reader*, 2nd ed., edited by Bill Ashcroft, Gareth Griffiths and Helen Tiffin. London and New York: Routledge, 2006: 447–450.

Müller, Max. *Lectures on the Science of Language*. London: Longmans Green and Co., 1882.

Peres da Costa, Suneeta. *Saudade*. Artarmon: Giramondo, 2018.

Pinto, Rochelle. *Between Empires: Print and Politics in Goa*. Oxford: Oxford University Press, 2007.

Rushdie, Salman. "Imaginary Homelands." In *The Post-Colonial Studies Reader*, 2nd ed., edited by Bill Ashcroft, Gareth Griffiths and Helen Tiffin. London and New York: Routledge, 2006: 428–434.

Steiner, George. *Extraterritorial: Papers on Literature and the Language Revolution*. New York: Atheneum, 1971.

Todd, Loreto. "The English Language in West Africa." In *English as a World Language*, edited by Richard W. Bailey and Manfred Görlach. Ann Arbor: University of Michigan Press, 1982: 281–305.

wa Thiong'o, Ngũgĩ. *Decolonizing the Mind: The Politics of Language in African Literature*. London: James Curry, 1981.

————. "The Language of African Literature." In *The Post-Colonial Studies Reader*, 2nd ed., edited by Bill Ashcroft, Gareth Griffiths and Helen Tiffin. London and New York: Routledge, 2006: 262–267.

Zabus, Chantal. "Relexification." In *The Post-Colonial Studies Reader*, 2nd ed., edited by Bill Ashcroft, Gareth Griffiths and Helen Tiffin. London and New York: Routledge, 2006: 285–288.

IV

Embattled Englishes

Revolt, Emancipation,
Transformation

14

"THE INDIAN QUEER"

For Lack of a Better Term

Umesh Patra

In the year 1860, an English periodical named *Cornhill Magazine* carried four controversial essays by John Ruskin. Notwithstanding the severe criticism, or due to it, these essays were later published in form of a book titled *Unto This Last*. Forty-four years later, a young Indian barrister in South Africa found this book recommended by a friend at a vegetarian restaurant. He completed the book in one go on a train journey from Johannesburg to Durban. The barrister, named Mohandas Karamchand Gandhi, who would later be hailed as the father of the newly independent nation India, could not sleep a wink the night he read the book. Four years later, in 1908, he would translate the book into his mother tongue Gujarati under the title *Sarvodaya*, literally meaning "the welfare of all."[1] Ruskin's upholding of the dignity of labour and vision of a world where everyone, irrespective of their job title, had an equal dividend on the output, had a profound impact on Gandhi's theory of "Trusteeship, economic equality, relationship between the employer and the employees and the use of modern technology."[2] Gandhi envisioned an Indian *sarvodaya* possible only through the development of the last person standing, designated by another similar term *antodaya*. The concept of *antodaya* became the core of the philosophical and political writings of another Indian scholar Pundit Deen Dayal Upadhyay, who laid out an indigenous path through which the development of all could be achieved. The popular slogan of "*Sabka Sath, Sabka Vikas*," literally meaning the "fellowship of all and the welfare of all," popularised by the incumbent government of India today, seems to pay homage to the idea of *antodaya* and *sarvodaya*. Most people in India would know *sarvodaya* and *antodaya* as political and economic reform movements, without being aware of their distant roots.

DOI: 10.4324/9781003464037-19
This chapter has been made available under a CC-BY-NC-ND 4.0 license.

230 Umesh Patra

Another term that gained a life of its own in India was "civil disobedience," which was the title of an essay by Henry David Thoreau published in 1849. In the essay, Thoreau exhorted the abolitionists of the United States to withdraw their support from the American government by refusing to pay taxes. Thoreau embraced the penalty of incarceration and urged others to do so by actively relinquishing the yoke of the state on their shoulders. He wrote: "Under a government which imprisons unjustly, the true place for a just man is also a prison."[3] Gandhi translated this essay, too, and sought to use its principles in the Indian freedom struggle. Thousands of men courted prison by joining rallies and symbolically making salt, which was against the salt law that at the time provided the British government the monopoly to produce salt. In India, "civil disobedience," also known as "*sabinay abagya*," is more famous as a chapter of the Indian freedom movement than as an essay by an American transcendentalist philosopher. Today, while conducting a gheraos (encirclement) or dharna (strike) in which non-violent protesters willingly disobey the government and actively disrupt the status quo, few would harken back to the contributions of Thoreau.

One way or the other, the contribution of the philosophers across the globe impact social, cultural, and political transformations. Many times, people would not (or perhaps do not need to) realise the distant roots of a fruit that is available at hand. "Sarvoday" and "civil disobedience" are two of the many Indian appropriations of Anglophone philosophical and political musings. Similarly, several works of Anglophone literature and literary movements have inspired literary and cultural upheavals in India. One such movement is on a subtle yet perceptible rise today. For the lack of a better term, I would identify this development as the rise of "the Indian queer."

The term "queer" sounds incongruous with any adjective like "Indian," "French," or "German." "Queering" is a technique used to problematise any essentialist categorisation of an individual's identity in terms of gender, sexuality, and sexual orientation. To be queer is to be free from all sorts of identity markers. How can such a term accept a nationalistic dominion over an unchartered body? Being "queer" entails the risk of a deliberate destabilising of all conservative norm-assigning systems. It means to be radically anti-establishment like the notorious 19th-century dilettante Oscar Wilde. To be queer is to assume the persona of an outlaw like the Indian author R. Raj Rao, who would lament the decriminalisation of homosexuality in India by the Hon'ble Supreme Court of India, as it would put an end to the thrill of being a chronic rebel.[4] Historically speaking, the term queer was a term of abuse that was reinvested with new meaning by its victims.[5] The pejorative and non-normative sense of the word "queer" was alarming not only to the heterosexual community but also to the gay and lesbian communities, many of whom would declare themselves gay but not queer.[6] As a methodological technique, "queering" or "queer analysis" challenges the understanding of sexual identity by focusing not only on the historically constructed nature and hence contingent nature of the homosexual/heterosexual binary but also on the many ways in which individual desires, practices and affiliations cannot be accurately defined by the sex of object choice.[7]

Queer theory entails a theoretical framework and an academic discipline concerned with these historically contingent identities. The word "queer" is part of the assemblage of many sexual identities, including lesbian, gay, bisexual, transgender, and intersex in the abbreviation LGBTQIA+, yet assumes a meaning that covers all non-heterosexual identities that are forged on the axis of gender, sex, or sexual orientation. It is in this sense I use the word "queer" in this chapter.

India has shown an ambivalent relationship to the use of the terminology associated with queer theory. One of the reasons for the ambivalence is the distrust of a western label to connote Indian identities. I am using the term "the Indian Queer" to connote a community that does not yet have a significant political formation, nor a clearly formulated agenda, nor even a pan-Indian solidarity. Yet it exists, and has its ramifications in three distinct yet intersecting dimensions. It takes the shape of an academic discourse proliferating in the urban centres of higher education in India, especially in the domain of the humanities through conferences, lectures, elective papers, and overt and covert study groups. It flourishes as a branch of literature comprising coming out narratives, confessional interviews in print and audio-visual media, stand-up acts, anthologies including translations of ancient to modern Indian literature, novels, poetry collections, and plays written especially by queer authors on themes pertaining to gender and sexuality. The Indian Queer is most visible on the streets of metropolitan cities in Pride marches, in jubilations, and despair after the three crucial verdicts of the Indian judiciary concerning Article 377 of the Indian Penal Code. The Indian Queer does not draw attention, yet it cannot be ignored. Unlike any other Indian movements inspired by the West such as feminism, Marxism, and even to some extent post-colonialism, the movement of the Indian Queer is yet to dissect its umbilical cords from its origin. The Indian Queer harkens back to its roots in Anglophone literature and theory. Attempts have been made to decolonise the "queer," but an indigenous model is yet to surface, largely, I contend, due to the dearth of appropriate Indian vocabulary. Let me illustrate this point by comparing the Indian Queer movement with the rise of Dalit literature.

In the year 1972, several writers and activists in the state of Maharashtra in India formed a group named "Dalit Panthers." The formation of the group signified their common agenda to write voraciously against the caste-based discrimination in India and to actively participate in social reform movements that can eventually lead to a casteless society. This group was inspired by the

life and writings of Dr B. R. Ambedkar who relentlessly fought for the uplift-
ment of the downtrodden community. The group was paying homage to a
similar literary forum named "Black Panthers" which fought against racial
discrimination in the United States. Even though the nature of racial discrimination is different from that of caste-based discrimination, the naming of the
group itself not only showed a solidarity to the African-American cause but
also demanded a similar resolve from its members.[8] The rise of the "Dalit Panthers" led to the blossoming of a canon of literature named "Dalit literature"
with its own aesthetics and debates. Many Dalit writers wrote autobiographical narratives following the western model. It is not that prior to the emergence of Dalit literature, there was no literature that spoke against caste-based
discrimination. Gandhi had used the word "Harijan," literally meaning "god's
people," to describe the castes on the lower rungs of the Indian varna system. Ambedkar was more direct in using the word "untouchables" to describe
those people whose very touch or even shadow could be perceived to pollute
a higher-caste person. The choice of the word "Dalit" led to the acceptance
among people united by a common history of suffering. The Dalits of Maharashtra were very different from the Dalits in Uttar Pradesh. The Dalits did not
necessarily belong to the Hindu fold either. After the massive conversion of
Dalits to Buddhism by Ambedkar himself, many Dalit writers from Maharashtra were Buddhists. The pariah community in Kerala consisted of lower-caste
Hindu people who had converted to Christianity. Despite the promise of
equality, they were meted out a similar treatment with a pariah church and a
pariah parish. Writers from these communities also adopted the term "Dalit."
Even though the word "Dalit" did not literally mean "lower-castes," today
"Dalit literature" connotes the body of literature that is either produced by or
talks about the experiences of caste-based discrimination.

The term "Dalit" therefore consolidated a community that shared neither
the same religion nor the same language. Yet they were united in the commonality of their victimhood by an identical system of oppression which
drew its sustenance from the ancient varna system. There is to my knowledge
no such word that could unite the people who stand diametrically opposed
to the heteronormative system in India except, alas, the term "queer." Unlike
the terms "civil disobedience" or "Sarvoday," the term "queer" has neither
received an in toto acceptance nor a proper translation. Many leading gay
and lesbian theorists, litterateurs, and activists from India such as R. Raj
Rao, Hoshang Merchant, Suniti Namjoshi, and Giti Thandani hail from
metropolitan cities of India and had direct western exposure. Many have
attempted to apply the concepts germinating in the West to Indian settings
with varying degrees of success since the 1990s. Over the last three decades,
there have been many attempts to supply an Indian equivalent of the terminology of queer theory, yet no such term like "Dalit" or "Sarvodaya" has
emerged which would be acceptable to a diverse multilingual country like

"The Indian Queer" **233**

India to designate diverse identities on the axis of gender, sex, and sexual orientation. The "Indian Queer" is in desperate search for its pre-20th-century foremothers or forefathers. In search of ancestry, anthologies have emerged to trace same-sex love in ancient Indian literature. Yet, the bulk of the theory is still imported from the west.

Among the identities represented by the alphabet soup LGBTQIA+, the only identity that has a rich Indian mythological history is that of the transgender. In 2009, the Supreme Court of India recognised the transgender as the third gender. In the judgement, the Hon'ble court accentuates the Indian concept of transgender:

> It is to be emphasized that Transgender in India have assumed distinct and separate class/category which is not prevalent in other parts of the World except in some neighbouring countries. In this country, TG [sic] community comprise of Hijaras, enunch, Kothis, Aravanis, Jogappas, Shiv-Shakthis etc. In Indian community transgender are referred as Hizra or the third gendered people. There exists wide range of transgender-related identities, cultures, or experience – including Hijras, Aravanis, Kothis, jogtas/Jogappas, and Shiv-Shakthi.[9]

The verdict also distances itself from any wider implication of the term derivable from the onset of queer theory. Usually referred to as "hijra" and "*kinner*" (a term which has lately gained wider acceptance), the transgender community is believed to have spiritual powers. Their blessings are sought in family events such as birth and marriage ceremonies. Otherwise, they are subjected to various hardships, compelling many of them to work as low-paid sex-workers. In Indian trains, one often finds groups of hijras collecting money from passengers either by bestowing benedictions or threatening abuse. The novel *The Ministry of Utmost Happiness* by acclaimed Indian author Arundhati Roy is perhaps the most significant work in recent times that features a hijra protagonist. Discarded by parents, and with no qualification for any respectable profession, Anjum, the protagonist, sets out to establish a home near a graveyard for all those who belong nowhere in heteronormative society. Roy's gripping narrative introduces many transgender characters, each with a unique story, yet all designated by the umbrella term hijra.[10] The term hijra is also used to designate intersex people, leading to a conflation of categories. Annie Banerji writes, "Being intersex – born with a body that does not conform to gender norms – is very different from transgender people's profound sense of being assigned the wrong gender at birth, which usually results in a transition to the opposite sex."[11] Being clubbed with transgender people, the intersex community, which in many cases requires consensual medical assistance, suffers from acute invisibility among the queer community in India.

Apart from "transgender" and "intersex," another term that finds an Indian equivalent is "asexual." The Sanskrit term brahmachari, which literally means one who treads the path of Brahma or God, connotes a spiritual seeker who practices abstinence from all sensual pleasures, including sexual ones. "Baal Brahmacharis" are sworn to lifelong celibacy since childhood. In Jainism, Buddhism, and Hinduism, there is a rich tradition of monks and sages who take an ascetic path of renunciation and are not lured by amorous enterprises. The term brahmachari has strong indigenous roots with an austere spiritual dimension, not denoted in the term "asexual."

The rest of the terms, such as lesbian, gay, bisexual, and queer, do not find any indigenous terminology that captures their essence without losing significant features in translation. The most important reason for the absence of appropriate Indian equivalent terminology for these identities is the lack of a straightforward movement for their rights in India, as was seen in the United States. In India, while there was no legislation banning homosexual relations prior to the advent of the British, there was no overt acknowledgement of them either. Section 377 in the Indian Penal Code was the first nationwide prohibition of homosexuality adopted in 1861. This archaic law criminalised "carnal intercourse against the order of nature" which also included homosexuality.[12] In India, the first time this act came to wide public purview was when the Delhi High Court, in a historic verdict on 2 July 2009, declared this section unconstitutional in so far as it criminalised "consensual sex among adults."[13] Nearly four years later, on 12 December 2013, a two-judge bench of the Hon'ble Supreme Court of India (the apex court in India) upturned the Delhi High Court's decision and upheld Section 377 of the IPC. In 2018, the Hon'ble Supreme Court of India overturned the ruling of 2013 and decriminalised all consensual sex among adults. Even though consensual sex among adults of all genders was decriminalised eventually, the initial demands were made by an NGO named NAZ Foundation which viewed Section 377 as a hindrance in curbing the menace of HIV/AIDS. The 2013 judgement of the Hon'ble Supreme Court of India includes the following:

> Respondent No.1 is a Non-Governmental Organisation (NGO) registered under the Societies Registration Act, 1860 which works in the field of HIV/AIDS intervention and prevention. Its work has focussed on targeting 'men who have sex with men' (MSM) or homosexuals or gays in consonance with the integrationist policy. Alleging that its efforts have been severely impaired by the discriminatory attitudes exhibited by State authorities towards sexual minorities, MSM, lesbians and transgender individuals and that unless self-respect and dignity is restored to these sexual minorities by doing away with discriminatory laws such as Section 377 IPC it will not be possible to prevent HIV/AIDS.[14]

"The Indian Queer" **235**

Only after gaining support from various groups with the passage of time did the petitioners, representing 7–8% of the Indian community, become vociferous for their rights without a medical alibi. They submitted in the court that "homosexuality, bisexuality and other sexual orientations are equally natural and reflective of expression of choice and inclination founded on consent of two persons who are eligible in law to express such consent."[15] Thus, in the absence of a unified systematic oppression that handed out terms of abuse, which could have been later used as empowering labels, the Indian queer community resorted to the West in the adoption of their terminology. What follows is a study of the complications and implications of such attempts in the field of academia, literature, and social activism.

In academia, the humanities, especially departments of English and allied disciplines, have championed the cause of queer theory in the metropolitan centres of higher education. The figure of R. Raj Rao, former head of the Department of English at Savitribai Phule Pune University, Pune, looms large in India. In an interview to *The Times of India*, Rao speaks of his experience in the UK during his post-doctoral fellowship. This exposure provided him with the necessary impetus for an unapologetic embracing of his sexuality:

> In the UK, I realised that being a homosexual was not just about having sex or a different sexual preference. It was about identity and politics as well. The UK had student as well as faculty LGBT societies then. The year that I spent there taught me a lot and once I was back in India, I decided to plunge completely into gayness. I realised there was nothing to be ashamed or scared of.[16]

A prolific author, poet, and novelist, Rao has delivered lectures at various Indian universities on Queer theory. He has also delivered a Tedx talk titled "What Does It Mean to Be Queer."[17] In the preface of his book *Criminal Love? Queer Theory, Culture, and Politics in India* published in 2017, he admits that "Queer theory *still* largely comes to us from the West" (emphasis added) and attempts to apply these theories in the Indian context.[18] In a chapter in the book titled "Normativities," Rao discusses at length the homosexuality of Oscar Wilde in opposition to Andre Gide, interspersed with quotations from Eve Sedgewick, Michael Foucault, and Judith Butler. The fact that he had to take recourse not only to the theories but also to the lives of famous western literary figures while talking about sexuality in India shows the dearth of such personas or their life accounts available in India. In response to a claim that Indian academia in the 21st century backed off "when it came to gay and lesbian studies," he states that "in the humanities and liberal arts, with topics such as postcolonialism, women's studies, and Dalit studies having reached saturation point, researchers have had to parasitically and opportunistically turn to queer studies for succour."[19]

236 Umesh Patra

The choice of the term "Criminal Love" as the title of Rao's book has a telling story. It is part of a tradition of Indian queer writings that has taken recourse to "love" and "friendship" to define identities instead of sexual orientation. The title of Rao's novel *Lady Lolita's Lover* follows the same route. In the novel, Rao fuses the plot of two Western literary masterpieces, *Lady Chatterley's Lover* and *Lolita*, and situates them in India. He narrates the story of a bored middle-class Indian housewife married to a homosexual naval officer. She seduces an under-age working-class boy who finds an alliance with such a lady heroic rather than exploitative.[20] Ruth Vanita, a former reader in the Department of English, and Saleem Kidwai, a former professor at the Department of History at Delhi University, compiled an astounding anthology titled *Same-Sex Love in India: A Literary History*. The first section of the preface of the book is appropriately titled "Love." Vanita and Kidwai justify the use of such a title:

> This book traces the history of ideas in Indian written tradition about love between women and love between men who are not biologically related. [...] A primary and passionate attachment between two persons, even between a man and woman, may or may not be acted upon sexually. For this reason our title focuses on love, not sex.[21]

The book is an extraordinary achievement in the field of literary exploration of homosexuality. The book deliberately uses "Same-Sex Love" instead of "gay" and "lesbian" in its title. Another anthology on homosexual literature in India was edited by Hoshang Merchant, an openly gay poet from Mumbai, who also served as professor of English at the University of Hyderabad. Merchant's anthology titled *Yaraana: Gay Writing From South Asia* chooses the Punjabi word *"yaarana"* to stand as an Indian equivalent for "gay."[22] "Yaarana" is a word that is used for male-male homosocial bonding as well as heterosexual love. To call a person of an opposite gender *"yaar"* would imply the possibility of a passionate attachment. Merchant is quick to repudiate any insinuation that this book is the product of a literary-political cause and warns against such a reading:

> The new gay academic mafia, like the feminist or communist academic mafia, tends to fit all literature into a form of their own special pleading. Yes, Virginia, there is a Santa Claus and there is a literature above one's own special pleading, the sonnets of Shakespeare for example, being products of genius rather than homosexual mania.[23]

The individual writings in the volume may be the product of genius and not of "homosexual mania" – if at all there is a perceptible difference – but the very attempt to anthologise these pieces does serve a purpose. However watchful it may be towards the lures of an emergent "gay academic mafia," the anthology boosts queer visibility in print by the very use of the word "gay" in its subtitle. "*Yaarana*" was also the name of the famous 1981 Bollywood movie featuring Amitabh Bachchan and Amjad Khan, telling the story of male friendship and sacrifice. A similar word, "*Dostana*" (a Hindi word meaning friendship), was the name of a 2008 Bollywood movie deliberately used to signify male homosexual bonding. In this comic film, the two protagonists, played by Abhishek Bachchan (the son of Amitabh Bachchan) and John Abraham, pretend to be gay without having any passionate attachment. The first gay magazine in India, founded in 1990 by Ashok Row Kavi, was named *Bombay Dost*. The use of the words "*yaar*"/"*yaarana*" and "*dost*"/"*dostana*" is a deliberate attempt to find an Indian substitute for the word "gay." Bombay is also the inspiration for the coinage of the word Bollywood, an Indian response to the Hollywood film industry. Together, "Bombay" and "Dost" provide a filmy glitter to male homosexual bonding. An issue of *Bombay Dost* in 1995 carried an interview with Akshay Kumar, a famous Bollywood actor and a symbol of masculinity, bringing the world of Bollywood and homosexuality together.[24] One of the famous poems by R. Raj Rao was made into a short film titled "Bomgay," a more courageous coinage demonstrating that the Indian metropolis is a perfect place to transplant homosexuality.[25]

The magazine *Bombay Dost* was earlier meant only for homosexual men – or so it was understood. There was thus the need for a forum of Indian lesbians. This was the task for Delhi-based Giti Thandani, who, along with three other members, founded the organisation Sakhi, the first lesbian collective in India.[26] The term "*sakhi*" served as the female equivalent of "*yaar*" and "*dost*" and an Indian equivalent of "lesbian." "*Sakhi*" is used exclusively for a female friend, yet it does not necessarily connote a homosexual attachment as forcefully as "lesbian" does. A male can also have a "*sakhi*," and so can a female. Nonetheless, Sakhi became the first forum where homosexual females in India, especially English-educated ones, found a patient and sympathetic listener. Letters poured into Sakhi from unexpected quarters, and they were responded to by its members. Many of these letter-writers identified themselves as lesbians. Naisargi N Dave, in her article "To Render Real the Imagined: An Ethnographic History of Lesbian Community in India," discusses at length the politics related to the word "lesbian" in feminist circles in India. Interestingly, she claims that the women who identify themselves as "lesbians" do not find any colonial tint and are blithely unaware of academic hullaballoos on the nomenclature. She writes: "Contrary, then to the doxa that Indian women outside of urban, activist networks will not, and cannot feel hailed by the term "lesbian," the above letters demonstrate that "lesbian" functioned as a welcome invitation to wider belonging."[27] Dave also cites a letter in which the writer seeks help regarding techniques that she and her friends could learn: "I hope Sakhi will take the lead and guide

238 Umesh Patra

us. Do foreign ladies come there and mingle with our ladies? Can you please send an educational note about lesbianism and female bisexuality?"[28] The desire for education about lesbianism and bisexuality as well as the interest to meet foreign women shows the wider implication of the word "lesbian." The writer sought a belongingness to a transnational community of lesbians.

Giti Thandani, the founder of Sakhi, authored a book titled *Sakhiyani: Lesbian Desire in Ancient and Modern India*. As the title of the book Thandani chose the word "*sakhiyani*," a derivative of "*sakhi*," (as "*yaarana*" is of "*yaar*"). Yet, she used the word "lesbian" in the subtitle to ward off any ambiguity. She justifies the use of the subtitle thus:

> The subtitle of this book, *Lesbian Desire in Ancient and Modern India*, might seem at first glance to be somewhat naïve and essentialist, a reductive category subsuming and homogenising different histories, geographies and disciplines. As a deliberate choice, however, it raises the problematic of lesbian invisibility in non-'Western' histories.[29]

The preface shows the necessity of using the word "lesbian" despite her apprehensions of a reductive categorisation. *Sakhi/sakhiyani* joins the list of similar words such as "*yaar*"/"*yaarana*" and "*dost*"/"*dostana*," yet goes only halfway. The immense success of the Sakhi forum led to the formation of another group named "Women to Women," which provided the letter-writers the rare possibility of meeting each other in person for the first time in Bombay in 1995. Co-founded by Lesley, a Catholic girl from Bombay, this group broke away from Sakhi and held meetings for its members who wrestled with the name of their group:

> At their first retreat, a majority of members decided to replace the English women to women with Stree Sangam (confluence of women). And in place of "lesbian," the collective began shifting to the phrase "women who love women." Granted, the latter phrase is English, but unlike "lesbian," it evokes no extranational genealogy of speciated perversity, no immediate accusation of bourgeois irrelevance.[30]

Like "Same-Sex Love in India" and "Criminal Love," "women who love women" became one more term to define identity based on the idea of love. In her article, Dave occasionally uses the term "same-sex desiring women." While all such words are foreign, some words are more foreign than others. Regarding the naming of the group Stree Sangam, Shals Mahajan, one of its members, says: "We didn't want to make it even more difficult for repressed women to reach out to us. Having a radical moniker at that time would've warded them off."[31] Later, the group was named LABIA which was an acronym of "Lesbians and Bisexuals in Action." Today, according to Mahajan,

"The Indian Queer" **239**

"It [LABIA] is no more an acronym, we describe ourselves as a queer feminist LBT collective."[32] The change of name from "Women to Women" to "Stree Sangam," and finally to "LABIA" sans its acronymic value represents a growing sense of strength among its members.

Among literati, Indian playwright Mahesh Dattani is one of the first authors to represent queer issues on stage with staggering success. His English play *On a Muggy Night in Mumbai* shows the struggles of an elite gay subculture in Mumbai. The title of the play highlights its metropolitan setting.[33] His other play, *Bravely Fought the Queen*, is a brilliant experiment in queering the middle-class Hindu household. It narrates the lives of two sisters, married against their will to two brothers who constantly ignore and bully them. Passing days in utter ennui, they long for sensual pleasures and cook up stories of non-existent extra-marital affairs which they are not bold enough to carry out. Throughout the play, it appears as if the women were the sole victims of patriarchy in a middle-class Hindu household. The final scene reveals, to the surprise of the audience, that the younger brother named Nitin was a homosexual who was ashamed to come out of the closet and was forced to marry an unwilling wife.[34] Dattani's title "Bravely Fought the Queen" is usually understood as the literal translation of the Hindi phrase "*Khub Ladi Mardani Wo To Jhasnsi Wali Rani Thi.*" The phrase is the title of a popular Hindi folksong that narrates the life of Queen Lakhsmi of Jhansi who chose to fight against the British on horseback, with her child attached to her back, instead of relinquishing her kingdom. The term "Queen" here could also mean the struggle of Nitin, who finds it hard to fight against homophobia, largely the result of a rule imposed by the British. This play is also set in a metropolitan city, Bangalore.

Nitin's identity is like that of many men who do not identify themselves as gay and continue to marry and beget children. In effect, they could be called bisexual. Due to their resentment of the heterosexual lifestyle which has forced them to stay closeted throughout their lives, they often subject their wives to domestic abuse. R. Raj Rao defines these men by another term: "Men Who Have Sex With Men" (MSM). These are men who have sex on the sly with other men, cautious not to identify either as gay or bisexuals. They are conscious of their gendered selves, and do not see occasional sex as a marker of identity:

> What is important, however, is that the proportion of such men in relation to the total population is so high, that Indian queer theory cannot afford to ignore them. Though MSMs reject the notion of identity based on sexual desire, they have over time come to constitute an identity and have added to the plethora of queer sexual identities already available in this country, such as gay, lesbian, bisexual, transgender, koti, panthi, hijra, and so on.[35]

The husband of Lolita in Rao's novel *Lady Lolita's Lover* can be called an MSM. According to Rao, this community became the chief reason for the spread of the HIV/AIDS in India. MSM becomes one more Indian equivalent for gay and bisexual men. Terms such as "women desiring women," "women who love women," "men who have sex with men" sound less foreign than "gay," "lesbian," "bisexual," or "queer." The appropriation of Indian language words such as *sakhi*, *yaar*, and *dost* are attempts to generate new meanings with familiar words. Yet, no such word exists as an umbrella term for *sakhi*, *yaar*, *hijra*, and other identities denoted by LGBTQIA+. Thus, the term "the Indian Queer" becomes a necessary heuristic tool to bring these diverse communities together under a common cause. The decriminalising of homosexuality, the official recognition of transgender as the third gender, and the banning of gender normalising procedures for intersex children show signs of hope. The growth of queer visibility in academia, literature, and social activism exhibits a growing acknowledgement of, if not empathy with, the Indian Queer. Yet, as many of these activities are carried out in metropolitan cities like Delhi, Mumbai, Bangalore, or Hyderabad, Indian Queer risks being a largely urban phenomenon. Yet it posits a hope that a day will come when the winds of change will gradually reach the last person standing, and that would be, in the truest form, Sarvodaya, or the Welfare of All.

Notes

1 Mohandas Karamchand Gandhi, *Unto this Last: A Paraphrase* (Ahmedabad: Navjivan Publishing House, 1956): 1–22, www.mkgandhi.org/untothislast/untothislast.htm.
2 M. L. Dantwala, "Gandhiji and Ruskin's *unto this Last*," *Economic and Political Weekly* 30.44 (1995): 2793, www.jstor.org/stable/4403395.
3 Henry David Thoreau, "Civil Disobedience," 1849. https://archive.vcu.edu/english/engweb/transcendentalism/authors/thoreau/civil/.
4 Mihir Bhanage, "R Raj Rao: Happy that Sec 377 is Scrapped, but Will Miss Being an Outlaw," *Times of India*, 2018, https://timesofindia.indiatimes.com/life-style/spotlight/r-raj-rao-happy-that-sec-377-is-scrapped-but-will-miss-being-an-outlaw/articleshow/65730733.cms.
5 "Queers Read This: A Leaflet Distributed at Pride March in NY Published Anonymously by Queers," *qrd.org*, 1990, www.qrd.org/qrd/misc/text/queers.read.this.
6 Adam Isaiah Green, "Gay but Not Queer: Toward a Post-Queer Study of Sexuality," *Theory and Society* 31.4 (2002): 521.
7 Stephen Valocchi, "Not Yet Queer Enough: The Lessons of Queer Theory for the Sociology of Gender and Sexuality," *Gender & Society* 19.6 (2005): 754.
8 Janet A. Contursi, "Political Theology: Text and Practice in a Dalit Panther Community," *The Journal of Asian Studies* 52.2 (1993): 320–339.
9 "National Legal Services Authority v. Union of India and Others," *South Asian Translaw Database* (2014): 109–110, https://translaw.clpr.org.in/wp-content/uploads/2018/09/Nalsa.pdf.
10 Arundhati Roy, *The Ministry of Utmost Happiness* (New Delhi: Hamish Hamilton, 2007).
11 Annie Banerji, "Job Snubs to Forced Surgery: India's 'Invisible' Intersex People," *Reuters*, 16 August 2019, www.reuters.com/article/india-lgbt-intersex-idINKCN1V60ZO.

"The Indian Queer" **241**

12 "Section 377 in the Indian Penal Code," *indiankannon.org*, https://indiankanoon.org/doc/1836974/.
13 "Indian Court Overturns Ban on Gay Sex," *Reuters*, 2 July 2009, www.reuters.com/article/us-india-gay-idINTRE5611VE20090702.
14 "Suresh Kumar Koushal and Another v. NAZ Foundation and Others," *Supreme Court of India*, 2013: 3, https://main.sci.gov.in/jonew/judis/41070.pdf.
15 "Navtej Singh Johar & ORS v. Union of India," *The Hindu*, 2016: 16, www.thehindu.com/news/national/article24880700.ece/binary/Sec377judgment.pdf.
16 Bhanage, "R. Raj Rao."
17 R. Raj Rao, "What Does it Mean to be Queer," *TedxVITPune*, *YouTube*, 16 April 2019. www.youtube.com/watch?v=SMIuFl3m_U4&t=340s.
18 R. Raj Rao, *Criminal Love? Queer Theory, Culture, and Politics in India* (New Delhi: Sage, 2017): ix.
19 Rao, *Criminal Love*, 28.
20 R. Raj Rao, *Lady Lolita's Lover* (New Delhi: HarperCollins, 2015).
21 Ruth Vanita and Saleem Kidwai, *Same-Sex Love in India: A Literary History* (Gurugram, Haryana: Penguin India, 2008): xxiii.
22 Hoshang Merchant, *Yaraana: Gay Writing from South Asia* (Gurugram, Haryana: Penguin India, 2011).
23 Merchant, *Yaraana*, xvii.
24 Vikram Phukan, "Bombay Dost, India's First LGBT Magazine, Turns 25!" *Mid-Day*, 6 October 2015, www.mid-day.com/mumbai/mumbai-news/article/Bombay-Dost--India-s-first-LGBT-magazine--turns-25--16587189.
25 Bhanage, "R. Raj Rao."
26 Naisargi N. Dave, "To Render Real the Imagined: An Ethnographic History of Lesbian Community in India," *Signs* 35.3 (2010): 601.
27 Dave, "To Render Real," 604.
28 Dave, "To Render Real," 609.
29 Giti Thandani, *Sakhiyani: Lesbian Desire in Ancient and Modern India* (New Delhi: Bloomsbury, 2021): vii.
30 Dave, "To Render Real," 614.
31 Vikram Phukan, "LABIA Celebrates 20th Birthday," *The Hindu*, 18 December 2015.
32 Phukan, "LABIA Celebrates."
33 Mahesh Dattani, "On a Muggy Night in Mumbai," in *Collected Plays* (New Delhi: Penguin India, 2000): 43–112.
34 Mahesh Dattani, "Bravely Fought the Queen," in *Collected Plays* (New Delhi: Penguin India, 2000): 227–316.
35 Rao, *Criminal Love*, 19–20.

Bibliography

Banerji, Annie. "Job Snubs to Forced Surgery: India's 'Invisible' Intersex People." *Reuters*, 16 August 2019. www.reuters.com/article/india-lgbt-intersex-idINKCN1V60ZO (last accessed 10 October 2023).
Bhanage, Mihir, "R Raj Rao: Happy that Sec 377 is Scrapped, but Will Miss Being an Outlaw." *Times of India*, 8 September 2018. https://timesofindia.indiatimes.com/life-style/spotlight/r-raj-rao-happy-that-sec-377-is-scrapped-but-will-miss-being-an-outlaw/articleshow/65730733.cms (last accessed 10 April 2024).
Contursi, Janet A. "Political Theology: Text and Practice in a Dalit Panther Community." *The Journal of Asian Studies* 52.2 (1993): 320–339.
Dantwala, M. L. "Gandhiji and Ruskin's *Unto This Last*." *Economic and Political Weekly* 30.44 (1995): 2793–2795.
Dattani, Mahesh. "Bravely Fought the Queen." In *Collected Plays*. New Delhi: Penguin, 2000: 227–316.

———. "On a Muggy Night in Mumbai." In *Collected Plays*. New Delhi: Penguin, 2000: 43–112.

Dave, Naisargi N. "To Render Real the Imagined: An Ethnographic History of Lesbian Community in India." *Signs* 35.3 (2010): 595–619.

Gandhi, Mohandas Karamchand. *Unto this Last: A Paraphrase*, translated by Valji Govindji Desai. Ahmedabad: Navjivan Publishing House, 1956. www.mkgandhi.org/untothislast/untothislast.htm (last accessed 10 April 2024).

Green, Adam Isaiah. "Gay but Not Queer: Toward a Post-Queer Study of Sexuality." *Theory and Society* 31.4 (2002): 521–545.

"Indian Court Overturns Ban on Gay Sex." *Reuters*, 2 July 2009. www.reuters.com/article/us-india-gay-idINTRE5611VE20090702 (last accessed 10 April 2024).

Merchant, Hoshang, ed. *Yaraana: Gay Writing from South Asia*. Gurugram, Haryana: Penguin India, 2011.

"National Legal Services Authority v. Union of India and Others." *South Asian Translaw Database*, 2014. https://translaw.clpr.org.in/wp-content/uploads/2018/09/Nalsa.pdf (last accessed 10 April 2024).

"Navtej Singh Johar & ORS v. Union of India." *The Hindu*, 2016. www.thehindu.com/news/national/article24880700.ece/binary/Sec377judgment.pdf (last accessed 10 April 2024).

Phukan, Vikram. "Bombay Dost, India's First LGBT Magazine, Turns 25!" *Mid-Day*, 6 October 2015. www.mid-day.com/mumbai/mumbai-news/article/Bombay-Dost--India-s-first-LGBT-magazine--turns-25--16587189 (last accessed 22 February 2024).

———. "LABIA Celebrates 20th Birthday." *The Hindu*, 18 December 2015. www.thehindu.com/news/cities/mumbai/labia-celebrates-20th-birthday/article8003123.ece (last accessed 10 April 2024).

"Queers Read this: A Leaflet Distributed at Pride March in NY Published Anonymously by Queers." *qrd.org*, 1990. www.qrd.org/qrd/misc/text/queers.read.this (last accessed 10 April 2024).

Rao, R. Raj. *Criminal Love? Queer Theory, Culture, and Politics in India*. New Delhi: Sage, 2017.

———. *Lady Lolita's Lover*. New Delhi: HarperCollins, 2015.

———. "What Does it Mean to be Queer." *TedxVITPune, YouTube*, 16 April 2019. www.youtube.com/watch?v=SMIuFl3m_U4&t=340s (last accessed 10 April 2024).

Roy, Arundhati. *The Ministry of Utmost Happiness*. New Delhi: Hamish Hamilton, 2007.

"Section 377 in the Indian Penal Code." *indiankannon.org*. https://indiankanoon.org/doc/1836974/. (last accessed 15 July 2023).

"Suresh Kumar Koushal and Another v. NAZ Foundation and Others." *Supreme Court of India*, 2013. https://main.sci.gov.in/jonew/judis/41070.pdf (last accessed 10 April 2024).

Thandani, Giti. *Sakhiyani: Lesbian Desire in Ancient and Modern India*. New Delhi: Bloomsbury, 2021.

Thoreau, Henry David. "Civil Disobedience." 1849. https://archive.vcu.edu/english/engweb/transcendentalism/authors/thoreau/civil/.

Valocchi, Stephen. "Not Yet Queer Enough: The Lessons of Queer Theory for the Sociology of Gender and Sexuality." *Gender & Society* 19.6 (2005): 750–770.

Vanita, Ruth and Saleem Kidwai, eds. *Same-Sex Love in India: A Literary History*. Gurugram, Haryana: Penguin India, 2008.

15

TRICKSTERS, HUSTLERS, AND MORAL SAINTS

Students and Other Strangers in Post-Apartheid South African Literature

Ibrahim Abraham

Introduction

The "Rhodes Must Fall" and "Fees Must Fall" student protests, which engulfed South Africa's prestigious University of Cape Town and Wits University in 2015 and 2016, were impassioned expressions of youthful frustration with the ongoing cultural and socio-economic inequalities of post-apartheid society, making headlines around the world. Not all South African students are revolutionaries, however, and alienation from the "rainbow nation" usually appears in less unified and incendiary forms. Engaging with post-apartheid South African *bildungsromane*, in dialogue with social scientific literature on contemporary African youth and "Fallist" student movements, this chapter analyses the subjectivities of black South African students and young graduates.[1] As post-apartheid literature seeks to rediscover "the ordinary,"[2] including experiences of individuals at odds with their communities and everyday English vernaculars removed from the political rhetoric of the anti-apartheid struggle, this chapter explores a threefold typology of subjectivities – tricksters, hustlers, and moral saints – locatable in novels about struggling students and graduates of Wits and Cape Town universities: Niq Mhlongo's *Dog Eat Dog* and *After Tears* and Songeziwe Mahlangu's *Penumbra*.[3]

The focus on student and graduate experiences is neither accidental nor indulgent. For while Mhlongo and Mahlangu draw on their own experiences, they continue a long tradition of semi-autobiographical black South African literature, following writers such as Es'kia Mphahlele. Education, moreover, has been the *sine qua non* of black social mobility from the colonial era onwards. Therefore, at the risk of resurrecting old arguments about

DOI: 10.4324/9781003464037-20
This chapter has been made available under a CC-BY-NC-ND 4.0 license.

244 Ibrahim Abraham

national allegories in postcolonial fiction,[4] black education and aspiration has deep social significance.

The focus on students as individuals has social significance also. For while Michael Chapman observes that South African literature evinces a longstanding "thematic and stylistic impulse to belong to a common society,"[5] albeit a dysfunctional society, the post-apartheid society Mhlongo and Mahlangu narrate is particularly alienating and anomic. Mahlangu's narrator seeks personal meaning and Mhlongo's narrators seek personal advantage, while the writers themselves seek readers in a society of spectacles that no longer even pretends to revere black writers. In a democratic culture that now offers a cacophony of black voices – the upwardly mobile mainstream on radio, television and social media, usually adept at codeswitching between boardroom English and indigenous languages – even writers that capture the voices of their communities or generations struggle for the status of comparable black writers of the apartheid era. The protagonists and authors of the key texts in this chapter all find themselves at arm's length from an economy (if not a whole society) that, after the fall of apartheid, should be theirs as aspirational black bourgeois. The world of strangers this volume explores is experienced by many such South Africans as Mhlongo's titular *Dog Eat Dog* society.

While Sarah Nuttall finds *Dog Eat Dog* comparable to David Lodge's campus novels,[6] where the university is a "small world" generating comedy rather than tragedy,[7] the university itself is not a concern for Mhlongo or Mahlangu, as it is for Lodge who influenced the turn to theory in British literary studies. Mhlongo and Mahlangu's protagonists experience university liminally, as strangers passing through spaces that often alienate black students, as Fallist activists observed. These novels are *bildungsromane* in a broader sense, taking "*youth* as the most meaningful part of life," especially in a rapidly changing society in which youth is a period of "uncertain exploration of social space," rather than socialisation into continuity.[8] There is profound uncertainty about the society the novels' protagonists are coming of age within and which subjectivities might succeed in the new South Africa.

After contextualising contemporary South African literature within a cultural context of depoliticisation and individualisation, this chapter begins with the work of Niq Mhlongo, a leading figure among the "kwaito generation" of writers, named for a local hedonistic music genre.[9] Analysing Mhlongo's *Dog Eat Dog* and *After Tears* reveals the apartheid-era "trickster," outwitting racist oppressors, transforming into the post-apartheid "hustler," outwitting anyone they can. In stark contrast, the figure of the "moral saint" emerges as a youth overly burdened by ethical deliberation. Although glimpsed in apartheid-era writing, the moral saint emerges clearly in Songeziwe Mahlangu's anguished autofiction, *Penumbra*, and among some Fallists' demands for total social transformation. Mhlongo and Mahlangu's writing – and writing careers – reveals a post-apartheid youth "bereft of signature literature or heroes in the present,"[10] now seeking bite-sized inspiration on social media. The "impulse to belong to a common society,"[11] Chapman observes, now seems to be the need to delve deep into isolated individual psyches, even as they crumble, as in Mahlangu's *Penumbra*. For as this chapter will suggest, South African society appears as the increasingly incommensurate experiences of anomic individuals seeking their own paths, between the cynicism of the hustler and the performative certainty of the moral saint.

Rediscovering the Ordinary in Post-Apartheid Literature

In his influential lecture, "The Rediscovery of the Ordinary," Njabulo S. Ndebele critiqued anti-apartheid writing focused on the "spectacular" nature of black South African struggle and suffering.[12] Whereas spectacular protest literature "keeps the larger issues of society in our minds obliterating the details," the "ordinary" focuses attention on those details, for even those living "under oppression" are capable of complexity.[13] Not all apartheid-era writers celebrated "heroic narratives" of the struggle, but the "typical" could supersede the "individual,"[14] such that André Brink's relief in the changing culture of post-apartheid literature is relief at the turn to the individual and ordinary:

> [T]here were always stories placed on the back burner, waiting for "one day" when we could return to them and explore them more deeply without any inner compulsion other than the urge to tell a story. That day has now come. And it is the recognition of this new freedom of choice that characterizes much of the exhilaration of the inner liberation embodied in the new South Africa.[15]

In Brink's *The Rights of Desire*, a retired librarian reigniting his sex life describes a packet of condoms in his sock drawer as "like a freedom fighter keeping sticks of dynamite in his room,"[16] centering individual pleasures and displacing radical politics.

This individual turn is evident in Mhlongo and Mahlangu's novels, exemplifying the "post-transitional aesthetics" of contemporary South Africa.[17] After apartheid, literature fragmented along various social trajectories, recognising the diversity and intersectionality of black experience.[18] As Brink observed, citing Mhlongo specifically, semi-autobiographical writers seemed to react especially strongly against narratives explained through "grand ideology," treating stories as "the intensely lived personal experience of specific individuals."[19] Post-apartheid life, in short, cannot be reduced to political slogans. In *Dog Eat Dog*, when a Marxist lecturer tries, denouncing democracy as "an ideological phantasm invented by the bourgeoisie," students are baffled: "Can you speak in English please, sir?"[20] There is obvious irony in

246 Ibrahim Abraham

these young, multiracial students acting as commonsense guardians of English expression. More profoundly, however, language emerges again as a site of youthful alienation, albeit perhaps as farce. Just as students rose up in 1976 against the ideological imposition of Afrikaans in the school curricula, these students are piping up against the ideological imposition of language that is politically, not linguistically incomprehensible.

A broader reconsideration of the political possibilities of literature has also occurred. Whereas apartheid-era debates assume literature's political power, post-apartheid writers focus more on individual ethics, and express "modesty" about literature's impact.[21] Mhlongo's third novel, *Way Back Home*, illustrates this, focusing on a corrupt black businessman literally haunted by the violence of the armed anti-apartheid struggle: "Comrade, I see dead people."[22] Like race, politics remains relevant, but it is now indexed to individual questions and values, rather than prescriptively imposed.

Mhlongo therefore rejects explicit ideological affiliations, telling a literary festival audience:

> I'm just a writer, and I write about whatever I experience. I write about gossip, I write about hearsay, I write about my view of the world. I'm sure you want me to come with big political terms, but I'm not like that [...] I know you want me to say I'm a Black Consciousness person. I might be. But I'm a writer.[23]

Mahlangu has similarly rejected the notion that "literature is expected to be an extension of the social sciences."[24] In *Penumbra*, Manga bristles at a friend's criticism of his autofiction about student struggles: "You should avoid this egocentric writing. Any book of importance touches on the politics of the time. My advice to you is that if you ever want to write, you must represent people."[25]

Mhlongo and Mahlangu would dismiss this notion that writing about embattled middle-class individuals is "egocentric writing," as both are open about their professional difficulties, sometimes mirroring their narrators, given literature's limited reach among black South African readers. Mahlangu expresses embarrassment about his "romantic" ideas of being a writer and neglecting his career as a chartered accountant: "I would have been much further had I qualified as a CA. I would have been able to rent a decent apartment and have a car."[26] *Penumbra* presents these ideas in another self-critique, with a different friend telling Manga:

> We should be seeing practical progress now. [...] There does not need to be any grand ideas. There's no reason for you not to have a small car; or to be able to save a bit each month. You see those kids I was with at Capello? They also did accounting at UCT. They stay in nice apartments and drive decent cars.[27]

He is also uncomfortable with the self-promotion required from South African writers. Mhlongo relishes this role, conversely, but in an effervescent and self-effacing manner. He depicts trips to African literary festivals as low-budget adventures uniting writers and their readers,[28] no matter how few attend – rare opportunities to create community among a reading public of strangers.

Niq Mhlongo's Tricksters and Hustlers

Mhlongo's work is set in Soweto, the Johannesburg township juxtaposing recent wealth and established poverty. Mhlongo's first novel, *Dog Eat Dog*, is set during South Africa's first democratic election in 1994 and focuses on a Soweto student, Dingz, at risk of failing his studies at Wits. His second novel, *After Tears*, is set five years later and focuses on Bafana, who has failed his legal studies in Cape Town and returned to Soweto, pretending he has graduated. Whereas *Dog Eat Dog*'s title clearly criticises South Africa as a society of competitive strangers, the title of *After Tears* is more particular, referring to parties that often follow funerals in Black African communities. Demonstrating *Ubuntu*, southern African communitarianism, after tears parties are "joyful events where the living crack jokes about the dead, and get sloshed and dance to loud music."[29] Mhlongo documents ordinary township life, but hardly celebrates its precarity, with his protagonists often despising the townships.[30] *Dog Eat Dog* contrasts Soweto with Wits; "there is no sexual harassment here in the township," one character jokingly remarks about different moralities, but differences are also material, with university offering the "luxury" of free toilet paper.[31]

A decade before Fallism, Mhlongo depicted the struggles activists would campaign against. Although the "uncertain exploration of social space" which epitomises youth in modernity underpins the entire *bildungsroman* genre,[32] social spaces are unusually uncertain in Mhlongo's novels, and although university is "to some extent a foreign country for all new students," elite South African universities can be downright "hostile" to black students.[33] The University of Cape Town's former Vice-Chancellor, Max Price, admitted his university created "an environment which does communicate that the colour of excellence is white [...] it valorises European culture still."[34] While we might assume that this extends to its use of English, language-related Fallist protests occurred at traditionally Afrikaans-language universities.[35] These protests did not call for equal status for indigenous languages, but for English, as the *linga franca* of the black middle class. Much like the students of the 1976 uprising, their preference for English expressed pragmatic personal ambition. At English-language universities, protests were primarily focused on black students' material poverty: inadequate housing and nutrition, but also inadequate prior education.[36] This is prefigured in Mhlongo's protagonists, who are poor students in multiple senses of the word. Dingz and Bafana have low incomes

248 Ibrahim Abraham

and low discipline, but underinvestment in black education and the disruptions of anti-apartheid activism left them unprepared for university; Dingz recalls rote learning the Psalms and "pass one–pass all" protests at school.[37]

Dog Eat Dog also illustrates the challenges for universities in addressing inequalities without disempowering students further. Fallism presented black students as historical victims, demanding "recognition of the student as [an] individual whose collective 'genealogy' has been one of oppression and subordination,"[38] without presenting them as helpless. Activists drew attention to the "shameful" process of applying for needs-based bursaries by proving one's vulnerabilities, not one's capabilities as with merit-based bursaries.[39] Indeed, *Dog Eat Dog* opens with a letter informing Dingz that his bursary application has been rejected:

> *Did anybody even read my applications?* I wondered angrily. I thought that I had supplied everything that the Bursary Committee needed: copies of my father's death certificate and my mother's pension slip, an affidavit sworn at our local police station giving the names and ages of the nine other family members who depend on my mother's pension, as well as three other affidavits confirming all movable and immovable property that we owned. [...] *What more information do these people want about the poverty that my family is living in?*[40]

Situated within a system unable to respond effectively to his material situation that makes him feel like a stranger to the university, the narrative shifts between the structural and subjective, trying to make sense of an environment in which the potentialities of individual agency are unclear.

Dingz and Bafana resort to elaborate schemes to further their ambitions and compensate for their structural positions and poor personal decisions. These novels have been theorised as "novels of deception," therefore, with multiple levels of deceit; although Dingz and Bafana are self-interested, readers can consider whether their deceit is legitimised by social injustices.[41] In *Dog Eat Dog*, Dingz requests a deferred examination after failing to study for an exam. Like one of Moretti's working-class students, who manipulated him into awarding an "A" for an essay about Stendhal and the Black Panthers he claimed to be too busy to actually write,[42] Dingz combines self-interest and black politics. He lies about a death in his family and bribes an official to obtain the death certificate of someone with the same family name. Facing scrutiny from the faculty dean, Dingz cites cultural taboos and social problems to explain discrepancies in his story, "to put the dean as far into his corner of white ignorance as possible."[43] In doing so, Dingz exploits the cultural ignorance fostered by the apartheid system, which enshrined ethnic differences, not merely racial inequalities, seeking to create communities that were strangers to each other, a situation which has hardly been fully resolved.

Mhlongo's narrative shows the dean is right to question Dingz, but for the wrong reasons. The reader knows Dingz is lying, but the dean is ignorant of the truth adjacent to Dingz's lies:

> I never thought that a man of his calibre would be so ignorant about the cancer of poverty that cripples so many families. Poverty means that you cannot give your loved one a proper burial. It also means you cannot contact your relatives who live far away in times of need. [...] Although I had produced a sham certificate, I was angry that the dean was talking arrogantly to me. I didn't feel sorry that I lied to get it. Lying to get a certificate was a practical affair to me.[44]

Dingz is also angry that his white classmate received a deferred examination after the death of her dog,[45] referencing a literary trope going back to Mphahele's famous story "Mrs Plum," that whites' pets rank above black people.[46] Two decades later, activists at the University of Cape Town were similarly angered over exam exemptions for philosophy students whose exam coincided with a music festival, citing black students' difficulties receiving exemptions to attend funerals, and Muslims' obligations to sit exams on religious holidays.[47] Still, it seems, South Africans are living as strangers, ignorant or indifferent to each other's cultures.

Given Mhlongo's protagonists' trickery, his novels suggest continuity with apartheid-era trickster narratives.[48] African trickster stories celebrate small victories of the weak over the powerful, but unlike Christianised African American trickster stories, African stories are cyclical, with tricksters ending up back where they began.[49] Bafana's scheme is uncovered, but at the end of the novel he travels to Durban with his fake diploma to try again.[50] Since personal advantage is also extracted from one's own impoverished community and family, the trickster transforms into a hustler in Mhlongo's narratives, signalling a breakdown of community, or at least of commonality, and the emergence of a society of exploitable strangers no longer unified by oppression.

Tricksters were certainly roguish in apartheid-era literature, but trickster narratives revealed the illegitimacy of apartheid, and no such certainty is possible, after apartheid, in a social system that is democratic, but deeply flawed. A good example is Mphahlele's apartheid-era story, "Grieg on a Stolen Piano,"[51] illustrating a middle-class trickster in the figure of the narrator's uncle. Despite working as a school inspector, he is in constant search of money, illicitly trading stolen goods during his school rounds, depicted as compensation for the disrespect he receives from white peers and justified by the illegitimate social order.[52] Mocking his wife's "policy of non-collaboration" in his schemes, the trickster cannot understand why she should worry about the titular stolen piano when life is built upon dishonesty: "Don't we steal from

250 Ibrahim Abraham

each other, lie to each other every day and know it, us and the whites? [...] [W]e keep stealing from the white man and lying to him and he does the same. This way we can still feel some pride."[53] Mhlongo's post-apartheid protagonists are cynical about the democratic transition but not antagonistic, despite an explicit justification for deceit by one of Dingz's friends: "You haven't read *Africa My Music* by Professor Mphahlele? He says exactly what I am saying; that you must lie to the whites in order to survive in this country because the whites themselves already live in the web of a big lie.[54] So while Dingz and his friends mock Mandela's "faltering language" and the almost regal English expressions of a man who loved his Shakespeare, this is intergenerational disrespect rather than radical refusal of the democratic compromise.[55]

Whereas tricksters outwitted a system unworthy of respect, post-apartheid hustlers seek advantages in a democratic system with limited opportunities. As in Mhlongo's fiction, ethnographic studies depict hustling as a "waithood" survival strategy, a period of uncertainty between adolescence and adult self-sufficiency that may never arrive.[56] Comedian Trevor Noah reflects upon hustling in his autobiography about his youth in Johannesburg in the 1990s, contemporaneous with Mhlongo's early novels.[57] He echoes a sociological definition of hustling as "capitalizing on *every opportunity* to procure a good or a service to supplement income and symbolic capital,"[58] explaining that "someone's always buying, someone's always selling, and the hustle is about trying to be in the middle of that."[59]

Unlike apartheid-era narratives, Mhlongo never implies his protagonists are forced into deceit, nor that honest success is impossible. Although Dingz justifies his deceit as necessary,[60] Mhlongo's narrative reveals that despite the injustice and inequality he was born into, he contributes to his own failures. The situation is more pronounced in *After Tears*, with Bafana beset by mounting feelings of guilt, not only over his hustles, but also over missing the "opportunity to be the first in my family to have a university degree."[61] Although aware of the corrupt state of society and historical injustices, pondering politics on occasions – "If the IMF and World Bank were willing to cancel the debts owed to them by poor African countries, why couldn't our government scratch out the loans owed to it by poor African students like me?"[62] – he acknowledges the consequences of his actions. Mhlongo is not a neoliberal moraliser; he does not suggest South Africa offers easy or equal opportunities, simply that the greater freedoms of the post-apartheid era impose greater individual accountability.

Songeziwe Mahlangu's Moral Saints

Like *After Tears*, Mahlangu's *Penumbra* focuses on a former Cape Town student, Manga, but unlike Bafana, Manga legitimately graduated. The university remains relevant for Manga, and as he sits near the statue of Cecil Rhodes that inspired the "Rhodes Must Fall" protests, he recalls "someone once wrote some graffiti on the statue of the ancestor: 'Fuck you and your ideas of empire.'"[63] Manga benefits from the affirmative action policies Dingz sought to manipulate in *Dog Eat Dog*, but he is embarrassed about visibly wasting his days "doing nothing" in a corporate graduate scheme which itself manipulates affirmative action policies.[64] Despite winning the Etisalat Prize for African literature in 2014, *Penumbra* has been rather overlooked, but it is nevertheless a significant novel in which the subjective entanglements of religion, politics and pop culture, constitutive of the moral ecology of contemporary South African youth,[65] are explored evocatively.

In contrast to the tricksters and hustlers previously, *Penumbra*'s protagonist Manga can be theorised through Susan Wolf's figure of the moral saint,[66] in the South African context a student or youth (in particular) for whom questions of morality unduly dominate in a self-destructive manner. Wolf's moral saint is an analytical construction, a theoretical person striving for every action to be "as morally good as possible, a person, that is, who is as morally worthy as can be," and someone who "pays little or no attention to his [sic] own happiness in light of the overriding importance he [sic] gives to the wider concerns of morality."[67] This quest for moral perfection undermines "the enjoyable in life," because life is "dominated by a single, all-important value under which all other possible values must be subsumed."[68] Ndebele's novella "Fools" features an apartheid-era moral saint in the figure of Zani, a student activist.[69] There are few things Zani does not condemn in his anti-apartheid activism, and the novel's protagonist, a morally compromised teacher, discovers the moral saint can be a "nauseating companion."[70] There is something performative about Zani: "Whenever he spoke that way, it seemed as if there was something, some disembodied essence, speaking through him."[71] There is also something invigorating about his uncompromising radicalism: "There was something painfully immediate yet strangely liberating about him. [...] That boy! He was pure fear, pure concern, pure indignation, pure conceit, pure profligacy, pure reason, pure irrationality."[72]

Manga presents a different morality to Zani; he drinks, takes drugs, sleeps with prostitutes, and wastes time at work. Both nevertheless require an all-important value to make sense of life, and both stand apart from the cynical prudence of the hustler. However, what is jarring about Wolf's initial figuration of the moral saint, four decades later, is the centrality of self-denial. In contemporary expressive individualist cultures, including South Africa's middle-class cultures, individual identity and personal pleasure are vital sites of political contestation, even political perfectibility, not detachable distractions. After both the post-apartheid and expressive individualist turn, the moral saint is no longer a self-denying subject. The contemporary moral saint

252 Ibrahim Abraham

is an obsessively self-monitoring and even self-regarding subject, concerned with the moral meanings of personal pleasure as foundational to individual identity.

This contemporary moral saint can be glimpsed in Sara Ahmed's figure of the killjoy,[73] who similarly refuses to compromise with injustice for pleasure or convenience, albeit with moral scrutiny focused outward rather than inward. The contemporary moral saint can also be glimpsed in "woke" language, prevalent among black graduates of Wits and Cape Town, that is often intimidatingly incomprehensible to graduates of less elite institutions.[74] Whereas Mhlongo's generation seemed to want to banish dogma – recalling the request, previously, to a Marxist lecturer to "speak in English please"[75] – perhaps moral saints are reviving sophisticated radical rhetoric, with all that entails.

For Carl A. Grant, writing in an African American context, wokeness is constituted by constant alertness; "maintaining heightened consciousness," "calling-out friends and family," and "recognizing duplicity or deception."[76] In an article for the *Mail & Guardian*, a progressive, middle-class South African weekly, J.S. Smit compares wokeness to being a child at Christmas who realises that Santa Claus is just a fat relative in a costume.[77] As this definition recognises, the saintly refusal to suspend disbelief produces a self-righteousness that can be profoundly unsettling. By necessity, therefore, moral saints are social outsiders – even if they ironically require elite education to reach moral sainthood. Rather than seeking to connect with one's society, as Chapman argues has been the case in South African literary culture,[78] moral saints become conspicuous strangers standing in sometimes incomprehensible condemnation of their society.

While Manga is frustrated with work and his creative endeavours, he is also dissatisfied with society, searching for political or religious values to make sense of everything. A sincere spiritual seeker, Manga's attention drifts throughout the novel between forms of Christianity, creative self-expression and radical politics, seeking the saint's "all-important value."[79] The antithesis of moral sainthood also loiters on the margins of Manga's life, his hustler friend Mfundo whose hustling presents a form of amorality as absolute as any concrete morality: "I was fascinated by Mfundo: how someone could make a living out of crime; once money was in his hand it did not matter how it got there."[80]

Manga shifts from the Black Consciousness of student radicalism to a form of spiritual searching, moving between different forms of evangelical Christianity, including African Pentecostalism with its openness to claims of spiritual possession and empowerment.[81] "My acceptance of Christianity has required me to get out of my mind, for spirituality is not an exercise of intellect. It's like Paul says: 'These battles are not of the flesh and blood.'"[82] Manga is someone who senses that there is "something in everything,"

Tricksters, Hustlers, and Moral Saints **253**

identifying signs and deeper meanings in the most quotidian of experiences: "The cab driver's name was Paul. Perhaps the message was in the Bible. In my Bible I couldn't find the book of Paul. It could be that I had bought a faulty Bible."[83] Whereas Dingz and his friends speculate about casual racism in interactions with whites, Manga is more likely to consider absolute condemnation or supernatural evil.[84]

This emotional and political turmoil is reminiscent of a passage in Mphahlele's autobiography, *Down Second Avenue*, depicting his years of tertiary education as a period of:

> chronic emotional upsets, so that the more I tried to think things out the faster my spleen seemed to fill up. I woke up at nights in a cold sweat; sat up all night in the dark and tried to remember an unpleasant experience with whites during the day. An eternal dialogue spun around in my mind, in which I imagined in the things I should have said to the white man. [...] My personality was simply a whirlpool of currents and cross-currents of ambition and idealism.[85]

The values of ambition and idealism certainly apply to Manga, but his worldview is also a symptom of spiralling mental illness and certainty-seeking moral sainthood:

> I once read Alice Walker who said dying is like being pressed to pee and not being able to. I understand this. It is about absorbing too much self-righteousness and not being able to release. I have been bitter for most of my life, looking for wrong in the world [...] looking to condemn the world.[86]

Manga accumulates half-remembered quotes, like the ones previously, offering bite-sized values, but not a deep value system. Indeed, the educationalist Jonathan Jansen was critical of Fallist activists searching the radical canon for "fighting words" – fragments of Fanon were favoured – without serious study.[87]

Whereas Mphahlele's ambitions and idealism targeted the oppressive racial system and the pressing need to earn a living to support himself and his family, Manga is emblematic of radical middle-class black youth who are bereft of not only a "signature literature," as Jansen argued,[88] but of a unifying worldview in the absence of apartheid. A form of moral insecurity is therefore locatable among contemporary moral saints, and arguably constitutive of contemporary moral sainthood. Manga is certain of the significance of life's miseries, but unable to settle on values to make sense of life amidst an array of contradictory ideas, and in the absence of any community of practice or authority other than his anomic self.[89] This is of course emblematic of the

254 Ibrahim Abraham

post-apartheid condition wherein race is relevant, but not wholly determinative, and politics is pertinent, but not the most obvious way to address individual problems; prosperity-focused religion or the amoral material self-help of the hustler are common, too. It is hard to be a moral saint in the post-apartheid city, therefore, when assertiveness cannot eclipse uncertainty.

Conclusion

Focusing on black university students and graduates, active and aspirational individuals, this chapter has sketched a threefold typology of subjectivities locatable in black South African literature: tricksters, hustlers, and moral saints. Focusing on Mhlongo's *Dog Eat Dog* and *After Tears*, and Mahlangu's *Penumbra*, certain continuities were demonstrated with the earlier apartheid-era literature of Mphahlele and Ndebele, in spite of the fact that the tricksters and moral saints of the apartheid era were able to set themselves in unifying opposition against the apartheid system. Certain continuities were also demonstrated between the fictional lives of the protagonists and the lives of their creators, Mhlongo and Mahlangu, who also experienced difficulties at university and frustrations in their professional creative lives, as well as continuities with the lives of Fallist activists who campaigned on many of the issues referenced in the novels. Placing these novels in the *bildungsroman* genre, it was shown that post-apartheid society reflects the social uncertainty that makes the genre valuable, as the novels' protagonists come-of-age into communities in which commonalities born of shared oppression are no longer apparent, and in which race remains relevant but not predictive. As the novels conclude, Dingz, Bafana and Manga have not found settled places for themselves in their unsettled society in which individuals appear to hold ever less in common. South African writers' desires to connect with communities is increasingly challenging in this fragmenting culture, but this chapter has suggested that the semi-autobiographical struggles of young individuals, drifting through social spaces as strangers and exploring unsettled subjectivities, reflects post-apartheid reality.

Notes

1 In South African discourse, "white" refers to those of exclusively European ancestry and Levantines who litigated their way to whiteness, while "black" encompasses the subcategories "African" (or "Black African"), "Indian" and "Coloured." This chapter focuses on Black African experiences.
2 Njabulo S. Ndebele, *South African Literature and Culture: Rediscovery of the Ordinary* (Manchester: Manchester University Press, 1994).
3 Songeziwe Mahlangu, *Penumbra* (Cape Town: Kwela, 2013); Niq Mhlongo, *Dog Eat Dog* (Cape Town: Kwela, 2006); Niq Mhlongo, *After Tears* (Cape Town: Kwela, 2010).

Tricksters, Hustlers, and Moral Saints 255

4 Aijaz Ahmad, "Jameson's Rhetoric of Otherness and the 'National Allegory,'" *Social Text* 17 (1987): 3–25.
5 Michael Chapman, "Literature Struggles: To Belong in South Africa?" *Matatu* 50.2 (2018): 238.
6 David Lodge, *The Campus Trilogy* (London: Vintage, 2011).
7 Sarah Nuttall, *Entanglement: Literary and Cultural Reflections on Post-Apartheid* (Johannesburg: Wits University Press, 2009): 164.
8 Franco Moretti, *The Way of the World: The Bildungsroman in European Culture*, new ed. (London: Verso, 2000): 3–4.
9 Christopher Warnes, "Welcome to Msawawa: The Post-Apartheid Township in Niq Mhlongo's Novels of Deception," *Journal of Postcolonial Writing* 47.5 (2011): 548–557.
10 Jonathan Jansen, *As by Fire: The End of the South African University* (Cape Town: Tafelberg, 2017): 79.
11 Chapman, "Literature Struggles," 238.
12 Ndebele, *South African Literature and Culture*, 49.
13 Ndebele, *South African Literature and Culture*, 49.
14 Chapman, "Literature Struggles," 242.
15 André Brink, "Post-Apartheid Literature: A Personal View," in *J.M. Coetzee in Context and Theory*, edited by Elleke Boehmer, Katy Iddiols and Robert Eaglestone (London: Continuum, 2009): 12.
16 J.M. Coetzee, *Disgrace* (London: Secker and Warburg, 1999): 89; André Brink, *The Rights of Desire* (London: Secker and Warburg, 2000): 100.
17 Miki Flockemann, "Little Perpetrators, Witness-Bearers and the Young and the Brave: Towards a Post-Transitional Aesthetics," *English Studies in Africa* 53.1 (2010): 21–34.
18 Christopher Heywood, *A History of South African Literature* (Cambridge: Cambridge University Press, 2004): 218–219.
19 André Brink, "Articulating the Inarticulate – an Interview with André Brink," in *Trauma, Memory, and Narrative in South Africa: Interviews*, edited by Ewald Mengel, Michela Borzaga and Karin Orantes (Amsterdam: Rodopi, 2010): 16.
20 Mhlongo, *Dog Eat Dog*, 167.
21 Lily Saint, *Black Cultural Life in South Africa: Reception, Apartheid, and Ethics* (Ann Arbor: University of Michigan Press, 2018): 115–117.
22 Niq Mhlongo, *Way Back Home* (Cape Town: Kwela, 2013): 135.
23 Jennifer Malec, " 'I'm not Philosophical, I'm Just a Writer' – Niq Mhlongo Tells it Like it is at Time of the Writer," *Books Live*, 19 March 2016.
24 Songeziwe Mahlangu, "I've Become Emboldened and do not Give a Shit Anymore," *Johannesburg Review of Books*, 15 January 2018, https://johannesburgreviewofbooks.com/2018/01/15/conversation-issue-ive-become-emboldened-and-do-not-give-a-shit-anymore-award-winning-author-of-penumbra-songeziwe-mahlangu-talks-to-mbali-sikakana/.
25 Mahlangu, *Penumbra*, 65–66.
26 Mahlangu, "I've Become Emboldened."
27 Mahlangu, *Penumbra*, 132.
28 Mahlangu, "I've Become Emboldened"; Niq Mhlongo, "Hardly Working under the Apricot Tree in Harare," *Johannesburg Review of Books*, 7May2018,https://johannesburgreviewofbooks.com/2018/05/07/city-editor-hardly-working-under-the-apricot-tree-in-harare-niq-mhlongo-reports-back-from-his-joint-book-tour-with-zukiswa-wanner/.
29 Zakes Mda, *Black Diamond* (Johannesburg: Penguin, 2009): 1.
30 Warnes, "Welcome to Msawawa," 549–550.
31 Mhlongo, *Dog Eat Dog*, 8–10, 101.

256 Ibrahim Abraham

32 Moretti, *The Way of the World*, 4.
33 Gillian Godsell and Rekgotsofetse Chikane, "The Roots of the Revolution," in *Fees Must Fall: Student Revolt, Decolonisation and Governance in South Africa*, edited by Susan Booysen (Johannesburg: Wits University Press, 2016): 69.
34 Jansen, *As by Fire*, 57.
35 Stephanie Rudwick, "Language Politics at Stellenbosch University, South Africa," in *Interests and Power in Language Management*, edited by Marek Nekula, Tamah Sherman and Halina Zawiszová (Berlin: Peter Lang): 101–122.
36 Godsell and Chikane, "The Roots of the Revolution," 60–68.
37 Mhlongo, *Dog Eat Dog*, 60–65, 75–76.
38 Lis Lange, "20 Years of Higher Education Curriculum Policy in South Africa," *Journal of Education* 68 (2017): 49.
39 Gillian Godsell, Refiloe Lepere, Swankie Mafoko and Ayabonga Nase, "Documenting the Revolution," in *Fees Must Fall: Student Revolt, Decolonisation and Governance in South Africa*, edited by Susan Booysen (Johannesburg: Wits University Press, 2016): 117.
40 Mhlongo, *Dog Eat Dog*, 8.
41 Warnes, "Welcome to Msawawa."
42 Moretti, *The Way of the World*, xi.
43 Mhlongo, *Dog Eat Dog*, 245–247.
44 Mhlongo, *Dog Eat Dog*, 248.
45 Mhlongo, *Dog Eat Dog*, 188–191.
46 Es'kia Mphahele, "Mrs Plum," in *The Unbroken Song* (Johannesburg: Ravan Press, 1981 [1967]): 216–261.
47 Lisa Isaacs, "Uproar over UCT Concession to Miss Test for Rocking the Daisies," *Cape Times*, 29 September 2017, www.iol.co.za/capetimes/news/uproar-over-uct-concession-to-miss-test-for-rocking-the-daisies-11397717.
48 Rebecca Fasselt, "Versatile Kinship: Trans-African Family Formations and Postcolonial Disillusionment in Niq Mhlongo's *After Tears*," *Social Dynamics* 43.3 (2017): 477.
49 John Roberts, *From Trickster to Badman: The Black Folk Hero in Slavery and Freedom* (Philadelphia: University of Pennsylvania Press, 1990): 22–23, 37.
50 Mhlongo, *After Tears*, 219–221.
51 Es'kia Mphahlele, "Grieg on a Stolen Piano," in *The Unbroken* Song (Johannesburg: Ravan Press, 1981 [1967]): 171–196.
52 Mphahlele, "Grieg on a Stolen Piano," 178–179.
53 Mphahlele, "Grieg on a Stolen Piano," 194–195.
54 Mhlongo, *Dog Eat Dog*, 196; Es'kia Mphahlele, *Africa My Music: An Autobiography, 1957–1983* (Johannesburg: Ravan Press, 1984).
55 Mhlongo, *Dog Eat Dog*, 251.
56 Tatiana Thieme, "The Hustle Economy: Informality, Uncertainty and the Geographies of Getting By," *Progress in Human Geography* 42.4 (2018): 529–548.
57 Trevor Noah, *Born a Crime: Stories from a South African Childhood* (New York: Spiegel and Grau, 2016).
58 Jairo Muniva, "The Army of 'Unemployed' Young People," *Young* 18.3 (2010): 331.
59 Noah, *Born a Crime*, 148.
60 Mhlongo, *Dog Eat Dog*, 22, 248.
61 Mhlongo, *After Tears*, 59.
62 Mhlongo, *After Tears*, 55–56.
63 Mahlangu, *Penumbra*, 187.
64 Mahlangu, *Penumbra*, 65, 68, 135.
65 Ibrahim Abraham, *Race, Class and Christianity in South Africa: Middle-Class Moralities* (London: Routledge, 2021).
66 Susan Wolf, "Moral Saints," *The Journal of Philosophy* 79.8 (1982): 419–439.

67 Wolf, "Moral Saints," 419–420.
68 Wolf, "Moral Saints," 424, 431.
69 Njabulo S. Ndebele, "Fools," in *Fools and Other Stories* (Harlow: Longman, 1985): 152–278.
70 Wolf, "Moral Saints," 428.
71 Ndebele, "Fools," 177.
72 Ndebele, "Fools," 196.
73 Sara Ahmed, *Willful Subjects* (Durham: Duke University Press, 2014).
74 Joonji Mdyogolo, "The Language of Identity Politics," *City Press*, 26 March 2017, www.news24.com/news24/columnists/guestcolumn/the-language-of-identity-politics-20170324.
75 Mhlongo, *Dog Eat Dog*, 167.
76 Carl A. Grant, "A Better Multicultural Society: Woke Citizenship and Multicultural Activism," *Multicultural Education Review* 10.4 (2018): 327–331.
77 J.S. Smit, "Wake up to What Woke Is," *Mail & Guardian*, 15 June 2018, https://mg.co.za/article/2018-06-15-00-wake-up-to-what-woke-is/.
78 Chapman, "Literature Struggles," 238.
79 Wolf, "Moral Saints," 431.
80 Mahlangu, *Penumbra*, 36.
81 Abraham, *Race, Class and Christianity in South Africa*.
82 Mahlangu, *Penumbra*, 53.
83 Mahlangu, *Penumbra*, 171, 173.
84 Mhlongo, *Dog Eat Dog*, 170; Mahlangu, *Penumbra*, 11–12.
85 Es'kia Mphahlele, *Down Second Avenue* (Johannesburg: Picador Africa, 2004 [1959]): 139.
86 Mahlangu, *Penumbra*, 17.
87 Jansen, *As by Fire*, 79.
88 Jansen, *As by Fire*, 79.
89 Abraham, *Race, Class and Christianity in South Africa*, 53–72.

Bibliography

Abraham, Ibrahim. *Race, Class and Christianity in South Africa: Middle-Class Moralities*. London: Routledge, 2021.
Ahmad, Aijaz. "Jameson's Rhetoric of Otherness and the 'National Allegory.'" *Social Text* 17 (1987): 3–25.
Ahmed, Sara. *Willful Subjects*. Durham: Duke University Press, 2014.
Brink, André. "Articulating the Inarticulate – an Interview with André Brink." In *Trauma, Memory, and Narrative in South Africa: Interviews*, edited by Ewald Mengel, Michela Borzaga and Karin Orantes. Amsterdam: Rodopi, 2010: 3–18.
———. "Post-Apartheid Literature: A Personal View." In *J.M. Coetzee in Context and Theory*, edited by Elleke Boehmer, Katy Iddiols and Robert Eaglestone. London: Continuum, 2009: 11–19.
———. *The Rights of Desire*. London: Secker and Warburg, 2000.
Chapman, Michael. "Literature Struggles: To Belong in South Africa?" *Matatu* 50.2 (2018): 237–257.
Coetzee, J.M. *Disgrace*. London: Secker & Warburg, 1999.
Fasselt, Rebecca. "Versatile Kinship: Trans-African Family Formations and Postcolonial Disillusionment in Niq Mhlongo's *After Tears*." *Social Dynamics* 43.3 (2017): 470–486.
Flockemann, Miki. "Little Perpetrators, Witness-Bearers and the Young and the Brave: Towards a Post-Transitional Aesthetics." *English Studies in Africa* 53.1 (2010): 21–34.

Godsell, Gillian, Refiloe Lepere, Swankie Mafoko and Ayabonga Nase. "Documenting the Revolution." In *Fees Must Fall: Student Revolt, Decolonisation and Governance in South Africa*, edited by Susan Booysen. Johannesburg: Wits University Press, 2016: 101–124.

Godsell, Gillian and Rekgotsofetse Chikane. "The Roots of the Revolution." In *Fees Must Fall: Student Revolt, Decolonisation and Governance in South Africa*, edited by Susan Booysen. Johannesburg: Wits University Press, 2016: 54–73.

Grant, Carl A. "A Better Multicultural Society: Woke Citizenship and Multicultural Activism." *Multicultural Education Review* 10.4 (2018): 327–333.

Heywood, Christopher. *A History of South African Literature*. Cambridge: Cambridge University Press, 2004.

Isaacs, Lisa. "Uproar over UCT Concession to Miss Test for Rocking the Daisies." *Cape Times*, 29 September 2017. www.iol.co.za/capetimes/news/uproar-over-uct-concession-to-miss-test-for-rocking-the-daisies-11397717 (last accessed 25 April 2024).

Jansen, Jonathan. *As by Fire: The End of the South African University*. Cape Town: Tafelberg, 2017.

Lange, Lis. "20 Years of Higher Education Curriculum Policy in South Africa." *Journal of Education* 68 (2017): 31–57.

Lodge, David. *The Campus Trilogy*. London: Vintage, 2011.

Mahlangu, Songeziwe. "I've Become Emboldened and do not give a Shit Anymore." *Johannesburg Review of Books*, 15 January 2018. https://johannesburgreviewofbooks.com/2018/01/15/conversation-issue-ive-become-emboldened-and-do-not-give-a-shit-anymore-award-winning-author-of-penumbra-songeziwe-mahlangu-talks-to-mbali-sikakana/ (last accessed 25 April 2024).

———. *Penumbra*. Cape Town: Kwela, 2013.

Malec, Jennifer. "'I'm not Philosophical, I'm Just a Writer' – Niq Mhlongo Tells it Like it is at Time of the Writer." *Books Live*, 19 March 2016.

Mda, Zakes. *Black Diamond*. Johannesburg: Penguin, 2009.

Mdyogolo, Joonji. "The Language of Identity Politics." *City Press*, 26 March 2017. www.news24.com/news24/columnists/guestcolumn/the-language-of-identity-politics-20170324 (last accessed 25 April 2024).

Mhlongo, Niq. *After Tears*. Cape Town: Kwela, 2010.

———. *Dog Eat Dog*. Cape Town: Kwela, 2006.

———. "Hardly Working Under the Apricot Tree in Harare." *Johannesburg Review of Books*, 7 May 2018. https://johannesburgreviewofbooks.com/2018/05/07/city-editor-hardly-working-under-the-apricot-tree-in-harare-niq-mhlongo-reports-back-from-his-joint-book-tour-with-zukiswa-wanner/ (last accessed 25 April 2024).

———. *Way Back Home*. Cape Town: Kwela, 2013.

Moretti, Franco. *The Way of the World: The Bildungsroman in European Culture*, new ed. London: Verso, 2000.

Mphahlele, Es'kia. *Africa My Music: An Autobiography, 1957–1983*. Johannesburg: Ravan Press, 1984.

———. *Down Second Avenue*. Johannesburg: Picador, 2004 [1959].

———. "Grieg on a Stolen Piano." In *The Unbroken Song*. Johannesburg: Ravan Press, 1981 [1967]: 171–196.

———. "Mrs Plum." In *The Unbroken Song*. Johannesburg: Ravan Press, 1981 [1967]: 216–261.

Muniva, Jairo. "The Army of 'Unemployed' Young People." *Young* 18.3 (2010): 321–338.

Ndebele, Njabulo S. "Fools." In *Fools and Other Stories*. Harlow: Longman, 1985: 152–278.

———. *South African Literature and Culture: Rediscovery of the Ordinary*. Manchester: Manchester University Press, 1994.

Noah, Trevor. *Born a Crime: Stories from a South African Childhood*. New York: Spiegel and Grau, 2016.

Nuttall, Sarah. *Entanglement: Literary and Cultural Reflections on Post-Apartheid*. Johannesburg: Wits University Press, 2009.

Roberts, John. *From Trickster to Badman: The Black Folk Hero in Slavery and Freedom*. Philadelphia: University of Pennsylvania Press, 1990.

Rudwick, Stephanie. "Language Politics at Stellenbosch University, South Africa." In *Interests and Power in Language Management*, edited by Marek Nekula, Tamah Sherman and Halina Zawiszová. Berlin: Peter Lang, 2022: 101–122.

Saint, Lily. *Black Cultural Life in South Africa: Reception, Apartheid, and Ethics*. Ann Arbor: University of Michigan Press, 2018.

Smit, J. S. "Wake Up to What Woke is." *Mail & Guardian*, 15 June 2018. https://mg.co.za/article/2018-06-15-00-wake-up-to-what-woke-is/ (last accessed 25 April 2024).

Thieme, Tatiana. "The Hustle Economy: Informality, Uncertainty and the Geographies of Getting By." *Progress in Human Geography* 42.4 (2018): 529–548.

Warnes, Christopher. "Welcome to Msawawa: The Post-Apartheid Township in Niq Mhlongo's Novels of Deception." *Journal of Postcolonial Writing* 47.5 (2011): 546–557.

Wolf, Susan. "Moral Saints." *The Journal of Philosophy* 79.8 (1982): 419–439.

16

SPOKESWOMEN

African Authors' Historical-Fictional Witnessing in the Literary Anglosphere

Annie Gagiano

The central issue in the ongoing literary-theoretical debate focused particularly on works of postcolonial fiction and/or in World Anglophone Studies remains (this chapter contends) the matter of representational authority as it concerns *both* creative fiction *and* critical-theoretical positions addressing the latter. A chapter like the present one is no less subject to this question than any other related writing, and its own assumption of representational authority is indeed open to challenge, but to understand that does not remove the scholarly duty to take up a moral-intellectual interpretative position and to explain how and why it has been taken. The literary-political discursive struggle takes place within the context and against the background of previously established and contemporary accounts and studies of 'non-Western' societies, a majority of which were probably (though clearly not exclusively) written in English and at a time when a probable preponderance of contemporary creative fiction by authors of African origin or with roots in African countries is appearing in English.

The position assumed in this chapter is that Anglophone African novels (broadly speaking) respond to a felt need to decentralise colonial-era and postcolonial outsiders' histories and depictions of African societies. To do so, the novelists need to present the world, by using their access to the literary Anglosphere, with authoritative, detailed and compelling accounts written from African perspectives. Decades ago Trinh T. Minh-ha reminded us to be aware of the "distance" between speaking as "we, the natives" on the one hand and referring to "they, the natives" on the other.[1] Maria Pia Lara correctly insists that "recognition must come first as a struggle over resignifying the spaces of appearance."[2] Rita Felski observes that "literature, like other cultural forms, is thus a key *mechanism* of recognition."[3] In the density,

DOI: 10.4324/9781003464037-21
This chapter has been made available under a CC-BY-NC-ND 4.0 license.

fullness and complexity of their evocations of African characters and societies, authors like Atta, Forna, and Mengiste evoke lives and communities within various and turbulent contexts in ample and subtle representations exhibiting these authors' command of the English language and their skill as verbal artists. Retaining close emotional links with the African countries in which they have roots, these authors use English as a medium sufficiently capacious and adaptable to portray the African experiences, encounters, and settings their novels contain. Their representations can be seen as both caring and critical, and texts like the three discussed subsequently have been referred to as exhibiting "affiliative critique."[4]

Concerning African authors' choice and use of English for their creative endeavours, I invoke what I see as pertinent remarks concerning non-English though European linguistic contexts described by Mikhael Bakhtin and Franz Kafka, respectively. Bakhtin, in his 1936 essay given the (translated) title "Discourse in the Novel,"[5] states that

> language, for the individual consciousness, lies on the borderline between oneself and the other. The word in language is half someone else's. It becomes "one's own" only when the speaker [or writer?] populates it with his own intention, his own accent, when he appropriates the word, adapting it to his own semantic and expressive intention.[6]

This is very useful (despite the androcentric phrasing) when read as applying both to African authors 'entering' the discourse of pre-existing accounts of the African societies and situations they depict, and to the way they evoke African characters' speech in English. In the same essay, Bakhtin notes:

> The novel begins by presuming a verbal and semantic decentering of the ideological world, a certain linguistic homelessness of literary consciousness, which no longer possesses a sacrosanct and unitary linguistic medium for containing ideological thought; it is a consciousness manifesting itself in the midst of social languages that are surrounded by a single [(inter-) national] language, and in the midst of [other] national languages that are surrounded by a single culture (Hellenistic, Christian, Protestant), or by a single cultural-political world.[7]

This passage, too, in my view inadvertently, appears to anticipate the literary-linguistic situation in which authors like the three whose novels are addressed here produce and publish their work in an international English-dominated context. Bakhtin also describes how "there takes place within the novel an ideological translation of another's language, *an overcoming of its otherness*."[8] This evokes the title of the present collection, where English functions within "a world of strangers." Kafka, even earlier

262 Annie Gagiano

(in 1921) referred to the "linguistic impossibilities" presented by the culture within which Jewish German authors like himself had to write, listing "the impossibility of not writing, the impossibility of writing German, the impossibility of writing differently."[9] There are parallels in this wry utterance to the Anglophone linguistic context within which African novelists write; feeling compelled to write of African locations inhabited overwhelmingly by speakers to whom English is not a native tongue, yet wishing to evoke such speakers with authenticity of expression and with authorial integrity.

Yet the importance of writing what could be termed 'corrective' representations of African societies and histories *in English* is unmistakeable, since this is the predominant medium that has been (and sadly, still is) employed in denigratory, condescending and distorting accounts of their lives and deeds. And while the novels appear in the international Anglosphere, it must be recognised that this includes readers who are native to the depicted societies, and that as renditions of contemporary life in these locations and/or of their histories from a predominantly local perspective, the novels matter to and impact upon such readers (albeit a likely minority, given the economic as well as educational constraints prevailing in these areas), in ways distinct from one another and from readers from non-African regions. The issue of whose episteme (among writers as much as literary theorists) is more persuasive, recognisable, complex and "de-othering" is much more important than where novelists reside or by which publishing houses in which countries their works get published. Achieving, at last, acknowledgement of the full human diversity of African experiences and histories remains a difficult task, but is (as the evidence of the best texts prove) a duty and a responsibility an increasing number of African writers in English have assumed. What can be termed 'deep' knowledge of a part of the world (an area and its people) comes from interpreted experience presented from perspectives to be found within such places and in voices (albeit rendered in the English language participants do not speak, or not primarily) that are locally contextualised. These authors enable and enlarge the literary Anglosphere in meaningful ways.

I argue that African authors' choice of English manifests, perhaps even insists upon the presented novelistic accounts being worthy of international attention – and I point out that the latter adjective pertains inclusively to intra-African as well as to non-African parts of the Anglosphere. Novels like the three discussed here are arduously produced, carefully structured African contributions to the worldly store of knowledge and (more importantly) its enlargement, circulation, and interpretation. Such novels contribute to an archive that testifies to locally rooted African forms of knowledge, to moral understanding, aesthetic vision, and social awareness, building self-esteem among African subjects along with lodging appropriate criticism of the political and social ills besetting this vast continent and how these are enabled both locally and by the powerful and enduring presence of the continent's non-African exploiters[10] – for its predators are plentiful and function in intra-African as well as international webs of lucrative co-operation. Allison Mackey has noted "the vast networks of responsibility and complicity that reach far beyond the borders of African nations."[11] Mathis Stock notes that "for a person to be considered as an insider he or she has to have an involved relation to a place."[12] The authors on whose texts this chapter draws are, as insiders to the societies their novels depict while resident outside/elsewhere in the international centres of economic power, particularly well located to recognise the political and broadly capitalist networks within which societies function and/or to identify the historical roles of non-African persons and societies that have had decisive impact on the African sites. Stock's remark can be complemented with a wise observation of Trinh T. Minh-ha's, that "the moment an insider steps out from the inside she's no longer a mere insider. She necessarily looks in from the outside while also looking out from the inside."[13] This, I feel, indicates that African authors entering the literary Anglosphere can be considered as doubly equipped and empowered, rather than weakened and compromised, by their footholds inside and outside African localities and with access to both spheres of opportunity. Because of my personal, but certainly also scholarly conviction of the significance of novels like those addressed in this paper, as well as my admiration of their authors' literary art and integrity as writers in depicting societies from which they and their families originate, I find a number of recent influential critical-theoretical responses to contemporary postcolonial and African texts – responses that cumulatively practise a "hermeneutics of suspicion"[14] towards the texts, their authors, and the latter's choice of publishers – deeply troubling. These responses are distinctly part of the broad frame of international English Studies and represent a specific area in postcolonial academic endeavour, as evaluators (inter alia) of African creative writing.

Recurrently and emphatically, the theorists and critics indicated claim that throughout the process of production of broadly contemporary postcolonial and African novels in English the single most influential consideration is the text's *marketability*, within the margins of which some authorial manoeuvres are said to remain possible. This position reflects clearly in the titles of the pertinent scholars' texts, in nearly every one of which some form of the word "market" appears (see subsequently), as in the texts of the commentaries. The highly influential initiator of what I term this 'school' of postcolonial and African literary analysis is Graham Huggan, whose 2001 book *The Postcolonial Exotic: Marketing the Margins* does qualify the last word of its main title by referring to "strategic exoticism" allowing the novelists, while "working from within exoticist codes of representation," opportunities "to subvert those codes" or at least to "[redeploy] them" for the "purpose of uncovering differential relations of power."[15] *Postcolonial Writers in the Global Literary Marketplace* by Sarah Brouillette followed in 2007; making the point that "any postcolonial industry depends upon the very market-ability of self-consciousness about the production and consumption of what circulates within it."[16] In 2012 Akin Adesokan's article "New African Writing and the Question of Audience" strongly drew (inter alia) on Huggan's and Brouillette's books. Adesokan claimed that African "writers perceive to be the market of their works [...] predominantly the metropolitan West where [...] African otherness (or cultural difference in general) remains a serviceable idea."[17] A 2016 Brouillette article, "World Literature and Market Dynamics," appeared in the collection *Institutions of World Literature: Writing, Translation, Markets*,[18] followed by the 2021 piece named "On the African Literary Hustle," containing her claim that the

> field of contemporary Anglophone literature relies [...] on private donors, mainly but not exclusively American, supporting a transnational coterie of editors, writers, prize judges, event organizers, and workshop instructors. The literary works that arise from this milieu of course tend to be targeted at British and American markets.[19]

My final example is Isaac Ndlovu's 2021 article "Writing and Reading Zimbabwe in the Global Literary Market: A Case of Four Novelists," in which Ndlovu states that the authors to whom he refers (Brian Chikwava, NoViolet Bulawayo, Petina Gappah and Tendai Huchu) "self-consciously depict Zimbabwe in stereotypical terms to secure publishing contracts" in order to "ensure the international marketability of their fiction," adding that "[a]t the same time, they show that they are conceptually decolonized by employing insurrectionary tactics of self-exorcism which register [the writers'] resistance to banal profit-driven portrayals of Zimbabwe."[20] (Binyavanga Wainaina's mocking piece, "How to Write about Africa,"[21] remains well known.)

Concerning marketability, I begin with the reminder that every manuscript presented to a publisher needs to persuade the business that it has that quality – whether it is from Africa or anywhere, and whether fictional or academic. Overemphasising market matters obscures the fact that verbal art and profundity of insight are serious considerations for publishers or readers of fiction. Theorists' and critics' analyses should avoid homogenising African writing and distinguish consistently between superficial and complex, subtle portrayal; whether a novelist, critic or theorist writes with respect for Africans' efforts is a major concern in the continuing battle for anti-racist restitution. Reading words such as "exotic" and references to "exotic codes of representation" in the previous examples of contemporary academic texts, I raise the question of perspective – are the portrayed conditions so rated in these texts not (unfortunately, indeed) everyday realities to Africans like the fictional characters? One person's "margin" is another's centre; the place from which they perceive the world, and depicting African circumstances in detail, even if strange or terrible in the view of 'outside' readers, is as valid and necessary as are portrayals of other settings and conditions. Proclaiming the 'Western' reading market as primarily determining what and how African novelists' write is demeaning to the authors who assume the grave and difficult task of lodging African persons' accounts of local histories and interpretations of conditions and their causes in the international knowledge archive of the world, from which such accounts have been so often excluded – with African verbal art and the power of its implicit, complex analyses still neglected or condemned or the gaps and deficiencies of understanding of African realities and its written representations still going widely unnoticed. 'Readings' of African societies from the perspective of caring, careful insiders need to replace and be allowed to replace skewed and superficial records that 'outsiders' have so abundantly produced. Language is perhaps not in the first place a matter of the medium (with the previous references and what follows restricted to English and to Anglophone texts), but a matter of attitude and affect; conveyed in words *and* in tone as aspects that definitively colour the information conveyed.

Chinua Achebe, in a 2009 essay, acknowledged: "Disaster parades today with impunity through the length and breadth of much of Africa: war, genocide, military and civilian dictatorships, corruption, collapsed economies, poverty, disease, and every ill attendant upon political and social chaos!" But while he said that it was "necessary" for these conditions to be "reported, because evil thrives best in quiet, untidy corners," he also observed how much depended upon "the character and attitude of the correspondent;" on "the presence or absence of respect for the human person."[22] The poet and scholar Michael Jackson notes that "the politics of storytelling [...] involves [...] the question of *whose* story will be told, and *which* story will be recognised as true and given legitimacy."[23] I do endorse Francesca Orsini's recommendation of "approaches that explore the pluralities of space and time, hold together local and wider perspectives, work multilingually, and take in hierarchies of language and literary value, but are not blinded by them," as "both productive for and *appropriate* to the work of world literature,"[24] but do so with the proviso that literary scholars should recognise that (since "world literature" is "[situated] in world history")[25] English necessarily *functions* multilingually both in representing other, local (e.g. African) languages, and offers opportunities of achieving "intermediation" that permits the "translation" of "the strange into the familiar, the far into the near"[26] – as the African novels discussed subsequently seek to do. It seems imperative and overdue for Anglophone academic literary critics and theorists to begin interpretation and response from the assumption that novels by African authors are more probably attempting such 'normalisation' of the local conditions portrayed than 'exoticising' vulgarly to ensure publication.

266 Annie Gagiano

Of course respectful reception needs to be earned by means of writing of high quality. Hence the relevance of Maria Pia Lara's insistence that, in a context of what she terms the "institutionalized languages of disrespect," the attempt to gain "esteem and recognition" for a novel (as well as for those whom it represents) "requires entering into the convoluted, interlarded language of public life with illocutionary force."[27] The latter phrase refers to writing of affective intensity, representational vividness and aesthetic eloquence.[28] It jars to sense alienating complacency and condescension in the utterances of some of the critical commentaries on recent African novels in view both of the difficulty and necessity of producing these narratives, and their unobtrusive aesthetic fineness. In brief comments on three selected novels by women writers of African origin, the rest of this chapter will analyse examples of the insight and verbal art contained in these texts and attempt to disprove the "false consciousness"[29] ascribed (in 2012) to "contemporary African writing," referring to such writing as characterised by "the productive foreignness of a sensibility that is estranged from its own interests."[30] The problem may arise to some extent from failure to consult African writers' own ideas about their fiction and relying on 'Western-facing' literary theories, but chiefly (I believe) from reading imperceptively as a result of prioritising theoretical generalisations.

Although the text was widely noted, initial responses tended to group Sefi Atta's *Everything Good Will Come*[31] with other novels deemed examples of "Third-Generation Women Writers"[32] and of "The New Nigerian Novel."[33] Such generally respectful reception contrasts with Akin Adesokan's condescending-seeming reference to Atta's text in his article, which in turn should be juxtaposed with the serious thematic readings by other Nigerian critics such as Sola Owonibi and Olufunmilayo Gaji, and Kayode Ogunfolabi.[34] Remarks by Atta herself concerning this novel confirm her desire to "portray characters that Nigerians could recognize, not stereotypes that others expect" and a refusal to yield to the "rewards" available "in America for writing under the Western gaze" – as if the author anticipated the criticisms that superficial readings of her work would later produce.[35] Atta was raised by her southern Nigerian Christian Yoruba mother but does not speak the language; they lived in a house overlooking Lagos lagoon, like the family of her main character, when Atta's father, an Igbirra Muslim, died in 1972. She attended boarding schools in Nigeria and the UK, also like Enitan, and has no strong ethnic allegiances; she emphasises her aspiration to "perspective and dimension" in fiction and her recoil from banal, hackneyed notions of 'Africa' foreign to her own experience.[36] In Enitan's boarding school there are Moslem, Catholic, Anglican and Methodist girls, and one Hindu; the girls are Hausa, Yoruba, and Igbo, but speak English "with different accents," mispronouncing names, but this (and the stereotypes flung about) "provided jokes" rather than conflict.[37] Atta deliberately imitates "the flavour and rhythm of the way we speak at home" (i.e. in Nigeria, where conventional English or its Nigerian pidgin version serve as *lingua franca*); as Atta states, "there are different ways of using English."[38] A few brief snatches must suffice to exemplify how deftly Atta demonstrates the ease with which Nigerians communicate across supposed class and culture barriers – when Enitan says "good evening" to her boyfriend's Yoruba landlord, he replies " 'evuh-ning,' rubbing his belly"; a teacher cruelly whipping a child angers Enitan, so she speaks "with an English accent to offend him," knowing that he'll assume "I was trying to be superior"; the firebrand activist-writer who befriends Enitan responds warmly upon hearing that she is pregnant, saying: "*Na wa*, congratulations."[39]

While Nigerians are thought to be 'loud,' and inhabitants of Atta's Lagos ready to comment wittily on anyone and everything, Owonibi and Gaji in their article comment perceptively on the attention the author pays to the different kinds of silence in which some of her characters are immersed or which they invoke. Niyi, Enitan's husband, wields silence like a weapon against her when she defies him to associate herself with anti-government activists. Owonibi and Gaji call the "military era" in which much of Atta's novel is set, "the era of silence"; they say of Enitan's neighbours in "Sunrise Estate" that their lives are "subdued," ruled by "silences [...] to avoid confrontation" with the state that has issued a decree against "speculation" – which is what political criticism and attempts to uncover corruption and tyranny are called.[40] Enitan detests most women's silent submissiveness in accepting her society's patriarchal practices; this, she notices, happens because "women are praised the more they surrender the right to protest," leaving the daughters only the legacy of "selflessness [...] like tears down a parched throat."[41] Enitan herself succumbs to the ruthless smothering of voices in her society and to her initial 'failure' to get pregnant – stating that by her thirties, she had been reduced to "a silent state."[42] As these two critics notice, the deepest silence is Enitan's mother's – a point taken further in Kayode Ogunfolabi's excellent article, in which he analyses that it is "because she speaks in silence and solitude that Enitan is [eventually] able to hear her [mother's] voice."[43] In briefly delineating how issues of silencing and speaking centralise communicability issues structuring the text and tie in with the present collection's focus and the section theme of "revolt, emancipation and transformation," I take the analysis further with the help of Atta's own declaration that hindsight brought her the insight that her novel is "a study of power" evoking "the route Enitan takes towards empowering herself."[44] Atta's task of using a novel in English to demonstrate African intellectual self-analysis and an African verbal artist's ability to craft a work of beauty and insight, making anger and love audible, in its achievement establishes the importance of a text of this kind.

In *Everything Good Will Come*, silencing is the form power takes in both tyrannical political power and familial or social oppression. It takes

268 Annie Gagiano

Enitan years to see, as her mother did, that by indulging Enitan and manoeu-vring her mother into the disciplinarian's role, her father was separating them; making Enitan deaf to her mother. While outspoken in her feminist opinions, she for years fails to 'hear' her father's humiliating smothering of her mother's voice and personality (abandonment, betrayal, and underfund-ing her after they split); that she "doesn't speak" to him *for* silencing her by the things he did; "never saying a word to support" her against his family's pressure and having a secret 'second family.'[45] Similarly, Nigerian "children of the oil boom" studying in the UK (like Enitan) don't respond to news of a military coup, believing "talk of political protest was the talk of mad English people."[46] "I would not let go until I was heard," Enitan declares, but does so as a middle-class feminist.[47] It is when her father's imprison-ment for "advocating a national strike" against detention without trial for the military regime's opponents pushes a fearful Enitan into voicing protest that she begins to hear her society's most unheard voices. Her father's aged gardener, Baba, a former victim of a brutal state eviction, nonplussed by the ending of democratic rule, stammers hesitantly: " 'It's as if they hate us.' "[48] But it is only when she is detained overnight in a stinking, overcrowded cell with "the sick and the mad with their sores and ringworm and tuberculosis" that Enitan learns the full extent of female subjugation and silencing in the rawest and most compelling section of this text.[49] The cell bully who names herself "Mother of Prisons" was separated from her children and thrown out of home by her in-laws when her husband died – later she became a victim of rape, jailed for six years for killing her attacker in the act but never given a hearing. Bildungsroman is not the appropriate label for *this* kind of learning through listening – for the character *and* the reader.

Enitan's life-changing experiences – her father's imprisonment, her hus-band's refusal to 'allow' her to campaign for his release, her mother's death from expired medication, her daughter's birth, being jailed and encountering women who remain there – endow her at last with the courage to speak out against the brutal regime on behalf of political detainees and to "advocate for women prisoners."[50] If she does not find her voice she might die, still silent; to speak out is to "revive" herself.[51] It is this that Enitan celebrates in her roadside song and dance at the novel's end, along with her father's release. Enitan's witnessing accords with Atta's; as Grace Ameh testifies: " 'writing is activism.' "[52]

Aminatta Forna's *Ancestor Stones*[53] was also its author's first novel. Per-haps because Forna's literary status grew so rapidly *after* her subsequent fic-tion appeared, it has not (if enthusiastically reviewed) to date received much critical attention.[54] Forna had a Sierra Leonean father who was executed by the corrupt Siaka Stevens regime.[55] She has a Scottish mother, is Lon-don based, and has moved into broadly non-African settings since her third book, but *Ancestor Stones* is very much the product of an African writer and assumes that perspective, with the nominal, London-based protagonist as a scribe to her four aunts, whose stories in concert make up a sort of Sierra Leonean oratorio – with the four stories of each narrator together constituting a familial-national history in chronological instalments. Forna's captivating and vivid gynocentric narratives make the lives of her West African characters fully recognisable by taking us into the many facets, settings, circumstances, and encounters that constitute the difficulties faced and pleasures enjoyed by the women. I suggest that its *not* being trauma focused makes Forna's text another clear example of African fiction that does not yield to any vaunted 'Western' readerly appetite for postcolonial 'trauma porn.' Early in the novel, Forna inserts a sardonic allusion to what is clearly Graham Greene's novel, *The Heart of the Matter*:[56] "I used to read the things written about us" (Sierra Leoneans), says Mariama, noting "one book [...] by a Very Famous Author" who, she says, "lived in our country for a very short time and then he wrote a story that would make sure nobody ever wanted to come here."[57] Abie, after realising that the "story" about "how Europeans discovered us [...] was really about [...] different ways of seeing," with 16th-century Portuguese sailors "blind to the signs" of cultivation as they picked fruit onshore, sees this as proving them lacking in "the African way of seeing."[58] Two pages further, Abie narrates how "as a spectator," she "watched" on television, during the Sierra Leonean '90s Civil War, "screen images of my country bloodied and bruised," realising eventually that "witnessing, from a distance" how her compatriots suffered was unbearable, and that she had to "go to them."[59] Forna in person contrasted "reportage," which "allows us to observe," with literature, through which we can "live with" the characters.[60] The contrast she draws reconfirms a point made previously concerning inaccuracy and injustice in critics imputing a spectacularising perspective to Africa's postcolonial novelists – an insulting generalisation, even if qualified. Forna (like Atta and Mengiste) eschews mere "spectacle" to allow the "discovery of complexity" in characters that seem "ordinary and faceless" Africans to outsiders, to cite Njabulo Ndebele.[61]

Abie's aunts have, like women do, kept their "most precious" knowledge "hidden in the safest place of all," which are the "stories" that are "remembered, until they are [...] ready to be heard." So their "guarded" accounts could not be divulged until Abie returned to the aunts in 2003, receptive at last to their revelations. Their tales are encompassing, ranging from the deeply personal to the familial (bearing in mind the extent of the paterfamilias Gibril Kholifa's marital reign), communal, social, and political dimensions of their own and their mothers' experiences over a seventy-three-year span. In an interview, Forna has said that her interest lies in "describing what [a situation] might look like *from elsewhere*," and awareness of this central issue of representational perspective is what is required if one wishes to have access to the wealth of knowledge capital available in African fiction. Forna

270 Annie Gagiano

has often indicated that she wants not only to put into her fiction what she knows but strives to write as a discovering, uncovering process: to "write about what [she] want[s] to understand."[62] Such deeper knowing is accessible to readers, critics, and theorists only by means of empathetic reading practices.

Forna's 'story' of Sierra Leone does not start with European 'discovery' but with the arrival of men on horseback, centuries ago, overland, from the northern Futa Djallon highlands.[63] The composite familial-historical account that constitutes the novel starts with the founding of Rofothane estate by making a clearing in the forest as recounted in the first story, one of Asana's, dated 1926. The title of the novel is derived from one of its saddest stories, told by Mariama, about how her father Gibril, under the influence of Haidera Kontorfili – preaching a fanatically purist form of Islam – deprived her mother Sakie (exiled from her family in the marriage) of her most precious possessions: a collection of small, individually named stones, each of them representing one of her female ancestors, which Sakie had used to commune with those women and for divination. This punishment for 'idolatry' is what drove her mother away, into the forest, and caused her insanity, as Mariama learns from her 'dumb' dearest friend, the 'boy' Bobbio, by means of speechless narration. Chapters three and four also concern aunts' mothers' stories, Hawa's and Serah's, revealing harsh experiences of co-wives' destructive viciousness and envy and of social-marital 'policing' causing accusations of infidelity to a woman nevertheless trapped in a loveless union. Asana's first marriage is another entrapment for a young woman foolishly misled by the initial, superficial attractiveness of a sadist – a situation from which one of her co-wifely fellow captives generously releases her. Mariama like her mother stays true to the ancient gods of her culture; resisting (in her case) the Christian doctrine taught by the Catholic nuns in the convent school where she (like her half-sister Serah) acquires a Western education.

Hawa's second story contains an account of how the African 'resource curse' through a combination of cunning and greed on European (here, British) and African sides strip African lands and people.[64] A brilliant short story, it remains throughout within the perceptive but politically and technologically non-educated perspective of its young female narrator. Serah's second chapter introduces her first (later lost) love, Janneh and initiates this aunt's more overtly national-political perspective. She remarks of the initial pseudo-independent elections in Sierra Leone that the British colonial rulers "gave us the cow but kept hold of the tether" and recognises that, even though she respects Janneh for his passionate idealism, he is naïve, so that "talking to him felt like chasing butterflies."[65] The story of Mariama's breakdown brought on by loneliness and racial ostracism in the coldness she was exposed to while studying in Britain concludes with Serah coming to her rescue – a kindness Mariama returns when her half-sister's marriage to a

Spokeswomen **271**

cynical, unfaithful lawyer, deep in the pockets of the corrupt postcolonial rulers, breaks down. By contrast, Janneh (a journalist) is murdered or (like other dissidents) 'disappeared'; "his empty car, the headlights dying" symbolically represents all political victims of this terrible time in Sierra Leone, "like lights going off all across the city," in one haunting image.[66] Serah will later say that the bloody mayhem of the 90s erupted in their country because "nobody heeded the warnings," blinkered in bubbles of privilege and chosen ignorance. The horror of the war period is not evoked in detail, but its presence haunts the last part of the novel, in which the aunts all acknowledge the extent of local failures and faults in bringing on the disaster. A superb tapestry of vivid narration, *Ancestor Stones* refuses to reduce its multiple layers to cheap thinness for public consumption. Its complex English conveys Sierra Leonean *understood* experience.

In an enlightening essay concerning her writing practice and philosophy, Maaza Mengiste recalls one journalist's taunting question: " 'How does it feel to put another book about African violence into the marketplace?' "[67] Such arrogant, ill-considered complacency requires refutation on two points. First, Michael Jackson's admonitory reminder that "violence must be seen as a product of our humanity, not of some vestigial, instinctual, or repressed animality" but as "tak[ing] place against a backdrop of injustice, humiliation, and marginalization."[68] Second, in Mengiste's own words, "*what if* [post-colonial/African writers] are interested in stories of people struggling to survive war and poverty?"[69] With particular pertinence to *The Shadow King*[70] discussed here, Mengiste – who left Ethiopia at age four with her family during the Ethiopian Revolution – has emphasised the task of "artists and scholars to record and memorialize what has slipped away."[71] This second novel evokes an earlier Ethiopian war: the guerrilla resistance to the second Italian invasion of 1935–1941 and subsequent temporary claimed colonisation by the vastly larger and better equipped Fascist army (assisted by a mass of *ascari* or African mercenaries from surrounding countries), which notoriously used mustard gas-spraying aeroplanes to subdue the local population. Mengiste's novel is remarkable for evoking the deep class and gender fissures of Ethiopian society *predating* the war; for its unsparing yet also lyrical writing that focuses simultaneously on war's horrific ugliness and the exhausting heroism of those fighting in and contributing to a just cause. Italy has been slow to acknowledge its colonial past, and Mengiste is conscious of the need to " 'talk about the brutalities [...] people had to endure under occupation [...] the racial segregation, etc.'," adding: " 'there's a lot there still to unearth.' "[72]

Mengiste's novel opens in 1974 with Hirut, her central character as a young woman, sitting, middle-aged, at the Addis Ababa train station, awaiting the Jewish-Italian photographer Ettore Navarra; the *ferenj* who nearly forty years ago took humiliating photos of her and the many, many Ethiopians his commander, Fucelli, ordered flung to fall to their deaths without trial

272 Annie Gagiano

or court martial – atrocities he wanted recorded as heroic achievements. On her lap Hirut holds the box containing letters, photos, and newspaper clippings reporting the war, which Ettore entrusted to her safekeeping as he fled the final defeat of the occupying force. These documentary traces represent the reductive Italian view of the occupation and those resisting it; a distorting, false history that still fills Hirut with fury. She will refuse to shake the hand Ettore (now forced to flee Addis as the Revolution erupts) extends to her – instead saluting to insist on maintaining her role as patriotic Ethiopian soldier and telling Ettore in a whisper, " '*Vatene* [...] You're not welcome in this place.'"[73] Speaking, years before the publication of her second novel, of the wrongness of staring at photos of the "humiliation, pain, degradation, and suffering of people of color with dispassionate eyes," Mengiste emphasises the need "to complicate our understanding of what we are looking at."[74] Especially admirable about the way Mengiste does just that is that, juxtapositioned with Italian cruelty and Ethiopian bravery, she shows us instances of humanity on the Italian side and of cruel violence by Ethiopian men and women, and does so *even as* she evokes the entangled feelings and histories of oppression that erupt in such vicious violence.

The brutal class cleavages in pre-war Ethiopia are registered in the words of Hirut's fellow servant in the aristocratic household of Kidane and Aster, by choice only ever known as the cook, who tells her: " 'My father was killed by those people who came to steal us away to work in rich houses. I saw it.'"[75] It is there, too, in Aster's greeting to the newly orphaned girl, Hirut, as she "dragged the long nail of her little finger across Hirut's cheeks: You are less than the dirt in my nail."[76] Jealously observing how naturally Hirut and the brave fighter Aklilu (his cousin's son) relate, Kidane sneers: "They are simple people, tillers of land. They hold nothing dear except what is directly in front of them."[77] But it is in the sexual exploitation of 'lowly' women that class disdain takes its ugliest form as it is maintained over generations. Hirut's mother was so abused by Kidane's father; she will be raped by Kidane in his role as her commander and acts with a complex emotional background in Kidane's own fears, shame, and anguish under the burdens of this time and his strained marriage. Mengiste makes brilliant use of an object, the outdated Wujigra (a rifle) that is confiscated from Hirut by Aster and Kidane early in the narrative. Only near the end do we learn that this used to be Aster's gun and that she gave it to Hirut's mother to defend herself against Kidane's father – explaining Hirut's memory of her mother pointing a gun at a strange man at whose feet her father lay pleading. This confiscated gun is later given to one of the best Ethiopian snipers, young Dawit, but it fails and he is himself shot. Anguished by his own failure to have tested it first, Kidane makes Hirut's retrieval of the gun, her only heirloom, from the cave where Dawit lies dying, the excuse for his first rape of her. But after "the blackest night of [her] life,"[78] Kidane's second and most brutal assault, one of the novel's tenderest moments shows Aklilu bringing Hirut a blanket, food, and the gun; this restorative, gentle ministering is the opposite of the ugly mimicry in Kidane's nauseating "Little One, let's go" as he summons the "quaking" girl to rape.[79] "Wujigra," she will later say to Ettore, attempting to 'befriend' the (then) imprisoned Hirut, "because it contains the full range of the disgust that she feels for him."[80] At the novel's end, we learn that Hirut still polishes the old gun (now with five notches) every day: memory embodied.

Mengiste's account eschews mere partisan harshness; she includes contextual humanising detail in portraying Ettore's familial history and even concerning the childhood of arrogant, vicious Fucelli, as she does concerning the tribulations and terrors faced by Kidane. War's sheer grimness is indelibly, even viscerally felt throughout the narrative. Hirut's witnessing of the shot Ethiopian boy soldier Beniam's death from mustard gas poisoning haunts her, for she had to flee the dying youth, "trying foolishly to stand on legs that hang as so sloppily from the hipbone" and telling her his name – the memory she pretends to have forgotten.[81] By contrast, the photos taken of individually described Ethiopians that Ettore takes before and even while they fall to their deaths below the mountain precipice, are named "An Album of the Dead," and he himself is called an "archivist of obscenities."[82] Contrasted with desecration of this kind is the anguishing compassion of Hirut's un-erasable glimpse of "an inconsolable mother pressing a dead hand against her womb" as the body of the young fighter hanged by Fucelli is brought back to the Ethiopian camp. From the safety of his foreign exile, Emperor Haile Selassie orders Kidane and other men to continue fighting the Italians even after the Europeans' declared victory – warfare Kidane and many others know they cannot survive. But it is the demoralising hollow created by their country's revered leader's absence that leads to Hirut's brilliant discovery of the near-identity in appearance between Selassie and a shy musician among them, a man named Minim. As figurehead, dressed up like the emperor and groomed to bear himself regally, guarded by a uniformed Hirut (and Aster, who mustered Ethiopian women to battle from the start), the masquerade re-inspires the disheartened people and brings about eventual, bloodily hard-won victory for the Ethiopians. Both Fucelli and Kidane are struck down in the final battle before they are executed in righteous vengeance – Fucelli by a father whose son he had hanged and Kidane (secretly) by Hirut.

Heroism takes different forms, Mengiste shows, not all of it in battle – the woman Fifi, who is really Faven, riskily living with Fucelli as his Ethiopian lover, spies for her people and saves many lives; she tells the Italian: "We are older than this Roman culture you're so proud of."[83] Moments of kindness and self-sacrifice offset the grimness of the wartime narrative; not only Aklilu's defiance of Kidane's possessive lust in his tender care for Hirut, but the cook's volunteering to be the concubine of a French gun trader – so stepping

274 Annie Gagiano

in for Hirut whom the man wants in exchange for badly needed guns – later on preparing tranquillising herbs she secretly gives to the doomed Ethiopian captives who are soon to be flung to death, urging them: "do not give them your fear" and "do not beg."[84] There is heroism, too, in Fifi's public encouragement to Hirut in the very presence of an already distrustful Fucelli (who forces his mistress and the cook to observe his humiliating exhibition of Hirut to the Italian soldiers and *ascaris*) as Fifi steps courageously forward, saluting the young captive in the stance of an Ethiopian soldier – rallying Hirut to salute in return.[85] Even Ibrahim, proud *ascari* leader under Fucelli, orders his men not to shoot Ethiopian children; later on he facilitates the rescue of Aster and Hirut from Fucelli's camp – incurring a near-fatal beating.[86] When Hirut expresses her realisation, at the end of the narrative, that the "shadow king" that stood in for the absent emperor was not only Minim, his impersonator, but a composite of those who together held up the Ethiopian standard, her honour roll of heroism foregrounds the women warriors (like Mengiste's own grandmother) – for in "the story of war [...] women have been there, we are here now."[87] In the gravitas of her text, Mengiste achieves that "terrible beauty" that W.B. Yeats ascribed to another war elsewhere.[88]

To evoke African lives with the compelling authority and profound respect that authors like Atta, Forna, and Mengiste do in the three novels discussed previously requires their deep connectedness to the places that and the people whom they evoke. The novels are *original* in the fullest sense of that term: coming from where whatever is evoked, originated; unprecedented and non-derivative; productive of further creation. To see this is to see the writers' contribution to the difficult struggle that Fanon termed "do[ing] battle for the creation of a human world – that is, a world of reciprocal recognitions."[89]

Notes

1 Trinh T. Minh-ha, *Woman, Native, Other: Writing Postcoloniality and Feminism* (Bloomington and Indianapolis: Indiana University Press, 1989): 52.
2 Maria Pia Lara, *Moral Textures: Feminist Narratives in the Public Sphere* (Berkeley: University of California Press, 1998): 143.
3 Rita Felski, "Recognizing Class," *New Literary History* 52.1 (2021): 103 (original emphasis).
4 Annie Gagiano, "Women Writing Nationhood Differently: Affiliative Critique in Novels by Forna, Atta and Farah," *Ariel: A Review of International English Literature* 44.1 (2013): 1–27.
5 M. M. Bakhtin, "Discourse in the Novel," in *The Dialogic Imagination: Four Essays*, edited by Michael Holquist (Austin: University of Texas Press, 1981): 259–422.
6 Bakhtin, "Discourse in the Novel," 293 [insertion added].
7 Bakhtin, "Discourse in the Novel," 367, containing two editorial insertions, to the first of which I added "(inter-)" to fit it to my context.
8 Bakhtin, "Discourse in the Novel," 365, italics added.

9 Franz Kafka, in *The Basic Kafka*, reissue ed., edited by Erich Heller (New York: Pocket Books, 1984): 292.
10 Cf. Annie Gagiano, "Book-Keeping in Africa," in *Mapping Africa in the English-Speaking World*," edited by Kemmonye Collete Monyaka, Owen S. Seda, Sibonile Edith Ellece and John McAllister (London: Cambridge Scholars Publishing, 2010): 43–68.
11 Allison Mackey, "Troubling Humanitarian Consumption: Reframing Relationality in African Child Soldier Narratives," *Research in African Literatures* 44.4 (2013): 117.
12 Mathis Stock, "Classics in Human Geography Revisited," *Progress in Human Geography* 24.4 (2000): 616.
13 Trinh T. Minh-ha, "'Not You/Like You': Postcolonial Women and the Interlocking Questions of Identity and Difference," in *Dangerous Liaisons: Gender, Nation, and Postcolonial Perspectives*, edited by Anne McClintock, Aamir Mufti and Ella Shohat (Minneapolis: University Press, 1998): 418.
14 G D Robinson, "Paul Ricoeur and the Hermeneutics of Suspicion: A Brief Overview and Critique," *Premise* 2.9 (1995): 12.
15 Graham Huggan, *The Postcolonial Exotic: Marketing the Margins* (London and New York: Routledge, 2001): 32 [elisions and adaptations added].
16 Sarah Brouillette, *Postcolonial Writers in the Global Literary Marketplace* (New York: Palgrave, 2007): 7.
17 Akin Adesokan, "New African Writing and the Question of Audience," *Research in African Literatures* 43.3 (2012): 15.
18 Sarah Brouillette, "World Literature and Market Dynamics," in *Institutions of World Literature: Writing, Translation, Markets*, edited by Stefan Helgesson and Pieter Vermeulen (New York: Routledge, 2016): 93–106.
19 Sarah Brouillette, "On the African Literary Hustle," *Blind Field: A Journal of Cultural Inquiry*, 5 September 2017, https://blindfieldjournal.com/2017/0 8/14on-th-african-literary-hustle/.
20 Isaac Ndlovu, "Writing and Reading Zimbabwe in the Global Literary Market: A Case of Four Novelists," *Journal of Postcolonial Writing* 57.1 (2021): 106.
21 Binyavanga Wainaina, "How to Write about Africa," *Granta* 92 (2005): 92–95.
22 Chinua Achebe, "Africa's Tarnished Name," in *The Education of a British-Protected Child*, edited by Chinua Achebe (Harmondsworth: Penguin Classics, 2009): 93.
23 Michael Jackson, *The Politics of Storytelling: Variations on a Theme by Hannah Arendt* (Copenhagen: Museum Tusculanum Press, 2013): 133.
24 Francesca Orsini, "The Mutilingual Local in World Literature," *Comparative Literature* 67.4 (2015): 351 (original emphasis).
25 Shu-mei Shih, "World Studies and Relational Comparison," *PMLA* 130.2 (2015): 437.
26 Boaventura de Sousa Santos, *The End of the Cognitive Empire: The Coming of the Epistemologies of the South* (Durham and London: Duke University Press, 2018): 79.
27 Lara, *Moral Textures*, 136.
28 Writing with "illocutionary force ... has the 'disclosive' ability to envision normatively," Lara states (6).
29 Friedrich Engels, "Letter to F. Mehring," in *Karl Marx and Friedrich Engels: Selected Works Vol. II* (Moscow: Foreign Languages Publishing House, 1949): 451.
30 Adesokan, "New African Writing," 1.
31 Sefi Atta, *Everything Good Will Come*, 2nd ed. (Cape Town: Double Storey, 2006 [2004]).
32 Jane Bryce, "'Half-and-Half Children': Third-Generation Women Writers and the New Nigerian Novel," *Research in African Literatures* 39.2 (2008): 49–67.

276 Annie Gagiano

33 Ogaga Okuyade, "Weaving Memories of Childhood: The New Nigerian Novel and the Genre of *Bildungsroman*," *Ariel* 41.3–4 (2010): 137–165.

34 Akin Adesokan, "New African Writing," 4; Sola Owonibi and Olufun Milayo Gaji, "Identity and the Absent Mother in Sefi Atta's *Everything Good Will Come*," *Tydskrif vir Letterkunde* 54.2 (2017): 112–121; Kayode Ogunfolabi, " 'The Lives of Others': Trauma and Precariousness in Sefi Atta's *Everything Good Will Come*," *Postcolonial Text* 13.4 (2018): 1–14.

35 Sefi Atta, "Something Good Comes to Nigerian Literature," interview by Ike Anya, *African Writer Magazine*, 23 May 2005, www.africanwriter.com/sefi-atta-something-good-comes-to-nigerian-literature.

36 Sefi Atta, "Interview with Sefi Atta," interview by Walter Collins, *English in Africa* 34.2 (2007): 123–131.

37 Atta, *Everything*, 44–45.

38 Atta, "Interview with Sefi Atta," 131.

39 Atta, *Everything*, 109–110, 130, 257.

40 Owonibi and Gaji, "Identity," 118.

41 Atta, *Everything*, 179.

42 Atta, *Everything*, 189.

43 Ogunfolabi, "The Lives," 7 [inserts added].

44 Atta, "Something Good," n.p.

45 Atta, *Everything*, 108, 173.

46 Atta, *Everything*, 77.

47 Atta, *Everything*, 200.

48 Atta, *Everything*, 313–314.

49 Atta, *Everything*, 264–281.

50 Atta, *Everything*, 332.

51 Atta, *Everything*, 333.

52 Atta, *Everything*, 263.

53 Aminatta Forna, *Ancestor Stones* (London: Bloomsbury, 2006).

54 Gagiano, "Affiliative Critique," 1–27 and Yunusy Ng'umbi, "Re-Imagining Family and Gender Roles in Aminatta Forna's *Ancestor Stones*," *Tydskrif vir Letterkunde* 54.2 (2017): 86–99, give prominent placing to this novel, but other critics tend to pass quickly from this to Forna's later writings – e.g. Françoise Lionnet and Jennifer MacGregor, "Aminatta Forna: Truth, Trauma, Memory," in *The Contemporary British Novel Since 2000*, edited by James Acheson (Edinburgh: Edinburgh University Press, 2017): 199–208; placing Forna among British writers.

55 Aminatta Forna, *The Devil that Danced on the Water: A Daughter's Quest* (London: Grove Press, 2003), her first book, describes her investigation into the causes of her father's execution and of her own 'digestion' of these painful and horrifying facts.

56 Graham Greene, *The Heart of the Matter* (London: Heinemann, 1948).

57 Forna, *Ancestor Stones*, 35 (cf. "tales of cannibals and juju," 300).

58 Forna, *Ancestor Stones*, 6.

59 Forna, *Ancestor Stones*, 8–9.

60 Aminatta Forna, "Secrets and Lies," *BBC Podcast*, 28 June 2013, bbc.com/culture/article/20130628-aminatta-forna-secrets-and-lies.

61 Njabulo Ndebele, *South African Literature and Culture: Rediscovery of the Ordinary* (Manchester: Manchester University Press, 1994): 52, 53.

62 Aminatta Forna, "The View from Elsewhere," interview by Parsinnen, *World Literature Today* 93.3 (2019): 24–27 (emphasis added): 25; and Aminatta Forna, cited in Lionnet and MacGregor, "Truth," 200.

63 Forna, *Ancestor Stones*, 5.

64 Cf. Jon Schubert, ed., *Extractive Industries and Changing State Dynamics in Africa: Beyond the Resource Curse* (New York: Routledge, 2018).
65 Forna, *Ancestor Stones*, 170–171.
66 Forna, *Ancestor Stones*, 233.
67 Maaza Mengiste, "Creative Writing as Translation," *Callaloo* 35.4 (2012): 940. The remark pertains to her first novel, *Beneath the Lion's Gaze* (New York: Vintage, 2010); its evocation of revolution and tyranny.
68 Jackson, *Politics of Storytelling*, 135.
69 Mengiste, "Creative," 941.
70 Maaza Mengiste, *The Shadow King* (New York: W.W. Norton, 2019).
71 Maaza Mengiste, "A New 'Tizita,'" *Callaloo* 34.3 (2011): 854.
72 Maaza Mengiste, "Maaza Mengiste and Nadifa Mohamed," interview by Shringarpure, *Warscapes*, 29 January 2012, www.warscapes.com/conversations,maaza -mengiste-nadifa-mohamed.
73 Mengiste, *Shadow King*, 422.
74 Mengiste, "Creative Writing," 939.
75 Mengiste, *Shadow King*, 21.
76 Mengiste, *Shadow King*, 70.
77 Mengiste, *Shadow King*, 179.
78 Mengiste, *Shadow King*, 184.
79 Mengiste, *Shadow King*, 187.
80 Mengiste, *Shadow King*, 366.
81 Mengiste, *Shadow King*, 160–162.
82 Mengiste, *Shadow King*, 284; 291.
83 Mengiste, *Shadow King*, 331.
84 Mengiste, *Shadow King*, 104–108, 289.
85 Mengiste, *Shadow King*, 350.
86 Mengiste, *Shadow King*, 109, 382–385.
87 Mengiste, *Shadow King*, 423; n.p. "Author's Note."
88 W. B. Yeats, "Easter 1916," in *Collected Poems* (London: Macmillan, 1933): 202–205.
89 Frantz Fanon, *Black Skin, White Masks* (St Albans: Paladin, 1970): 155.

Bibliography

Achebe, Chinua. *The Education of a British-Protected Child: Essays*. Harmondsworth: Penguin Classics, 2009.

Adesokan, Akin. "New African Writing and the Question of Audience." *Research in African Literatures* 43.3 (2012): 1–12.

Atta, Sefi. *Everything Good Will Come*, 1st ed. Cape Town: Double Storey, 2006 [2004].

———. "Interview with Sefi Atta." Interview by Walter Collins. *English in Africa* 34.2 (2007): 123–131.

———. "Something Good Comes to Nigerian Literature." Interview by Ike Anya. *African Writer Magazine*, 23 May 2005. www.africanwriter.com/sefi-atta-something-good-comes-to-nigerian-literature (last accessed 20 April 2024).

Bakhtin, M. M. "Discourse in the Novel." In *The Dialogic Imagination: Four Essays*, edited by Michael Holquist. Austin: University of Texas Press, 1981: 259–422.

Bryce, Jane. "'Half-and-Half Children': Third-Generation Women Writers and the New Nigerian Novel." *Research in African Literatures* 39.2 (2008): 49–67.

Brouillette, Sarah. "On the African Literary Hustle." *Blind Field: A Journal of Cultural Inquiry*, 5 September 2017. https://blindfieldjournal.com/2017/08/14/on-the-african-literary-hustle/ (last accessed 20 April 2024).

278 Annie Gagiano

———. *Postcolonial Writers in the Global Literary Marketplace*. New York: Palgrave, 2007.

———. "World Literature and Market Dynamics." In *Institutions of World Literature: Writing, Translation, Markets*, edited by Stefan Helgesson and Pieter Vermeulen. New York: Routledge, 2016: 93–106.

Engels, Friedrich. "Letter to F. Mehring." In *Karl Marx and Friedrich Engels: Selected Works in Two Volumes, Vol. II*. Moscow: Foreign Languages Publishing House, 1949: 451.

Fanon, Frantz. *Black Skin, White Masks*. St Albans, Hertfordshire: Paladin, 1970.

Felski, Rita. "Recognizing Class." *New Literary History* 52.1 (2021): 95–117.

Forna, Aminatta. *Ancestor Stones*. London: Bloomsbury, 2006.

———. *The Devil that Danced on the Water: A Daughter's Quest*. London: Grove Press, 2003.

———. "Secrets and Lies." *BBC Podcast*, 28 June 2013. bbc.com/culture/article/201 30628-aminatta-forna-secrets-and-lies (last accessed 20 April 2024).

———. "The View from Elsewhere." Interview by Keija Parsinnen. *World Literature Today* 93.3 (2019): 24–27.

Gagiano, Annie. "Book-Keeping in Africa." In *Mapping Africa in the English-Speaking World*, edited by Kemmonye Collete Monyaka, Owen S. Seda, Sibonile Edith Ellece and John McAllister. London: Cambridge Scholars Publishing, 2010: 43–68.

———. "Women Writing Nationhood Differently: Affiliative Critique in Novels by Forna, Atta, and Farah." *Ariel: A Review of International English Literature* 44.1 (2013): 45–72.

Greene, Graham. *The Heart of the Matter*. London: Heinemann, 1948.

Huggan, Graham. *The Postcolonial Exotic: Marketing the Margins*. New York: Routledge, 2001.

Jackson, Michael. *The Politics of Storytelling: Variations on a Theme by Hannah Arendt*. Copenhagen: Museum Tusculanum Press, 2014.

Kafka, Franz. *The Basic Kafka*, Reissue ed., edited by Erich Heller. New York: Pocket Books, 1984.

Lara, Maria Pia. *Moral Textures: Feminist Narratives in the Public Sphere*. Los Angeles and London: University of California Press, 1998.

Lionnet, Françoise and Jennifer MacGregor. "Aminatta Forna: Truth, Trauma, Memory." In *The Contemporary British Novel Since 2000*, edited by James Acheson. Edinburgh: Edinburgh University Press, 2017: 199–208.

Mackey, Allison. "Troubling Humanitarian Consumption: Reframing Relationality in African Child Soldier Narratives." *Research in African Literatures* 44.4 (2013): 99–122.

Mengiste, Maaza. *Beneath the Lion's Gaze*. New York: Vintage, 2019.

———. "Creative Writing as Translation." *Callaloo* 35.4 (2012): 939–942.

———. "Maaza Mengiste and Nadifa Mohamed." Interview by Bhakti Shringarpure. *Warscapes*, 29 January 2012. www.warscapes.com/conversations/maaza-mengiste-nadifa-mohamed (last accessed 20 April 2024).

———. "A New 'Tizita.'" *Callaloo* 34.3 (2011): 853–854.

———. *The Shadow King*. London: W.W. Norton, 2019.

Minh-ha, Trinh T. "Not You/Like You: Postcolonial Women and the Interlocking Questions of Identity and Difference." In *Dangerous Liaisons: Gender, Nation and Postcolonial Perspectives*, edited by Anne McClintock, Aamir Mufti and Ella Shohat. Minneapolis: University of Minnesota Press, 1997: 415–419.

———. *Woman, Native, Other: Writing Postcoloniality and Feminism*. Bloomington and Indianapolis: Indiana University Press, 1989.

Ndlovu, Isaac. "Writing and Reading Zimbabwe in the Global Literary Market: A Case of Four Novels." *Journal of Postcolonial Writing* 57.1 (2021): 106–120.

Ndebele, Njabulo. *South African Literature and Culture: Rediscovery of the Ordinary*. Manchester: Manchester University Press, 1994.

Ng'umbi, Yunusy Castory. "Re-imagining Family and Gender Roles in Aminatta Forna's *Ancestor Stones*." *Tydskrif vir Letterkunde* 54.2 (2017): 86–99.

Ogunfolabi, Kayode Omoniyi. "'The Lives of Others': Trauma and Precariousness in Sefi Atta's *Everything Good Will Come*." *Postcolonial Text* 13.4 (2018): 1–15.

Okuyade, Ogaga. "Weaving Memories of Childhood: The New Nigerian Novel and the Genre of *Bildungsroman*." *Ariel* 41.3–4 (2010): 137–165.

Orsini, Francesca. "The Multilingual Local in World Literature." *Comparative Literature* 67.4 (2015): 345–374.

Owonibi, Sola and Olofunmilayo Gaji. "Identity and the Absent Mother in Sefi Atta's *Everything Good Will Come*." *Tydskrif vir Letterkunde* 54.2 (2017): 112–121.

Robinson, G. D. "Paul Ricoeur and the Hermeneutics of Suspicion: A Brief Overview and Critique." *Premise* 2.9 (1995): 12–20.

Santos, Boaventura de Sousa. *The End of the Cognitive Empire: The Coming of Age of Epistemologies of the South*. Durham and London: Duke University Press, 2018.

Schubert, Jon. *Extractive Industries and Changing State Dynamics in Africa: Beyond the Resource Curse*. New York: Routledge, 2018.

Shih, Shu-mei. "World Studies and Relational Comparison." *PMLA* 130.2 (2015): 430–438.

Stock, Mathis. "Classics in Human Geography Revisited." *Progress in Human Geography* 24.4 (2000): 613–619.

Wainaina, Binyavinga. "How to Write about Africa." *Granta* 92 (2005): 92–95.

Yeats, W. B. "Easter 1916." In *The Collected Poems of W.B. Yeats*. London: Macmillan, 1933: 202–205.

17

TOWARD A "MOST SUBTLE AND FLUENT SELF"

Indigenous Englishes and the Pursuit of Self-Sovereignty in *The Translation of Dr. Apelles*

Vanessa Evans

Introduction

David Treuer's (Leech Lake Ojibwe) *The Translation of Dr. Apelles* begins with a "Translator's Introduction" that states: "I was looking for a book. A very particular book in a vast and wonderful library. I found what I was looking for."[1] Shoved within this book are the loose pages of another text, written in a language the Translator does not understand. Finding someone who could "make sense of those words," the Translator listens "as [they] sp[eak] the story out loud."[2] Eventually, the Translator tries to "render that story into English and into a language, an idiom that, God willing, can be translated into other languages as easily as we shed one set of clothes only to don another. [They] have also tried to paint a portrait of the body underneath those clothes that is beautiful even in its smallest part and that will be beautiful no matter what language it wears."[3] Emergent here is the novel's central extended metaphor: that of the text as a body that can not only be read but can be translated as easily as people change their clothes. The novel itself proceeds to mirror, albeit suggestively, the book found by the Translator, containing two separate oscillating metafictional narratives: (1) the story of Native American translator Dr. Apelles, his work at the Research Collections and Preservation (Consortium) known as RECAP, his developing relationship with fellow employee Campaspe Bello, and his bimonthly Fridays spent in an archive translating a text written in an Indigenous language only he can speak, and (2) the story readers are led to believe is being translated by Apelles: a pastoral romantic satire of two Ojibwe foundlings, Bimaadiz and Eta, who grow up and fall in love on Ojibwe lands in the early 19th century.[4] As the parallel narratives develop,

DOI: 10.4324/9781003464037-22
This chapter has been made available under a CC-BY-NC-ND 4.0 license.

the meaning of the word translation becomes steadily more ambiguous, at one moment figurative, at another literal, and oftentimes both. Readers of *Translation* work to decipher which of these two stories is Dr. Apelles's translation, which is the translation of Dr. Apelles, and who amidst all of this is the novel's translator.

When readers meet Apelles in the early pages of *Translation* he is working in an archive and has discovered "a document that only he can translate" (23). In this moment he realizes "he has never been in love" and that there is "a connection between the translation and love" (24). This revelation bonds Apelles to the translation, affirming the presence of the novel's core metaphor and deepening its meaning by comparing the process of translation to that of falling in love. Here, Apelles is forced to reckon with the reality that he "has no reader for his heart. And he never has" (25). Like the translation, Apelles is unread and untranslated, fearful of being mistranslated and misread: "it is one thing to translate a thing, and something else completely to have that thing read. It is one thing to love someone, and something else entirely to be loved in return" (27). For Apelles as a Native American man, translation is complicated not only by his native language of Anishinaabemowin not being widely spoken, but by his subject position. In more ways than one, Apelles is written in a language that only he can understand, making falling in love appear as an impossible act of translation.

As a Native American, Apelles is reluctant to be read by others, "to give up that *sovereign part of himself*," because he is always already "measured against the stories that were told about Indians by those who did not know Indians" (204–5, emph. add.). Apelles's trepidation extends from the deficiency narratives about Native Americans told by the Eurowestern imaginary. These narratives locate Indigenous Peoples "in a state of constant lack," through "colonial reduction[s]" that originate in the long historical tendency to interpret Indigenous cultural expression as sociological or anthropological artifact, as clues to a bygone "primitive" past with no referent in the "advanced" civilizations of the present.[5] Deficiency narratives are just one of the ways that Indigenous Peoples have been "bathed in a vat of cognitive imperialism" that enforces assimilation to perpetuate a settler future.[6] Apelles contemplates these very stories when he considers the risks of finding a lover who might misread him.

This chapter is specifically concerned with the assumption, and colonial reduction, that in speaking English Indigenous Peoples are complicit in their own erasure because English cannot be an Indigenous language. This reduction places the blame for Indigenous cultural 'disappearance' on Indigenous Peoples, ignoring and eliding the settler 'civilizing' process whereby Indigenous languages were violently eroded by government-sanctioned cultural genocide. Discussions around the politics of English as an Indigenous language often slip dangerously into arguments about authenticity – code

282 Vanessa Evans

for the view that English is not *for* contemporary Indigenous Peoples. This perspective occludes the reality that the very language used in processes of oppression can be taken back and reimagined as a means of strengthening Indigenous cultures. As this chapter will underscore, English belongs to Indigenous Peoples, too, indigenized by centuries of use in longstanding efforts of self-determination and sovereignty.

Self-Sovereignty

For Apelles, the threat to that "sovereign part of himself" is a risk that comes with falling in love and being (mis)translated within the English language. Exploring the relationship between what this chapter calls *self*-sovereignty and the English language is therefore central. As a term, sovereignty does the important work of highlighting the complex history of Native American self-determination in what is currently the United States, a history that reaches back long before European arrival. I follow Jace Weaver's (Cherokee) theorization of sovereignty as a form of self-determination that has always already been central to Indigenous ways of life.[7] While scholars such as Gerald Taiaiake Alfred (Kahnawake Mohawk) have taken issue with sovereignty's fraught nature as a Euroamerican concept wielded against Indigenous Peoples, other scholars such as Weaver, Craig Womack (Creek-Cherokee), Robert Warrior (Osage), and Daniel Heath Justice (Cherokee) have taken the term back for their own purposes. In this chapter, self-sovereignty is observed in the *acts* Indigenous Peoples like Apelles undertake to maintain control of their language(s) and their individual bodies.

Writers such as Billy-Ray Belcourt (Cree) and Sherman Alexie (Spokane-Coeur d'Alene) have sought to bring sovereignty into this more intimate and individual setting by aligning it with the self. This chapter is indebted to Belcourt who invokes the term "self-sovereignty" in the epilogue for his collection of poems *This Wound Is a World*, tying it to the body and to the ability to love: "If I know anything now, it is that love is the clumsy name we give to a body spilling outside itself. It is a category we've pieced together to make something like sense or reason out of the body failing to live up to the promise of self-sovereignty."[8] Bodies fail to live up to this promise precisely *because* they love, and that love necessitates a spilling outside of the self. Here, being "unbodied" is "love's first condition of possibility."[9] Belcourt's words are reminiscent of the politics of vulnerability so familiar to conversations about the risks that come with falling in love. According to Belcourt, for queer and/or Indigenous Peoples, love is a complex negotiation that threatens sovereignty at its most individual level. Apelles contends with this very problem as he works to translate a text that only he can read from a language that only he speaks, all while falling in love

Toward a "Most Subtle and Fluent Self" **283**

and risking mistranslation as a body and text "spilling outside" itself. The pursuit and maintenance of self-sovereignty is therefore an ongoing promise to live and maintain control of the body while being vulnerable to the reality that to love means to embrace a lesser state of self-determination. It is my contention that English can help, rather than hinder, this process. To theorize the relationship between English and self-sovereignty, then, I seek to answer two questions Apelles asks himself in the novel: "What language could he use for himself that had not become part of those stories about his people, the sad ones and the funny ones and the ones about the ways and days of the past[?] What could he say that would exist on its own, that represented only him and his life?"[10] By indigenizing the English language and authoring his own reality, Apelles makes English his own and in so doing allows it to be a force of resistance against colonial reductions that enable the mistranslation and misreading that compromise self-sovereignty. Ultimately, *Translation* demonstrates one way that the relationship between English and self-sovereignty can be understood as essential to the contemporary lives of Indigenous Peoples.

Literature Review

Engaging with issues of language and sovereignty situates this chapter in a broader dialogue with the nationalist stream of Indigenous literary criticism. Characterized as tribally specific and affirming of Indigenous methodologies and approaches, Indigenous literary nationalism sees Native American literatures as 'separate and distinct' from other national literatures (American included) and is dedicated to supporting and serving the interests and identities of Native nations with regard to their own separate sovereignties, particularly intellectual sovereignty.[11] Literary nationalism operates with "a pluralist separatism [...] splitting the earth, not dividing up turf."[12]

In many ways, this literary nationalism was inaugurated by Simon Ortiz (Acoma Pueblo) in "Towards a National Indian Literature: Cultural Authenticity in Nationalism."[13] In the article, Ortiz tells the story of an Acqumeh ceremony that has become blended with Catholic Christian rituals because of the history of Spanish colonialism in the region. These originally Spanish rituals, brought to the Southwest in the 16th century, are no longer Spanish because of the creative development applied to them by local Native Peoples. For Ortiz, "Native American or Indian literature is evidence of this in the very same way" (8). Indigenous Peoples bring meaning and meaningfulness to aspects of colonial culture as a way to survive colonization by protecting "the indigenous mind and psyche" (9). Speaking about Indigenous authors writing in English, Ortiz gestures at the colonial reduction present in the belief that those writers have "succumbed" to English and forgotten or been

284 Vanessa Evans

forced to leave behind their Indigenous subjectivity, a reality that is "simply not true" (10). Ortiz puts this plainly:

> it is entirely possible for a people to retain and maintain their lives through the use of any language. There is not a question of authenticity here; rather it is the way that Indian people have creatively responded to forced colonization. And this response has been one of resistance; there is no clearer word for it than resistance.
>
> *(10)*

Ortiz also underscores the indigenization of English as a form of resistance in his Foreword for *American Indian Literary Nationalism*.[14] Written by Weaver, Womack, and Warrior, this book coalesced ideas about literary nationalism, of which language is a key element. For these scholars,

> Ortiz, brilliantly, lays claim to English as an Indian language instead of the omnipresent cliché that Indian people are the victims of English. Claiming English as an Indian language is one of the most important, if not *the* most important step toward insuring Indian survival for future generations.[15]

The belief among Native Americans that they are somehow less Native because they only speak English is an unfortunate symptom of internalized colonialism, of following suit with how Indigenous Peoples are viewed by settlers and the government.[16] Ortiz underscores the importance of resistance through language so that Indigenous Peoples can continue to move forward with strength.

Centering English as an Indigenous language within processes of resistance and cultural affirmation makes explicit the connection between English and sovereignty. Issues pertaining to Indigenous sovereignty also permeate Indigenous literatures in English, suggesting ways forward that affirm Indigenous ways of knowing and being. While discussions around the intersection of sovereignty and the English language have done much work at the communal level, a gap remains for further thinking about how sovereignty functions for the individual. This chapter contributes to bridging this gap by considering the relationship between English and self-sovereignty in *Translation*.

Placing David Treuer within these conversations makes it important to note that when *Translation* and its 'companion piece' *Native American Fiction: A User's Manual* were published,[17] the latter sparked controversy because of its cosmopolitan approach and opposition to literary nationalism.[18] *User's Manual* reignited arguments on what Treuer calls "the terrible twins of identity and authenticity"[19] – key issues at the intersection of Indigenous literary nationalism and cosmopolitanism – while *Translation* was left to languish by comparison. In *User's Manual*, a work of non-fiction, Treuer argues that

Toward a "Most Subtle and Fluent Self" 285

what readers know as Native American literature written in English "does not exist," or, as Matthew L. M. Fletcher (Grand Traverse Band) writes, what does exist is invoked by Native American writers "as a 'memory,' not 'reality,' [...] 'the longing for culture, not its presence.'"[20] Critical responses to *User's Manual* have been varied, with multiple scholars accusing Treuer of taking his argument too far.[21] Critics took issue with what they found to be a brazen disengagement from decades of scholarship attending to the issues Treuer was reflecting upon. *User's Manual* appears to embrace a false binary, that of the aesthetic/ethnographic dichotomy which contemporary criticism has moved beyond, and which suggests Treuer is ignoring the last two decades of scholarship on Native American literature.[22] Concerns relating to aesthetics and identity politics populated debates between nationalist and cosmopolitan criticisms but have more recently shifted into dialogue about the ethics of Indigenous and non-Indigenous methodologies.[23] Those who did appreciate Treuer's approach, however, noted his incisive and controversial argument as a relevant and legitimate form of engagement.[24] Scott Richard Lyons (Ojibwe/Dakota) praised Treuer's ability to "invoke our anxieties regarding the proper place of tribal nations and cultures in a rapidly globalizing world" where the "sexy" selling points of Native American literature obscure its aesthetic value.[25] Daniel Heath Justice suggested that the value in *User's Manual* can more readily be found by embracing its "both/and" potential rather than a much simpler "either/or" paradigm.[26]

As a result of the eclipse caused by this controversy, *Translation* has received relatively little critical attention. The treatments that do exist tend to focus on the novel's affirmation of the "value of love and self-realization for a Native man torn between cultures and understood through stereotypes" and a decoding of the novel's shifting styles and complex intertextuality.[27] Central among critics is the consensus that *Translation* does not reward quick reading, instead putting the reader through a complex series of "metafictional gymnastics."[28] Colleen Eils's work on *Translation* demonstrates how the novel resists the role of the native informant, a central concern of Treuer's, by embracing dissimulation as a mode of resistance.[29] Proving Eils correct, some critics found the novel – particularly the Bimaadiz and Eta section – to be "preposterous," "Disneyesque and Cooperesque," "flirting [...] insistently with bad writing."[30] These critics fail to recognize the text's dissimulating nature, as the absurdity is precisely the point: Bimaadiz and Eta's story is a satirical retelling of Longus's 2nd-century Greek novel *Daphnis and Chloe*. Treuer himself admits that the Bimaadiz and Eta section is a "buyer beware" moment that "loo[ks] like Indian myth" and is therefore seductive to certain "lazy or inattentive readers" who miss out on the "real meaning and real beauty of the book."[31] David Yost and William K. Freiert each advance nuanced close readings of *Translation's* intertexts that attend to the novel's satire.[32] Their readings struggle, however, to fully comprehend how the novel

286 Vanessa Evans

"insists upon its own fictionality."[33] This insistence appears in the breaking of traditional narrative distance in *Translation's* final pages when Apelles reveals himself to have been the author of his own reality all along. My reading of *Translation* is indebted to Eils for her consideration of dissimulation as a form of resistance, a thread that I carry forward as this chapter explores English's role in strengthening negotiations of self-sovereignty that, like dissimulation, resist settler colonial logics of Indigenous erasure and disappearance.

Analysis

Under *Translation's* extended metaphor, Apelles is imagined as an unreadable, untranslatable text, in desperate need of a translator and a reader. Apelles is described as having "no language" of his own, a lack that renders him unable to articulate the "lush foliage of what he already knows – other languages, other landscapes, other stories" (23–24). Ever since leaving his reservation to join the predominantly English-speaking world where very few speak Anishinaabemowin, Apelles has had the sensation that he "was leaving himself behind" (26). Even as a child mourning the death of his younger sister, Apelles could not cry, because "he had no language for his grief. And no way to translate his sorrow" (28). Speaking literally, of course Apelles has *language*, but this imposed lack felt by Apelles results from an internalized colonialism that de-legitimates Indigenous languages just as it renders English an impossible possession. Apelles finds himself in a bind, then, between speaking many languages as a translator, while simultaneously having no language. After all, according to the settler project Indigenous Peoples and their languages are nearly if not already extinct.

These complications have left Apelles without a reader for his heart who can engage in this complex process of recognition with him. Apelles feels suddenly and acutely that "[i]f he were to die [...] he would die as languages do: with no one left in the world to speak him" (52). This realization moves Apelles to risk a breach of his self-sovereignty by making himself vulnerable to love, a difficult task for a man who has kept to himself "in order to survive" (133). He knows that "[a]s an Indian in the world, he was, as far as most were concerned, a little ghost in living colors, with a reality of his own that was written out in the tenses of the remotest past" (133). Apelles's solitary lifestyle has been a method of maintaining self-sovereignty by avoiding stereotyping by non-Indigenous people. Upon discovering the translation, however, Apelles realizes that he "had been forced to hide his most subtle and fluent self. He was tempted now to let that self come out" (133). To do so means perforating the careful borders of self-sovereignty by falling in love, by finding a language with which he can express himself and in which he can be read. It is in Campaspe, an English speaker and Italian-American, that Apelles finds a possible translator and reader.

Toward a "Most Subtle and Fluent Self" **287**

Apelles's attraction to Campaspe had long been simmering, but it is not until an ice storm cancels the train service from RECAP back into the city that the two share conversation over drinks and realize their attraction is mutual. Campaspe asks Apelles where he goes every second Friday. He responds, "'I am a translator of Native American languages. 'Oh!' she cried. 'So *that's* what you are!' 'A translator or an Indian?' 'Both,' she said" (132). This disclosure of Apelles's subjectivity begins the process of letting his "self come out" (33). Sleeping with Campaspe for the first time later that night, Apelles engages in a process of recognition wherein he "sees the translation, the meaning available only to him, vulnerable only to him, in a language belonging only to him. [...] *I've been waiting to read you.* [...] And what a story it is to read" (149, orig. emph.). Campaspe also sees him as a text to be read: "she longed to lift his cover and read him, to bring him home and read him immediately and completely, and, ultimately, to shelve him in her most private and intimate stacks in her warm, cozy, red-hued apartment" (144). This scene further tightens the metaphor of text/translation and body in the novel, suggesting that if the body is a text to be read, then making love is an act of reading. As Campaspe and Apelles read one another "[h]is translation bec[omes] even more *his* translation, and it beg[ins] to include her – all of it held between the soft cover of his sheets" (207).

Apelles starts to face the repercussions of his new vulnerability when he senses the people in his life behaving differently towards him. Intuiting that his coworkers Jesus and Ms Manger are talking about him and Campaspe, Apelles feels that "[t]his [is] a disaster. Dr Apelles was not interested in being interesting. He did not want to be noticed" (211). He feels what any text might feel: "scanned, read, and consumed, and he had no control over how they read him or what they told themselves about him. They could be saying anything. They probably were saying anything" (211). He feels "defenseless" against the surveilling eyes of others because "he had no language for his present self, no Indians do" (211). The past that stalks Native Americans threatens to keep them in some always already anterior temporal realm where the only languages they can speak are those of the past. Apelles's life has always been "in relation to, always in conversation with, always gauged by, what everyone thought they knew about Indians" (211). He reflects on the dark undercurrent of what it means to be read by those around him:

the whole of his adult and very modern world was so strange, so strangely out of his language. The white people haunted him just as he haunted his own past. They excursed into the sanctity of his own self. It was that way for all Indians. Indians were the past that everyone else visited as a way to check on the development of something deep and long dormant.

(215)

Apelles knows that revealing his Native American self to Campaspe and the wider world means that his subjectivity can be recruited into white fantasies of how an Indigenous person should or should not appear. In saying that the "modern world" is "out of his language," Apelles is assigning himself to the anterior realm that "white people haun[t]," that "everyone else visit[s]" when they want to confirm their definitions of modernity. What is "deep and long dormant," then, is the racist belief that Indigenous Peoples are somehow less human and more "savage," that they need to be removed in the name of Western progress. White people, and settlers more broadly, need the concept of the savage to legitimate their continued presence on the land, to rationalize their alleged racial superiority. Apelles knows that his presence as a Native American man, going about his life and living in the contemporary moment, unsettles people and moves them to project their racist assumptions onto him in service of their own narratives of innocence.

Part of these wider assumptions is the belief that Indigenous Peoples cannot make English their own, that it will always belong (under settler logics of ownership) to the colonizer. Apelles has internalized this assumption and feels its impacts acutely, referring to English as his "everyday language" in an attempt to categorize it away from his native languages (35). Only on the two Fridays a month at the archive, or when he "occasionally meets with Indians from his tribe, or other tribes," does he "bring those beautiful languages to the front of his mind" (35). For Apelles, these Indigenous languages "lend themselves to memory" much more easily than English, as "English has no credit, can make no purchase" there (36). He recognizes each of his languages "have different values and those values change according to what he is doing or what he is thinking about, and when he bothers to think about his feelings, there is a kind of linguistic arbitrage that takes place wherein English loses all its value" (36). In finding a reader for his heart in Campaspe, however, Apelles has little choice in the language of his expression. He must fall in love in English and through this process make it his own, make it serve him and his self-sovereignty.

Literally changing the narrative, then, is what allows Apelles to take greater control of his story as the novel's metafictional nature simultaneously places Apelles as the protagonist of the story told by the novel's narrator, and the narrator himself – a revelation that only appears in the final pages. In this way, Apelles is able to try on different language styles in search of an English that feels comfortably his own. As Apelles slowly embraces his feelings for Campaspe, the novel transits "three archetypal Western styles – English, French, and Hemingway-esque."[34] In an early dream sequence, these styles and the events of the novel are foreshadowed as Apelles finds himself in the Stacks at RECAP with the sense that in order to escape, he must sort the texts in front of him. The stress of where to start is overwhelming, until Campaspe appears to tell Apelles that it is more important for him to begin than to

Toward a "Most Subtle and Fluent Self" **289**

worry about which text to choose (75). After making his selection, Apelles is confronted by scene after scene from canonical English language novels, amidst which he begins to glimpse familiar scenes from his past:

> Was that the landscape of his childhood home? Or was it only a copy of the landscapes one finds in books? Dr Apelles couldn't say. [...] What he could see and sense, however, was that each episode has its own tone and style – and thus, a different reality. The dream and the scenes of his early affair with the girl at the round dance hall had something French, something simple-hearted about it, while his boyhood had the hard cast of Hemingway.
>
> *(79)*

This dream "literalizes" Apelles's anxiety over the "mélange of styles" he must transit.[35] As the novel continues to unfold, readers watch Apelles, and the parallel narrative of Bimaadiz and Eta, move through the three archetypal styles in search of one Apelles can call his own. Slowly, he begins to shift his previous position from a translator "standing outside *all* stories, written and lived [...] accustomed to the idea that stories happened to other people, not to him" (25–26, orig. emph.) to an active and sovereign participant in the living and writing of his own story.

Throughout the dream one thing is clear to Apelles: "It seemed to be very important that he find a way to control those styles" (80). As a result, Apelles begins to enact greater control (and thus self-sovereignty) by infusing the western styles with untranslated Anishinaabemowin. When Apelles narrates memories of his childhood – the scenes told with "the hard cast of Hemingway" – several passages appear in Anishinaabemowin (79). For example, young Apelles follows his father and uncle as they help some white hunters retrieve their friend from the tree where he committed suicide. Apelles's uncle speaks in Anishinaabemowin, offering a false translation to the white hunters:

> "Mii geget igo giiwanaadiziwaad chimookomaanag. Gaawiin wiikaa giwii-niisaabiiginaasiinaan," he said.
>
> "What'd you say?" asked the white man with the cigarette. He seemed like a nice man.
>
> "I say it's a long way up there. Long way up." He toed the snow with his boot.
>
> *(190)*

Treuer translates this passage in an email to Yost, revealing the humor hidden in this untranslated moment: "For sure those white people are crazy. You'll never get him down."[36] Moments like this pepper Apelles's memories

290 Vanessa Evans

and offer a contrast to the Bimaadiz and Eta pastoral romance where Anishi-naabemowin is "ornamentaliz[ed]" and made decipherable through the English context.[37] For example, when Bimaadiz and Eta's friend Gitim, whose name means "he is lazy," is introduced, it is immediately mentioned that "Gitim was so lazy."[38] According to Treuer in *User's Manual*, this contrast is a direct critique of one way in which Native American fiction performs the role of the native informant by feeding translations to the reader. For Treuer, "understanding must be earned by the reader," so much so that even with the English language context those who cannot read Anishinaabemowin are not privy to its translation.[39] Apelles's infusion of the text with his native language can be seen as one way of indigenizing English and making it his own. These moments also offer an effective example of Apelles demonstrating how his English can be indigenized. That is, in a way that maintains tribal specificity or, under *Translation's* extended metaphor of body as text to be read, self-sovereignty.

Apelles is described as unsure of how to initiate the processes of translation, of falling in love, but he knows it requires a reader because "[a]ny story, all stories, suppose a reader" (24). Encouraging himself, Apelles reflects: "Stories are meant to be heard and are meant to be read. And translations, no matter what the subject, are like stories in that regard, only more so. Twice the effort has been put into a translated document than has been put into the original" (24). The ideal reader has to be willing to put in the work to avoid misreading Apelles's translation and the translation of Apelles. Campaspe proves to be up to the challenge, approaching both translations with the dedication found in one who is comfortable with vulnerability. Campaspe loves that Apelles "could not be, or seem to be, anything other than Apelles" (143). He is complete unto himself, entirely whole precisely because of his solitary existence and self-sufficiency. To her, he is "like some kind of animal – a badger or a woodchuck or a beaver – who needs nothing else, who need not do anything in particular at all for us to recognize him" (144). The politics of recognition brought to bear on Apelles by Campaspe are complicated by her Euroamerican settler subject position. Campaspe could represent the very thing Apelles fears, someone who will only see him as stereotype, as inauthentic by virtue of his very presence. Instead, she dedicates herself to reading and understanding Apelles and the translation, to seeing beyond the settler imaginary's overdeterminations.

Campaspe's efforts ultimately bring the novel to its climax. Since Apelles does not "feel he can tell her about his present or past life because of the fear of being mistranslated," he talks endlessly about the translation instead, "which is to say that he talks about his life because they are the same thing" (206). But it is not enough, and Campaspe has to take matters into her own hands by stealing the translation. She "reads and rereads" the text "that Sunday. Once. Twice. Three times" (252). Upon bringing the translation to

Toward a "Most Subtle and Fluent Self"   **291**

RECAP so she can return it to Apelles, the translation is stolen by Jesus who, jealous of their love, shoves the translation into a copy of *Daphnis and Chloe* that is shelved "far up the stacks, on a shelf, in a box, in a book, in a place [they] could never find again even if [they] were to try" (308). After all, while RECAP is technically a library, it more readily "resembled a prison" for books (58). It was designed in response to a "surplus of books in the world" for books with no current use that might someday be important (57–58). What should be the terrible loss of the translation is actually the completion of Apelles's translation, as upon being read by Campaspe the text finds its place within the literatures of the world just as Apelles is finding his own place within the English language.

It is no coincidence that a curious breakdown in formal conventions occurs within Apelles's narrative at the very moment when the translation is stolen and shelved at RECAP: Apelles has found a way to make the novel's language – English – his own, and as narrator he is enacting self-sovereignty. This shift is evidenced by: fading capitalization, save for the names of characters and the first-person pronoun "I"; the erasure of quotation marks, indicating that signaling voice is not important because Apelles knows who is speaking, and a turn away from long paragraphs to clear and simple sentences that "could not be, or seem to be, anything other than" what they are (143). Having embraced his omniscience, Apelles also reveals that he has been the narrator all along and that everything from the " 'Translator's Note' forward has been 'make-believe,' not an actual account [or translation] of [Apelles's] life."[40] When Campaspe confesses to losing the translation and to knowing the "translation is really [Apelles's] translation. it is [Apelles's] story," Apelles reassures her that he already knew this would take place (309–310). Campaspe listens to Apelles as he confesses to "know[ing] everyone here better than they know themselves," because he is the author of this reality:

> this all feels like make-believe [...] everyone is going to think you made all this up. I can't believe it's actually happening.
>
>   it is happening, he says, his eyes wild. it *is* happening and what's wrong with make-believe? isn't that how it works: we make belief? besides, happiness is more real than any illusion.
>
> *(312, orig. emph.)*

To find a language for himself, Apelles has had to engage in make-believe whereby he constructs their novel reality to make himself believe in the potential of English as an Indigenous language. Campaspe reflects, "I was wondering why each section sounded so different," to which Apelles replies, "I did not know yet who I was. I had no language for myself" (312). In allowing his body to spill outside itself and risk "failing to live up to the promise of self-sovereignty," Apelles has found a language for himself, a

292 Vanessa Evans

way to mobilize English and protect his self-sovereignty.[41] Apelles "feels free of all earthly weight. All his habits and thoughts and styles, the ponderous words that were so heavy in his mind, have dropped away [...] The rules are different here" (268).

Conclusion

In *This Wound Is a World*, Belcourt reminds readers that while "loneliness is endemic to the affective life of settler colonialism [...] loneliness in fact evinces a new world on the horizon."[42] Apelles glimpses this new world as author of his own reality when he finds a way to make the English language work for him and his self-sovereignty. Apelles chooses to reimagine the potential of English for resistance in alignment with Ortiz's assertion that it is possible for people to maintain their ways of being and knowing in any language.[43] By indigenizing his English and making it his own, Apelles responds to and resists the colonial conditions of his reality.

Notes

1 David Treuer, *The Translation of Dr. Apelles* (New York: Vintage Books, 2008): 1 (orig. emph.).
2 Treuer, *Translation*, 1.
3 Treuer, *Translation*, 1.
4 For the specific distinction between Ojibwe and Anishinaabe, see: Gregory Young-ing, *Elements of Indigenous Style: A Guide for Writing by and about Indigenous Peoples* (Edmonton, Alberta: Brush Publishing, 2018): 70.
5 Daniel Heath Justice, *Why Indigenous Literatures Matter* (Waterloo, Ontario: Wilfrid Laurier University Press, 2018): 2; Gerald Vizenor, *Manifest Manners* (Hanover: University Press of New England, 1994): 72.
6 Leanne Betasamosake Simpson, *Dancing on Our Turtle's Back* (Winnipeg: Arbeiter Ring Publishing, 2013): 32.
7 Jace Weaver, Craig S. Womack and Robert Warrior, *American Indian Literary Nationalism* (Albuquerque: University of New Mexico Press, 2006): 6.
8 Billy-Ray Belcourt, *This Wound is a World* (Calgary, Alberta: Frontenac House Poetry, 2018): 59.
9 Belcourt, *This Wound*, 59.
10 Treuer, *Translation*, 205.
11 Weaver, Womack and Warrior, *Nationalism*, 15.
12 Weaver, Womack and Warrior, *Nationalism*, 74.
13 Simon Ortiz, "Towards a National Indian Literature," *MELUS* 8.2 (1981): 7–12, https://doi.org/10.2307/467143.
14 Simon Ortiz, "Foreword: Speaking-Writing Indigenous Literary Sovereignty," in *American Indian Literary Nationalism*, edited by Jace Weaver, Craig S. Womack and Robert Warrior (Albuquerque: University of New Mexico Press, 2006): vii–xiv.
15 Weaver, Womack and Warrior, *Nationalism*, xviii (orig. emph.).
16 Weaver, Womack and Warrior, *Nationalism*, xii.
17 David Treuer, *Native American Fiction: A User's Manual* (Saint Paul: Graywolf Press, 2006).

18 Virginia Kennedy and David Treuer, "A Conversation with David Treuer," *Studies in American Indian Literatures* 20.2 (2008): 57, www.jstor.org/stable/20739549.
19 Treuer, *User's Manual*, 4.
20 Treuer, *User's Manual*, 195; Matthew L. M. Fletcher, "A Perfect Copy: Indian Culture and Tribal Law," *Yellow Medical Review* 95 (2007): 96.
21 See John D. Kalb, "Review," *Studies in American Indian Literatures* 20.2 (2008): 113–116, www.jstor.org/stable/20739556; Karl Kroeber, "Review: A Turning Point in Native American Fiction?" *Philosophical Review* 8.3 (1995): 63–88, www.jstor.org/stable/20479860; Arnold Krupat, "Culturalism and Its Discontents: David Treuer's 'Native American Fiction: A User's Manual'," *American Indian Quarterly* 33.1 (2009): 131–160, www.jstor.org/stable/25487921; Duane Niatum, "The Fiction of a New Reality," *American Book Review* 28.6 (2007): 25, https://muse.jhu.edu/article/485267; Gerald Vizenor, "Aesthetics of Survivance: Literary Theory and Practice," in *Survivance: Narratives of Native Presence*, edited by Gerald Vizenor (Lincoln, Nebraska: University of Nebraska Press): 1–24.
22 Lisa Tatonetti, "The Both/and of American Indian Literary Studies," *Western American Literature* 44.3 (2009): 278, www.jstor.org/stable/43022745.
23 Christopher Taylor, "North American as Contact Zone," *SAIL* 22.3 (2010): 27, https://doi.org/10.5250/studamerindilite.22.3.0026.
24 William Gillard, "Native American Fiction," *Literary Review* 50.3 (2007): 155–156.
25 Scott Richard Lyons, "Battle of Bookworms," *Indian Country Today*, August 2007, https://indiancountrytoday.com/archive/lyons-battle-of-the-bookworms.
26 Daniel Heath Justice, "Currents of Trans/National Criticism in Indigenous Literary Studies," *American Indian Quarterly* 35.3 (Summer 2011): 350, www.jstor.org/stable/10.5250/amerindiquar.35.3.0334.
27 Colleen Eils, "The Politics of Make-Believe," *SAIL* 26.4 (2014): 39, www.jstor.org/stable/10.5250/studamerindilite.26.4.0039.
28 Eils, "The Politics," 39.
29 Eils, "The Politics," 41.
30 John D. Kalb, "Review," *SAIL* 20.2 (2008): 116, www.jstor.org/stable/20739556; Douglas Robinson, "The Translation of Dr. Apelles," *California Literary Review*, 2020, https://calitreview.com/174/the-translation-of-dr-apelles-a-love-story-by-david-treuer/.
31 Kennedy and Treuer, "Conversation," 58.
32 William K. Freiert, "An Ojibwe Daphnis and Chloe: David Treuer's *The Translation of Dr. Apelles*," *Mediterranean Studies* 21.1 (2013): 57–66; David Yost, "Apelles's War: Transcending Stereotypes of American Indigenous Peoples in David Treuer's *The Translation of Dr. Apelles*," *Studies in American Indian Literatures* 22.2 (2010): 59–74.
33 Eils, "The Politics," 35. Eils's article provides a detailed critique of both Yost and Freiert's readings.
34 Yost, "Apelles's War," 70.
35 Yost, "Apelles's War," 69–70.
36 Yost, "Apelles's War," 63.
37 Yost, "Apelles's War," 64.
38 Yost, "Apelles's War," 63; Treuer, *Translation*, 88.
39 Kennedy and Treuer, "Conversation," 54.
40 Eils, "Politics," 40–41.
41 Belcourt, *Wound*, 59.
42 Belcourt, *Wound*, 59.
43 Ortiz, "Towards a National Indian Literature," 10.

Bibliography

Belcourt, Billy-Ray. *This Wound is a World: Poems*. Calgary, Alberta: Frontenac House Poetry, 2018.

Eils, Colleen G. "The Politics of Make-Believe: Dissimulation and Reciprocity in David Treuer's *The Translation of Dr. Apelles*." *Studies in American Indian Literatures* 26.4 (2014): 39–58.

Fletcher, Matthew L. M. "A Perfect Copy: Indian Culture and Tribal Law." *Yellow Medical Review* 95 (2007): 95–118.

Freiert, William K. "An Ojibwe Daphnis and Chloe: David Treuer's *The Translation of Dr. Apelles*." *Mediterranean Studies* 21.1 (2013): 57–66.

Gillard, William. "Native American Fiction: A User's Manual/The Translation of Dr. Apelles: A Love Story." *Literary Review* 50.3 (2007): 152–156.

Justice, Daniel Heath. "Currents of Trans/National Criticism in Indigenous Literary Studies." *American Indian Quarterly* 35.3 (Summer 2011): 334–352.

———. *Why Indigenous Literatures Matter*. Waterloo, Ontario: Wilfrid Laurier University Press, 2018.

Kalb, John D. "Review." *Studies in American Indian Literatures* 20.2 (2008): 113–116.

Kennedy, Virginia and David Treuer. "A Conversation with David Treuer." *Studies in American Indian Literatures* 20.2 (Summer 2008): 47–63.

Kroeber, Karl. "Review: A Turning Point in Native American Fiction?" *Philosophical Review* 8.3 (1995): 63–88.

Krupat, Arnold. "Culturalism and its Discontents: David Treuer's 'Native American Fiction: A User's Manual.'" *American Indian Quarterly* 33.1 (2009): 131–160.

Lyons, Scott Richard. "Battle of Bookworms." *Indian Country Today*, August 2007. https://indiancountrytoday.com/archive/lyons-battle-of-the-bookworms (last accessed 25 April 2024).

Niatum, Duane. "The Fiction of a New Reality." *American Book Review* 28.6 (2007): 25.

Ortiz, Simon. "Foreword: Speaking-Writing Indigenous Literary Sovereignty." In *American Indian Literary Nationalism*, edited by Jace Weaver, Craig S. Womack and Robert Warrior. Albuquerque: University of New Mexico Press, 2006: vii–xiv.

———. "Towards a National Indian Literature: Cultural Authenticity in Nationalism." *MELUS* 8.2 (1981): 7–12.

Robinson, Douglas. "The Translation of Dr. Apelles: A Love Story-by David Treuer." *California Literary Review*, 2020. https://calitreview.com/174/the-translation-of-dr-apelles-a-love-story-by-david-treuer/ (last accessed 25 April 2024).

Simpson, Leanne Betasamosake. *Dancing on Our Turtle's Back: Stories of Nishnaabeg Re-Creation, Resurgence, and New Emergence*. Winnipeg: Arbeiter Ring Publishing, 2013.

Tatonetti, Lisa. "The Both/and of American Indian Literary Studies." *Western American Literature* 44.3 (2009): 276–288.

Taylor, Christopher. "North American as Contact Zone: Native American Literary Nationalism and the Cross-Cultural Dilemma." *Studies in American Indian Literatures* 22.3 (2010): 26–44.

Treuer, David. *Native American Fiction: A User's Manual*. Saint Paul, Minnesota: Graywolf Press, 2006.

———. *The Translation of Dr. Apelles: A Love Story*. New York: Vintage Books, 2008.

Vizenor, Gerald. *Manifest Manners: Postindian Warriors of Survivance*. Hanover: University Press of New England, 1994.

———. *Survivance: Narratives of Native Presence*. Lincoln: University of Nebraska Press, 2008.

Weaver, Jace, Craig S. Womack and Robert Warrior. *American Indian Literary Nationalism*. Albuquerque: University of New Mexico Press, 2006.

Yost, David. "Apelles's War: Transcending Stereotypes of American Indigenous Peoples in David Treuer's *The Translation of Dr. Apelles*." *Studies in American Indian Literatures* 22.2 (2010): 59–74.

Younging, Gregory. *Elements of Indigenous Style: A Guide for Writing by and about Indigenous Peoples*. Edmonton, Alberta: Brush Publishing, 2018.

INDEX

Note: *Italic* page numbers refer to figures and page numbers followed by "n" denote endnotes

Achebe, Chinua 200, 206–208, 219, 265; *Things Fall Apart* 201
Achino-Loeb, Maria-Luisa 187, 193
Adesokan, Akin 264
aesthetics: dichotomy 285; fineness 266
Africa/African: authors 263; characters and societies 260–261; colonial educational policy 4; communitarianism 247; creative writing 263; cultural nationalists 200; descent 72; Eurocentric stereotypes of 207; fiction 264–265, 269–270; French colonies in 135; intellectual self-analysis 267; linguistic realities in 4–5; literary festivals 247; literature 197–198; novels 265; Pentecostalism 252; realities 265; 'resource curse' 270; situations 261; societies 260–261; stereotypes 197; traditions of verbal poetry 78; Urban Youth Languages 153; writers in English 262
Africa My Music (Mphahlele) 250
Afro-Caribbean cultures 124–125
Afropolitanism 197
After Babel (Steiner) 222
After Tears (Mhlongo) 243, 247, 250–251
Ahmed, Sara 252

Alameddine, Rabih: *An Unnecessary Woman* 91; *The Hakawati* 91
Alexie, Sherman 282
Algeria/Algerian 138–139; colonial languages 135; debates 139; English in 140–141; higher education system 134–135; identity 142; knowledge and events 141–142; languages in 134–135; universities in 139
Al-Maleh, Laila 91
Ambedkar, B. R. 231–232
Ancestor Stones (Forna) 268–269, 271
And Now the Poets Speak (Zimunya and Kadhani) 199
Anglo-American: 'chick-lit formula' 177; literary market 166
Anglophilia 3, 8, 98–99
Anglophobia 3, 98–99
Anglophone 56, 61, 74–75; academic literary critics 265; African novels 260; Arab writings 90–91; audience 105; colonies 9; cultures 3, 89; hegemonic pedagogies of 99; imaginaries 3, 95–96, 98; immigrant fiction 54–55; Indian appropriations of 230; influence on Balkans 106; journalism and academic knowledge 96; literary canon 111; literature 55, 106, 116, 231; media products

99; mediation of 97; metaphors 89; modernities 93; popular culture 98; readers 96–97; studies, conceptualisations of 116; writing 7–8, 27

Anglosphere: international 262; literary 260, 262–263

Angola/Angolan: colonial cultural hierarchy 215; colonial hierarchy 218; independence of 215–217; independentist writers 222; social hierarchy 215–216

Anishinaabemowin language 281, 286, 289–290

anti-apartheid: activism 251; struggle 246; writing 245

Antoon, Sinan 92

apartheid system 248–249; narratives 250; writers 245

Appadurai, Arjun 154

Arab/Arabic: Anglophone context 90; community 91; linguistic traditions 95; nationalism 90

Arab Spring 11, 88–89, 92–93, 97, 100

Ashcroft, Bill 153, 213, 220, 222–223

Atta, Sefi 274; *Everything Good Will Come* 266–268

Attwell, David 52–53

Australia/Australian 24, 52, 104, 108, 111–114, 212, 223

authenticity: arguments about 281–282; of expression 262

Bafana 247–250, 254

Bakhtin, Mikhaïl 138, 154, 157–159; *Rabelais and His World* 154, 261

Bakshi, Sandeep 185, 190

Balkans/Balkanism 105–106, 109–110, 116, 112; Anglophone literature from 105–106; liminal status of 106; stereotypical tropes of 109; Western conception of 109

Bandaranaike, Sirimavo 3

Bantu language 213, 220

Barnes, Juliet 161

Basu, Manisha 169, 172–173

Bauman, Zygmunt 183

Beck, Zeina Hashem 223

Belcourt, Billy-Ray 282; *This Wound Is a World* 292

Belize/Belizean 71, 75, 77; culture 74; discourses 74–75; English in 68, 75, 78; historical ties 76; of Indian descent 76; language situation of 78; sociolinguistic context of 75–76; status of 74

Benjamin, Walter 190–191

Bennett, Louise 7

Bhagat, Chetan 169–173; *Half Girlfriend* 171–172

bildungsroman genre 16, 185, 212–213, 215–216, 247, 268

bilingual/bilingualism 12, 77, 104, 108, 111, 115, 143, 185, 193; French-Arabic 143; silence 111

Billingsgate genres 154–159, 163

Black American English 175

Black Anglophone students 144

Black Rock White City (Patrić) 111–115

Bombay Dost (Kavi) 237

Bonilla, Yarimar 136, 140

bookstalls *170*

Bosnia 12, 104, 108–111

Bourdieu, Pierre 27–28

Brathwaite, Kamau 31

Brink, André 245; *The Rights of Desire* 245

British colonialism 69, 88, 90

Brouillette, Sarah: *Postcolonial Writers in the Global Literary Marketplace* 263–264

Buddhism 232, 234

Bushnell, Candace: *Sex and the City* 166

Butler, Judith 235

Cape Malay Muslims 63

Caribbean: cultures 122; Examination Council 73; tongue 32; women's writings 122, 127

Caribbean Voices BBC radio programme 29–34

Casanova, Pascale 28–30; conceptual framework 30; *The World Republic of Letters* 29

caste-based discrimination 232

Chakrabarty, Dipesh 4, 6, 87

Chapman, Michael 52, 244–245, 252

Charwe 199–201

Chauhan, Anuja 169–170, 172

Cheah, Pheng 63–64; *What Is a World? On Postcolonial Literature as World Literature* 9, 56

chick lit of Global South: aspiration 177–178; de-familiarisation 175–177; description of 166–169; Englishes 175–177; formal transformations

298 Index

177–178; India 169–173; nicknames 175–177; Nigerian 173–175; social mobility 177–178

Chikwava, Brian 198, 264; *Harare North* 201

Chirere, Memory 198, 202

civil disobedience 230, 232

Cliff, Michelle 56

Coetzee, J.M. 52

collective 'genealogy' 248

colonial/colonialism 1, 60; culture, aspects of 283; hierarchies 73

Commonwealth 9, 23–26

communication: problems 112–113, 115–116; theories of 28

consciousness 15, 43, 94, 193, 200, 213, 216, 224

contact zone(s) 1, 9, 17, 89, 104–107, 109–116

Coovadia, Imraan: *High Low In-Between* 52

Cornhill Magazine 229

cosmopolitan/cosmopolitanism 44–46, 54, 56, 153, 284–285

Costa, Suneeta Peres da: *Saudade* 212

creole/creolization 9, 64 n7, 68–77, 137, 217, 220,

Criminal Love? Queer Theory, Culture, and Politics in India (Rao) 235, 238

cross-cultural 26, 60–64, 125, 222

cultural/culture: affirmation 284; difference/differentiation 7–8, 110–111, 217; forms of 78; gravity 26; hegemony 54; identities 123; modernities 6; motifs 213; nationalism 90; reorganization of 55; shocks 110; and society 158–159; standard language 68

Dalits 4, 232–233; literature 231–232; of Maharashtra 232; in Uttar Pradesh 232

Dangor, Achmat 53; *Kafka's Curse* 53, 56–62; material circumstances of 54

Daphnis and Chloe (Longus) 285

Datta, Durjoy 169–170, 173

decolonisation: description of 134–136; discourses of 142; methodology methods and ethics 138–140; relocalisation in practice 140–144; world Englishes 136–138

defamiliarisation 114, 175–177

deficiency narratives 281

de Klerk, F.W. 52

democratic: culture 244; language 107–108; transition 250

Desai, Gaurav 8–9

Dias, Bartholomeu 214–215, 218

digital: literary 8; platforms using Sheng 154; storytelling 8; technologies 166–167

Dimock, Wai Chee 59

discrimination 110; forms of 108; in United States 232

disruptive force 121, 124, 126–128

Dog Eat Dog (Mhlongo) 243–245, 248, 251

doing English 5, 13

dress and ethnicity 217–219

Eastlands 13, 151–152

Ebonystory, Nigerian literary platform 174

Effendi, Abu Bakr 63

Egypt/Egyptian: Anglophone writers from 88; cultural psyche 98; literature in English 87–92; observations about and critiques of 89; political elite and mainstream media 99; service of demystifying 97; social classes 89

Eju'ojo, Joy: *The Reunion* 174–176

emancipation 79, 87, 193, 207, 267

emigration, individual experience of 91

Empson, William 183

English/Englishes 1–2, 115, 143, 152, 173, 244, 289; African authors 261–262; African characters' speech in 261; African writers 262; Arab-speaking world's relationship with 90; Balkan literature in 105; colonial and imperial 3, 9; constructions of 144; context of dominance of 135; discourses and practices of 136; discursive violence of 128; exogenous norms of 75; explanatory frameworks for 136; formal use of 156; forms and functions of 137; founded and unfounded fears about 87; as global language 116; 'global' status of 136; grammatical structures of 152; hypocritical treatment of 2; indigenization of 284; Indigenous authors writing in 283–284; Indigenous Peoples 281; internal norms of 73; international standards of 68; learning 141; literary productions 23–24; literatures 23, 30, 54, 284; mediated technology 143; as medium 261; metropolitan norms of 69–70; national Englishes (*see also* national Englishes); national norms of 70; national varieties of 68, 79; partial knowledge of 186; performance of learners of 152–153; in post-liberalisation India 167; practices of 73; Rasa's tactile use of 95; reading 24; in semiotic landscape 144; Shona language in 198; and sovereignty 284; speaking environment 144; strategic use of 141; symbolic functions of 69; translations from Arabic 90; in world of strangers 6–9; in world of vernaculars 4–6; writing 24, 104

Englishing 11, 67

ethnicity 71, 217–219

Ette, Ottmar 8

European: languages 70, 209n1; linguistic contexts 261; modernist literary print culture 68–69

Everything Good Will Come (Atta) 266–268

Fallism in South Africa 247–248

Fanon, Frantz 253, 274

Faqir, Fadia: *Pillars of Salt* 91; *Willow Trees Don't Weep* 91

Farah, Nuruddin 56, 89

Felski, Rita 219, 260

feminism/feminist 120, 168, 231; articulation of 123; bodies 127–128; Caribbean women's identity 122–123; Cristina García 121; description of 120–121; determination 125–127; *Dreaming in Cuban* and *Sonar en cubano* 124–125; hegemonic 124; literary 120; translation and 123–124

Fielding, Helen: *Bridget Jones's Diary* 166

Finding Mr. Right (Oyinkansola) 174, 176

food 42–46, 67 n24, 156, 198, 205, 298, 213–221

Forna, Aminatta 274; *Ancestor Stones* 268–269, 271; literary status 268–269; story of Sierra Leone 270

Sao Miguel Fort 221

Foucault, Michel 235

Francophone/Francophonie 13, 135–138, 141

francophonie

Freiert, William K. 285–286

French: and Arabic bilingualism 143; colonisation 143; explanatory frameworks for 136; neo-colonialism 135

Gaji, Olofunmilayo 267

Gandhi, Mohandas Karamchand 230, 232; principles in Indian freedom struggle 230; *Sarvodaya* 229

García, Cristina 12; *Dreaming in Cuban* 120–125, 128

gay and lesbian communities 230

gender 230–231. *see also* feminism/feminist; conservatism 169; identities 122, 154; oppression 123–124; relationship between 120

genre fiction 168, 170–171

Ghosh, Amitav 56, 169

Gibbs, James 208

Githiora, Chege 151

Glissant, Éduard 191

global Anglophone 24; analysis of 29; description of 23–25; framework for 25–30; literature 8–9; material and imaginative existence to 25; *Miguel Street* (case study) 30–34

Global South 3; popular cultures of 166; writers in 178

Goa/Goan: ethnic and cultural origins 219; hybrid linguistic community of 219; identity 218

Greene, Graham: *The Heart of the Matter* 269

grotesque humour 156–157

Guillory, John 27–28

Haddad, Saleem: *Guapa* 88, 92

The Hakawati (Alameddine) 91

Halaby, Laila: *Once in a Promised Land* 91

Half Girlfriend (Bhagat) 171–172

Hall, Stuart 122, 213, 218

Hammond, Andrew 106

Harlow, Barbara 52–53

The Heart of the Matter (Greene) 269

hegemonics: feminisms 124; masculinities 154, 162; patriarchal discourses 128; patriarchal literary 120

300 Index

Hemon, Aleksandar 104, 107–111
hermeneutics of suspicion 263
heroism 62, 271, 273–274
heterosexual community 230
Hindi 2, 39, 42, 45–47, 53, 89,
   171–173, 237–239
Hindu/Hinduism 170, 234
Hoffmann, Eva 212, 222
homosexual/homosexuality:
   decriminalising of 240; mania
   236–237; prohibition of 234;
   relations 234
Hong, Cathy Park 184–186, 188,
   191; limited vocabulary 186;
   *Minor Feelings: An Asian American
   Reckoning* 189
Hove, Chenjerai 197–198, 203, 207;
   Ancestors 198–200, 202, 204–205,
   207–208; art in national and global
   context 199–201; *Blind Moon* 199;
   Bones 199–201, 208; narrative
   techniques 201; *Rainbow in the
   Dust* 199; *Red Hills of Home* 199;
   Shonalised English 202; Shona
   lyricism 202; Shonglish 206–208; *Up
   in Arms* 199
Hove, L.M. 199–200
Hybrid/hybridity 5, 9, 54, 56, 89, 91,
   98, 122, 125, 128
Huggan, Graham 264; *The Postcolonial
   Exotic: Marketing the Margins* 263
hustlers 243, 251

Ilaiah, Kancha: *Why I'm Not a
   Hindu* 5–6
imperialism 90, 97, 217, 281
India/Indian 178; Anglophobic
   nationalists of 3; caste-based
   discrimination in 231–232; chick
   lit texts 168; civil disobedience
   230; commercial fiction 168–169;
   community 235; concept of
   transgender 233; ecologies of chick
   lit in 167; economy, liberalisation
   of 170; English-language publishing
   in 169; equivalent terminology 234;
   freedom movement 230; Hindu
   nationalist regime in 2; Indian Penal
   Code 231, 234; literature 170–171;
   post-liberalisation 167, 169; queer
   community in 233; Queer movement
   231, 233; queer writings 236;
   Urdu in 89

indigenization of English 284
indigenous: cultural 'disappearance'
   281; cultural expression 281;
   languages 198, 244, 247, 281–282,
   286, 291; literary 283–285; peoples
   283; subjectivity 283–284
internalized colonialism 284, 286
international literary space 28–29
intersex 231, 233–234

Jackson, Michael 265, 271
Jacobson, Roman 106–107
Jones, Bridget 166

Kachru, Braj 69, 136–137
Kadhani, Mudereri: *And Now the Poets
   Speak* 199
Kafka, Franz 261
Kavi, Ashok Row: *Bombay Dost* 237
Kemal, Yaşar: *Memed, My Hawk* 62
Kenya/Kenyan: articulating transnation
   153–154; commemoration 159;
   contemporary cultural artefacts
   153; cultural celebrations 161;
   geographical border 154; languages
   151; memes on social media in 161;
   Men's Conference *160*, 160–161;
   National Transport and Safety
   Authority 162; popular culture in
   159; public festivities 159; Publishers
   Association in 2006 153; society
   152–153, 158; transformation of
   154; transnation 157–158, 163;
   Valentine's Day 159–160; World
   Rally Championship 161
Kerala, pariah community in 232
Khan, Omar 57, 59, 62; metamorphosis
   60; monologue 60
Kimbundu 212–214, 216, 220–221
Kiswahili 13, 152–154, 156, 158, 163
Kriol 68, 71, 73, 78; community 77;
   culture 74; diglossic relation of
   77; discourses on 75–76; ethnic
   inclusiveness and transnational
   relations 76; L-code 77; popular
   function 75–76

Lady Lolita's Lover (Rao) 236
Landsman, Anne: *The Rowing
   Lesson* 52
language 265, 280, 282–283, 291.
   see also bilingual/bilingualism;
   multilingual/multilingualism;

abundance 188; of aspiration 167–168; change 137; choice 72; of colonial literature 223; of colonizing natives 206; concept of 77; of culture 221; discourses on 67, 69, 79, 138; of emancipation 87–88; ethnographic documentation of 71; excess 189–193; flurry of 187; functions of 106; hierarchies of 172, 178; ideologies 68, 70–71, 261; importance of 114; insufficiency 185; issues of 283; justice 5; levels of 106; metareflections on 111, 114–115; of migration and border-crossing 7; of modernity 137; negotiations of 105–106; oral, vernacular, literary 219–222; performance 74; permanent companion and normal condition 183; policy 153; reorganization of 55; scarcity 184–189, 192; schools 144; of science 137; structures, hierarchy of 4–5; of subjugation 207; transparencies 190–191

Lara, Maria Pia 260, 266

linguistics 7, 69. *see also* language; anthropology 70; arbitrage 288; difference 110–111; divides 172; gender representation 123; heritage 88; impossibilities 261–262; instability 177; modernities 6; nationalism 90; traditions 89–90

literary: analysis 158; culture 8, 221; domination 29; food studies 215–216; modernities 94; nationalism 283–284; production 26–27; strategies 105; studies 69

literature 28. *see also* writings; agentic capabilities of 57; political possibilities of 246; potentialities of 55–56; reorganization of 55; review 283–286; study of 154

Little Dog 184–186, 188, 191–193; conspicuous inaction 187; English falters 187; free associations 192; occasional bouts of impatience 190; transformative command of English 192

Lodge, David 244

Mahabharata 218

Mahlangu, Songeziwe 244–246; *Penumbra* 243–245, 250–251

Makerere Language Debate of 1963 209n1

Makoni, Sinfree 138

Malouf, David 223

Mandela, Nelson 52, 250

Mandelstam, Amina 57–58

Maphoto, Mike 167; *Diary of a Zulu Girl* 167

Marechera, Dambudzo: 200; *House of Hunger* 200; style 200

Marx, Karl 223

Marxism 231

Matar, Hisham: *Anatomy of a Disappearance* 91–92; *In the Country of Men* 91–92; *The Return* 91–92

Mazrui, Alamin 151

McMillan, Terry: *Waiting to Exhale* 166

Mengiste, Maaza 271–272, 274; *The Shadow King* 271

'men who have sex with men' (MSM) 234, 239–240

Merchant, Hoshang 232; *Yaraana: Gay Writing From South Asia* 236

metalanguage 106–107

metamorphosis 57–60, 62

metamultilingual/metamultilingualism: literature of 106–107; mode 107, 111; writing 116

metareflections 107, 111, 114–116

methodological nationalism 69, 79

Mhlongo, Niq 244–246; *After Tears* 243; *Dog Eat Dog* 243–244, 247; narrative 249; post-apartheid protagonists 250; protagonists' trickery 249; *Way Back Home* 246

migrants/migration. discrimination of 113; identities 184, 191–192; literature of 106–108; negotiations of 106; process of 105, 108; texts dealing with 107; in US 187; writing about 107

migrational metamultilingual mode 105, 110, 115–116; Anglophone literature, Balkans 107–108; Balkan spaces and Anglophone literature 105–107; bilingual silence and 108–111; familiar silence and defamiliarisation in exile 111–115; necessitates narration 104–105

Miguel Street (Naipaul) 30–34

Miller, Chris P. 189

Minh-ha, Trinh T. 260, 263

302 Index

The Ministry of Utmost Happiness
(Roy) 233
*Minor Feelings: An Asian American
Reckoning* (Hong) 189, 193
Miyoshi, Mayo 8
Mo, Timothy 56; *Redundancy of
Courage* 1
Modernity/modernities: 6, 70, 88,
93–94, 137,
Modi, Narendra 3, 41, 49 n11, 170
Momanyi, Clara 152–153
monolingual/monolingualism 55,
67, 79, 136; order 70; paradigm
111–112
moral saints 16, 243–245, 250–254
mother tongue(s) 4, 5–6, 7, 70, 88,
184–185, 188, 193, 199, 201,
223, 230
Mphahlele, Es'kia 243; *Africa My Music*
250; ambitions and idealism 253;
Down Second Avenue 253
Mubarak, Hosni 94
Mufti, Aamir R. 55; *Forget English!
Orientalisms and World Literatures* 8
Müller, Max 223
multilingual/multilingualism 58, 108;
cultural configurations 7; in India
167; postcolonial contexts 67;
practices 72, 140–141; setting
70, 78
Mungoshi, Charles 198
Mwangi, Evan 90
Myambo, Melissa Tandiwe
168–169, 178

Nagarkar, Sudeep 169–170
Naipaul, V. S. 29, 33; *The Adventures
of Gurudeva* 31; artistic motives
30; creative departure 32; literary
self-discovery 31; *Miguel Street*
30–34
Nairobi 161; colonial contours of 152;
Eastlands 152; multilingual situation
of 151; urban youth of 152
Namjoshi, Suniti 232
national Englishes: and 'languages'
as Western constructs 69–70;
and non-national language
71–78; non-teleological language
orientations 67–69; reading with
hyperlinked histories 62–63
national/nationalism: languages 5,
72–73, 75; literary 284; readerships 8

Native American: fiction 290;
literature 285; self 287–288;
self-determination 282
*Native American Fiction: A User's
Manual* (Treuer) 284–285
Native Americans 287; belief among
284; deficiency narratives about 281;
languages 287
native speakers 5, 13, 70, 76, 137, 144
nativism 88, 100
Ndebele, Njabulo S. 245, 251, 269
Nehanda, medium of 209n11
neo-colonialism 135, 139
Netflix: description of 38–40; *Little
Things* 45–47; politics of language
and cultural representation in
popular culture and 47–48;
streaming services 40–45
Ng, Adolph 1
Nguyen, Viet Thanh 187–188
Nigeria/Nigerian 178; chick lit
167–168, 173–175; commercial
fiction 168–169
Noah, Trevor 250
Nuttall, Sarah 244

Once in a Promised Land (Halaby) 91
On Earth We're Briefly Gorgeous
(Vuong) 185, 188; Blanks, silences,
stutters 185–189; description
of 183–185; spirals, cycles,
transparencies 189–193
oppression: identical system of 232;
systematic 235
Orientalist/Orientalism 8, 55, 90–91,
96–97, 106
Orsini, Francesca 265
Ortiz, Simon 283–284, 292
Othering/otherness 109, 135,
187, 264
Ottoman imperial legacy 62–63
Ovid: *Metamorphoses* 59–60
Oyinkansola, Olayemi: *Finding Mr.
Right* 174, 176

pan-Arab identity 91
patriarchal/patriarchy 91, 200; cultures
128; demands 122–123; expectations
126; materialisations of 120, 125;
norms and values 124
Patrić, A. S. 107–108, 111; *Black Rock
White City* 104, 111–115
Pennycook, Alastair 138, 141

Penumbra (Mahlangu) 243–246, 250–251
Peres da Costa, Suneeta 212–213, 223
Pessoa, Fernando 221
Phillips, Caryl: *New World Order* 7
pluralism/plurality: of aesthetic expressivity 56; challenges of 53; Englishes 173–175; novel spaces of 55
poems/poetry 205, 282
polycentricity 96
Ponzanesi, Sandra 168
Popescu, Monica 53; *South African Literature Beyond the Cold War* 53
popular culture 13, 41, 45–47, 98, 166
Portuguese: colonial administration 217; imperial monoglossia 220
post-apartheid: literature 243, 245; society 243–244, 254
postcolonial/postcolonialism. 3–4, 8, 23–25, 53–56, 67–71, 88, 104–105, 116, 171, 215–216, 235, 260, 263–264
The Postcolonial Exotic: Marketing the Margins (Huggan) 263
Postcolonial Writers in the Global Literary Marketplace (Brouillette) 263–264
post-liberalisation India 167, 169
power relations 4–5, 28, 109, 179
Pratt, Mary Louise 106
prejudices 109, 112, 207
publishing/publications 25–26, 28, 121, 140, 152, 177, 242, 264–265, 272

queer 230. *see also* sexual/sexuality; sexualities 184, 191–192; theory 231; translations 124

Rabelais, François 154
Rabelais and His World (Bakhtin) 154
Rao, R. Raj 230, 232, 237, 239; *Criminal Love? Queer Theory, Culture, and Politics in India* 235; *Lady Lolita's Lover* 236
recognition, process of 286–287
Redundancy of Courage (Mo) 1–2
Research Collections and Preservation (Consortium) (RECAP) 280
resistance, processes of 284
rhetorical ambiguity 183
The Rights of Desire (Brink) 245
Roman culture 273

romantic love 190
Roy, Arundhati 5–7, 88, 97; *The Ministry of Utmost Happiness* 233
Rushdie, Salman 25–26, 169, 171–173, 219, 222
Ruskin, John 229; dignity of labour and vision 229; *Unto This Last* 229

Safari Rally World Championship 163
Said, Edward 90, 95, 106
Same-Sex Love in India: A Literary History (Vanita and Kidwai) 236, 238
Saro-Wiwa, Ken: *Sozaboy* 201
Sarvodaya (Gandhi) 229, 232–233
Saudade (Costa) 212, 220–221, 223–224
Saussy, Haun 55
Selasie, Taiye 197
self-determination: efforts of 282; form of 282; state of 283
self-sovereignty 282–283, 286, 288, 291–292; borders of 286; pursuit and maintenance of 282–283
Serageldine, Samia: *The Cairo House* 91
Serbian/Serbia 108–115
settler colonialism 69, 292
Sex and the City (Bushnell) 166
sexual/sexuality 57, 126–127, 188, 230–231, 235
The Shadow King (Mengiste) 271
Shakespeare, William 4, 188; *The Tempest* 220
Sheng in Kenyan popular culture 151–152; Billingsgate genres 154–159; critical reception of 152–153; description of 151–152; festival humour in 159–163; institutional stigmatisation of use of 153; transnation 153–154; usage 155
Shona/Shonglish 202, 206–208; of *Ancestors* 201–206; concepts of ancestry, mamhepo 208; criticism of Hove's 206–208; culture 202, 204–205; definition of 198; description of 197–198; to English, translation from 198; forms of life of people 198; history of 199; Hove's art in national and global context 199–201; levels of 198; proverbs and idioms from 204–205; relationships with English 203; society 207; speech patterns 198–199

304 Index

Sierra Leone 268–269
social: categorisation 71; distance 76;
 diversity 72; immobility 168; marital
 policing 270; oppression 267–268;
 reform movements 231–232
social media 167; campaigns 2;
 platforms 154; popularisation of
 166–167
Soñar en cubano 12, 120, 124–125
South African fiction: Anglophone
 World Literary Studies 54–57;
 description of 52–54; *Kafka's Curse*
 57–61; post-apartheid 53; reading
 with hyperlinked histories 62–63
South Africa/South African: literary
 contexts 62; literature 56, 244;
 middle-class cultures 251;
 writers 247
Spanish: colonialism 283;
 language 128
Spivak, Gayatri 8, 173
Sri Lanka, Sinhala Only Act 3
Srinivasan, Ragini Tharoor 8–9, 24
Steiner, George: *After Babel* 222
Stewart, Jon 99; *The Daily Show* 97
strategic exoticism 263
sub-Saharan Africa 166–167
Swahili 13, 151–155
Syria, Salafists of 3

TallBear, Kim 139
Tan, Amy 192–193
target culture 123, 127
Telugu 5–6
Thandani, Giti 232, 238; *Sakhiyani:
 Lesbian Desire in Ancient and
 Modern India* 238
Things Fall Apart (Achebe) 201
This Wound Is a World (Belcourt)
 282, 292
Thoreau, Henry David 230
The Times of India 235
Todd, Loreto 222
Todorova, Maria 106
traditional masculinity 152
transcendental signifier 156–157
transcultural/transculturality 1, 7, 57,
 59, 61, 64, 91, 116
transgender 234
translanguaging 70
translation 126–127, 290–291;
 articulation of 123; discursive
 practice of 120; processes of 290

The Translation of Dr. Apelles (Treuer)
 280–282, 286–288, 291–292;
 anxiety 289; attraction to Campaspe
 287; complications 286; memories
 289–290; narrative 291; subjectivity
 287; translation of 290–291
translingualism 70
transnational/transnationalism
 123–124, 128, 207
transparency 190–192
Treuer, David 284, 289–290; *Daphnis
 and Chloe* 285; *Native American
 Fiction: A User's Manual* 284–285;
 The Translation of Dr. Apelles
 280–281
tricksters 243, 249–251
Trump, Donald 97–98
Tsernianski, Milosh: *Migrations* 115
Turkish literary contexts 62

universal language 136
An Unnecessary Woman
 (Alameddine) 91
'untouchability' in British India 4

Veit-Wild, Flora 208
Venuti, Lawrence 123
Verde, Cabo 220
vernacular: hegemonies 3, 9;
 languages 89
Vietnamese/Vietnam 192–193;
 formulation 192–193; migrant
 workers 189
Viswanathan, Gauri 54
Vuong, Ocean 189–190; *On Earth
 We're Briefly Gorgeous* 183–184;
 migrant and queer voice 184

"waithood" survival strategy 250
Walkowitz, Rebecca L. 8–9, 55, 116;
 Immigrant Fictions 54
Warrior, Robert 284
wa Thiong'o, Ngũgĩ 4, 69, 95, 98,
 200–201, 208, 209n1, 221, 223
Way Back Home (Mhlongo) 246
Western: authors 184; cultural influence
 93; culture, institutionalisation of
 152; discourses 79; epistemologies
 68; espionage 88; metropolitan chick
 lit 174; suburbs 94
whiteness 122, 144, 187–188
Winslet, Kate 98
Wordsworth, B. 33

World Anglophone Studies 3–4, 7–9, 38, 40, 47–48, 116, 260; mapping 9–17
World Englishes 67, 69–70
world literature 8–9, 23, 26, 29, 53–58, 61, 104,107, 111,115–116, 197, 264–265
'writing back' 8–9, 17, 96, 100

Yildiz, Yasemin 107
Youssef, Bassem 2, 11, 89, 97, 99; *Revolution for Dummies* 87–88, 96

Yugoslavia 107, 109–110, 115; novel of 115; process of emigrating from 113
Yunis, Alia: *The Night Counter* 91

Zabus, Chantal 222
Zimbabwe/Zimbabwean 198; discourses on patriarchal domination 199; English language in 203
Zimunya, Musaemura B.: *And Now the Poets Speak* 199
Žižek, Slavoj 106, 109

Printed in the United States
by Baker & Taylor Publisher Services